QuickBooks Premier 2018

Level 1

QuickBooks Product Registration for Students

- Students should sign up on the Intuit website to get their own license at http://education.intuit.ca/education-program/students.jsp.

- Students can download and use the product on two devices for the term specified.

If you have technical questions or concerns regarding the installation or activation of the software, please contact Intuit directly at IEPCanada@intuit.com or visit the Support page on the Intuit Education website at http://education.intuit.ca/education-program/support.jsp.

October 2018
© CCI Learning Solutions Inc.

CCI Learning™

QuickBooks Premier 2018 – Level 1

Funded by the Government of Canada | Canada

Published by CCI Learning Solution Inc., www.ccilearning.com.

Copyright © 2018 CCI Learning Solutions Inc. – All rights reserved.

Printed in Canada.

ISBN: 978-1-55332-532-1

CCI Courseware#: 1767-1

Courseware Development Team: Jean Selkirk, J.R. Veinot, Kim Williams, Irina Heer, Sue Wong, Ken Kozakis, Kelly Hegedus

QuickBooks is a registered trademark of Intuit, Inc.

Table of Contents

About This Courseware

Introduction

Lesson 1: Getting Started in QuickBooks

Lesson 2: Making Deposits

Lesson 3: Reporting and Examining Your Work

Lesson 4: Purchasing with Cash or Credit

Lesson 5: Receiving Cash Sales

Lesson 6: Entering and Exporting Business Names and Lists

Lesson 7: Credit Purchasing Transactions

Lesson 8: Creating Invoices for Sales

Lesson 9: Modifying the Chart of Accounts

Lesson 10: Banking and Bill Payments

Lesson 11: Reconciling Banking

Appendices

Course Description

QuickBooks Premier Accountant Edition 2018 Desktop version (Canadian) is an integrated accounting package suitable for most small- to medium-sized businesses that require functions such as the general ledger, accounts receivable, accounts payable, Canadian payroll, and inventory accounting.

Utilizing real-world scenarios, *QuickBooks Premier 2018 – Level 1* introduces the basic features of QuickBooks Premier Accountant Edition 2018 Desktop version (Canadian). The course reviews basic accounting principles and procedures to increase your proficiency and enhance your level of understanding as you work through the exercises.

Note: Course content was accurate at the time of publishing. Intuit may change, update, or enhance the product and/or program described herein at any time. The companies used are fictitious – the dates, screen captures, tax tables, and other content may vary at time of use.

Payroll for QuickBooks Premier Accountant Edition 2018 Desktop version (Canadian) will be supported until June 30th, 2019.

Course Series

QuickBooks Premier 2018 – Level 1 is the first course in the MasterTrak Accounting series for QuickBooks Premier (Canadian). The MasterTrak Accounting series consists of the following two courses:

- **QuickBooks Premier 2018 – Level 1:** teaches you how to use QuickBooks to make deposits and purchases, work with cash, credit, and invoices, add general ledger accounts, perform reconciliation, and generate reports.
- **QuickBooks Premier 2018 – Level 2:** teaches you how to create new company files, work with inventory, collect and remit taxes, and work with payroll, templates, and file permissions.

The series is designed to reinforce your existing knowledge of accounting terms and concepts by associating bookkeeping with the specific accounting tasks you learn.

Course Length

QuickBooks Premier 2018 – Level 1 is a 30 to 60 hour course depending on the depth of coverage.

Course Prerequisites

You must possess basic computer skills (know how to navigate and launch programs within Microsoft Windows) and beginner accounting skills. No prior knowledge of QuickBooks is required; however, an understanding of fundamental accounting concepts is essential for successful completion of the course.

Course Setup

This course was developed using the Microsoft Windows 10 operating system and QuickBooks Premier Accountant Edition 2018 Desktop version (Canadian). All updates available at the time of development were installed.

As you work with QuickBooks, consider the following:

- QuickBooks versions for other countries differ from the Canadian version, primarily in how you work with payroll and taxes.

- This course does not cover QuickBooks Online.

- For best results, your computer must meet or exceed the system requirements specified by Intuit for the use of the software. Visit https://quickbooks.intuit.com/ca/desktop/premier/ to view the system requirements to run QuickBooks 2018.

  Note: Because Intuit may update or change the minimum system requirements for the software, it is important to check their web site and ensure that your computer meets or exceeds the latest posted requirements prior to starting the course.

- QuickBooks Premier Accountant Edition 2018 (Canadian), should be installed, updated with the currently available updates, and activated. The default software settings should be maintained, including the setting to receive automatic updates.

  Note: Installing available updates before beginning class and keeping automatic updates turned on is recommended. If you keep updates turned on, you will be prompted to update the provided data files (created in 2018) when you open/restore them, and you may safely do so. If you do not update, you will be prompted to update QuickBooks each time you open the data files.

- Exercises in Lesson 3 provide an option to email reports to the instructor. To successfully email reports, Microsoft Outlook must be installed and configured.

- Exercises in Lessons 6 and 11 require that Microsoft Excel be installed and configured.

- Exercises in Lessons 3, 4, 5, and 10 direct students to print output. You may want to have a classroom printer available. You may also opt to have students send printed output to a file.

Some information that appears in the courseware screen captures may differ from the results you encounter depending on:

- the operating system on your computer.

- the tax deduction tables you use.

The data files used in this course have been created for fictitious companies in various Canadian provinces using the GST/HST rates relevant to those provinces at the time the data files were created.

Note: If you change the GST/HST or PST tax rates used as you work through the exercises, the results you encounter will differ from the results that appear in the courseware screen captures.

Course Objectives

After completing this course, you will be able to:

⚐ Describe the purpose of the Accounting Cycle.

⚐ Identify Transaction Cycles used in QuickBooks.

⚐ Find, open, save, rename, and close QuickBooks files.

⚐ Navigate forms.

⚐ Verify data entry settings.

⚐ Customize the Home page.

⚐ Describe how revenue, investments, and loans differ.

⚐ Discuss QuickBooks classes.

⚐ Match GL accounts to financial reports.

⚐ Produce detail and summary reports.

⚐ Find and correct transactions.

⚐ Enter purchases using cheques.

⚐ Enter credit card purchases.

⚐ Process petty cash reimbursements.

⚐ Identify when an accrual is required as opposed to a cash-based sale.

⚐ Enter sales receipts.

⚐ Make deposits.

⚐ Issue cash refunds.

⚐ Create and edit vendor and customer name records.

⚐ Memorize and export reports.

⚐ Understand how customer and vendor credit transactions differ in QuickBooks.

⚐ Understand how credit purchases affect reports.

⚐ Enter credit purchases.

⚐ Understand how credit sales affect reports.

⚐ Enter credit sales and charge correct sales tax.

⚐ Apply the accounting equation to the Chart of Accounts.

⚐ Enter and modify GL accounts.

⚐ Pay bills according to terms, receive and deposit multiple payments, and adjust customer invoices.

⚐ Reconcile the chequing, credit card, and merchant accounts.

Course Design

This courseware was designed to be part of an instructor-led training course. You will be introduced to the concepts and features of QuickBooks that you can use to perform day-to-day accounting transactions.

The courseware is organized by lesson. Each lesson begins with Lesson Objectives that list what's covered in the lesson. The lesson narrative text presents in-depth conceptual information that explains the 'how' and the 'why' of accounting concepts using real-world examples.

Step-by-step hands-on exercises reinforce the application of QuickBooks skills.

Each lesson in the courseware includes an end-of-lesson (EOL) section designed to reinforce the concepts presented in the lesson and provide additional opportunities for you to apply your skills. The EOL section includes the following components:

- **Lesson Summary** – reviews the list of the covered learning objectives.
- **Key Terms** – lists the vocabulary terms and definitions introduced in the lesson.
- **Activities** – multiple choice, fill-in-the-blank, true/false, matching, or short answer assessments designed to reinforce understanding of the learning objectives.
- **Practice the Skill** – a hands-on exercise that enables you to practice applying your newly-acquired skills based on the concepts introduced in the lesson.
- **Course Project Exercise** – another hands-on exercise that utilizes a different company file and challenges you to determine what steps you need to take to achieve the desired outcome.
- **Quiz Questions** – a series of multiple-choice questions to assess your understanding of lesson concepts.

At the end of the course, the **Capstone Project** is included as Appendix A. The Capstone Project is an exercise that encompasses many of the skills taught in the course and results in a finished product that allows you to showcase what you have learned. In the Capstone Project, you will be presented with a starter file and a list of tasks and desired outcomes. It is up to you to determine how to perform the tasks necessary to reach those outcomes. Your teacher may assign the Capstone Project at his or her discretion.

Additional appendices at the end of the courseware include a courseware mapping, a glossary of terms, and an index.

The courseware is organized as follows:

- 📖 MasterTrak Accounting Series
  - 📑 Table of Contents
  - 📑 Lesson
    - 📄 Lesson Objectives
    - 📄 Narrative Text
      - ✓ Graphics
      - ✓ Tips and Tricks
      - ✓ Notes
    - 📄 Exercises
      - ✓ Graphics
      - ✓ Tips and Tricks
      - ✓ Notes
    - 📄 Lesson Summary
    - 📄 Key Terms
    - 📄 Activities
    - 📄 Practice the Skill
    - 📄 Course Project Exercise
    - 📄 Quiz Questions
  - 📑 Appendices
    - 📄 Capstone Project
    - 📄 Courseware Mapping
    - 📄 Glossary of Terms
    - 📄 Index

When you return to your home or office, you will find this courseware to be a valuable resource for reviewing concepts and applying the skills you have learned.

Lessons Overview

Throughout the lessons in this courseware, you'll see how you might use QuickBooks in the workplace by following the progress of one company from its start through various stages of growth. Your role during the course will be that of an intern at an accounting firm. This scenario will allow you to learn how to enter many types of business transactions.

Within our course scenario, the company you are responsible for is Best Custom T-Shirts. They operate several business lines: production of finished product on screen printing equipment, a retail store, design services, and a program that aids in supplying trained workers and creating jobs with the support of the city. In each lesson, the business undertakes different types of business activities that you will enter as transactions into the accounting software. You'll complete these transactions as exercises and turn in the results of your work.

This courseware consists of an Introduction and 11 lessons.

- **Introduction** – You will learn how QuickBooks compares to other accounting packages. You will also review basic accounting terms and principles and learn about the Transaction Cycles in QuickBooks, which provide the framework for the accounting activities you will perform as you work your way through the course.

- **Lesson 1: Getting Started in QuickBooks** – You will learn about the fundamentals of working in QuickBooks, including how to launch the program, navigate the interface, and work with files. You will also work with file settings and preferences.

- **Lesson 2: Making Deposits** – You will learn about the Banking Cycle and how to make deposits. You will learn about the different types of income and learn how to use QuickBooks classes.

- **Lesson 3: Reporting and Examining Your Work** – You will learn the skills you need to review, correct, and report the results of your work. You will also use the administrative Reports Cycle in QuickBooks to present relevant information.

- **Lesson 4: Purchasing with Cash or Credit** – You will learn how to enter cash, debit, and credit card expenses, and learn how to work with petty cash.

- **Lesson 5: Receiving Cash Sales** – You will learn to enter and identify cash sales, enter sales receipts, make deposits, and issue cash refunds.

- **Lesson 6: Entering and Exporting Business Names and Lists** – You will learn about Administrative Cycle lists. These lists reveal how QuickBooks manages information, such as the names and terms associated with monetary transactions.

- **Lesson 7: Credit Purchasing Transactions** – You will learn how the element of timing affects the Purchases Cycle, work with payment terms, and examine Accounts Payable reports.

- **Lesson 8: Creating Invoices for Sales** – You will learn how the element of timing affects the Sales Cycle, enter credit sales, and examine Accounts Receivable reports. You will also learn how to collect sales tax.

- **Lesson 9: Modifying the Chart of Accounts** – You will learn how to apply the accounting equation to the Chart of Accounts and enter and modify GL accounts.

- **Lesson 10: Banking and Bill Payments** – You will learn about the final stages of the Purchases and Sales Cycles, as well as their connections to the Banking Cycle. You will also learn about paying bills, receiving payments, and adjusting customer invoices.

- **Lesson 11: Reconciling Banking** – You will learn about the Banking Cycle and how to reconcile accounting records with bank and credit card statements.

Downloading the QuickBooks Data Files

The exercises in this courseware require you to use the data files provided for the course. To download the data files for this course, perform the following steps.

1. Launch your browser and navigate to the Student Data Files page on CCI Learning's website, located at http://www.ccilearning.com/data.

2. Type: **1767** in the *Courseware #* field, then click **Find Data**.

3. Depending on the browser you are using, the ZIP file may be automatically saved in your Downloads folder, or you may be prompted to open or save the file. Save (or move) the downloaded ZIP file to your Desktop.

4. Right-click the **ZIP file** on your Desktop, then click **Extract All** to display the Extract Compressed (Zipped) Folders dialog box.

5. Click the **Browse** button, navigate to the Desktop, click the **Select Folder** button to confirm the Desktop as the location for extracting the files, then click the **Extract** button. A folder named *1767-Student-Files* should now reside on your Desktop.

Within the 1767-Student-Files folder, you will find a folder for each lesson, and within each of these, a *StarterFiles*, *PTS*, and *MyProjects* folder. The StarterFiles folder contains data file(s) you are directed to open at the beginning of an exercise. The PTS folder contains the data file for the Practice the Skill exercise. The MyProjects folder will be empty. As you perform the exercises for a lesson, you will be directed to save your work in that lesson's MyProjects folder.

Course Conventions

The following conventions are used in CCI Learning materials:

Key Terms – Vocabulary terms that are presented in the narrative text appear in *__bold, italic__* font style.

Objective L-1.1, L-1.2 – Indicates the numbered learning objective being covered in the topic. Refer to the Appendices for a complete listing of learning objectives.

Screen Areas – Names of areas on the screen to which you need to direct your attention to perform a task during an exercise appear in *italic* font style.

Data-Entry Text – Text or values to be entered during an exercise appear in **bold, 10-pt, Times New Roman** font style.

Action Items – Commands, buttons, keys, and items on which you perform actions during an exercise appear in **bold** font style.

Keyboard Keys – Keys to be pressed on the keyboard during an exercise appear in **bold, UPPERCASE** font style. For example, **TAB**, **ENTER**, **DELETE**.

Notes – point out exceptions or special circumstances that may be present when working with a procedure or may indicate there is another method to complete the task.

Lesson Exercise

This signals the start of step-by-step hands-on exercises.

Key Terms

This signals the start of the Key Terms table found at the end of each lesson, which lists the vocabulary terms and definitions presented in the lesson.

Activity

This signals the start of multiple choice, fill-in-the-blank, true/false, matching, or short answer assessments found at the end of each lesson. They are designed to reinforce your understanding of the concepts and may be completed in class or on your own.

Practice the Skill

This signals the start of the Practice the Skill exercise found at the end of each lesson. They are included as extra practice and may be completed in class or on your own. Omission of the Practice the Skill exercise will not affect future lessons.

Course Project Exercise

This signals the start of the Course Project Exercise found at the end of each lesson. It is included as extra practice and may be completed in class or on your own.

Teacher Resources

The Teacher Resources provided with CCI courseware include several components you can use to plan and deliver your course effectively.

Teacher Resources include:

- **Using the 1767 Teacher Resources** – a document that describes in detail how to use the supplied Teacher Resources to complement the courseware.
- **Lesson Notes** – provide a heading-by-heading "map" of each lesson. For each heading, the notes indicate the corresponding:
    - page number.
    - slideshow slide (if any).
    - learning objective(s).
    - teaching tips and/or suggestions.
    - data file(s) used and/or saved during the exercise.
    - suggested time (in minutes) to spend on each topic.

  You can use the Lesson Notes to create lesson plans.

- **Lesson Slideshows** – follow the general flow of each lesson, highlight important concepts and interfaces, and provide supplemental information and graphics for presenting accounting concepts. No animations or transitions have been applied to the slides, so you can customize them as desired. You can use the slideshows to familiarize yourself (or your students) with the course content.
- **Student Files** – are the data files students open and work with in the hands-on exercises. These are organized by lesson and located in the StarterFiles and PTS folders within each lesson folder. These are the same files described in the *Downloading the QuickBooks Data Files* section.
- **Completed Files** – show how each lesson exercise data file should appear after the exercise steps have been performed correctly. You can compare these properly-completed files to those that students have completed to determine how successful they were in performing the exercise steps. These files are organized by lesson.

  Note: The StarterFiles provided for each lesson are all a student needs to proceed regardless of whether the previous lesson's files were completed correctly. Use caution when making any completed files available to students. Consider providing printed copies to students for reference.

- **Capstone Project Solution File** – this is the correctly completed version of the Capstone Project data file.

- **End of Course Practice Test** – a customizable pen-and-paper test that you can print and distribute to your students at the end of the course. A suggested time limit to complete the test is provided. You may adjust the time appropriately for your class. The test covers the course learning objectives and includes an answer/grading key.

- **End of Course Final Exam** – a hands-on assessment that covers the course learning objectives and includes a grading key.

- **Answer Keys** – provide answers for activities, quiz questions, and the end of course practice test. You can use the answer keys to review the correct answers with students and explain why the incorrect options are incorrect.

Downloading Teacher Resources

To download a Teacher Resources ZIP file and extract the files, perform the following steps.

1. Launch your browser and navigate to the Teacher Resources page on CCI Learning's website, located at http://ccilearning.com/teacher-resources/.

2. Enter the Teacher Resource Package (TRP) code you received as part of your fulfillment package in the *TRP Code:* field, then click **Find Data**.

3. Depending on the browser you are using, the ZIP file may be automatically saved in your Downloads folder, or you may be prompted to open or save the file. Save the downloaded ZIP file and note its location.

4. Right-click the **ZIP file**, then click **Extract All** to display the Extract Compressed (Zipped) Folders dialog box.

5. Click the **Browse** button, navigate to the folder to which you want to extract the files, click the **Select Folder** button to confirm the folder location, then click the **Extract** button.

Help Us Improve!

Feedback

We'd love to hear from you. Share your thoughts about this book by emailing us at feedback@ccilearning.com.

Errata

Help us keep this course accurate and up-to-date. You can submit a correction or check for updates by visiting our Errata page at QuickBooks 2018 Level 1.

Introduction

Lesson Objectives

In this lesson, you will be introduced to QuickBooks and its purpose and function in the workplace. You will also review some basic accounting concepts and how they relate to bookkeeping with QuickBooks.

Upon successfully completing this introduction, you should be able to:

☐ Understand how QuickBooks is used in the workplace.

☐ Understand that there are various QuickBooks products, editions, and versions available.

☐ Describe the purpose of the Accounting Cycle.

☐ Identify Transaction Cycles used in QuickBooks.

Why Use QuickBooks?

Accounting software programs provide an easy way to perform **bookkeeping**. Because all accounting software applications perform the tasks required for ***double-entry bookkeeping***, they are suitable for use by professional accountants, interns, and amateur accountants alike. QuickBooks is one of many accounting systems available on the market today.

However, not all accounting systems are designed in the same manner or even for the same uses. Although QuickBooks can manage the needs of large businesses, certain businesses do require more complex software that can handle accounting distributed across many locations, sharing a centralized computing system.

QuickBooks offers certain advantages that some more powerful systems cannot provide. One is that QuickBooks allows you to compare several years of data in one report. Many accounting systems provide reporting for only a single year. Other systems are also often less flexible than QuickBooks is about allowing you to correct mistakes or customize the interface.

Additionally, QuickBooks has the capacity to connect to other applications and can be used as the accounting platform for custom applications; however, it cannot be modified except by its manufacturer, Intuit.

Companies with a large accounting staff and adequate technical support might be able to manage the more complex types of software, but for smaller businesses, the benefits offered by QuickBooks are clear. QuickBooks offers flexibility and relatively few restrictions so that a small accounting staff with little technical support can economically accomplish a great deal of accounting work in a stable software environment.

QuickBooks Products

QuickBooks provides online and desktop products. Desktop products include QuickBooks Pro, QuickBooks Premier, QuickBooks Accountant Edition, and QuickBooks Enterprise Solutions. There are several editions of each product available, as well as distinct versions within the editions. You can read about and compare products, editions, and versions at Intuit's web site: https://quickbooks.intuit.com/ca/small-business/.

It is wise to evaluate which accounting functions you require for your business before you decide which edition of QuickBooks to purchase. You will learn more about the available products in Level 2 of this courseware. Keep in mind, however, that while some products provide advanced capabilities, the software functions the same way across all versions for essential accounting tasks, so once you learn one, learning another is easy.

QuickBooks in this Course

Objective L-0.1 Recognize the edition of QuickBooks used in this course

The accounting software package used in this course is QuickBooks Premier Accountant Edition 2018. This package allows you to open and work with files created in QuickBooks Pro and QuickBooks Premier and includes all the functionality found in these two editions.

Additionally, the Accountant edition includes a powerful file process known as the Accountant Copy which allows an accountant to review and correct a client's files without interrupting the client's day-to-day business. Clients can export an Accountant Copy file for review and continue to update their daily accounting records. The accountant reviews and corrects the exported file and sends the corrections back to the client in a specialized import file. The client can then import the file to apply the accountant's corrections.

QuickBooks in the Workplace

As you perform accounting tasks, you will share responsibilities with other people. They may be interns, supervisors who may be licensed accounting professionals, known as **Chartered Professional Accountants** (CPAs), business owners, or their employees.

Remember that you are responsible to others as you participate in a team effort to complete the accounting tasks together. When these tasks are performed correctly, accurate reports about the financial condition of the business are available to guide business development.

Accounting Basics and QuickBooks

Objective L-0.2 Describe the purpose of the Accounting Cycle

In this section, you will review the purpose and phases of the Accounting Cycle and examine a visual overview of the QuickBooks Transaction Cycles.

The Accounting Cycle

The purpose of any accounting system is to represent all monetary activities of the business in the accounting records. The activities encompass the movement of money or orders for goods or services and the promise to deliver them. The accounting tasks, when complete, constitute the **Accounting Cycle**. The success or failure of a business depends on timely and accurate reports about the financial condition of the business entity based on the bookkeeping.

Bookkeeping takes place continually throughout the major phases in the Accounting Cycle. These phases take place during a *fiscal year* of a business. A fiscal year lasts for twelve months; it may follow a calendar year and start on January 1st or it may start at the beginning of another month and end on the corresponding twelfth month. Bookkeeping steps are performed in sequence and should follow *International Financial Reporting Standards (IFRS)*. IFRS are a common set of accounting principles and procedures. Following IFRS ensures that everyone can understand what is being entered and reported. At the level of accounting taught in this course, IFRS is identical to USA Generally Accepted Accounting Principles (GAAP).

When one Accounting Cycle is finished, all monetary transactions are entered and provide a total picture of the business during that year. The cycle begins with identifying the transactions that need to be entered. Then, you make or record the entries in the accounting system and proceed through the phases of the cycle until it is completed.

The following list summarizes the phases of the Accounting Cycle:

- Enter transactions.
- Examine results in reports.
- Determine and enter adjustments.
- Complete reports for review.
- Enter final transactions.
- Close the year.

Whether you are responsible for all these phases or not, paying attention to them allows you to participate responsibly in the team effort to complete the Accounting Cycle.

Visualizing Transaction Cycles in QuickBooks

Objective L-0.3 Identify Transaction Cycles used in QuickBooks

Transaction Cycles are the series of entries and activities that comprise the bookkeeping data entry portions of the Accounting Cycle. Verification steps may also be included in some of them.

A visual overview of the Transaction Cycles is presented in the QuickBooks Transaction Cycles Overview Diagram, shown in Figure I-1.

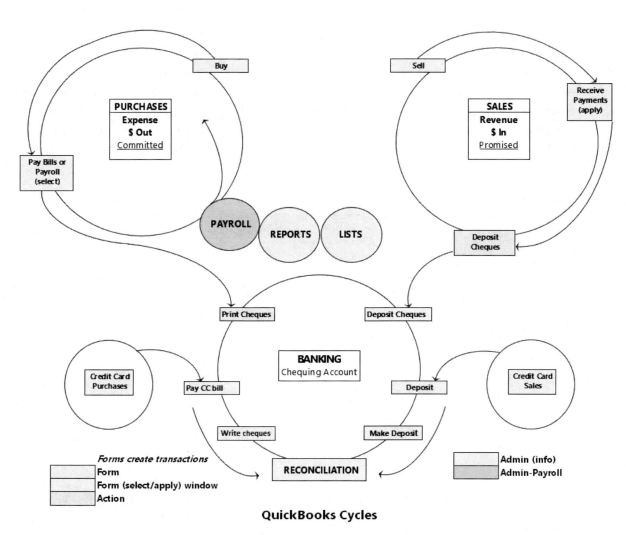

QuickBooks Cycles

Figure I-1: QuickBooks Transaction Cycles Overview Diagram

Note: You will see isolated sections of this diagram and learn how cycles intersect as you progress through the lessons. Referring back to this diagram at any time can assist you in finding what you need or in identifying what stage you have reached.

Table I-1 lists the three main Transaction Cycles and three Administrative Cycles, all of which appear in the QuickBooks Transaction Cycles Overview Diagram.

Table I-1: Transaction Cycles and Administrative Cycles

Cycle Name	Cycle Type
Purchases	Transaction
Sales	Transaction
Banking	Transaction
Reports	Administrative
Lists	Administrative
Payroll	Administrative

Follow the arrows around the Sales Cycle and the Purchases Cycle and notice that within each you perform comparable activities that are the reverse of each other: The Purchases Cycle covers money flowing out, while the Sales Cycle covers money flowing in.

The steps continue around the cycle through the stages unique to each, following the arrows until outgoing or incoming payments reach the Banking Cycle. Smaller cycles involving purchases and sales with credit also connect to the Banking Cycle.

The small, gray-colored Administrative Reports and Lists Cycles are placed in the center to indicate their support for and integration with other cycles. The third Administrative Cycle, Payroll, eventually becomes part of the purchase transaction and intersects with the Purchases Cycle.

You will learn more about the Transaction and Administrative Cycles throughout the course.

Lesson Summary

Now that you have completed this lesson, you should be able to:

☑ Understand how QuickBooks is used in the workplace.

☑ Understand that there are various QuickBooks products, editions, and versions available.

☑ Describe the purpose of the Accounting Cycle.

☑ Identify Transaction Cycles used in QuickBooks.

Key Terms

Term	Definition
Accounting Cycle	Period of time to complete one entire fiscal period of accounting.
Bookkeeping	The process of entering business transactions into the records of an accounting system.
Chartered Professional Accountant (CPA)	Licensed accounting professional.
Double-entry Bookkeeping	A system of bookkeeping that requires each business transaction be entered in two different accounts in the accounting records and that both entries are equal and have an "opposing" effect. Double-entry bookkeeping ensures that the accounting records stay in balance.
Fiscal Year	Refers to financial matters or items associated with taxation. In accounting, a fiscal year is the period of time in which the Accounting Cycle is completed and is the basis for filing taxes. A fiscal year may or may not follow a calendar year.
International Financial Reporting Standards (IFRS)	A common set of accounting principles, standards, and procedures. These principles ensure that everyone knows the accounting transactions accurately represent business activities and maintain integrity in reporting. Adherence to these principles ensures that financial reporting is transparent and consistent across organizations.

Quiz Questions

For each question, select the best answer.

1. Which statement about QuickBooks is true?

    a.   QuickBooks is available only in online versions.

    b.   The programming used within the QuickBooks application is easily modified by the user.

    c.   QuickBooks can connect to other applications.

    d.   QuickBooks is available only in desktop versions.

2. Donald sent his QuickBooks file to his accountant for corrections. The corrections are ready. How can Donald apply his accountant's corrections to his QuickBooks file?

    a.   Donald should import the file he receives from his accountant to apply the corrections.

    b.   Donald does not need to do anything; his QuickBooks file was automatically corrected while the accountant worked on it.

    c.   Donald should print a list of the corrections and apply them manually.

    d.   Donald should convert the file he receives from his accountant into an Excel spreadsheet, then import the spreadsheet.

3. Which statement about the Accounting Cycle is FALSE?

    a.   The Accounting Cycle takes place in one fiscal year.

    b.   Multiple Accounting Cycles take place each year.

    c.   Adjustments are part of the Accounting Cycle.

    d.   Reports are part of the Accounting Cycle.

4. Which cycle is NOT a Transaction Cycle in QuickBooks?

    a.   Banking

    b.   Purchases

    c.   Lists

    d.   Sales

Lesson 1:
Getting Started in QuickBooks

Lesson Objectives

In this lesson, you will prepare to enter transactions by accessing and opening the QuickBooks files you need while responding to pop up messages. You will also examine key forms in the Purchases and Sales Cycles and discover how forms relate to journal entries. Additionally, you will verify file settings that affect data entry.

Upon successful completion of this lesson, you should be able to:

☐ Launch QuickBooks, check your release number, and configure updates.

☐ Find, open, save, rename, and close QuickBooks files.

☐ Interpret and respond to pop up messages appropriately.

☐ Locate Purchases and Sales Cycle forms.

☐ Compare form usage to general journal entries.

☐ Navigate forms.

☐ Verify data entry settings.

☐ Customize the Home page.

Introducing the Story: Your First Day at Work

It's your first day at work as an intern at an accounting firm. At this firm, they use QuickBooks Premier Accountant Edition 2018. This desktop product provides all the features and functionality of QuickBooks Premier, plus the advanced features of the Accountant edition. You can read about and compare all QuickBooks products, editions, and versions at: https://quickbooks.intuit.com/ca/small-business/.

Your first task is to familiarize yourself with the QuickBooks files for some of the firm's clients, which include both individuals and businesses. You will need to locate and open their company files to enter transactions. QuickBooks uses the term *company file* to refer to the database file that it creates for an entity, whether the entity is an individual or a business.

At this accounting firm, you will share a computer, its software, and many QuickBooks company files with other interns and accountants. Because of this, many company files may have already been opened on your computer, so you may need to search for a specific company file, restore or decompress a backup file or portable file, or even close a company file that was left open. You may also need user names and passwords to log in to some of the company files.

Before You Begin

You will encounter the following items as you work with QuickBooks and they are important to understand for you to do your job effectively.

Note: Everything you learn in this lesson applies throughout QuickBooks. If additional global information is provided in later lessons, it will be marked in a note as *QuickBooks Global*.

Messages: When you open a QuickBooks company file for the first time, or take other actions while working in the file, various pop up messages may appear asking for your input. You can safely ignore some of these, but others require your attention and management. Messages appear at different process stages and we will summarize them in the next section.

Forms: Depending on the transactions you need to enter, you'll locate the correct forms. The forms used in this lesson will be in the Purchases and Sales Cycles. Within a *form*, transaction data is entered and stored in *fields*.

General Journal Entries: *General Journal Entries* are records of a financial transaction recorded in a company's General Journal. When you use a QuickBooks form to record a transaction, QuickBooks automatically makes the proper entries and properly debits and credits the appropriate accounts. You can also enter transactions into the General Journal manually, but you should have a thorough understanding of accounting principles and best practices. Manual entries are best left to qualified professionals.

User-customized Settings: Several data entry settings can be customized by the user to suit his or her working style and personal preferences. If you share QuickBooks with other users, you may be caught off guard by customized data entry settings. As you proceed through the course, you will learn how to adapt to choices made by others.

Understanding and Responding to Pop Up Messages

Objective L-1.2 Interpret message pop ups correctly

You may encounter many different messages or pop up forms in QuickBooks. This section explains the most common messages that you will encounter when accessing and working with QuickBooks company files. In this lesson, we have numbered these messages from one to five, to help you identify and properly respond to each. Some of the messages are purely informational, some provide helpful hints, while others may be warnings. Knowing what to do when you encounter each message type will save you time and reduce confusion. In some cases, after you respond to a message once, you will not see it again.

You can also permanently dismiss many messages by selecting the Do not display this message in the future check box in the message box. Be careful when marking this check box because QuickBooks will remember your preference. If you dismiss the message, QuickBooks will not display it again. Fortunately, you can reverse this behavior by displaying all previously hidden messages.

Messages-1: Updates

When you launch QuickBooks, it will automatically check for and ask if you want to install available updates by displaying a message such as the one shown in Figure 1-1a.

Figure 1-1a: Message about software updates

It is best practice to keep your software updated, and for this course we recommend that you install updates as they become available. However, your instructor has the final say on whether and when to install updates (it can be a very time-consuming process). If you receive a message like the one shown in Figure 1-1a, ask your instructor whether you should click Install Now or Install Later. QuickBooks will allow you to work with the company files we created for this course even if you skip the update.

Note: It is important to understand that IT policies at some companies are very strict regarding the installation of updates of any kind, and you should never arbitrarily update any software program at your place of employment without first enquiring about company policy and/or checking with the IT department.

Other Things to Know about Updates

If you elect not to update, you will likely see pop ups like the one shown in Figure 1-1b when you try to open the data files for this course. This message appears whenever you try to open a file that was created in a newer QuickBooks Desktop release than the one you are using.

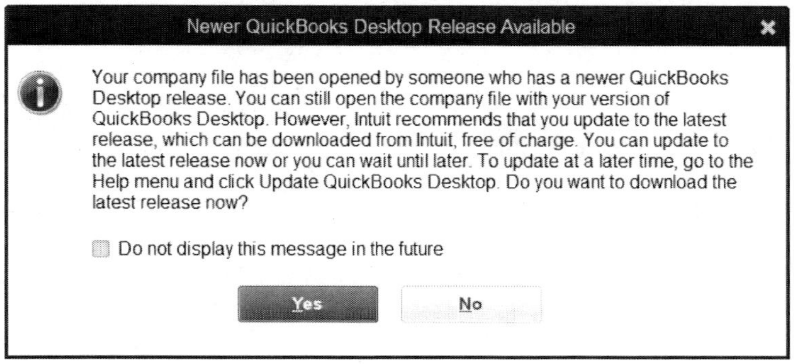

Figure 1-1b: Newer QuickBooks Desktop Release Available

You can safely select the Do not display this message in the future check box to suppress this message.

After you have selected the check box, as shown in Figure 1-1c, click No to close the message and proceed without updating.

Figure 1-1c: Newer QuickBooks Desktop Release Available, with message suppression check box selected

If you update QuickBooks and elect to keep receiving and installing updates automatically, you may encounter a message like the one shown in Figure 1-1d when you try to open a file created in an earlier release.

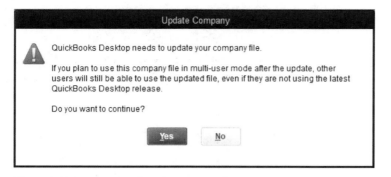

Figure 1-1d: Prompt to update the company file

You can safely click Yes and update the company file.

Messages-2: Payroll Update

When you first open a company file, you may receive a message similar to the one shown in Figure 1-2. This message notifies you that QuickBooks' tax information is out of date. This information is automatically updated when you update QuickBooks. For this course, click OK to dismiss the message. The company file will open, but you must address additional messages before you can start working with it.

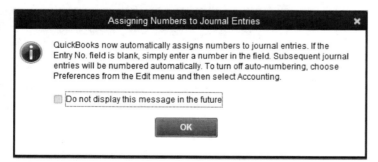

Figure 1-2: Payroll tax tables out of date

Messages-3: Helpful Hints

Note: You may dismiss the following series of messages as you encounter them. You will learn how to redisplay hidden messages later in this lesson.

The next message relates to assigning numbers to Journal Entries as shown in Figure 1-3. (Lesson 3 explains this in more detail.)

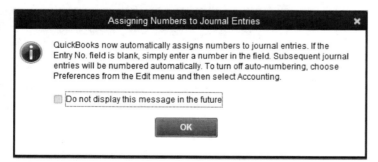

Figure 1-3: Assigning Numbers to Journal Entries, deselected

To suppress this message, select the Do not display this message in the future check box, then click OK to close the message.

Another message may appear informing you about collapsing and expanding transactions, as shown in Figure 1-4. This message is informational. You may select the Do not display this message in the future check box, and then click OK.

Collapsing and Expanding Transactions
QuickBooks combines (collapses) multiple items in a transaction into a single line on the report.
If you want to display the detail associated with a transaction, click Expand on the report toolbar.
Do not display this message in the future
OK

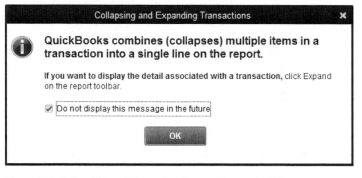

Figure 1-4: Collapsing and Expanding Transactions, selected

Messages-4: External Accountant

You will see the next message (Figure 1-5) only in the Accountant edition of QuickBooks. Select the Don't show this again check box, and then click the No button to avoid creating a new user.

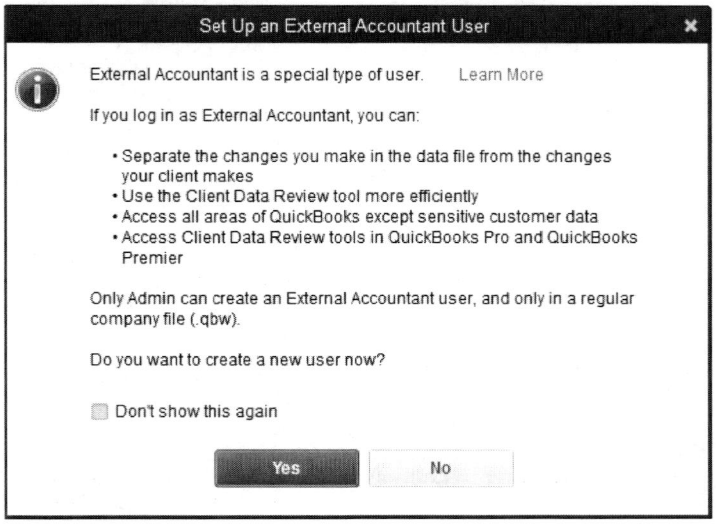
Set Up an External Accountant User
External Accountant is a special type of user.
Learn More
If you log in as External Accountant, you can:
• Separate the changes you make in the data file from the changes your client makes
• Use the Client Data Review tool more efficiently
• Access all areas of QuickBooks except sensitive customer data
• Access Client Data Review tools in QuickBooks Pro and QuickBooks Premier
Only Admin can create an External Accountant user, and only in a regular company file (.qbw).
Do you want to create a new user now?
Don't show this again
Yes
No

Figure 1-5: Set Up an External Accountant User

Messages-5: Memorized Reports

This message (Figure 1-6) differs from the helpful hints because it serves as a warning, indicated by the exclamation point within the triangle. QuickBooks allows you to customize most reports and save them for later use. Customized reports that you save are known as memorized reports.

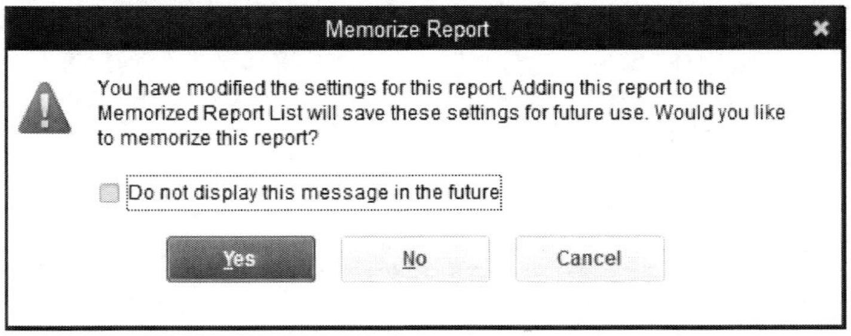
Memorize Report
You have modified the settings for this report. Adding this report to the Memorized Report List will save these settings for future use. Would you like to memorize this report?
Do not display this message in the future
Yes
No
Cancel

Figure 1-6: Memorize Report

You shouldn't see this message until you customize a report, which you will do in Lesson 3. Don't forget that if you suppress this message (by selecting the Do not display this message in the future check box), QuickBooks will remember this preference and will not display this warning message in the future. This could cause you to accidentally lose any customizations you have made to a report.

Note: Do not select the Do not display this message in the future check box in the message box for Memorized Reports. We will cover this message in Lesson 3 when we discuss reports.

Preparing to Use QuickBooks

In this section, you will learn how to recognize QuickBooks files and file types, launch the software, check your release number and check your update settings. You will also learn to access, open, and close company files.

Recognizing QuickBooks Files and File Types

The various file types in QuickBooks have their own file extensions. Table 1-1 lists the most common file types you may encounter in the Accountant edition of QuickBooks.

Table 1-1: QuickBooks File Types

File Extension	File Type	Description
.QBW	QuickBooks Company File	The QuickBooks "working" file for any entity, either individual or business. You perform your work in a company file.
.QBB	QuickBooks Backup File	A backup copy of a company file.
.QBM	QuickBooks Portable File	A compressed version of a company file that can be easily shared due to its smaller file size.
.QBX	Accountant's Transfer file (export file)	An exported copy of a QuickBooks company file that you send to your accountant for review and correction.
.QBA	QuickBooks Accountant Copy working file	After an accountant opens a .QBX file, it becomes a .QBA file. Your accountant works in this file to record all changes and corrections.
.QBY	QuickBooks Accountant Copy import file	After recording corrections, the accountant creates and returns a .QBY file. You import this file into your company file to apply the accountant's corrections.

Note: In this course, you will work primarily with .QBM and .QBW files.

Launching QuickBooks

When you installed QuickBooks, you may have opted to allow the program to place a QuickBooks icon (Figure 1-7) on your desktop.

You can double-click the icon to launch QuickBooks.

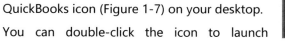

Figure 1-7: QuickBooks Premier - Accountant Edition 2018 icon

If you do not have an icon on your desktop, you can launch QuickBooks from the Windows Start menu by clicking **Start > QuickBooks > QuickBooks Premier – Accountant Edition 2018**.

Checking the QuickBooks Release Number

After you launch QuickBooks, you can view information about the product, including its release number. From the QuickBooks application window, press the F2 key to display the Product Information dialog box. The version of QuickBooks and the release number appear in the Product line at the top of the dialog box (highlighted in Figure 1-8). You may need this information if you call Intuit for technical support.

Product Information			✕
Product	QuickBooks: Premier Accountant Edition 2018 Release R1P		
Licence number		ACTIVATED	SERVICES INFORMATION
Product number	N/A	R1_38	AuthID
User Licences			Company Realm ID
			Online Billing Token

Figure 1-8: Product Information dialog box – release number

Checking the QuickBooks Update Settings

QuickBooks includes an Automatic Update feature that allows you to automatically receive product updates from Intuit to ensure that you have the latest product improvements. This feature is enabled by default; however, your classroom system may have the Automatic Update feature turned off. The setting used in your classroom will be determined by your instructor.

Regardless of the Automatic Update feature setting, you should be able to complete all the course exercises successfully. As discussed previously, you may need to dismiss pop up messages about updating QuickBooks if you have updates turned off, or you may need to update an exercise file before you can use it if you have updates turned on.

Note: To learn more about the Automatic Update feature, in the Menu Bar, click **Help > About Automatic Update**.

To check your current Automatic Update setting, in the Menu Bar, click **Help** > **Update QuickBooks Desktop.** The Update QuickBooks Desktop dialog box (Figure 1-9) appears.

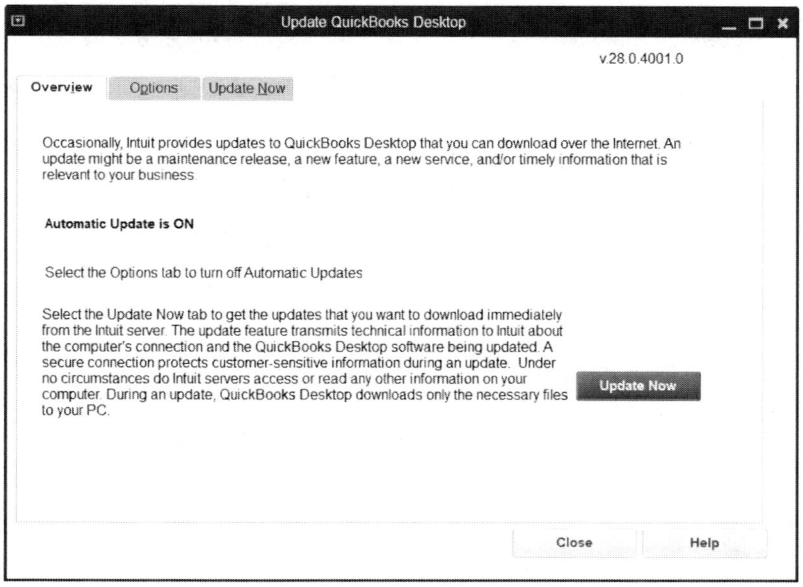

Figure 1-9: Update QuickBooks Desktop dialog box – Overview tab

The Overview tab shows the status of the Automatic Update setting. Click the Options tab to access the update settings (Figure 1-10).

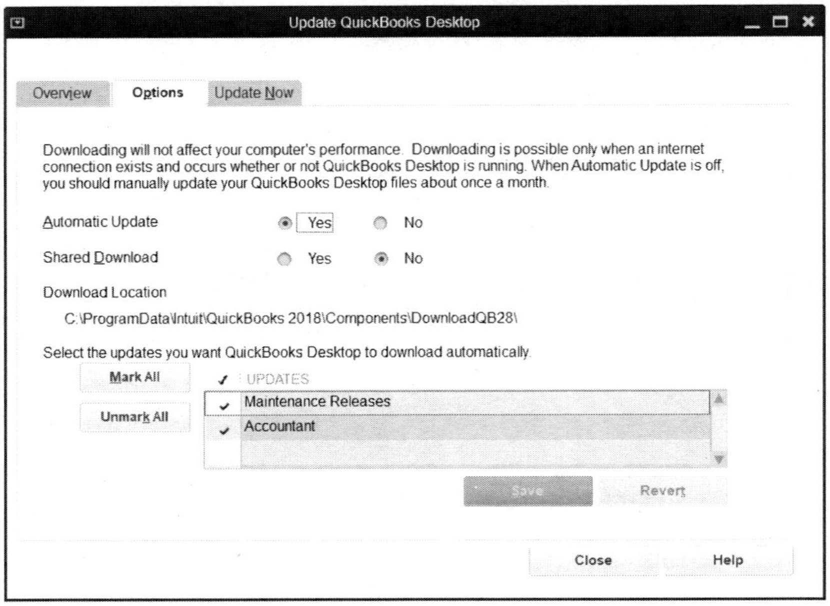

Figure 1-10: Update QuickBooks Desktop dialog box – Options tab

Use the Automatic Update radio buttons to specify the setting you want. If you change the setting, the Save button becomes available. Click the Save button to save the new setting. Click the Close button to close the dialog box.

Finding a File

Objective L-1.1 Find, open, save, rename, and close QuickBooks files

When QuickBooks opens, it may display the Welcome to QuickBooks Desktop screen shown in Figure 1-11a.

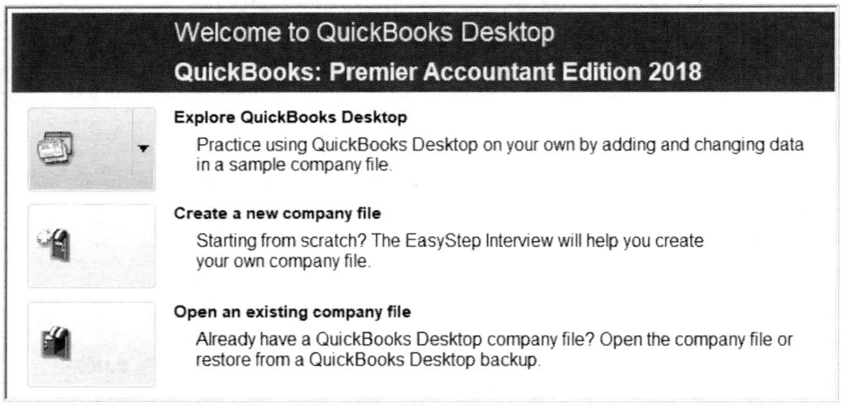

Figure 1-11a: Welcome to QuickBooks Desktop screen

This screen displays if you have not previously opened any company files; it provides options for exploring the application using a sample company file, creating a new company file, or opening an existing company file.

If you have already opened or created a file, QuickBooks may display a list of recently opened company files and prompt you to select a company file to open, as shown in Figure 1-11b.

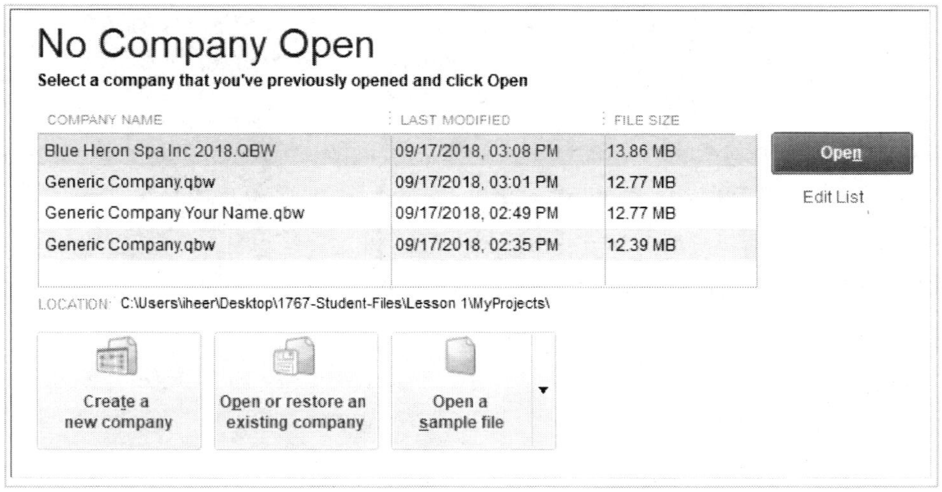

No Company Open

Select a company that you've previously opened and click Open

COMPANY NAME	LAST MODIFIED	FILE SIZE	
Blue Heron Spa Inc 2018.QBW	09/17/2018, 03:08 PM	13.86 MB	**Open**
Generic Company.qbw	09/17/2018, 03:01 PM	12.77 MB	Edit List
Generic Company Your Name.qbw	09/17/2018, 02:49 PM	12.77 MB	
Generic Company.qbw	09/17/2018, 02:35 PM	12.39 MB	

LOCATION: C:\Users\iheer\Desktop\1767-Student-Files\Lesson 1\MyProjects\

Create a new company | Open or restore an existing company | Open a sample file

Figure 1-11b: Open company options

Think of the list as a history of the files you have previously used. QuickBooks automatically adds files to this list after you open them. If the file you need is on the list, click its file name, and then click the Open button.

If you wish to change which company files are listed, click Edit List. The Edit List command allows you to remove a company file from the list but does not allow you to add files to the list.

If the company file you want to open does not appear in the list, then click the Open or restore an existing company button. This button displays the Open or Restore Company dialog box (Figure 1-12), where you can choose the type of file you want to open. The choice you make determines the type of company files that you will see when you click the Next button.

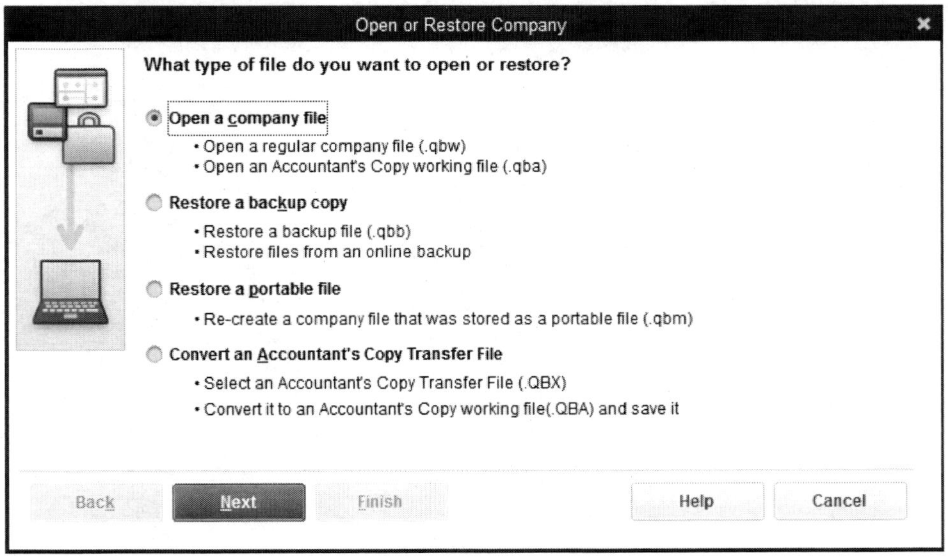

Open or Restore Company

What type of file do you want to open or restore?

● Open a company file
- Open a regular company file (.qbw)
- Open an Accountant's Copy working file (.qba)

○ Restore a backup copy
- Restore a backup file (.qbb)
- Restore files from an online backup

○ Restore a portable file
- Re-create a company file that was stored as a portable file (.qbm)

○ Convert an Accountant's Copy Transfer File
- Select an Accountant's Copy Transfer File (.QBX)
- Convert it to an Accountant's Copy working file(.QBA) and save it

Back | Next | Finish | Help | Cancel

Figure 1- 12: Open or Restore Company dialog box

To open a company file, click the Open a company file radio button, and then click the Next button to display your computer's files and folders. Only files with the .qbw file extension will appear in the file list, even if other files are stored in the same folder. By default, QuickBooks will open the folder C:\Users\Public\Public Documents\Intuit\QuickBooks\Company Files.

When you find the company file you want to open, double-click it. You may need to search another folder on your computer to locate the company files. If your office maintains a file server, the files may be located there. Ask your supervisor or IT person for help.

QuickBooks files can be password protected for additional security. Therefore, before you can start using a company file, QuickBooks may prompt you to enter a user name and password that is specific to that company file.

Note: The Generic Company .qbw file provided for this course does not have any users or passwords set up. Passwords are covered in more detail later in this lesson.

After you open the company file, QuickBooks may display one or more of the pop up messages we discussed previously. Keep in mind, however, that if the company file has been opened before, someone may have already dismissed some or all of the messages.

Viewing the Opened File

When the QuickBooks application window appears as shown in Figure 1-13, you have finished opening the company file. While difficult to see in detail except on your computer screen, it is important to identify the four main sections of the window (labeled in the figure).

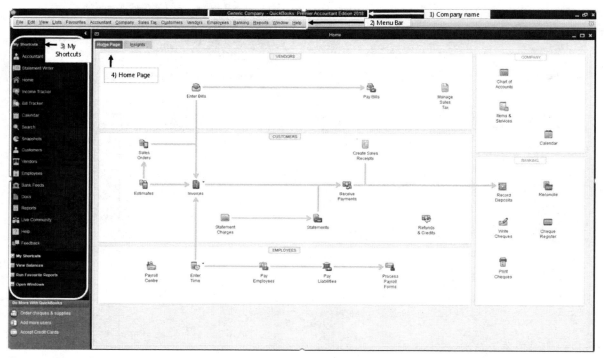

Figure 1-13: QuickBooks application window – company file opened

The four main sections of the window are:

1) **Company Name:**
   - This is the name of the person or business entity represented by the company file. The Company Name is editable, and often it is not the same as the file name of the company file. In Figure 1-13, the Company Name is *Generic Company*.

2) **Menu Bar:**

  – Each command that appears in the Menu Bar displays a pull-down menu of additional commands. You use these commands to perform actions in QuickBooks. (You can also access many actions in the menus using keyboard shortcuts.)

  – Many, but not all, commands have corresponding icons in the Home page.

3) **My Shortcuts:**

  – This panel is designed to display the shortcuts you use most often. Depending on your working style, you may like to use shortcuts instead of using the Menu Bar or the icons in the Home page.

  – You can customize this panel to include the shortcuts you want by scrolling to the bottom of the panel and clicking the Customize Shortcuts link.

  – You can click the small arrow just above and to the right of the My Shortcuts panel to hide it and open more working space.

4) **Home Page:**

  – The icons and arrows that display in the Home page indicate the workflow of the Accounting Cycle. That is, they show a flow chart of the main cycle steps.

  – Click an icon to open a form or perform an action.

  – You can also customize which icons appear in the Home page.

Notice that the Home page is separated into distinct sections. Each section is labeled in blue: there is a section for VENDORS, CUSTOMERS, EMPLOYEES, COMPANY, and BANKING. Each section includes icons for accessing the commands and tasks associated with it.

Closing the Company File

Objective L-1.1 Find, open, save, rename, and close QuickBooks files

When you finish using a company file, you should close it, and then if you are finished working for the day, you should exit QuickBooks. Although it is possible to exit QuickBooks while a company file is still open, that same company file will automatically load the next time you launch QuickBooks. This means that instead of prompting you for a company file to open, QuickBooks may prompt you to log in to a file, which can be very confusing if you regularly work with multiple QuickBooks files or share a computer with other accountants. It is good practice to close your company files every time you finish work, even if you will also exit QuickBooks.

You may also need to close a company file to log in as a different QuickBooks user. Some operations, such as changing the company name or creating a portable company file, can be performed only while logged in as the Admin.

To close a company file, in the Menu Bar, click **File > Close Company**, as shown in Figure 1-14.

File	Edit	View	Lists	Favourites	Accountant	Cor

New Company...
New Company from Existing Company File...
Open or Restore Company...
Open Previous Company   ▶
Open Second Company
Create Backup...
Restore Previous Local Backup   ▶
Create Copy...
Close Company

Figure 1-14: Close company file

When you close the company file, you may see a message asking if you want to back up the file. This message appears after a set number of file closings, which you can configure in QuickBooks settings. You may skip the backup operation by clicking the No button.

If you want to exit QuickBooks, in the Menu Bar, click **File > Exit**, or click the X at the top right of the QuickBooks application window.

Exercise 1.1: Launching QuickBooks and Opening and Closing the Company File

In this exercise, you will launch QuickBooks, determine the product release number, examine the Automatic Update feature, and then find, open, and close the Generic Company file.

Launch QuickBooks.

1. Double-click the **QuickBooks** icon on the desktop (or use your preferred method) to launch QuickBooks. If the QuickBooks software update message appears, ask your instructor if you should click **Install Now** to install the update, or **Install Later** to postpone it. The No Company Open dialog box appears.

    Note: Respond to all pop up messages appropriately (or as directed by your instructor) as they appear.

Determine the product release number.

2. Press the **F2** keyboard key. The Product Information dialog box appears. Notice that the QuickBooks version and release number appears in the Product line at the top of the dialog box. Write your release number on the line provided: _____

3. Click **OK** to close the Product Information dialog box.

Check the Automatic Update feature settings.

4. In the Menu Bar, click **Help > Update QuickBooks Desktop**. The Update QuickBooks Desktop dialog box appears.

5. Click the **Options** tab to access the update settings.

6. Is your product configured to receive automatic updates? _____.

7. Ask your instructor if you should change your setting. If necessary, select the appropriate Automatic Update radio button, click the **Save** button to save a new setting if applicable, and then click the **Close** button to close the dialog box.

    Note: If you do not make changes to the Automatic Update setting, the Save button will be unavailable. Click the **Close** button to close the dialog box.

Find, open, and close the Generic Company.

8. If Generic Company does not appear in the list in the No Company Open dialog box, click **Open or restore an existing company**, ensure that **Open a company file** is selected, click **Next**, navigate to the *1767-Student-Files\Lesson 1\StarterFiles* folder, click **Generic Company.qbw**, then click **Open**. Otherwise, double-click **Generic Company** in the list to open it.

If the Welcome to QuickBooks Desktop screen displays instead of the No Company Open dialog box, click **Open an existing company file**, ensure that **Open a company file** is selected, click **Next**, navigate to the *1767-Student-Files\Lesson 1\StarterFiles* folder, click **Generic Company.qbw**, then click **Open**.

9. If the Payroll Update warning message displays, click **OK** to dismiss it.

10. If the External Accountant message displays, select the **Don't show this again** check box, then click **No**.

11. If the Accountant Centre window opens, click the **Show Accountant Centre when opening a company file** check box to deselect it, then close the Accountant Centre window.

Close the Generic Company file.

12. In the Menu Bar, click **File > Close Company** to close the Generic Company file. The No Company Open dialog box appears.

Leave QuickBooks open for the next exercise.

Opening a Portable File

Objective L-1.1 Find, open, save, rename, and close QuickBooks files

QuickBooks allows you to save company files in several useful formats. One type you will often need to open is a portable QuickBooks file. In this course, you will use portable QuickBooks files in the exercises, and you will create them when submitting your work to your instructor. You have been given several portable company files, including one for the Generic Company, which has been configured with user names and passwords.

In the accounting world, you may be asked to restore a portable file that a client emailed to the accounting firm. There are two ways to open a portable company file. You can launch QuickBooks, then click the Open or restore an existing company button, or in the Menu Bar, click **File > Open or Restore Company**, as shown in Figure 1-15.

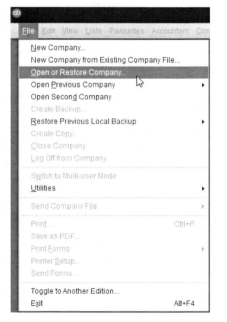

Figure 1-15: File > Open or Restore Company command

Both methods display the Open or Restore Company dialog box shown in Figure 1-16. To open a portable file, select the Restore a portable file radio button, and then click Next.

Note: When you do this, QuickBooks will close any company file you previously had open.

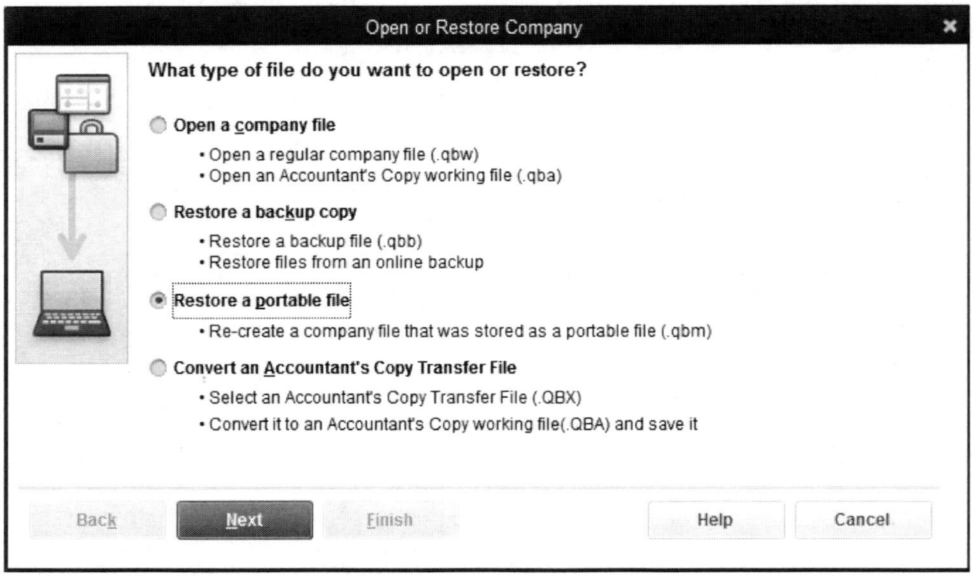

Figure 1-16: Open or Restore Company dialog box – restore a portable file

QuickBooks will then display your computer's files and folders. Only QuickBooks portable files will appear in the Open Portable Company File dialog box, as shown in Figure 1-17. Find your portable company file and double-click it to open the file.

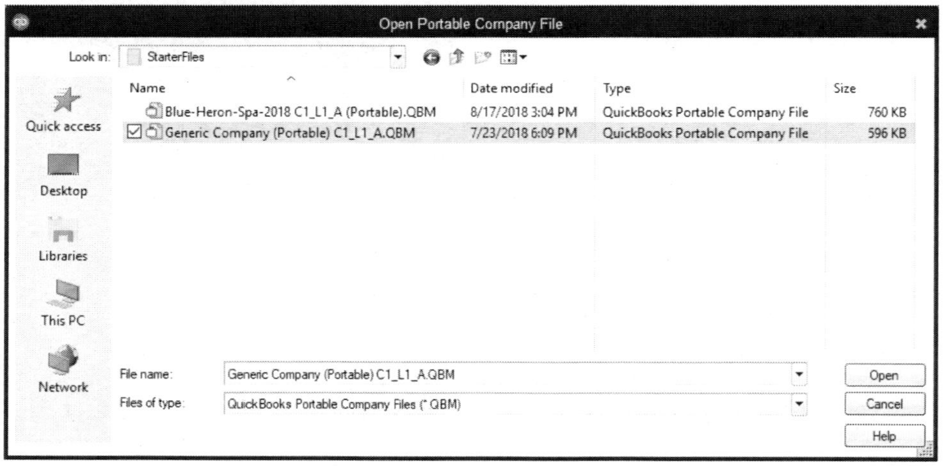

Figure 1-17: Open Portable Company File dialog box

After you open the portable company file, you need to specify where to save it. QuickBooks will advise you to think about the name you will use for the restored file, as shown in Figure 1-18.

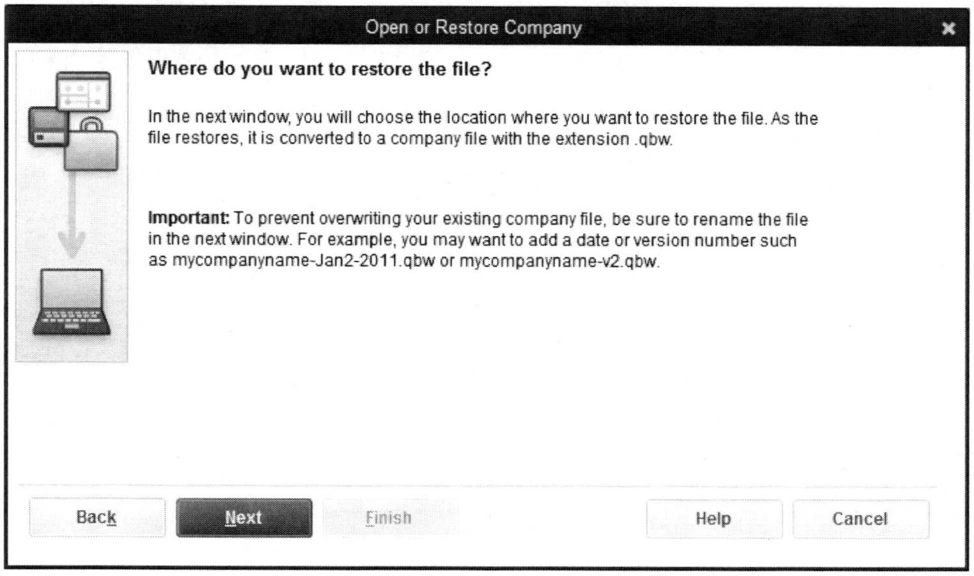

Figure 1-18: Open or Restore Company dialog box – file location and name message

You can select either a new folder or the default location. Then, in the File name field, enter the name of the restored company file, as shown in Figure 1-19. The file name can differ from the company name, but they are usually similar. Remember, the company name is the name that appears at the top of the QuickBooks application window when the company file is open; the file name is how you will identify different company files on your computer, as you saw in Figure 1-17. In this class, you will add your name to the end of the existing file name to show your instructor that this is your file for this lesson.

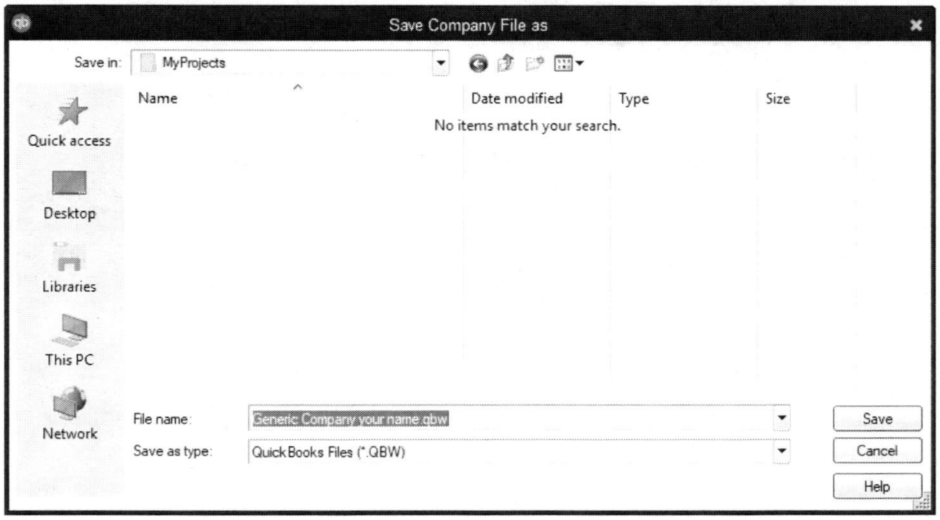

Figure 1-19: Save Company File as dialog box - name company file and choose location

When you click Save you will see a message that the file is opening (Figure 1-20).

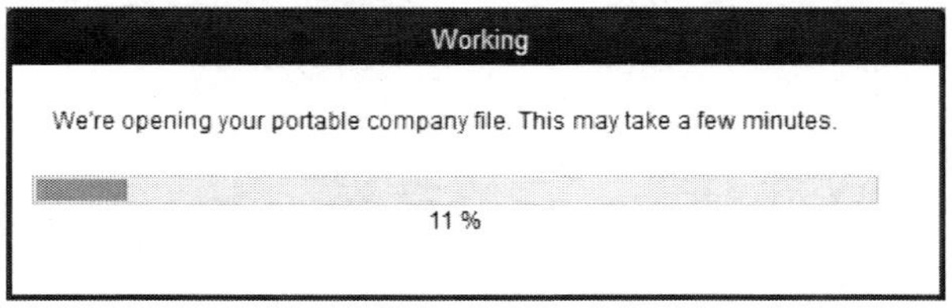

Figure 1-20: File is opening

After the file opens, you may be prompted to log in to it using a QuickBooks user name and password, as shown in Figure 1-21. If user names and passwords have not been configured in the company file, QuickBooks will display the Home page.

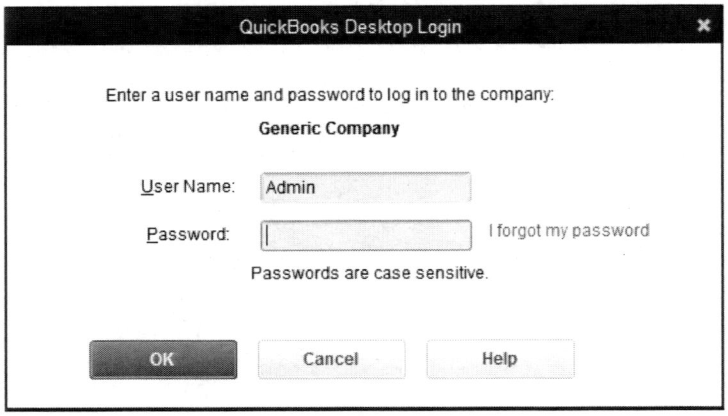

Figure 1-21: QuickBooks Desktop Login dialog box

Note: QuickBooks has a predefined user name called *Admin* that has unique permissions in QuickBooks company files. By default, this user name has no password associated with it.

The provided portable company file for the Generic Company has been configured with user names and passwords. The Admin user in this sample file does not have a password, so you may click the OK button to proceed to the Home page.

After the company file has successfully opened, you will see a confirmation message (Figure 1-22).

Figure 1-22: Portable file opened successfully

Exercise 1.2: Restoring Portable Files

In this exercise, you will restore the Generic Company portable file.

1. In the No Company Open dialog box, click **Open or restore an existing company**. The Open or Restore Company dialog box appears.

2. Click **Restore a portable file**, then click **Next**. The Open Portable Company File dialog box appears.

3. Navigate to the *1767-Student-Files\Lesson 1\StarterFiles* folder, click **Generic Company (Portable) C1_L1_A.QBM**, then click **Open**.

4. Read the prompt about how to avoid overwriting your existing company file in the Open or Restore Company dialog box, then click **Next**. The Save Company File as dialog box appears.

5. Navigate to the *1767-Student-Files\Lesson 1\MyProjects* folder, click in the **File name** field, at the end of the existing text type your name (it should read *Generic Company <your name>.QBW*), and then click **Save**. This step saves a company file with your name.

Note: This process may take a few minutes.

6.   When the QuickBooks Desktop Login dialog box appears, ensure that **Admin** appears in the *User Name* field, then click **OK** to log in as the Admin. Click **OK** again to close the message box informing you that the portable company file has been opened successfully.

Leave the company file with your name open for the next exercise.

Creating a Portable Company File

Objective L-1.1 Find, open, save, rename, and close QuickBooks files

A portable file is a compressed version of a company file that is small enough to send electronically. You can create a portable company file using the Menu Bar while the company file is open. You will frequently follow this process, which can be started in two ways: either by saving or sending the file.

Note: Only the Admin user can create a portable company file.

Saving a Portable Company File

If you want to save the portable file on your computer, in the Menu Bar, click **File > Create Copy**, as shown in Figure 1-23a.

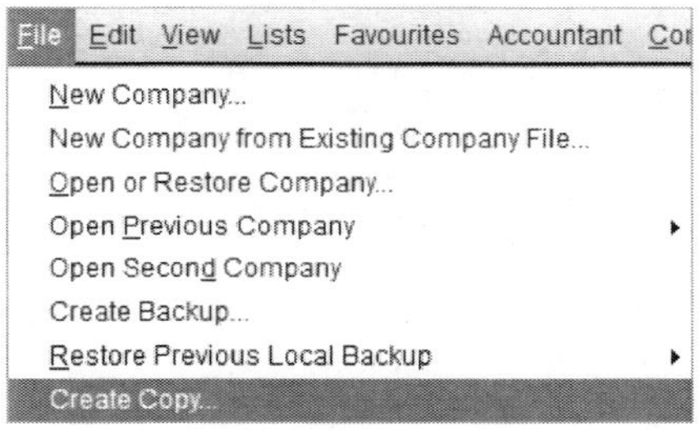

Figure 1-23a: File > Create Copy command

In the Save Copy or Backup dialog box, shown in Figure 1-23b, select the Portable company file radio button, and then click Next.

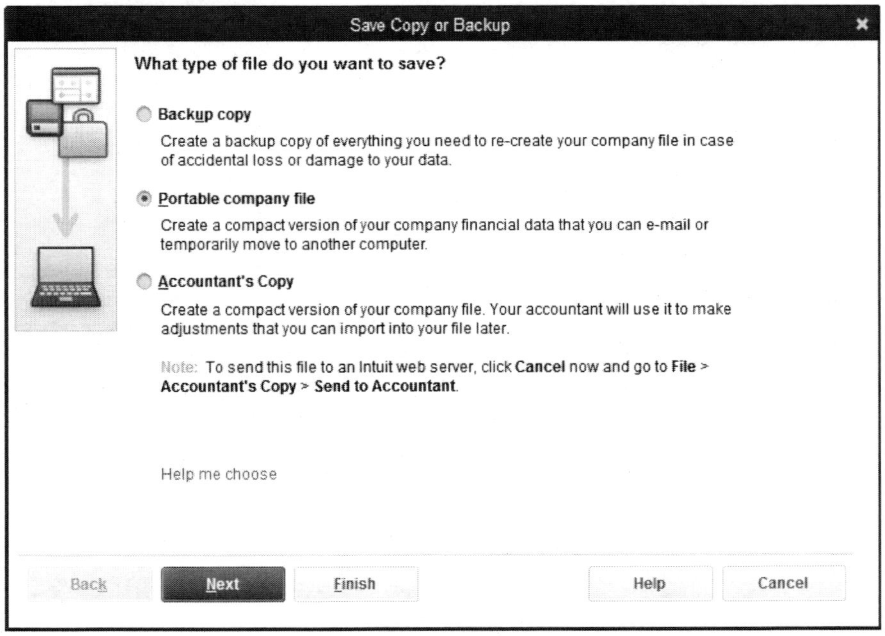

Figure 1-23b: Save Copy or Backup dialog box – Portable company file selected

QuickBooks displays your computer's files and folders, as shown in Figure 1-23c. Find the folder where you want to save your portable company file, enter a file name for the file, and then click Save.

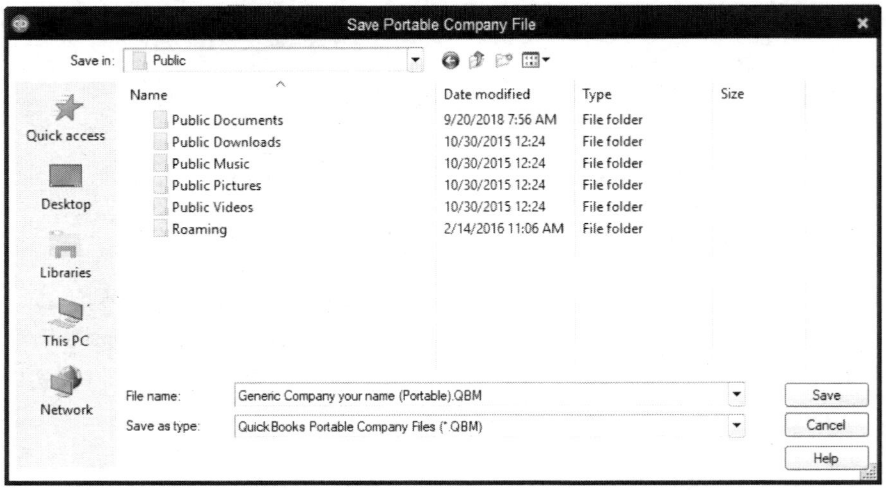

Figure 1-23c: Save Portable Company File dialog box – specify name and location

You'll see a message informing you that the company file must close and reopen (Figure 1-23d). Click OK to close the message.

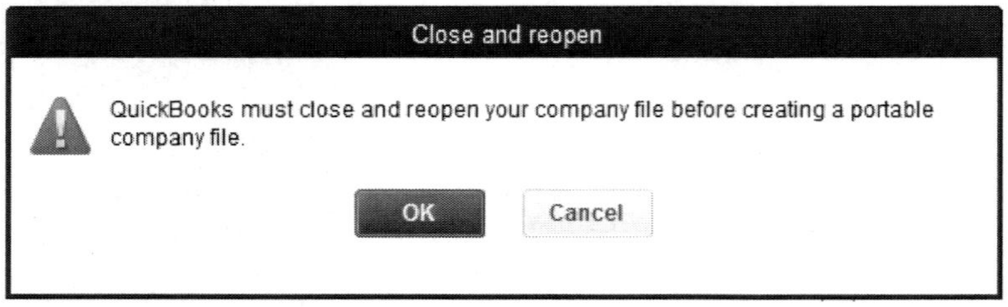

Figure 1-23d: Close and reopen message

When you have successfully saved the portable file, you'll see the informational message shown in Figure 1-23e. Click OK to close the message.

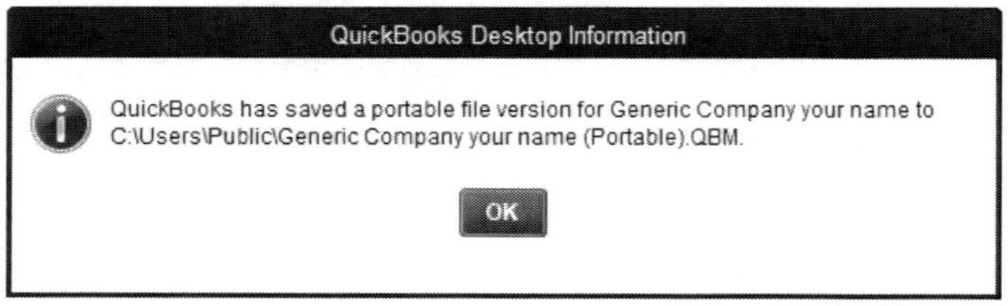

Figure 1-23e: Portable file successfully saved

Sending a Portable Company File

If you want to send the portable file to a location not on your computer, such as a commercial cloud storage site, in the Menu Bar, click **File > Send Company File > Portable Company File**, as shown in Figure 1-24a.

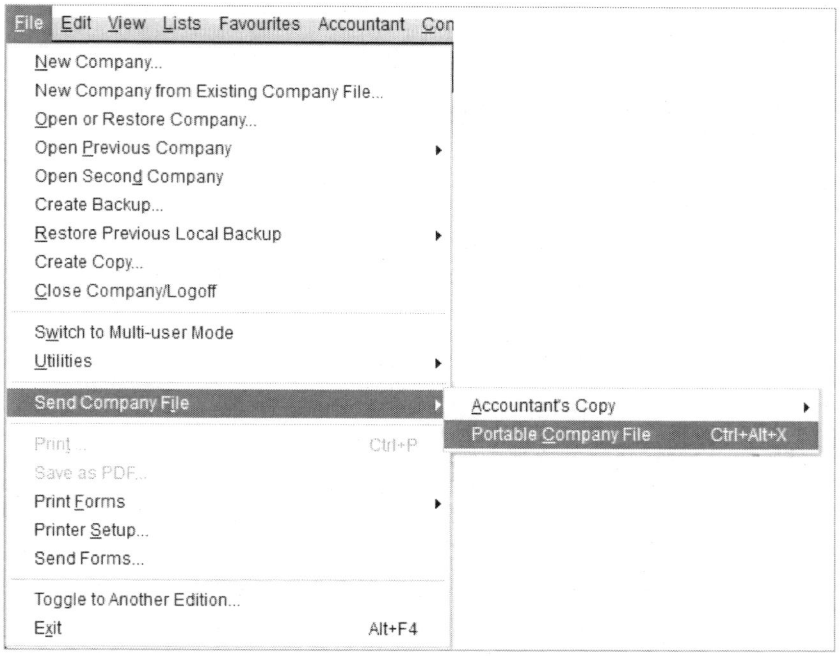

Figure 1-24a: File > Send Company File command and options

The Send Portable Company File dialog box appears (Figure 1-24b) and asks you where you want to send the portable file. The location shown in this example is on the local hard drive. Click the Browse button to find the folder where the file should be saved, select it, and then click the Send button.

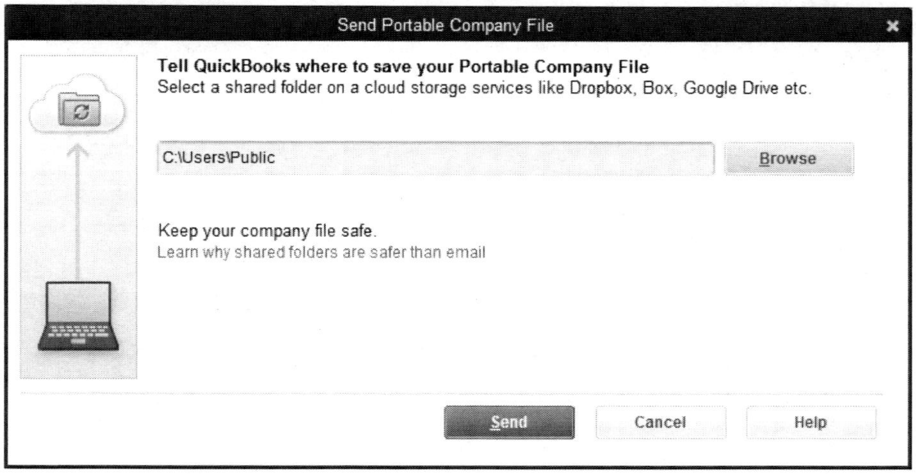

Figure 1-24b: Send Portable Company File dialog box

You'll see a message informing you that the company file must close and open (Figure 1-24c). Click OK to close the message.

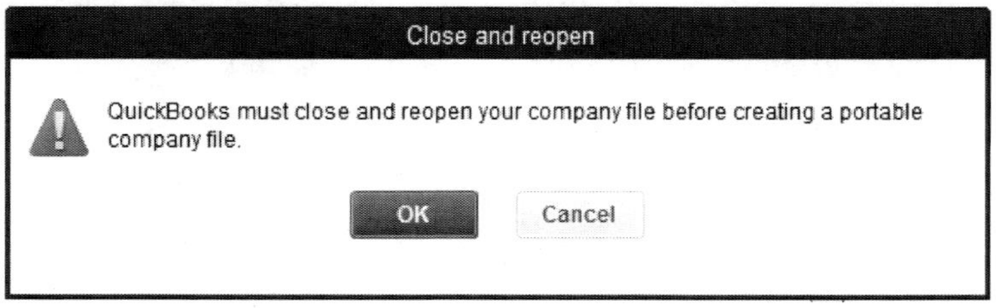

Figure 1-24c: Close and reopen message

When you have successfully sent the portable file, you will see the informational message shown in Figure 1-24d.

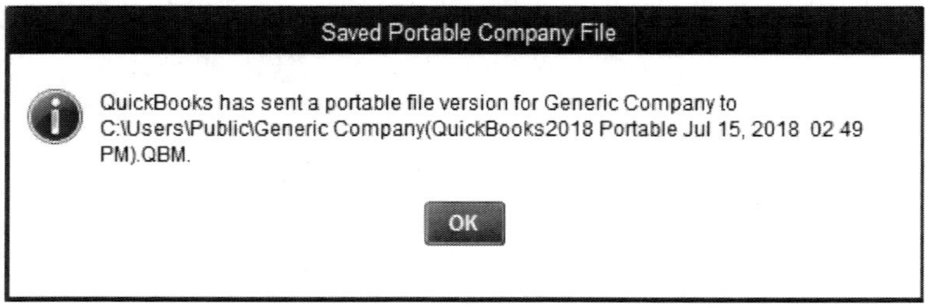

Figure 1-24d: Portable file successfully sent

Changing the Company Name

Sometimes a company changes names. A name change may occur when partners decide to incorporate or when, for marketing reasons, a company needs a new name other than the legal business name. For example, instead of Smith and Green, LLC, the partners may choose to operate under a different name such as Best Custom T-Shirts. The new name is called a **DBA**, short for *doing business as*, and is a registered legal alias for the business.

Note: Only the Admin user can change the company name.

To change the company name, in the Menu Bar, click **Company > Company Information**, as shown in Figure 1-25.

Figure 1-25: Company > Company Information command

The Company Information dialog box appears. Notice that the value in the Company Name field matches the name displayed in the title bar of the QuickBooks application window, as shown in Figure 1-26.

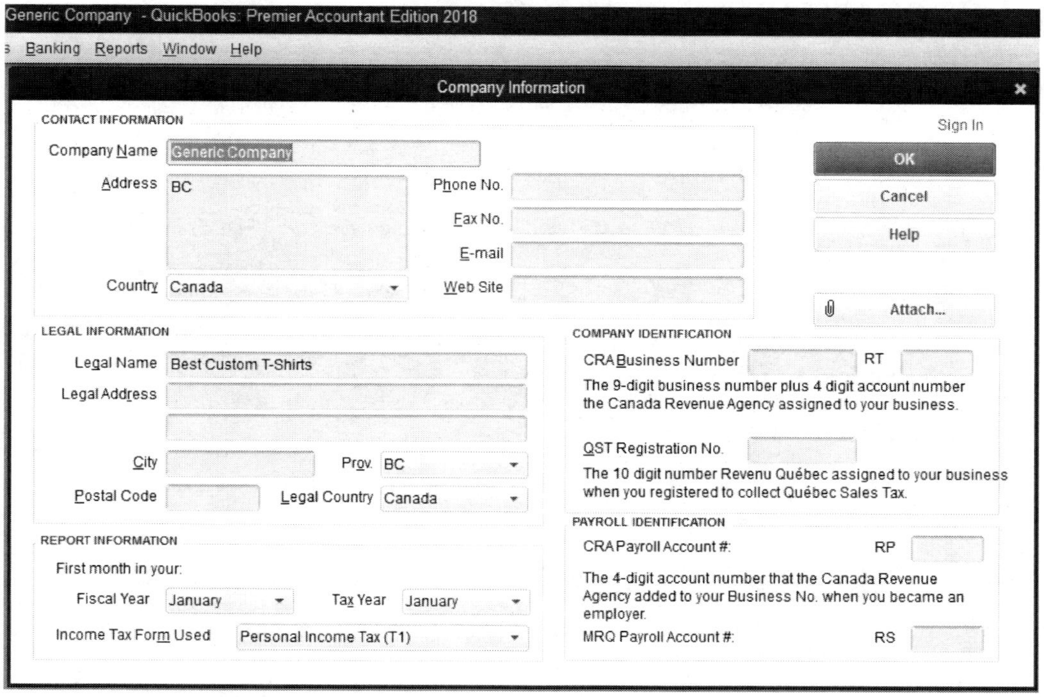

Figure 1-26: Company Information dialog box

To change the company name, enter the new name in the Company Name field (for example, Best Custom T-Shirts), as shown in Figure 1-27. Click OK to save the changes.

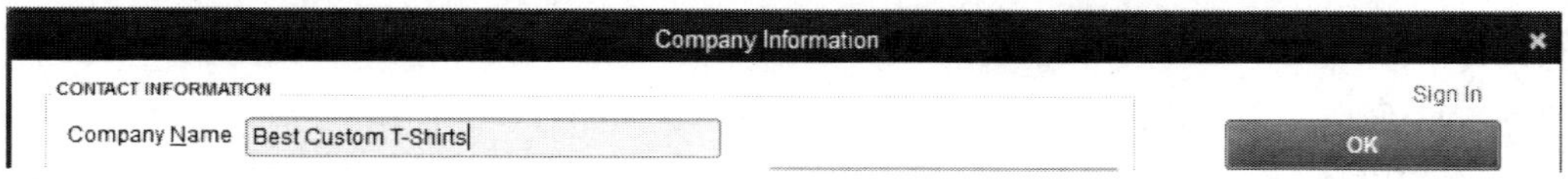

Figure 1-27: Change company name

The new company name appears in the title bar of the QuickBooks application window, as shown in Figure 1-28.

Figure 1-28: New company name

Exercise 1.3: Changing the Company Name and Creating Portable Company Files

In this exercise, you will change the company name, create a portable company file, close the company file, and then re-open and log in to it using the *Student* user name and password.

Rename the company with your name.

1. Ensure that the Generic Company file with your name that you restored in the previous exercise is still open.

2. In the Menu Bar, click **Company > Company Information**. The Company Information dialog box appears.

3. Click in the *Company Name* field and at the end of the existing text type your name (it should read *Generic Company <your name>*), then click **OK**.

Create a portable file to turn in as part of this lesson's assignments.

4. Click **File > Create Copy**. The Save Copy or Backup dialog box appears.

5. Select **Portable company file**, then click **Next**. The Save Portable Company File dialog box appears.

6. Navigate to the *1767-Student-Files\Lesson 1\MyProjects* folder, then click **Save**.

7. Click **OK** in the Close and reopen message box. QuickBooks closes the company file and creates a portable file with your name and the .qbm extension.

    Note: This is the file you will turn in.

8. Click **OK** to close the message box informing you that the portable file version has been saved. QuickBooks then reopens the company file.

Close the company file with your name so that you can log in again as a user other than Admin.

9. Click **File > Close Company/Logoff** to close the company file. The No Company Open dialog box appears.

Open the company file with your name and log in as the user named Student.

10. In the list, click the company file with your name, then click **Open**. The QuickBooks Desktop Login dialog box appears.

11. Select the text in the *User Name* field and type: **Student**.

12. Click in the **Password** field, type: **Student**, then click **OK**. This step opens the company file with your name using the student log in.

Leave the company file with your name open for the next exercise.

Examining QuickBooks Forms

Objective L-1.3 Locate the Purchases and Sales Cycle Forms
Objective L-1.4 Compare form usage to General Journal Entries
Objective L-1.5 Navigate forms

Now that you can open and close the company files successfully, you need to locate and open forms to start entering transactions in a QuickBooks cycle.

You will learn how QuickBooks forms affect your accounting records, including how form data automatically become journal entries. You'll also see how entering data in forms differs from manually creating general journal entries in QuickBooks.

After you complete a form, you may want to find it again quickly using the QuickBooks search form. You may also use keyboard shortcuts, which can help you open and navigate among connected forms. First, however, we'll learn more about using QuickBooks Cycles, how QuickBooks allows access to related forms in a cycle, and why using forms is so important compared to creating entries. We will also explore general journal entries in more detail.

Cycle Starting Points

The two cycles you'll explore in this section are Purchases and Sales. The Purchases and Sales Cycles each meet with the Banking Cycle when the arrows complete their circles, as shown in Figure 1-29.

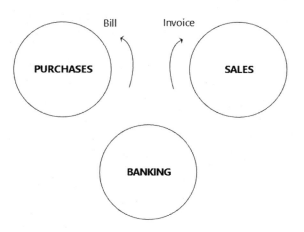

Figure 1-29: Bill and Invoice on Purchases and Sales Cycles

On each cycle, you'll see the name of each form you'll explore in this section—Bill and Invoice. Purchases are made from **vendors** using the Bill form. Sales are made to **customers** using the Invoice form. You use the **Bill** form to enter purchase transactions, and the **Invoice** form to enter sales transactions.

Form Connections and General Journal Entries

Every time you complete transactions in the QuickBooks Cycles, each form becomes connected to the form that preceded it. If you open any form in the cycle, you can easily find every form connected to it, whether a prior form or later form.

Figure 1-30 shows the Purchases Cycle with the Bill Payment step added. The next step is to Print Cheques, which is part of the Banking Cycle. After you pay the bill with a cheque, the bill is connected to the cheque.

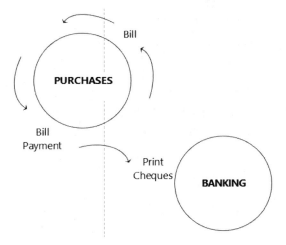

Figure 1-30: Purchases Cycle connects to Banking Cycle

You can use the CTRL+H keyboard shortcut to move among connected transactions. The H in this shortcut stands for History, as in the history of your forms. Later in this section, you will learn more about keyboard shortcuts.

Forms and General Journal Entries

In QuickBooks, whenever you use a form to record a transaction, the form automatically creates a journal entry in the accounting records. As you move through a cycle and continue to use forms, the transactions in these forms are linked together as you complete the series of transactions. In practical terms, you might want to know which cheque paid a certain bill. If you entered the transactions using forms, then you can find this information quickly using the form history, which is accessed using the keyboard shortcut CTRL+H.

You can also manually enter transactions as journal entries into the General Journal. However, unlike the QuickBooks forms, this process does not create any historical connections between the journal entries. This means that if you entered a transaction manually as a general journal entry, there is no quick way to find correlated entries.

Let's briefly review the basic parts of a general journal entry and how it looks.

General Journal Entries

The main general journal entry elements are the date, description, account, and amount. You will enter every amount into an **account** as a **debit** and a **credit**. This double entry is the reason accounting is called double-entry bookkeeping. Because you enter each amount twice for every transaction, the debits always equal the credits, which is how you keep the accounting system in balance.

However, debits and credits are neither positive nor negative. Either a debit or credit can increase or decrease the total amount, also called the **balance**, in any account. Where an account exists in the accounting records determines how the debit or credit behaves in that account. The account balance equals the difference between the total debits and total credits. In this lesson, we'll cover two of the three account types, assets and liabilities (Table 1-2). The third account type, equity, will be covered in Lesson 2.

Table 1-2: Account section and effects of debits and credits

Account Section	What increases the account	What decreases the account
Assets - What a business owns	Debit increases	Credit decreases
Liabilities - What a business owes	Credit increases	Debit decreases

This short general journal entry shows the preferred presentation. Debits are on the left and listed first. Credits are on the right and listed last. The date and description are located at the top, and the accounts are listed to the far left.

Date: Month, Day, Year

Description	Debit	Credit
Account A	100	
Account B		100

General Journal entries follow the same basic format as a T-account, showing all the debits and credits in the accounts in this same pattern. A T-account presentation of a general journal entry is useful for verifying that the results will correctly affect the accounts. The only difference is that the date and account switch places, because all the debits and credits are in the same account. This general journal entry looks like a set of T-accounts with the debit in Account A and the credit in Account B:

Account A		Account B	
100			100

Deciding whether an account is going to be debited or credited is the difficult part about entering a journal entry. The value of using a QuickBooks form is that the form automatically chooses either debit or credit. When you make a manual general journal entry, *you* need to make the choices.

Let's briefly review what the bill form and invoice form enter into the accounting records. You can see a summary of this in Table 1-3. You will record a bill when you purchase on credit and, therefore, owe a vendor. You will create an invoice when you sell on credit and a customer owes you.

Table 1-3: Types of forms and their effects on debits and credits

Form	Debit	Credit
Bill	Increases Inventory, Expenses, or Assets	Increases what is owed to others
Invoice	Increases what is owed from others	Increases sales

A general journal entry performs the exact same thing as the form, but in a general journal entry *you* must choose which account receives the debit and which receives the credit, as well as the corresponding accumulating account.

Opening a Bill and an Invoice

Objective L-1.3 Locate Purchases and Sales Cycle forms

You can open forms by clicking their representative icons in the Home page or accessing them from the Menu Bar. Figure 1-13 shows the Home page icons you click to open a bill (Enter Bills) and an invoice (Invoices > Create Invoices). Figure 1-31 shows the Menu Bar command to open an invoice form. Figure 1-32 shows the Menu Bar command to open a bill form.

Figure 1-31: Opening an invoice form

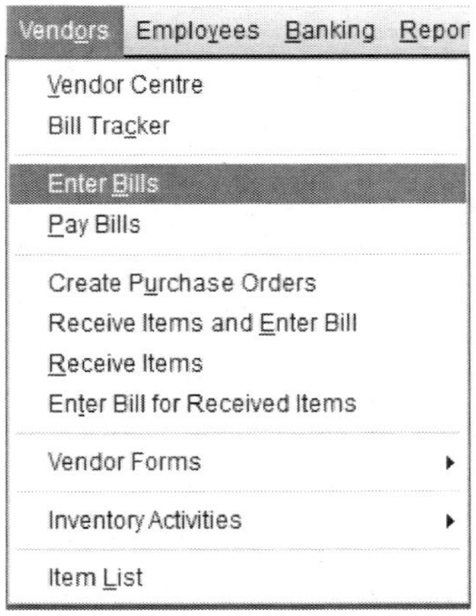

Figure 1-32: Opening a bill form

Figure 1-33 shows the Create Invoices form and Figure 1-34 shows the Enter Bills form. Each form has a ribbon at the top containing similar commands.

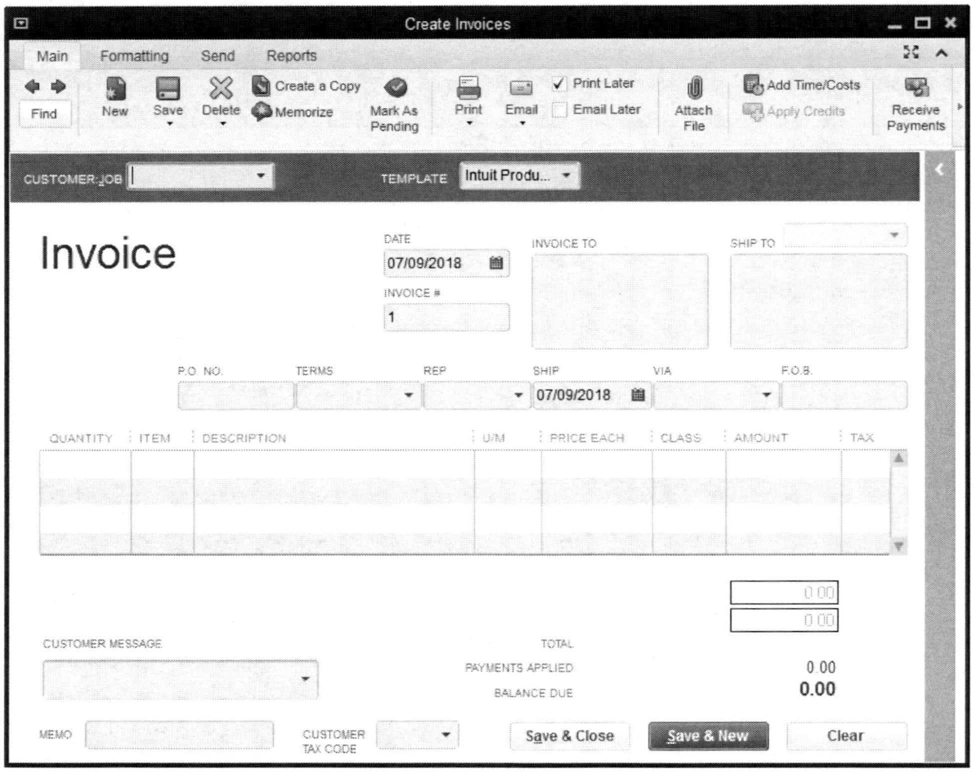

Figure 1-33: Create Invoices form

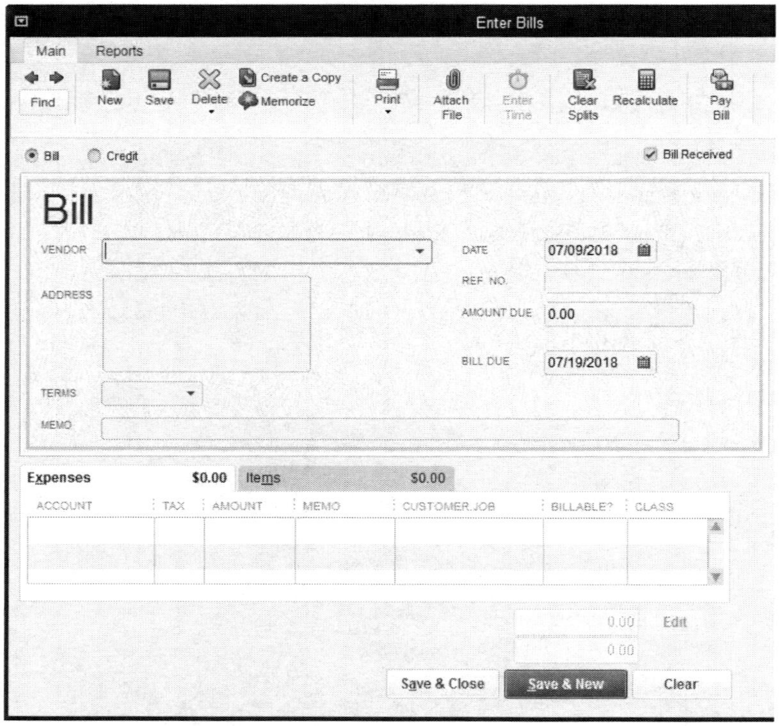

Figure 1-34: Enter Bills form

Each of the forms includes a ribbon and a detail area of blue and white lines and columns that looks like a grid for entering transactions. Buttons appear below the detail area. You can use multiple lines on any form. Each blue or white line becomes one entry line.

In the next exercise, you will explore the Invoice and Bill forms shown in Figures 1-33 and 1-34.

Exercise 1.4: Opening and Exploring Bills and Invoices

In this exercise, you will locate and open a bill and an invoice. You will also navigate and enter data in the form fields.

Open a bill and an invoice.

1. Ensure that the company file with your name that you used in the previous exercise is still open.

2. In the *VENDORS* section of the Home page, click **Enter Bills**. The Enter Bills window appears.

3. Click in an empty area in the Home page. In the *CUSTOMERS* section, click **Invoices**, then select **Create Invoices**. The Create Invoices window appears.

4. Toggle between the Enter Bills and Create Invoices windows to examine and compare their components.

Experiment with navigating fields and entering data in the forms.

5. Use the mouse to click in various fields in both forms. Then press the **TAB** key to move from field to field in each form. Notice that each form has a specific tab order.

6. Review the buttons and commands in each form and note their similarities.

7. In the *DATE* field in either form, select the existing date and enter a new date in the **mmddyy** format (for example: **081318**) and press **TAB**. Notice that it is not necessary to enter the forward slash characters, and the last two digits of the year are sufficient.

8. In the *DATE* field in either form, click the **calendar** icon and change the date using the calendar.

9. The *AMOUNT DUE* field in the Enter Bills window and the *AMOUNT* fields in the Create Invoices window contain a calculator you can use to enter amounts using arithmetic operators. In any of these fields, use the add, subtract, divide, or multiply operators to enter amounts (for example: **3+7**).

10. Type some words in either of the *MEMO* fields. Then, use the mouse to click, double-click, and triple-click to select various portions of text. Notice that, unlike in many programs, triple-clicking does not select all of the text in the field.

11. In the window in which you entered memo text, press the **ENTER** key. Because the form is not complete, an error message will appear. If the form were complete, pressing the ENTER key would save your transaction. It is good practice to use the buttons rather than the ENTER key to complete a form.

12. Click **OK** to close the error message.

13. In both forms, click their respective **CLEAR** buttons to remove the data you entered.

14. Close the **Enter Bills** and **Create Invoices** windows.

Leave the company file with your name open for the next exercise.

Finding a Transaction

Objective L-1.5 Navigate forms

Even with the connections between forms, you may still need to find a specific entry in the cycle. QuickBooks has a powerful lookup tool called Find. You can open it in either a bill or an invoice by using the Find button. Alternatively, in the Menu Bar, click **Edit > Find**, or use the keyboard shortcut CTRL+F.

Figure 1-35 shows the Advanced tab of the Find window, which you can use to find the exact amount of a transaction, $2.77. You can also use options in the Simple tab to look for specific transaction criteria. Press the ENTER key to run the search. Alternatively, you can click the Find button.

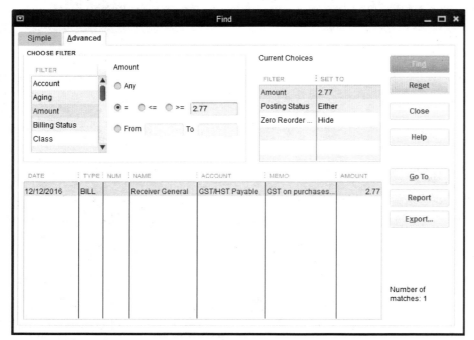

Figure 1-35: Find tool

Keyboard Shortcuts

Objective L-1.5 Navigate forms

You can use the ALT key in QuickBooks to provide keyboard shortcuts for displaying Menu Bar commands. In Figure 1-36, notice that some of the words in the Menu Bar have an underscored letter, such as File.

File   Edit   View   Lists   Favourites   Accountant   Company   Sales Tax   Customers   Vendors   Employees   Banking   Reports   Window   Help

Figure 1-36: Menu Bar

If you press and hold the ALT key, and then press an underlined letter in the Menu Bar, the drop-down menu for that command will appear. Figure 1-37 shows the result of pressing ALT+E, which displays the Edit menu.

```
 Edit  View  Lists  Favourites  Accounta
  Undo Typing            Ctrl+Z
  Revert

  Cut                    Ctrl+X
  Copy                   Ctrl+C
  Paste                  Ctrl+V

  Copy Line              Ctrl+Alt+Y
  Paste Line             Ctrl+Alt+V
  New Bill               Ctrl+N
  Delete Bill            Ctrl+D
  Duplicate Bill
  Memorize Bill          Ctrl+M
  Void Bill
  Copy Bill              Ctrl+O
  Go To Transfer         Ctrl+G
  Transaction History... Ctrl+H
```

Figure 1-37: ALT+E displays Edit drop-down menu

Note: The commands in the Edit menu vary depending on which window is open.

Once you have pressed the ALT key and the letter corresponding to the drop-down menu, press the underlined letter of the command you want to use. For example, after pressing ALT+E, press the H key to open the Transaction History window. This sequence will usually be the same as using the keyboard shortcut CTRL+<letter> outside of a menu; for example, you can press CTRL+H to open the Transaction History window. The Transaction History window allows you to move between connected forms within a cycle.

Changing Settings

While working in your company files, you can change the QuickBooks settings as you prefer. However, in the business world, you will often share files with others, and they may have different QuickBooks preferences. You need to understand how specific settings may affect your data entry process and how the company file behaves.

Checking User Mode

QuickBooks files allow multiple people to use them at the same time; this is called ***multi-user mode***. While in multi-user mode, some actions may be unavailable. You might also receive additional messages when saving forms. For now, we will focus on where to find the information and emphasize that if the company file is in multi-user mode, it's essential to close the file when work is completed.

Note: Some actions are possible only when the company file is open in ***single-user mode***. It is not possible to open a company file in single-user mode if any other user has the file open.

To check the mode of the file, in the Menu Bar, click File to display the File menu. You will see either Switch to Multi-user Mode, which means the file is in single-user mode, or Switch to Single-user Mode.

Accessing the Settings

Objective L-1.6 Verify data entry settings

To open QuickBooks settings, in the Menu Bar, click **Edit > Preferences**, as shown in Figure 1-38.

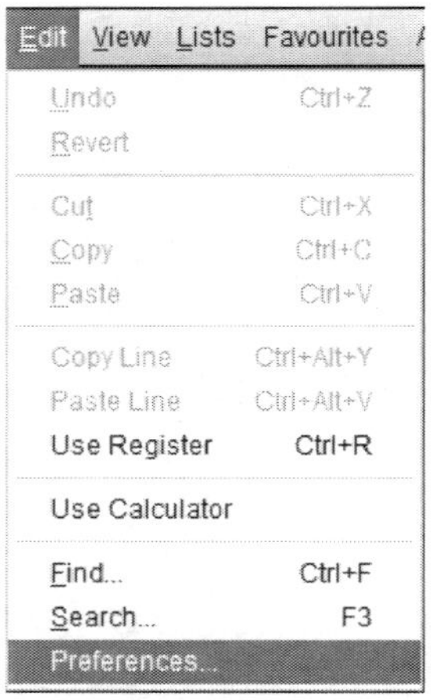

Figure 1-38: Edit > Preferences command

The Preferences dialog box will appear, displaying a list of categories in the left sidebar. Click a category in the sidebar to display the available preference settings for that category. The General preferences are shown in Figure 1-39.

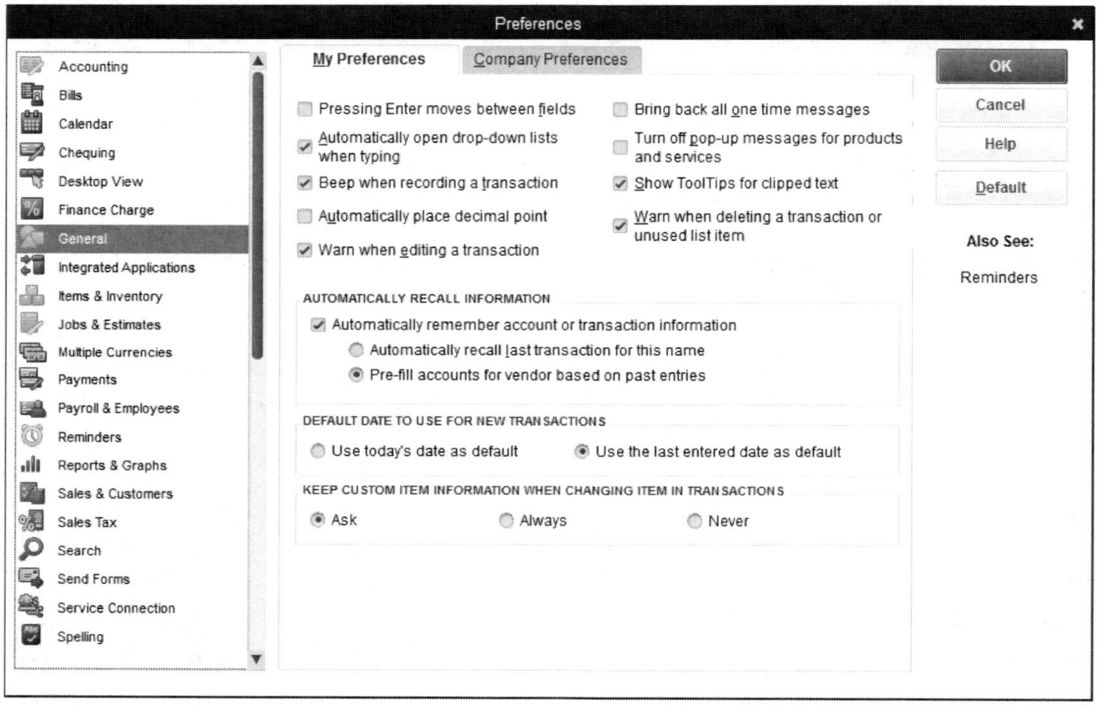

Figure 1-39: Preferences dialog box – General preferences

Notice that there are two tabs in the Preferences dialog box – the My Preferences tab and the Company Preferences tab. Settings on the My Preferences tab affect the current user logged in to the company file.

Preference settings specified on the Company Preferences tab affect all users who perform work in the company file. These settings control how company files behave and can affect which options are visible and accessible while performing various bookkeeping tasks. You must be an Admin to change settings on the Company Preferences tab.

For now, all the settings you want to check are in either the General or Desktop View preferences. In this section, we'll concentrate on the General preferences and how they affect data entry, navigation, and software views.

Setting General Preferences

On the My Preferences tab of the Preferences dialog box, there are four main options you need to know:

- **Pressing Enter moves between fields** – If this is selected, you will use the ENTER key in place of the TAB key. This means you will need to click the Save button, instead of pressing ENTER when you wish to save the data in a form.

- **Automatically place decimal point** – If this is selected, QuickBooks will automatically place the decimal point before the last two numbers entered, even if the decimal point key is not pressed. If this check box is not selected, then you must type the decimal point when entering numbers.

- **Bring back all one time messages** – If this is selected, QuickBooks will display any message you had previously dismissed, whether by accident or on purpose.

- **Default date to use for new transactions** – If the Use today's date as default radio button is selected, the current date will be entered in the date field of any new form. If the Use the last entered date as default radio button is selected, the date you used on the most recent form will be entered in the date field of any new form.

Note: You can select the **Bring back all one time messages** check box to reactivate message prompts for which you have checked the Do not display this message in the future check box.

Exercise 1.5: Changing Preferences

In this exercise, you will change preferences by specifying to automatically place the decimal point when you enter numeric data in forms.

1. Ensure that the company file with your name that you used in the previous exercise is still open.

2. In the Menu Bar, click **Edit > Preferences**. The Preferences dialog box appears.

3. In the list of categories in the left sidebar, click **General** if necessary.

4. In the My Preferences tab, click the **Automatically place decimal point** check box to select it, then click **OK** to save the setting.

5. Open the **Create Invoices** window.

6. In the first *AMOUNT* field, type: **10468**, and then press **TAB**. Notice that 104.68 appears in the field.

7. Delete the amount you just entered, type: **104.68** (using the decimal key), and then press **TAB**. Notice that, again, 104.68 appears in the field.

8. Click the **Clear** button and close the **Create Invoices** window.

9. In the Menu Bar, click **File > Close Company/Logoff** to close the company file with your name. If a message appears prompting you to create a backup, click **No**. The No Company Open dialog box appears.

Leave the No Company Open dialog box open for the next exercise.

Setting Desktop View Preferences

To change the desktop settings, select **Desktop View** in the Preferences dialog box, as shown in Figure 1-40.

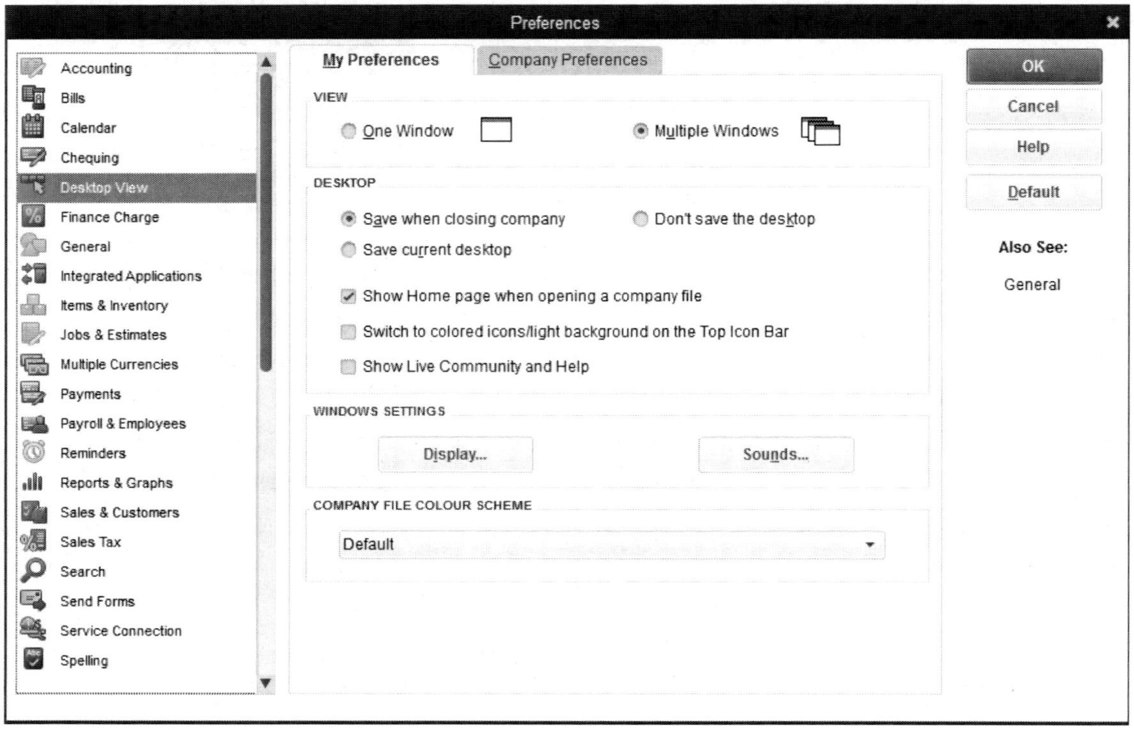

Figure 1-40: Preferences dialog box – Desktop View

While there are several useful options you might want to change for your files, you can use one of two ways to discover whether the file is set to display multiple windows or only one. If the One Window radio button is checked, you can click the Window command on the Menu Bar to show you which windows are open and then choose the one you want to see. The Window drop-down menu is shown in Figure 1-41.

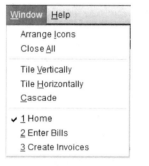

Figure 1-41: Window drop-down menu

You can check the window display setting in the Menu Bar. In the Menu Bar, click View, as shown in Figure 1-42. At the bottom of the drop-down menu, either One Window or Multiple Windows will be selected. Clicking either option toggles the window selection.

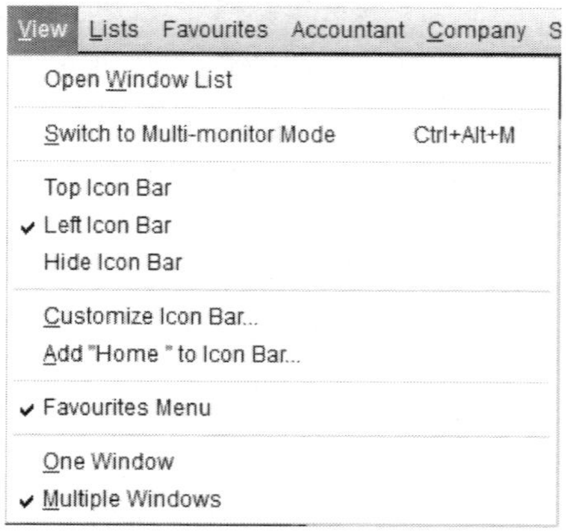

Figure 1-42: View drop-down menu

You can also change the location of the Icon Bar (which currently displays My Shortcuts), which appears in the QuickBooks application window. In the Menu Bar, click View, then select either Top Icon Bar or Left Icon Bar. Alternatively, you can select Hide Icon Bar if you want to hide it.

Customizing the Home Page

If you want to customize the features shown on the QuickBooks Home page, open QuickBooks Preferences, click Desktop View in the left sidebar, and then click the Company Preferences tab, as shown in Figure 1-43. You can activate or deactivate these features depending on the needs of the customer. You must be an Admin or an External Accountant to customize the Home page.

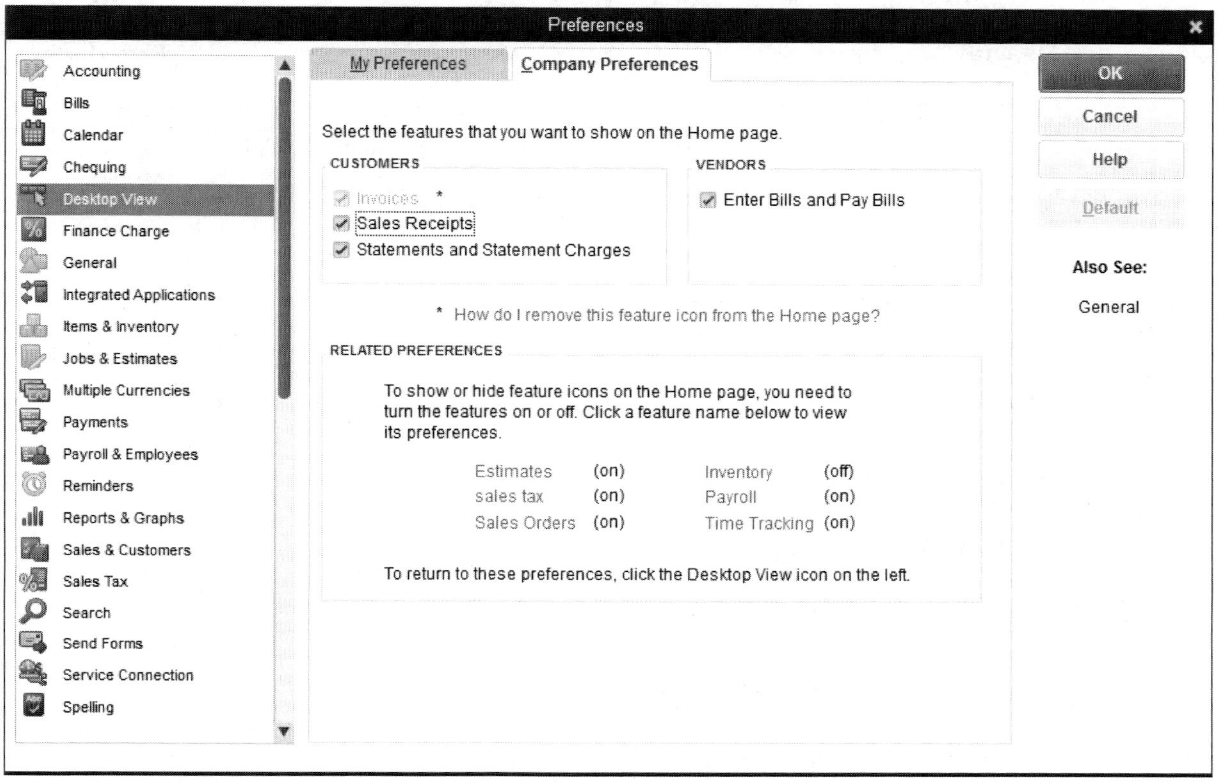

Figure 1-43: Preferences dialog box – Desktop View, Company Preferences tab

Exercise 1.6: Customizing the Home Page

In this exercise, you will customize the Home page by removing, then reinserting an icon.

Open the company file and log in as Admin.

1. In the No Company Open dialog box, click the company file with your name and then click **Open**. The QuickBooks Desktop Login dialog box appears.

2. Select the text in the *User Name* field, type: **Admin**, leave the *Password* field blank, then click **OK**. In the Home page, notice the Create Sales Receipts icon in the CUSTOMERS section.

Remove the Create Sales Receipts icon from the Home page.

3. In the Menu Bar, click **Edit > Preferences**. The Preferences dialog box appears.

4. In the list of categories in the left sidebar, click **Desktop View**, and then click the **Company Preferences** tab.

5. Click the **Sales Receipts** check box to deselect it, then click **OK**. Click **OK** in the message that appears informing you that QuickBooks must close all open windows to change the preference.

6. In the *My Shortcuts* section, click **Home** to redisplay the Home page. Notice that the Create Sales Receipts icon in the CUSTOMERS section no longer appears.

Redisplay the Create Sales Receipts icon on the Home page.

7. In the Menu Bar, click **Edit > Preferences**. The Preferences dialog box appears.

8. In the list of categories in the left sidebar, ensure that **Desktop View** is selected, and then click the **Company Preferences** tab.

9. Click the **Sales Receipts** check box to select it, then click **OK**. Click **OK** in the message that appears informing you that QuickBooks must close all open windows to change the preference.

10. In the *My Shortcuts* section, click **Home** to redisplay the Home page. Notice that the Create Sales Receipts icon now appears in the CUSTOMERS section.

11. Click **File > Close Company/Logoff** to close the file.

12. If you plan to perform the Practice the Skill exercise, leave QuickBooks open; otherwise, click **File > Exit** to close QuickBooks.

Lesson Summary

Now that you have completed this lesson, you should be able to:

☑ Launch QuickBooks, check your release number, and configure updates.

☑ Find, save, open, rename, and close QuickBooks files.

☑ Interpret and respond to pop up messages appropriately.

☑ Locate Purchases and Sales Cycle forms.

☑ Compare form usage to general journal entries.

☑ Navigate forms.

☑ Verify data entry settings.

☑ Customize the Home page.

Key Terms

Term	Definition
Account	A place in the accounting records for tracking funds.
Assets	What the business owns.
Balance	The value in an account at any given time. Balance can also refer to the total amount of money owed to a third party, such as a vendor or credit card company.
Bill	QuickBooks form used to record purchase transactions.
Company file	QuickBooks term that describes a QuickBooks file for any entity, either personal or business. The company file is a database that stores financial data, templates, transaction records, customizations, and preferences.
Credit	Usual Balances found in Sales and Liability accounts; used to decrease Asset accounts.
Customer	Company or individual that buys goods or services from a business.
DBA	Short for doing business as; a registered legal alias for the business.

Term	Definition
Debit	Usual Balances found in Asset accounts; used to decrease Liability accounts.
Field	Place to enter data on a form.
Form	Data entry window for transactions in QuickBooks.
Invoice	QuickBooks form used to enter sales transactions.
General Journal Entries	Records of a financial transaction recorded in a company's General Journal. When you use a QuickBooks form to record a transaction, QuickBooks automatically makes the proper entries and properly debits and credits the appropriate accounts. You can also enter transactions into the General Journal manually, but you should have a thorough understanding of accounting principles and best practices. Manual entries are best left to qualified professionals.
Liabilities	What a business owes.
Multi-user Mode	Setting that allows multiple users to work in a file at the same time.
QuickBooks Global	Information that applies everywhere in QuickBooks.
Single-user Mode	Setting that allows only one user to work in a file at a time.
Vendor	Company or individual that sells goods or services for you to purchase.

Activity 1: Opening Company Files

True or False: If the company file you need is not listed, clicking Edit List will allow you to find the needed file.

No Company Open

Select a company that you've previously opened and click Open

COMPANY NAME	LAST MODIFIED	FILE SIZE	
Blue Heron Spa Inc 2018.QBW	09/17/2018, 03:08 PM	13.86 MB	**Open**
Generic Company.qbw	09/17/2018, 03:01 PM	12.77 MB	Edit List
Generic Company Your Name.qbw	09/17/2018, 02:49 PM	12.77 MB	
Generic Company.qbw	09/17/2018, 02:35 PM	12.39 MB	

LOCATION: C:\Users\iheer\Desktop\1767-Student-Files\Lesson 1\MyProjects\

Create a new company   Open or restore an existing company   Open a sample file

Activity 2: Affecting Account Balances with Form Entries

In the second column in the table below, choose a statement that best describes the effect of a transaction that uses the given form. Then, in the third column, identify which type of accounting record is affected by the transaction.

Forms	Transaction Effect	Associated Accounting Record
Bill		
Invoice		

Transaction Effect:

1.   Entering a bill decreases expenses.

2.   Entering a bill increases what the company owes.

3.   Entering an invoice increases what the company is owed.

4.   Entering an invoice decreases sales.

Associated Accounting Record:

A.   Assets

B.   Liabilities

C.   Equity

Activity 3: Applying the Master Shortcut Keystroke

What is the correct sequence of keyboard shortcuts to close a company file?

a.   ALT+F then press the C key.

b.   ALT+F then press CTRL+C.

c.   CTRL+F then press the C key.

d.   CTRL+F then press ALT+C.

Practice the Skill

This Practice the Skill exercise is designed to reinforce the skills you have learned. In this exercise, you'll change two preferences, then create a portable file.

1.   If necessary, launch **QuickBooks**.

2.   Restore the **Student (Portable) C1_L1_B.QBM** portable company file from the *1767-Student-Files\Lesson 1\PTS* folder and log in as Admin.

3.   In the General preferences, change the setting to use today's date as the default.

4.   In the Desktop View preferences, change the setting that specifies to show only one window at a time.

5.   Save the company file as a portable file in the *MyProjects* folder. Name the new portable file **Generic Company <your name> PTS (Portable).QBM**. Turn this file in to your instructor.

Course Project Exercise

Starting with this lesson, you will begin your Course Project – maintaining the books for the Blue Heron Spa. For this exercise, you will perform a set of basic tasks to prepare your QuickBooks file for future lessons. Throughout the lessons, you will continue to make entries into this business.

Perform the following tasks:

1. Restore the **Blue-Heron-Spa-2018 C1_L1_A (Portable).QBM** portable company file from the *1767-Student-Files\Lesson 1\StarterFiles* folder.

2. Open and log in to the company file using the information in the table below.

3. Change the company name as indicated in the table below.

4. Save your work as a portable company file named **Blue-Heron-Spa-L1 <your name> (Portable).QBM** in the *1767-Student-Files\Lesson 1\MyProjects* folder.

Admin password:	BluSpa18
New company name:	Blue Heron Spa, Inc. L1<your name>

5. When you are finished, make sure that you close the company file and exit QuickBooks.

Quiz Questions

For each question, select the best answer.

1. What conditions need to be met before creating a portable file?

   a. You must log in to the company file using the user name Portable.

   b. You must log in to the company file using the user name Admin.

   c. You must install the latest QuickBooks software updates.

   d. You must rename the company to include the word Portable.

2. When you see the message QuickBooks Update Service, which statement about clicking the Install Now button is true?

   a. The installation may take a long time to perform.

   b. QuickBooks will not continue if you do not click Install Now.

   c. You must first open a company file before you can click Install Now.

   d. The entire software package reinstalls.

3. Which of the following statements is true?

   a. Every form is connected to every other form.

   b. Only forms in the same cycle are connected.

   c. Journal entries that are entered manually are not connected.

   d. Journal entries that are entered manually have the same capabilities as forms.

4. Which form do you use to get paid by a customer who purchased products from you?

    a. Invoice

    b. Bill

    c. Asset

    d. Liability

5. How can you change the automatic decimal placement setting in QuickBooks?

    a. Open the Preferences dialog box and click Accounting.

    b. Open the Preferences dialog box and click Desktop View.

    c. Open the Preferences dialog box and click General.

    d. Open the Preferences dialog box and click Payments.

6. Which keyboard shortcut displays a list of correlated transactions within an accounting cycle?

    a. ALT+H

    b. ALT+C

    c. CTRL+H

    d. CTRL+C

7. Which of the following tasks requires that you be logged in as the Admin?

    a. Customizing the Home page

    b. Creating a Bill

    c. Creating an Invoice

    d. Finding a transaction

8. Which keyboard key should you press to determine your QuickBooks product release number?

    a. F1

    b. F2

    c. F3

    d. F4

Lesson 2: Making Deposits

Lesson Objectives

In this lesson, you will learn about the different types of funds that need to be deposited to start a new business. You will also learn how to make a simple deposit entry in QuickBooks and describe the transaction using correct accounting language. Upon successful completion of this lesson, you should be able to:

☐ Describe how revenue, investments, and loans differ.

☐ Discuss QuickBooks classes.

☐ Determine information needed to enter transactions.

☐ Make bank deposits.

Identifying Income Sources

Objective L-2.1 Know how revenue, investments, and loans differ

There are many different sources of funds in the business world. In this course, we will focus on the fund sources you will likely encounter when starting a new business and when operational:

- Capital investment
- Loan proceeds
- Unrelated Income
- Revenue

Every business begins with a deposit of funds into a new business bank account at a financial institution. The business owners may use their own money, or they may borrow it from a bank. In either case, the initial deposit of funds by the owners is called a ***capital investment.*** They may also choose to loan money to the business which they have personally borrowed from the bank. This would be a ***Shareholder Loan***; the funds deposited would be loan proceeds. The capital may be provided by one or more owners or other investors.

Starting a business can require a lot of capital. If the business requires more money than the owners possess or borrow, the owners can obtain business ***loans*** from their banks and deposit the ***loan proceeds*** into the company's bank account. The business then needs to pay back the loan with ***interest***. Another type of loan is a ***line of credit***. Typically, a line of credit is set by the bank with a ceiling based on the business's financial position. The outstanding balance fluctuates with the business's cash flow requirements but cannot exceed the ceiling. Interest is generally calculated monthly and charged against the line by the bank.

Once the business is operational, it may also charge their customers interest for overdue balances, in which case the interest becomes a type of income, although not revenue. Instead, this interest is called **unrelated income** because it does not come from the business activities of selling products and services. A business earns **revenue** only when it sells products or services and then increases funds when it receives payment from customers.

When the business obtains the contribution of capital or shareholder loans, you will record the transactions as a deposit. Then the business may begin buying what it needs for its operations. The investments and loans affect banking records and the company's Balance Sheet, a type of financial report you will learn more about in a later lesson.

Let's put what you've learned into context by applying it to our example, Best Custom T-Shirts. Several people own the company as a partnership. Each of the partners provided investment funds. Part of these funds will be recorded as capital that the business retains, and part will be recorded as a loan that the business will later repay to the owners. Because the business has not yet begun its operating activities of buying and selling products or services, the initial contribution is not considered revenue. Figure 2-1 illustrates Best Custom T-Shirts' investment structure.

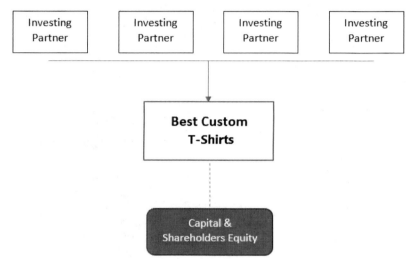

Figure 2-1: Best Custom T-Shirts' investment structure

Identifying Banking and Accounting Language

Objective L-2.1 Know how revenue, investments, and loans differ

When making deposits, it is important to understand that basic banking and accounting language are not the same. At first, the language used for banking transactions in accounting may seem backward. For example, when you deposit money into your chequing account, it is a bank credit to your account because the balance increases. Then, when you use your debit card or write cheques to spend money, called a bank debit, the balance decreases.

In accounting, the words credit and debit have specific meanings that define whether amounts are added to or removed from a **General Ledger (GL) account**. You use GL accounts to enter accounting transactions. Each GL account has its own ledger of transactions and is associated with either Assets, Liabilities, or Equity.

Note: In this course, whenever we use the word *account* to refer to a place within the accounting system (QuickBooks), we have written it as *GL account* to differentiate it from other uses of the word.

The behavior of the terms credit and debit is based on the accounting equation: Assets = Liabilities + Equity. In Lesson 1, you learned about two of the three parts of the accounting equation, Assets and Liabilities. Investments belong to the third part of the accounting equation, Equity. Figure 2-2 illustrates the effects of debits and credits on the Equity part of the accounting equation.

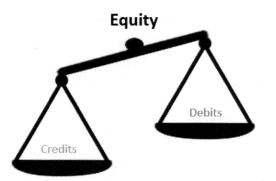

Figure 2-2: The Equity part of the accounting equation

Equity accounts are affected by debits and credits the same way Liability accounts are affected—credits increase the balance and debits decrease the balance.

Equity accounts are different from Assets and Liabilities; instead of representing the flows of money in and out of the business, Equity accounts represent the capital contributed to the business. Equity accounts also represent the difference between all sales and purchases since the business began in the Retained Earnings account. The sum of the two should equal the difference between Assets and Liabilities.

The **Chart of Accounts** contains the following GL accounts:

- **Asset accounts**
- **Liability accounts**
- **Equity accounts**

The type of account determines the effect of a debit or credit (Table 2-1).

Table 2-1: Debit/credit effect on different account types

Account Type	Debit behavior	Credit behavior
Asset account	Increases the balance	Decreases the balance
Liability account	Decreases the balance	Increases the balance
Equity account	Decreases the balance	Increases the balance

Because QuickBooks' forms automatically label a deposit as either a debit or credit, each deposit you make will debit the bank account you select for the deposit and credit the GL account(s) you select.

Identifying QuickBooks Classes

Objective L-2.2 Use QuickBooks classes

As a business grows, matching expenses to revenue streams becomes critical. Unfortunately, accounting systems may hold thousands or even millions of transactions. Determining how the transactions are related to different business units or departments can be a challenge. Fortunately, QuickBooks allows you to use classes to track cost centres or other transactions, making it easier to report on this information later. **Classes** allow you to categorize transactions in the accounting records within GL accounts.

Every line of every transaction lets you specify a class, allowing you to assign the amount of the transaction to logical areas within the business, such as locations, departments, or investors. Classes can be used with all types of transactions, including income, expenses, and administrative costs. For example, an investment deposit can be designated by a class that represents a specific investor.

Let's put this into practice. The partners know they plan to operate a retail store as well as a printing plant for their T-shirt business. These locations could be identified as classes, and you could later assign revenue and expenses to them.

To keep things simple, we'll add the store and plant later. For now, let's assume that a class has been created for each of the business partners as well as an Admin class. You will use the Admin class for miscellaneous entries not related to the other cost centres. The Admin class doesn't produce revenue and is sometimes called overhead or general and administrative expenses. Here are the current classes for Best Custom T-Shirts:

- Admin
- Taylor Green
- Jordan Smith

Entering Cheques and EFTs

Objective L-2.3 Correctly complete the QuickBooks Make Deposits form

Every transaction in an accounting system such as a cheque, invoice, or banking statement, is based on an action or item that exists in the physical world. For example, when a business receives a customer payment, it accepts a cheque that is deposited into a chequing account. Today, cheques are often scanned and electronically deposited instead of being physically taken to the bank.

After your first monetary transaction, you'll need to enter the transaction details in QuickBooks. To do this, you must first collect some information about the transaction. Some of the information you need is located on the provided documents, either cheques or **Electronic Funds Transfers (EFTs)**.

Let's determine the information you need to find on the cheque before making the deposit. If you lack certain information, such as the amount or the date of the deposit, you will not be able to enter the deposit. Keep in mind that additional information may be found on other documents, such as bank statements or receipts.

Locating Information for Cheque or EFT Entry

Figure 2-3 shows the information you need to find on a cheque before you can record the deposit in QuickBooks.

Name
Address
City, Province Zip Code

006

DATE 2 0 - -
Y Y Y Y M M D D

PAY TO THE
ORDER OF   <Your Business> $ 300.00

Three Hundred Dollars and no cents ---------------- /100 DOLLARS

coastcapital. COQUITLAM BRANCH
SAVINGS

MEMO   Purpose of payment   Signature   MP

"006" ⑈19130"809⑈ ⑈000000000000"

Cheque   Transit   Institution   Account Number
Number   Number   Number

Figure 2-3: Sample cheque

- From the cheque or EFT, you can find:
  - the name of the person or business who issued the cheque or EFT. The name is usually printed on the upper-left portion of the cheque.
  - the amount. The amount is usually entered in the middle of the cheque.
  - the document number. The document number is usually printed on the upper-right portion of the cheque and at the beginning of the string of numbers at the bottom.
- From other sources such as the deposit receipt or bank statement, you can find:
  - the date of the deposit.

  Note: This is *not* necessarily the date on the cheque.

  - the bank where you deposited the cheque or EFT.
  - the reason for the payment. This may be written in the memo field on the cheque or on paperwork that accompanies the cheque.
  - the categorization of the payment. This is the QuickBooks class that may be required or optional, depending on the configuration of your QuickBooks company file.

Making Deposits

Objective L-2.3 Correctly complete the QuickBooks Make Deposits form

You can use the **Make Deposits form** to enter bank deposit information from cheques and EFT deposits. You will use the form only in the Banking Cycle (Figure 2-4).

BANKING
Chequing Account

Deposit

RECONCILIATION

Figure 2-4: Banking Cycle showing deposit

Completing the Make Deposits Form

After you have collected and reviewed the information needed to enter the deposit, you should open and complete the Make Deposits form in QuickBooks. You can access the Make Deposits form from the QuickBooks Home page, or use the Menu Bar to click **Banking > Make Deposits**.

The Make Deposits form is shown in Figure 2-5. Every entry requires a date, account, and amount so that reports will be accurate.

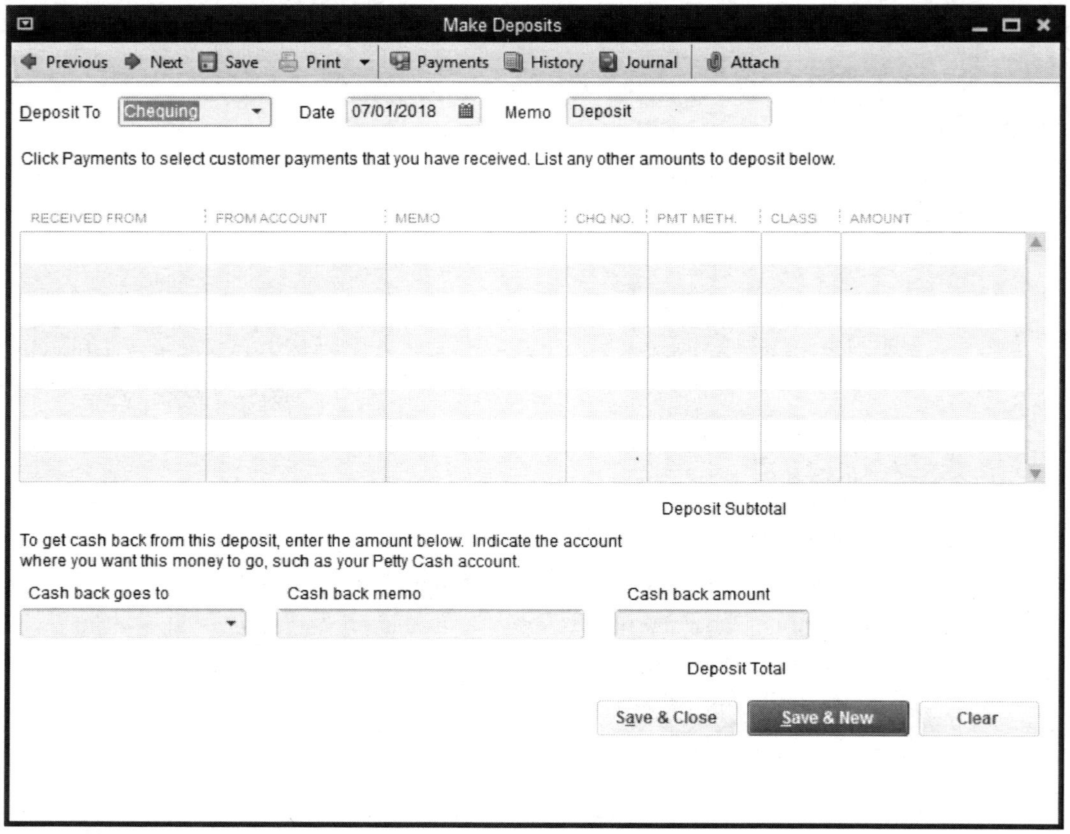

Figure 2-5: Make Deposits form

Let's look at the key components of the Make Deposits form, starting at the top, and note the actions needed for each field.

- **Deposit To:** Select the GL account where the funds were deposited.

- **Date:** Enter the date the funds were deposited in the bank account (this is not necessarily the date on the EFT or cheque).

- **Memo:** You may enter a description associated with this deposit. This field is optional, but it's a very good practice because it makes items easier to track. This text will appear only on the Bank Account Reconciliation report. It will not appear in any of the GL account entries. You would use this field to indicate why you made the deposit (for example, Partner Capital Contribution).

- **The detail table:** The table in the middle of the form is used to enter individual transactions with the GL accounts. Generally, each row represents a cheque or EFT; however, you can "split" a cheque or EFT across multiple GL accounts by using a separate line for each account and indicating its appropriate portion of the cheque total in the amount field. Each column represents a field associated with the transactions. The transactions are summed, and a subtotal is provided below the detail table. Fields in the detail table are:

  - **RECEIVED FROM:** Enter the name of the person or entity who wrote the cheque or initiated the EFT.

  - **FROM ACCOUNT:** Select the GL account associated with the person or entity.

  - **MEMO:** Enter a description of the transaction. This text will appear next to the transaction if you view the entries of a GL account. This field is optional.

  - **CHQ NO.:** Enter the cheque number or the transaction number of the EFT. This field is optional.

  - **PMT METH.:** Select the payment method (for example, cash, cheque, or credit card). This field is optional but handy for future reference.

  - **CLASS:** Select the class that should be assigned to this transaction. This is useful when categorizing expenses by cost centre or revenue by business line. This may be an optional field depending on the configuration of your QuickBooks company file.

  - **AMOUNT:** Enter the amount of the transaction.

- There are three Cash back fields below the detail table, which are used only if the person making the deposit requested cash back at the bank. Cash received in this manner does not decrease the amounts of the individual cheques or EFTs assigned to GL accounts in the detail table.

  - **Cash back goes to:** Select the *Petty Cash* account you want to use to track the money.

  - **Cash back memo:** This field is optional. For example, you could indicate why you received cash back instead of depositing the full amount of the cheques.

  - **Cash back amount:** Enter the amount of the cash received.

- **Save & Close:** Saves and posts the deposit, then closes the Make Deposits form.

- **Save & New:** Saves and posts the deposit, clears the Make Deposits form, and then leaves the form open for you to enter another deposit.

- **Clear:** Clears the contents of the Make Deposits form without posting the transaction. This is useful if you have made several mistakes and want to cancel recording the deposit.

Note: A properly completed Make Deposits form requires an entry in each of these fields: Deposit To, Date, Received From, From Account, and Amount.

Exercise 2.1: Making Deposits

In this exercise, you will work with the QuickBooks company file for Best Custom T-Shirts. You will restore the file, enter a deposit transaction using the Make Deposits form, and then save and export your work by creating a portable version of the QuickBooks file.

The scenario for this exercise:

- One of the business partners, Taylor Green, contributed $500 as a capital contribution to the new business. The cheque number was #6174 and was deposited on July 1, 2018.

- The Deposit type is Owner contribution and the GL account is an Equity account.

Restore the portable company file for this exercise.

1. Launch **QuickBooks** and close any message prompts that may appear.

2. In the Menu Bar, click **File > Close Company** if necessary to close any open company files. The No Company Open dialog box appears.

3. Click **Open or restore an existing company**. The Open or Restore Company dialog box appears.

4. Click the **Restore a portable file** radio button, and then click **Next**. The Open Portable Company File dialog box appears.

5. Navigate to the *1767-Student-Files\Lesson 2\StarterFiles* folder, then double-click **Best Custom T-Shirts C1_L2_A (Portable).QBM**. The Open or Restore Company dialog box reappears.

6. Click **Next**. The Save Company File as dialog box appears.

7. Click in the *File name* field, and then type: **Best Custom T-Shirts <your name>**. Navigate to the *1767-Student-Files\Lesson 2\MyProjects* folder, and then click **Save**. Respond to any message prompts that may appear. After a few minutes, your portable company file's Home page will appear in the QuickBooks Desktop.

Open the Make Deposits form.

8. On the *Home page*, in the *BANKING* section, click the **Record Deposits** icon. The Make Deposits form appears.

   Note: Alternatively, you may click **Banking** > **Make Deposits** to display the Make Deposits form.

9. Ensure that the *Deposit To* field is set to **Chequing** (the default account).

10. Double-click to select the information in the **Date** field, type: **07/01/2018**, and then press **TAB**.

    Note: You can also click the **calendar** icon in the Date field to display the calendar tool, which you can use to enter the date.

11. If necessary, double-click to select the information in the **Memo** field and type: **Deposit**.

    Note: This field appears only on the Bank Reconciliation view and is optional. The information is helpful if an explanation of the transaction is needed.

Enter deposit information in the first row of the detail table in the middle of the *Make Deposits* form.

12. In the *RECEIVED FROM* field, from the drop-down menu select **Green, Taylor**. This is the name of the person who wrote the cheque.

13. In the *FROM ACCOUNT* field, click the drop-down arrow, scroll down until you can see the *Equity* accounts, then select **Taylor Green, Capital**.

    Note: *FROM ACCOUNT* refers to the GL account you are crediting.

14. Leave the *MEMO* field blank because any text entered here will appear in the accounting entry.

15. In the *CHQ NO.* field, enter the cheque number: **6174**.

    Note: EFTs may not have a number.

16. In the *PMT METH.* field, from the drop-down menu select **Cheque**, which specifies the method type for the deposit.

17. In the *CLASS* field, from the drop-down menu select **Taylor Green**.

18. In the *AMOUNT* field, enter the dollar amount of the cheque: **500.00**.

Your finished form should appear as shown in the figure on the following page.

19. Click the **Save & Close** button.

Save your work as a portable company file that you can submit to your instructor.

20. In the Menu Bar, click **File > Create Copy**. The Save Copy or Backup dialog box appears.

21. Click the **Portable company file** radio button, and then click **Next**. The Save Portable Company File dialog box appears.

22. Navigate to the *1767-Student-Files\Lesson 2\MyProjects* folder.

23. In the *File name* field, enter: **Best Custom T-Shirts C1_L2 <your name> (Portable)**, and then click **Save**. Respond to any message prompts that may appear.

    Note: Check with your instructor for the appropriate file name.

24. If you plan to perform the Practice the Skill exercise, close the company file but leave QuickBooks open; otherwise, close the company file and exit QuickBooks.

Lesson Summary

Now that you have completed this lesson, you should be able to:

☑ Describe how revenue, investments, and loans differ.

☑ Discuss QuickBooks classes.

☑ Determine information needed to enter transactions.

☑ Make bank deposits.

Key Terms

Term	Definition
Asset accounts	General Ledger accounts that represent tangible objects such as inventory, machines, and buildings, as well as bank accounts that contain the funds the business has received. They also represent amounts owed to the business, prepaid amounts, and so on.
Capital investment	The funds or other assets that the owners of the business invest in the business.
Chart of Accounts	The list of all the different types of General Ledger accounts in your QuickBooks file.
Class	A QuickBooks category, such as a cost or income centre, to which you can assign a transaction. A class could represent a physical location, an entire line of business within the company, or one store among multiple stores the business operates.
Electronic Funds Transfer (EFT)	Money that is sent electronically from one bank account to another without the need for a person to write and mail a paper cheque.
Equity accounts	General Ledger accounts that represent the amount of money the owners invest in the business, plus the historical record of profitability over the life of the business.
General Ledger (GL) Accounts	The accounts into which accounting transactions are entered. GL accounts appear in the Chart of Accounts.
Interest	Fees charged by the lender for the use of the lender's funds.
Liability accounts	General Ledger accounts that represent obligations that must be paid to another person, business, or entity, such as payroll, credit card debt, or utility bills.
Line of Credit	A line of credit is set by the bank with a ceiling based on the business's financial position. The outstanding balance fluctuates with the business's cash flow requirements but cannot exceed the ceiling. Interest is generally calculated monthly and charged against the line by the bank.
Loan	Money borrowed from a lending institution that the borrower will repay with interest.
Loan Proceeds	The funds provided by the lender to the business.
Make Deposits form	A QuickBooks data entry form that allows you to enter bank deposits.
Petty Cash	An account that represents an amount of cash that the business keeps on hand for cash-based purchases.
Revenue	Funds a business receives as payment from customers for products or services.
Shareholder Loan	Money loaned to a business which the shareholder has personally borrowed from a bank.
Unrelated Income	Funds a business receives that do not come from the business activities of selling products and services.

Activity 1: Identifying Completed Deposit Forms

Following are two Make Deposits forms but only one contains enough data that it can be saved. Does the first or second form contain the required amount of information?

First Form

Make Deposits — ◆ Previous ◆ Next 🖫 Save 🖶 Print ▼ | 📇 Payments 🗐 History 📄 Journal 📎 Attach

Deposit To: Chequing ▼   Date: 07/01/2018 📅   Memo: Deposit

Click Payments to select customer payments that you have received. List any other amounts to deposit below.

RECEIVED FROM	FROM ACCOUNT	MEMO	CHQ NO.	PMT METH.	CLASS	AMOUNT
▼	Taylor Green, Capital ▼		6174	▼	Taylor Green ▼	500.00

Deposit Subtotal: 500.00

To get cash back from this deposit, enter the amount below. Indicate the account where you want this money to go, such as your Petty Cash account.

Cash back goes to   Cash back memo   Cash back amount

Deposit Total: 500.00

[Save & Close] [Save & New] [Revert]

Second Form

Make Deposits — ◆ Previous ◆ Next 🖫 Save 🖶 Print ▼ | 📇 Payments 🗐 History 📄 Journal 📎 Attach

Deposit To: Chequing ▼   Date: 07/01/2018 📅   Memo: Deposit

Click Payments to select customer payments that you have received. List any other amounts to deposit below.

RECEIVED FROM	FROM ACCOUNT	MEMO	CHQ NO.	PMT METH.	CLASS	AMOUNT
Green, Taylor ▼	Taylor Green, Capital ▼			▼	Taylor Green ▼	500.00

Deposit Subtotal: 500.00

To get cash back from this deposit, enter the amount below. Indicate the account where you want this money to go, such as your Petty Cash account.

Cash back goes to   Cash back memo   Cash back amount

Deposit Total: 500.00

[Save & Close] [Save & New] [Revert]

Activity 2: Knowing the Effects of Making a Deposit

Fill in the blanks:

1. Posting a loan in the accounting records _____ the loan account. (credits/debits)

2. When you deposit funds into a chequing account in the accounting records, the account is _____. (credited/debited)

Practice the Skill

This Practice the Skill exercise is designed to reinforce the skills you have learned. In this exercise, you will restore a portable file, enter two deposit transactions, and then save a portable file.

The following table contains the GL account information you need for the exercise.

Deposit type	GL account and section
Owner contribution	EQUITY: Partner X, Capital
Owner loan	LIABILITY: Loan - Partner X
Bank loan	LIABILITY: Loan - First Bank

1. If necessary, launch **QuickBooks** and open **Best Custom T-Shirts C1_L2_B (Portable).QBM** from the *1767-Student-Files\Lesson 2\PTS* folder.

2. Open the **Make Deposits** form.

3. Enter a new deposit into the Chequing account for Jordan Smith, who wrote cheque #8295 for $8,000. With this cheque, Jordan is giving $500 as a capital contribution to the new business, and $7,500 as a loan. The cheque was deposited on July 2, 2018. The deposit will have two lines. Use the GL account: **Loan – Jordan Smith** for the *FROM ACCOUNT* field on the second line.

4. Enter a second deposit into the Chequing account using the following information. The partners applied for a loan from First Bank for $10,000 and received it on July 15, 2018, via an EFT. Use the GL account: **Loan – First Bank** for the *FROM ACCOUNT* field.

5. Save and close the **Make Deposits** form.

6. Save the company file as a portable company file in the *1767-Student-Files\Lesson 2\MyProjects* folder and add the letters PTS to the end of the file name (*Best Custom T-Shirts C1_L2 <your name> PTS (Portable).QBM*). Turn this file in to your instructor.

Course Project Exercise

Begin your course project by recording a deposit from the new partner, Arlene Stohl. She will buy into the business with a capital contribution of $500 and a loan of $14,500 that will allow the business to expand. She has already been entered as a Customer in QuickBooks, and the accounts you will need for this exercise have been created for you. Arlene provided cheque #927 for $15,000 dated July 15, 2018 for deposit into the only chequing account for the business.

Perform the following tasks:

1. Restore the **Blue Heron Spa Inc 2018 C1_L2_A (Portable).QBM** file from the *1767-Student-Files\Lesson 2\StarterFiles* folder.

2. Log in and change the company name using the information in the table below.

Admin password:	BluSpa18
New company name:	Blue Heron Spa, Inc. L2<your name>

3. Enter a deposit as described in the opening paragraph.

4. Save your work as a portable company file named **Blue-Heron-Spa-L2 <your name> (Portable).QBM** in the *1767-Student-Files\Lesson 2\MyProjects* folder.

5. Close the company file and exit QuickBooks.

Quiz Questions

For each question, select the best answer.

1. Which statement about revenue is true?

    a. Every deposit brings revenue into the business.

    b. Revenue is earned by business activities.

    c. Only sales and interest are considered revenue.

    d. A capital contribution is a business's first revenue.

2. Which of the following is an optional field on the Make Deposits form?

    a. Date

    b. From Account

    c. Memo

    d. Amount

3. You can use a QuickBooks class to:

    a. identify revenue.

    b. name an account.

    c. designate investment deposits.

    d. categorize transactions in the accounting records within GL accounts.

Lesson 3: Reporting and Examining Your Work

Lesson Objectives

In this lesson, you will use QuickBooks' reporting capabilities to examine, correct, and review your bookkeeping. You will also identify the relationships among the financial reports, GL accounts, and the accounting equation. Upon successful completion of this lesson, you will be able to:

- ☐ Match GL accounts to financial reports.
- ☐ Produce detail and summary reports.
- ☐ Define non-accrual cash accounting.

- ☐ Find transactions.
- ☐ Correct transactions.
- ☐ Review your work.

Ending the Work Day

After you complete the bookkeeping for the day, you must review your work for correctness. Only by reviewing your work can you ensure its accuracy in the Accounting Cycle. This lesson covers the Reports Cycle and provides a bridge between what you enter in forms and how to locate your entries in reports so you can verify your work and submit reports when requested.

When you locate entries on detail reports, you will see how every form in QuickBooks converts the data entry into a journal entry of debits and credits. It is good practice to check the individual entries in summary reports, as well as their effects on the overall accounting records. Throughout your day, you may need one of the processes described in this lesson to find and check an entry you made.

Summary reports reflect the accounting equation that connects the three sections of the Chart of Accounts or Accounting Records: Assets, Liabilities, and Equity. The two main summary reports, the **Balance Sheet** and the **Income Statement** (also called the **Profit & Loss Statement** or P&L Statement), show the financial condition of the business and are together known as **financial statements**.Between them, they include every GL account with a balance during the period covered by the statements. A GL account will have a balance when the debits and credits within the account are not equal.

Each GL account belongs in one of the three sections of the accounting equation. The Equity section also has two main sub-sections that determine which financial report each account belongs to and how QuickBooks displays the transactions. Only the net (known as Net Income/Loss) of these two sub-sections ever appears in the Equity section of the Balance Sheet. We will maintain the concept of Equity sub-sections to ensure a complete understanding of the relationship between GL accounts and the accounting equation. All accounts are assigned a type that places them within the appropriate section of the equation and within a section of the Chart of Accounts.

QuickBooks Reports

Objective L-3.1 Match GL accounts to financial reports
Objective L-3.3 Define non-accrual (cash) accounting

QuickBooks offers reports for many different purposes. They provide different views of transactions, and often display them in detail or summary form. Usually, you can access the detail from the summary reports, which we will discuss in more detail below.

After you enter transactions, you can find every entry in the company file's journal, just as in pre-computer pen and paper accounting. The *journal* retains the detail of every transaction made. Other accounting software may store information from forms in one location and only produce a summary journal entry in the journal.

The *Journal report* is the detail report that includes all transactions in the accounting records. In manual systems there were several journals, such as Purchases, Payroll, and Sales journals, but in a computerized system it's all-in-one. You can run this report to display transactions either in numerical order by journal entry number or you may sort the journal entries by the transaction date.

Every report in QuickBooks draws from the journal to compile the requested results. Unlike using pen and paper, you do not need to enter or store transactions separately in the journal and the GL account ledger. Both reports show all entries and you can filter them by various criteria to display a limited set of transactions.

Whether you made the entries through a form or General Journal Entry, the entries can appear on all detail reports as journal entries showing debits and credits. The journal also retains and displays information about the type of form used to make the entry. QuickBooks refers to journal entries made without a form as *general journal* entries to distinguish them from the journal entries created by forms. Later in this lesson, we will locate the Make Deposits form entry you made in Lesson 2 in several different reports to demonstrate that you can always see the debits and credits for all forms in the reports.

Each entry you make is automatically assigned a sequential transaction number. QuickBooks assigns the transaction # and it cannot be changed. You only see this number on the Journal Report as the Trans # (transaction entry number) column header. Except for the Trans # column, each column header contains one field from the data entry forms. You can modify the number of columns that appear on all reports.

In Lesson 1, you learned that when you first open a Company File, you may see a pop up message like the one shown in Figure 3-1.

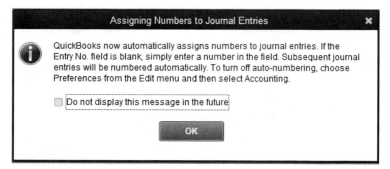

Assigning Numbers to Journal Entries   ✕

QuickBooks now automatically assigns numbers to journal entries. If the Entry No. field is blank, simply enter a number in the field. Subsequent journal entries will be numbered automatically. To turn off auto-numbering, choose Preferences from the Edit menu and then select Accounting.

☐ Do not display this message in the future

OK

Figure 3-1 Assigning Numbers to Journal Entries pop up

QuickBooks automatically numbers your journal entries based on the number that you assign to your first journal entry. The journal entry number appears on all detail reports, including the Journal Report, as the Num (number) column header.

There are cases when you may not want QuickBooks to automatically number your journal entries. For example, when you enter the final transaction entries for the year in the Accounting Cycle, you may want to manually enter the numbers to keep all the end of year general journal entries together in one numbered sequence to make your reports easier to read. You can disable the automatic numbering of journal entries by deselecting the Automatically assign general journal entry number check box in the Accounting Company Preferences tab of the QuickBooks Preferences dialog box.

You may also remember seeing a message about QuickBooks combining multiple items into a single line on a report, as shown in Figure 3-2.

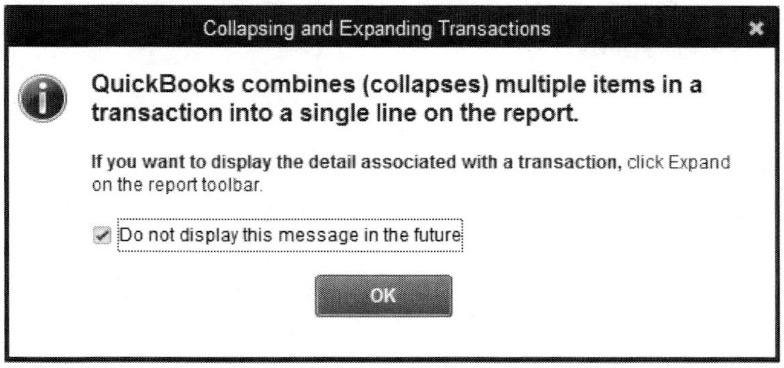

Figure 3-2: Collapsing and Expanding Transactions pop up message

QuickBooks provides the Expand/Collapse button that allows you to specify the level of detail to show about the transactions in your report. You can find the button in many reports and can use it to collapse the level of detail in some summary reports.

Note: In some reports, the Expand/Collapse button will appear but be disabled. Not all reports support this feature.

Reporting Business Finances

Financial reporting in any accounting system relies on the structure of the Chart of Accounts, shown in Figure 3-3.

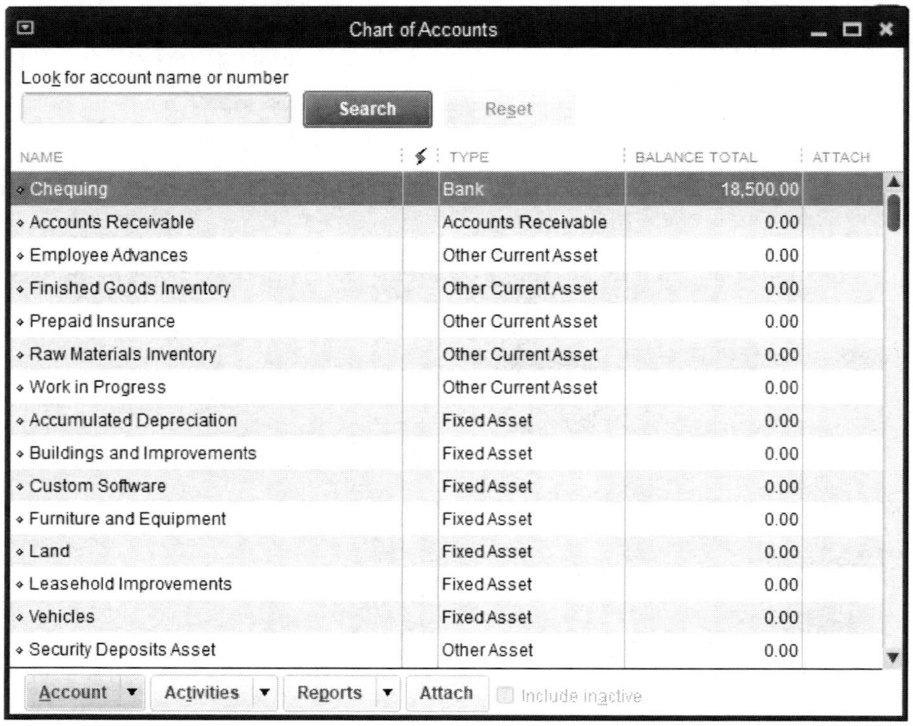

Figure 3-3: Chart of Accounts

All GL accounts are listed by section. The three main sections of the Chart of Accounts and the financial statements always follow the same order as the three parts of the accounting equation: Assets = Liabilities + Equity. Once you understand how to locate GL accounts in the three sections and the Equity sub-sections, you can easily move around the Chart of Accounts to find what you need. Each account also has other attributes that indicate where it belongs to help categorize it. For example, every time you select a GL account in QuickBooks, you can see from the account type where it belongs in the Chart of Accounts.

The two primary financial statements, or summary reports, are the Balance Sheet and the Income Statement. When submitting these reports, the Balance Sheet always goes first. The Balance Sheet contains all three sections of the accounting equation and gives a complete overview of the accounting records, although the equity sub-sections appear only in summary.

Every GL account with a balance, except for accounts in the Equity sub-sections, appears on the Balance Sheet. The GL accounts in the Equity sub-sections, Income and Expense, do not appear on the Balance Sheet, but on the Income Statement. The Balance Sheet summarizes the Equity sub-sections, as shown in Table 3-1. Therefore, the Income Statement is a partial summary report of Equity.

Note: Reports contain additional sections and sub-sections to those shown in Table 3-1. Table 3-1 is simplified to present the key relationships.

Table 3-1: Financial statements and equation/report sections and sub-sections aligned with GL account types

Financial Report	Equation Section	Equation Sub-Section	Report Sub-Section	Chart Sections and GL Account Type	Normal Balance
Balance Sheet	Assets		Current Assets	Bank	Debit
Balance Sheet	Assets		Current Assets	Accounts Receivable	Debit
Balance Sheet	Assets		Current Assets	Other Current Asset	Debit
Balance Sheet	Assets		Fixed Assets	Fixed Asset	Debit
Balance Sheet	Assets		Other Assets	Other Asset	Debit
Balance Sheet	Liabilities		Liabilities	Accounts Payable	Credit
Balance Sheet	Liabilities		Liabilities	Credit Card	Credit
Balance Sheet	Liabilities		Liabilities	Other Current Liability	Credit
Balance Sheet	Equity		Equity	Equity	Credit
Income Statement	Equity	Income	Ordinary Income and Expense	Income	Credit
Income Statement	Equity	Expense	Ordinary Income and Expense	Cost of Goods Sold (COGS)	Debit
Income Statement	Equity	Expense	Ordinary Income and Expense	Expense	Debit
Income Statement	Equity	Income	Other Income/Expense	Other Income	Credit
Income Statement	Equity	Expense	Other Income/Expense	Other Expense	Debit

One main difference exists between the Equity sub-section Income Statement GL accounts and every other GL account. The Income Statement accounts accumulate the posted debits and credits throughout the fiscal year. Then, they reset to zero for reporting purposes when the year ends. The rest of the accounts accumulate for the life of the business and accounting system.

In QuickBooks, the accounts that never reset are presented in a special window accessible directly from the Chart of Accounts, called a *register*. It is a compact view of the list of journal entries in every account, or the electronic equivalent of a ledger. The transactions in Income Statement accounts that reset don't display a balance on the Chart of Accounts at the end of a period but are accessible through reports (a double-click will provide access to every entry to that account for the period).

The difference in accumulating transactions also affects how to set and display the dates for the two financial statements. Because the GL accounts in the Income Statement reset at the end of the fiscal year, the Income Statement always shows a period with start and end dates. Usually, this encompasses the first day of the first month of the fiscal year to either a date during the year or the last day of the year. Any period during the year may be chosen. If whole months are selected, only the month and year will appear. The Balance Sheet is always set to a single end date during the fiscal year because all balances displayed began accumulating when the business started, not during the fiscal year.

The total of the two major Equity sub-sections in the Income Statement, Income and Expense, as well as any minor sub-sections, is called *Net Income*. The Equity section in the Balance Sheet includes net income because it summarizes all the GL accounts not on the Balance Sheet but that are required to balance the accounting equation.

Net income is one of the most important numbers for determining whether a business is succeeding or failing. You may recall that deposits are debits into the bank account. The effects of debits and credits on sections of the accounting equation can help you determine whether net income is good news or bad news for business owners and investors.

Net Income: A Little History

Prior to the advent of computerized accounting, a trial balance was prepared after all journal entries, including adjusting entries via the General Journal, had been made and sub-ledgers had been reconciled. From this trial balance, the accounts comprising the P&L Statement were selected and organized to form the statement. This was the first time the accountant would have knowledge of the amount of profit or loss for the period being measured. This derived amount was then posted to the Equity section of the Balance Sheet, constructed as of the last date of the P&L Statement, as Net Income. The accountant was sure the requirements of the accounting equation would be satisfied as the trial balance, constructed from the active Chart of Accounts, balanced.

In today's world, one of the efficiencies of computerized accounting is that the Net Income calculation is automatically performed instantly and with every entry into the system. If the entries are balanced, the calculation can be made accurately, and the system won't allow posting of entries that aren't balanced. Whatever entry is made, whether Balance Sheet only or P&L and Balance Sheet, The Net Income is calculated.

The downside of this efficiency is that the validity of the results is only as good as the timely maintenance of the inputs. If your business allows you to input transactions as they occur, great! Your financial statements will be up to date, except for adjusting entries. However, for many businesses this is not the case. You might sit down on the week-end to perform the posts, or the bookkeeper may come in once a month to do everything.

Do you post entries as of the date on the original document or the date of the posting? Is this an accrual entry or not? These are questions you might consider, and the guiding principle is the matching principle, which also infers a question of relevance. The best answer is that you post a transaction on the date it occurred, and you post it as if it was that day. Accounts that are set up as accruals will be updated as entries are made to them. At the end date of the P&L Statement you are interested in, you make adjusting entries. Your Net Income will then be accurate and up-to-date.

It is worthwhile to think of a perpetual Net Income as part of the Equity section of the Balance Sheet. A portion of the GL accounts include Revenues and Expenses. When a P&L Statement is calculated, the resultant Net Income must be posted to the Equity portion of the Balance Sheet to ensure the accounting equation is maintained. Also, the Net Income portion of the Equity account could be forced to balance the Balance Sheet, and then compared to the P&L up to the date of the Balance Sheet for accuracy.

Appraising Net Income

- When a business receives money for the sale of goods or services (as opposed to a capital contribution or investment), the money is considered revenue.
- When the revenue is deposited in the bank, the owner's equity must increase. For this to happen, the following actions occur simultaneously:
  - The asset GL account associated with the bank account is debited, which increases its balance (remember, debits increase asset accounts).
  - At the same time, the revenue GL account associated with Ordinary Income is credited, which increases its balance (remember, credits increase revenue, equity, or liability accounts).

- Therefore, this deposit transaction increases both sides of the accounting equation by increasing assets and increasing equity (via the Revenue sub-section).

- When a business spends money to pay for expenses, the owner's equity must decrease. For this to happen, the following actions occur simultaneously:

  - The asset GL account associated with the bank account is credited, which decreases its balance (because credits decrease asset accounts).

  - The expense account associated with the expense is debited, which increases its balance (because debits increase expense accounts).

- If the credits in income accounts are greater than the debits in expense accounts, then more money came in from business activities than went out, resulting in a *profit*. The credit balance becomes the Net Income value and is positive.

- If the debits in expense accounts exceed the credits in the income accounts, the business has a *loss*. The debit balance becomes the Net Income value and is negative.

- A common way of referring to Net Income describes the business as being "in the red" if Net Income is negative for that year. If Net Income is positive, the business is "in the black," which means that money is available for business growth and reinvestment.

- If the debits equal the credits in the Income Statement, the business is in a state known as *break-even*.

- When the fiscal year ends, the amount in Net Income automatically transfers to a special GL equity account called Retained Earnings. In a pen-and-paper accounting system, you would close each income and expense account with a journal entry. If, for example, the account had a debit balance, the account would receive a credit in the same amount and Retained Earnings would receive the debit. Some accounting systems still make this entry, but QuickBooks handles it with software programming.

- Retained Earnings shows the Net Income history for all years of the business, except for the current year because it is still considered Net Income. This summary of historical Net Income is also important for determining whether a business is successful or not.

- In the new fiscal year, before any transactions occur, Net Income is zero.

Accounting Basis

When you create financial statements and other reports, you also need to determine the *accounting basis* you will use to track revenue and expenses. The type of basis you specify determines when the tax authority recognizes revenue and expenses as eligible for inclusion in reporting. You can specify either the *accrual basis* or the *cash basis*.

The difference between the accrual basis and the cash basis depends on timing. Recognition of revenue and expenses occurs either when services or goods change hands (accrual basis), or when the payments for services or goods leave or arrive at the bank (cash basis).

In Canada, certain businesses such as self-employed farmers and fishers, professional business people, self-employed commissioned salespeople, and other small business as determined by the CRA may use either the cash basis or the accrual basis to report their income for tax purposes. Most entities in Canada, however, use the accrual basis of accounting. In some cases, a company may start on the cash basis, and then later change to the accrual basis. Fortunately, QuickBooks can always generate reports in either basis for any company file, even if the QuickBooks Preferences are set to Cash or Accrual (You can set the default basis in the Reports & Graphs Company Preferences section of the QuickBooks Preferences).

This lesson and Lessons 4 and 5 focus on the cash basis, which is best thought of as a non-accrual transaction posting. Later lessons cover the accrual basis and why it is the preferred basis for determining business success.

Checking Your Work

Objective L-3.2 Produce detail and summary reports
Objective L-3.4 Find transactions

In this section, you will learn how to access reports from the Menu Bar and via the Report Centre to check your work. You will open, customize, and memorize reports in QuickBooks. We'll look at the Journal report, Chart of Accounts registers, the Balance Sheet, and the Income Statement so you can see how transactions appear in summary reports.

Note: The directions for reports are **QuickBooks Global** information.

Accessing Reports

QuickBooks provides multiple ways to access reports. Figure 3-4 shows the drop-down menu that appears when you click Reports in the Menu Bar. Notice that the first command in the menu is Report Centre, which is one way to access reports. The *Using the Report Centre* section provides a detailed look at the Report Centre.

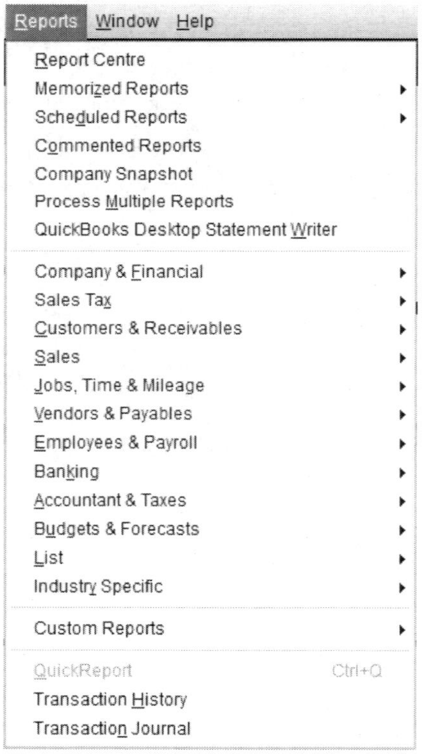

Figure 3-4: Reports drop-down menu

Notice that some of the commands have a small arrow to the right, which means sub-menus of additional commands are available. If you position the mouse pointer over Accountant & Taxes, the sub-menu shown in Figure 3-5 appears. Notice that the Accountant & Taxes sub-menu contains the Journal option (selected in the figure). Clicking the Journal command will display the Journal report.

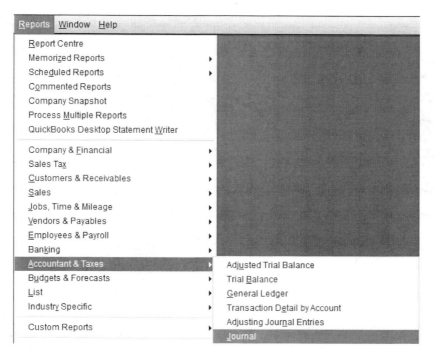

Figure 3-5: Reports > Accountant & Taxes command sequence with Journal selected

You can also access the Journal report (and all other reports) from the Report Centre, which we'll look at next.

Using the Report Centre

QuickBooks provides all the choices from the Reports drop-down menu in one accessible place, the Report Centre, shown in Figure 3-6. You can display the Report Centre by clicking **Reports > Report Centre**, or by clicking the Reports option in the My Shortcuts sidebar.

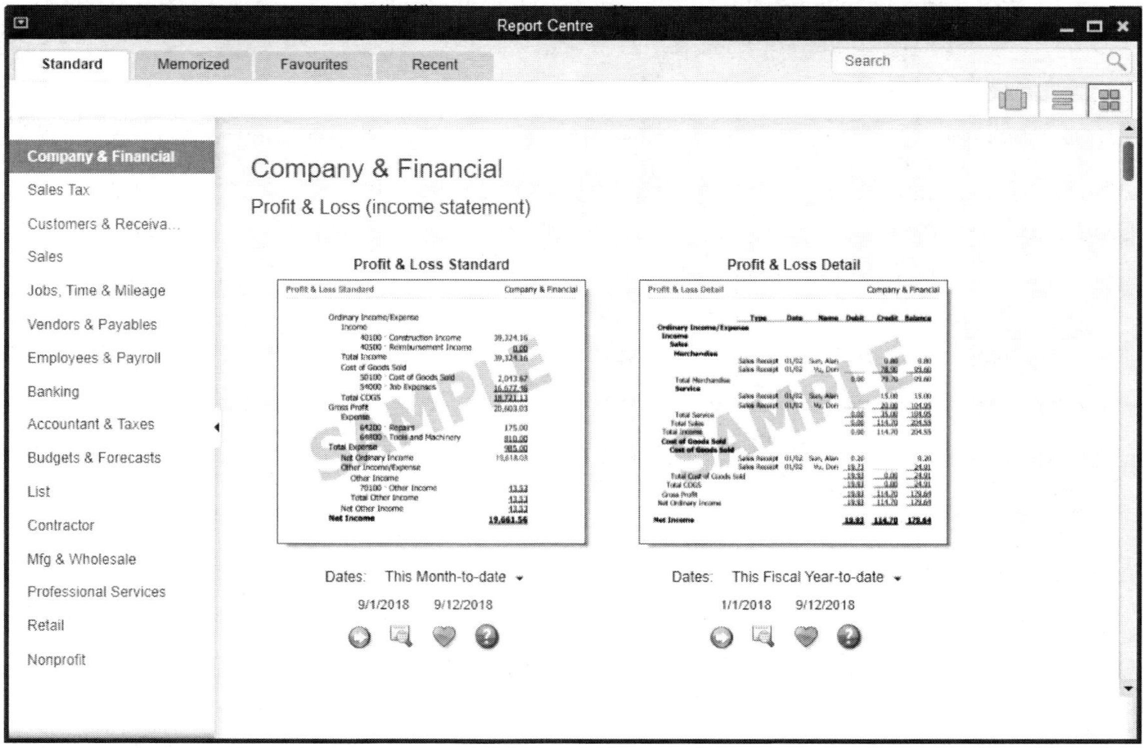

Figure 3-6: Report Centre

When you first open the Report Centre, you may see the message pop up shown in Figure 3-7, which suggests using the List View.

> **Report Centre**   ✕
>
> ⚠ Based on the graphics capabilities of your computer, some views in the
>   Report Centre may be slow. We recommend that you use the list view. To
>   switch, click the List View button located below the Search field. Click OK to
>   continue.
>
> ☐ Do not display this message in the future
>
>   OK

Figure 3-7: Report Centre pop up message

Click OK to display the Report Centre. Notice the icon bar (Figure 3-8) that appears immediately below the Search field in the upper right containing icons that reflect the three views you can specify.

Figure 3-8: Report Centre View icons

From left to right, the views are: Carousel View, List View, and Grid View.

Figure 3-6 above shows the Report Centre in Grid View. The grid view displays a sample report image for all reports in a category. Notice the four icons (Figure 3-9) that appear under each sample report image.

Figure 3-9: Report Centre report icons

- **Run** – displays the report as if you had clicked the report name in the Reports drop-down menu.
- **Info** – provides a description of the report.
- **Fave** – marks the report as a "Favourite."
- **Help** – displays the *Have a Question?* window, which presents help topics about the report you selected.

Also notice the four tabs that appear at the top of the Report Centre. The categories in the left sidebar change depending on which tab you select:

- **Standard** – lists all report categories. The categories match the options in the Reports drop-down menu. You can click a category to display all reports in that category. Figure 3-6 above displays the reports contained in the Company & Financial category.
- **Memorized** – displays a list of the memorized report categories in the left sidebar. You can click a category to display all memorized reports for that category.
- **Favourites** – displays a list of the reports you marked with the Fave icon. This allows you to put the reports you use frequently in one place.
- **Recent** – displays a list of date ranges for reports you have run. You can select a date range to display a list of reports you ran in that time span.

Figure 3-10 shows the Standard tab of the Report Centre in Carousel View.

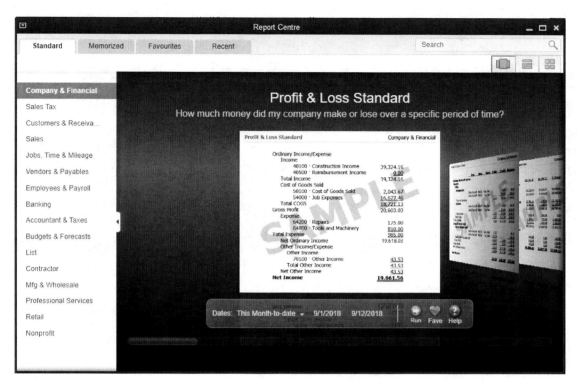

Figure 3-10: Carousel View

Notice the slider at the bottom. You can drag the slider to the left or right. This allows you to quickly see how all the reports look by sliding through them. Click a report to select it. Once you find what you want, you can use the date choices above the slider to open the report you want to view.

Note: The report images show only the report format; the content is generic. You do not see the actual report data until you run the report.

Figure 3-11 shows the Standard tab of the Report Centre in List View.

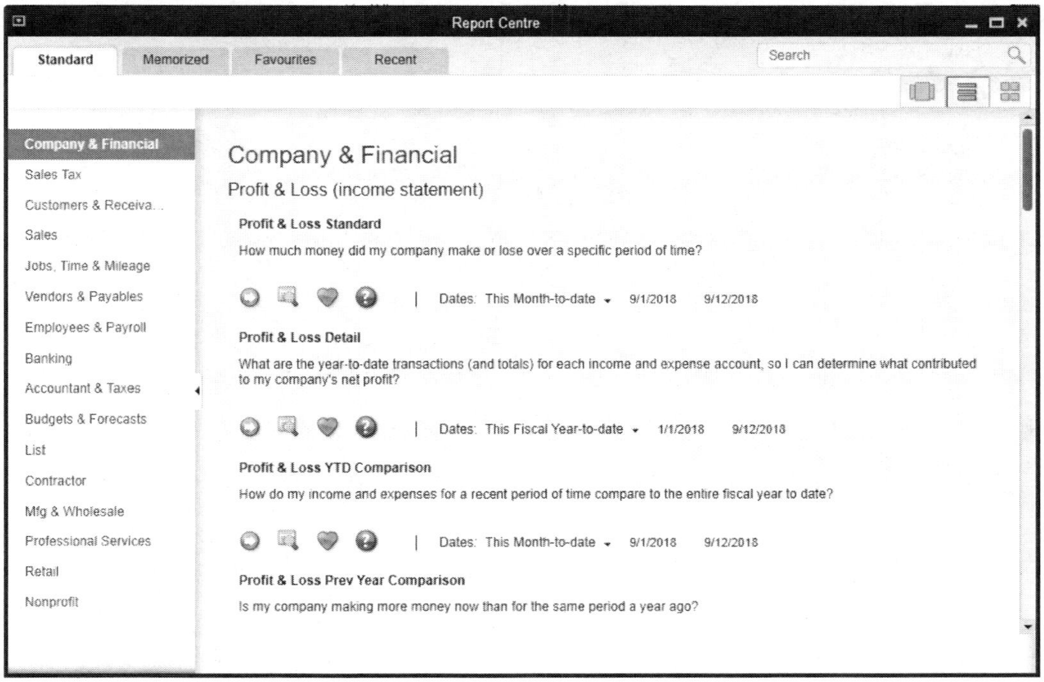

Figure 3-11: List View

List View displays reports vertically in a column. In this view, a description of the report appears below the report name. For example, in Figure 3-11, the description "How much money did my company make or lose over a specific period of time?" appears below the Profit & Loss Standard report. If you are unsure about what a report does, you can click the Info icon for more information about it.

Opening the Journal

To open the Journal report from the Menu Bar, click **Reports > Accountant & Taxes > Journal**. To open the Journal report from the Report Centre, select the Accountant & Taxes category in the left sidebar, then scroll to find and select the Journal report.

Figure 3-12 shows the Journal report. This example shows all the transactions you entered in Lesson 2.

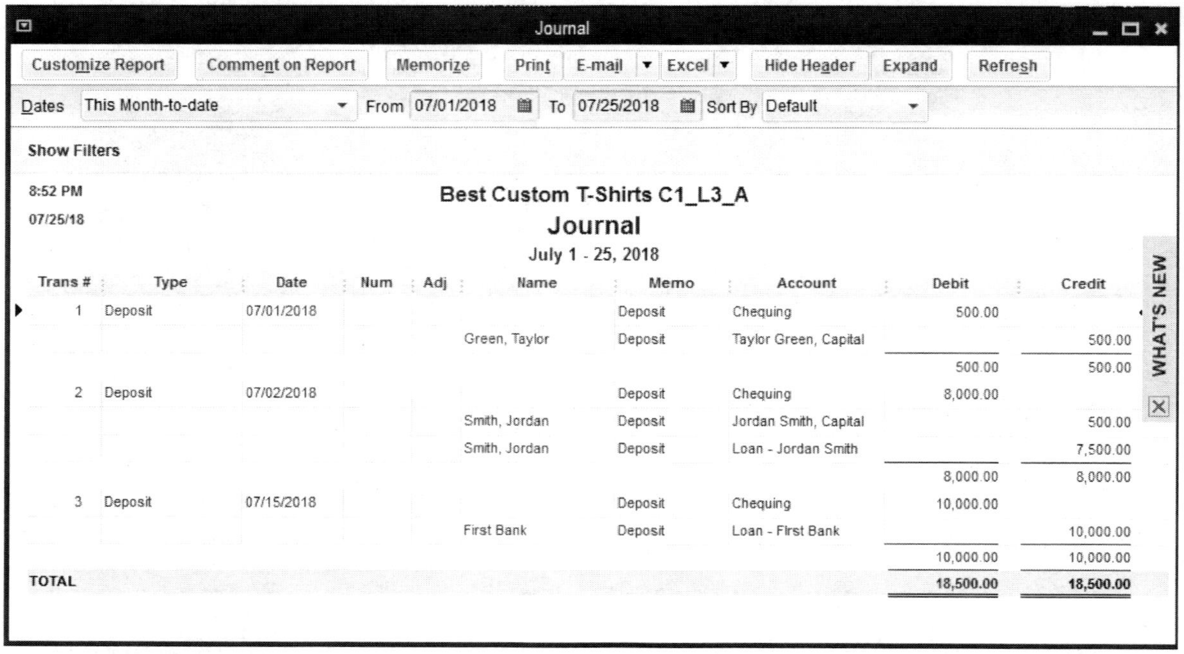
Journal
Customize Report | Comment on Report | Memorize | Print | E-mail | Excel | Hide Header | Expand | Refresh
Dates This Month-to-date | From 07/01/2018 | To 07/25/2018 | Sort By Default
Show Filters
8:52 PM
07/25/18
Best Custom T-Shirts C1_L3_A
Journal
July 1 - 25, 2018

Trans #	Type	Date	Num	Adj	Name	Memo	Account	Debit	Credit
1	Deposit	07/01/2018				Deposit	Chequing	500.00	
					Green, Taylor	Deposit	Taylor Green, Capital		500.00
								500.00	500.00
2	Deposit	07/02/2018				Deposit	Chequing	8,000.00	
					Smith, Jordan	Deposit	Jordan Smith, Capital		500.00
					Smith, Jordan	Deposit	Loan - Jordan Smith		7,500.00
								8,000.00	8,000.00
3	Deposit	07/15/2018				Deposit	Chequing	10,000.00	
					First Bank	Deposit	Loan - First Bank		10,000.00
								10,000.00	10,000.00
TOTAL								18,500.00	18,500.00

Figure 3-12: Journal Report

The first column header, Trans #, is the auto-number that QuickBooks adds to every transaction in the order you enter it. In this example, the first three transactions are also listed in order by date. The default setting for the Journal report is to list transactions by transaction number.

The second column header, Type, is the name of the form used to enter the journal entry. In this example, the Make Deposits form was used to enter the transactions.

The last two columns are Debit and Credit. You can see that each of the deposits placed a debit in the chequing account, even though that information was not explicitly identified in the Make Deposits form.

The Button Bar at the top contains most of the actions you might need. You can memorize the report settings (covered in the *Reviewing Your Work* section of this lesson), print the report, send the report via email, save the report to an Excel file, or, if the report has the capability, expand or collapse the detail view.

Below the Button Bar are the date parameter and sort options you can use to display specific Journal entries.

Another useful QuickBooks feature is the QuickZoom tool that appears when you position the mouse pointer over any of the numbers in the Debit or Credit columns. The QuickZoom tool looks like a magnifying glass with the letter z on it. When it appears, you can double-click the number to display the transaction in the form window. This is one of several ways you can locate a transaction without using the Find feature.

Note: The WHAT'S NEW flag is another type of message that you can dismiss. You can restore these messages by clicking **Help > New Features > What's New**.

Changing Settings

You can change many of the settings in the Journal (and any) report. Below the Button Bar are the date parameters and sort settings. The date options are shown in Figure 3-13.

This Month-to-date ▾	Fror
All
Today
This Week
This Week-to-date
This Month
✓ This Month-to-date
This Fiscal Quarter
This Fiscal Quarter-to-date
This Fiscal Year
This Fiscal Year-to-Last Month
This Fiscal Year-to-date
Yesterday
Last Week
Last Week-to-date
Last Month
Last Month-to-date
Last Fiscal Quarter
Last Fiscal Quarter-to-date
Last Fiscal Year
Last Fiscal Year-to-date
Next Week
Next 4 Weeks
Next Month
Next Fiscal Quarter
Next Fiscal Year
Custom

Figure 3-13: Date options

To change the settings for a report, click the Customize Report button on the Button Bar. The Modify Report dialog box for that report will appear, as shown in Figure 3-14.

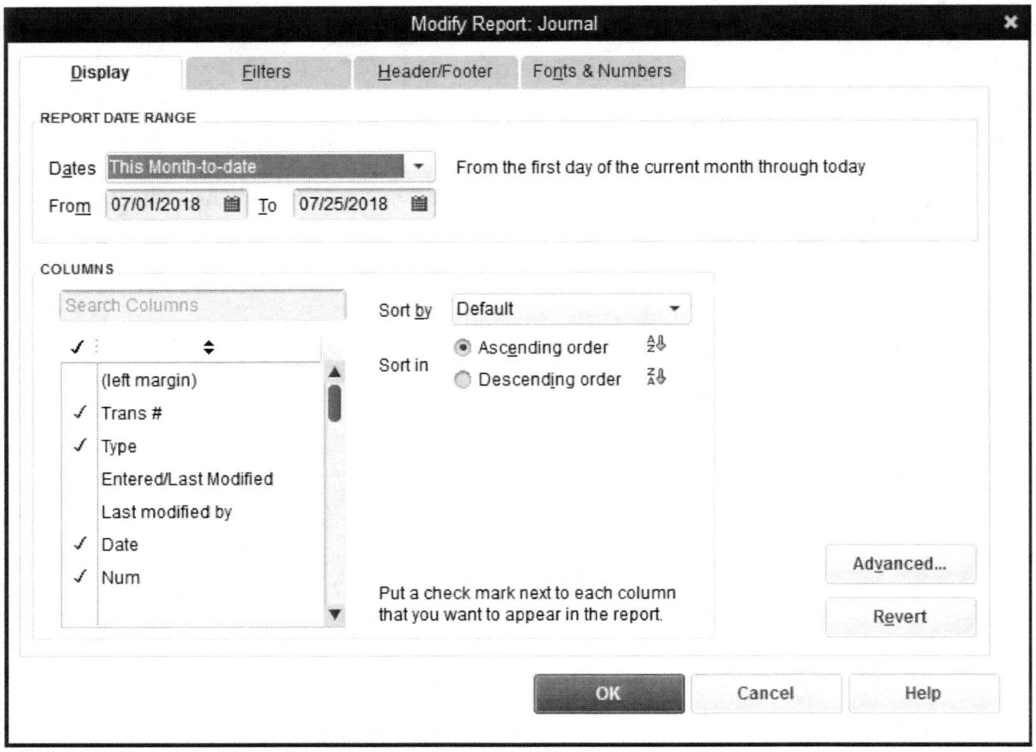

Figure 3-14: Modify Report dialog box: Journal, Display tab

The Modify Report dialog box for all reports contains settings you can change. For example, the Display tab contains options for modifying the dates for the report and the sort settings. The Sort by drop-down menu contains the options shown in Figure 3-15.

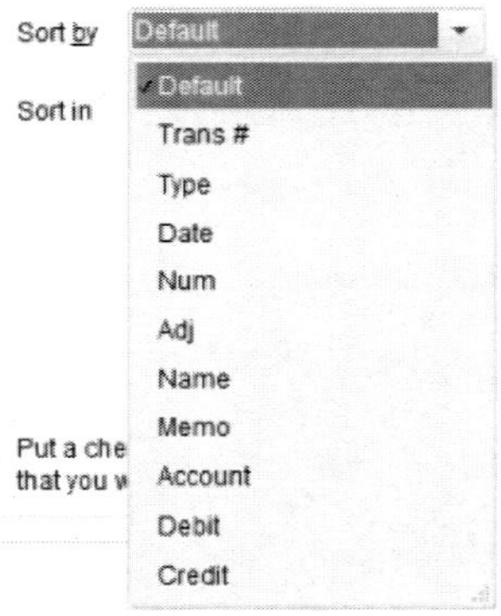

Figure 3-15: Sort by drop-down menu options

The Filters tab includes options for viewing only specific accounts or specific types of accounts. The Header/Footer tab includes options for specifying report header and footer information. The Fonts & Numbers tab includes options for selecting fonts for various report components, for specifying how to display negative numbers, and for specifying whether to show numbers without cents.

Note: The *Reviewing Your Work > Modifying the Journal Report* section of this lesson will cover the Modify Report dialog box in more detail.

Exercise 3.1: Investigating Reports

In this exercise, you will open reports, explore the Report Centre, and change report settings.

Open the portable file Best Custom T-Shirts C1_L3_A (Portable).QBM.

1. Launch **QuickBooks** and close any message prompts that may appear.

2. If necessary, close any open company files.

3. In the *No Company Open* dialog box, click the **Open or restore an existing company** button. Select the **Restore a portable file** radio button, and then click **Next**. Navigate to the *1767-Student-Files\Lesson 3\StarterFiles* folder, click **Best Custom T-Shirts C1_L3_A (Portable).QBM**, then click **Open**.

4. Click **Next**.

5. In the Save Company File as dialog box, navigate to *1767-Student-Files\Lesson 3\MyProjects* folder, then save the file as **Best Custom T-Shirts C1_L3_<your name>**. This may take a few minutes. A pop up message will appear saying the portable file opened successfully. Click **OK** to dismiss it.

Rename the company to add your name.

6. Click **Company > Company Information** to open the Company Information dialog box.

7. At the end of the text in the *Company Name* field, type your name, then click **OK**.

Open a report.

8. In the Menu Bar, click **Reports > Company & Financial > Balance Sheet Standard** to open the Balance Sheet report. By default, the report shows this fiscal year-to-date.

9. In the Button Bar, click the **E-mail** button. Notice that you can send the report as an Excel file or as a PDF.

10. In the Button Bar, click the **Excel** button. Notice that you can create a new Excel worksheet or update an existing one.

11. In the Button Bar, click the **Hide Header** button. The three title lines at the top of the report are hidden from view.

12. Click the **Show Header** button to redisplay them.

13. Click the Close (**X**) button at the upper-right corner of the report window to close the Balance Sheet report.

Open the Report Centre and find a report.

14. Click **Reports > Report Centre** to open the Report Centre.

15. In the View buttons at the upper-right corner of the window, click the **Carousel View** button if necessary to view the reports in Carousel View.

16. Ensure that the Standard tab is selected, then in the category list on the left, click **Accountant & Taxes** to view that specific set of reports.

17. Slowly drag the slider to the right until you find the Journal Report.

18. In the View buttons, click the **List View** button to change the view.

19. Scroll the list again to find the Journal report.

20. Position the mouse pointer over the Journal report, then click the **Info** icon to open a sample view of the report.

21. Click the Close (**X**) button in the sample view window.

22. In the View buttons, click the **Grid View** button to change the view.

23. Scroll to find the Journal report once more.

Set the date range and run the report.

24. Position the mouse pointer over the Journal report, display the **Dates:** drop-down menu, and then select **Last Month** to specify a new date range for the report.

25. Click the **Run** icon for the Journal report to open the report.

    Note: If the message about collapsing and expanding transactions appears, select the **Do not display this message in the future** check box, and then click **OK**.

Change the date range.

26. In the *From* field, change the date to **07/01/2018**.

27. In the *To* field, change the date to **07/25/2018**.

28. In the Button Bar, click the **Refresh** button to update the report data.

29. Resize the report window so that you can see all the data. The Journal report shows the deposits you made in Lesson 2.

Use the QuickZoom tool.

30. Position the mouse pointer over the Taylor Green transaction and double-click. The Make Deposits form appears showing the deposit details.

31. Close the Make Deposits form.

Close the Journal report.

32. Click the Close (**X**) button at the upper-right corner of the report window to close the Journal report and click **No** to avoid memorizing the report.

33. Close the Report Centre.

Leave the company file open for the next exercise.

Opening a Register

In this section, we will locate the same transactions you saw in the Journal report through the Chart of Accounts registers. Remember, only the Balance Sheet accounts that are not in the Equity sub-sections of the Income Statement have registers. You can click **Lists > Chart of Accounts** in the Menu Bar or click the Chart of Accounts icon in the COMPANY section of the Home page to open the Chart of Accounts.

Figure 3-16 shows the Chart of Accounts window with the Chequing account selected. Notice that the BALANCE TOTAL amount ($18,500) is the same as the Journal total for all the debits placed in the Chequing account at this point (see Figure 3-12). The TYPE column displays the account types (see Table 3-1).

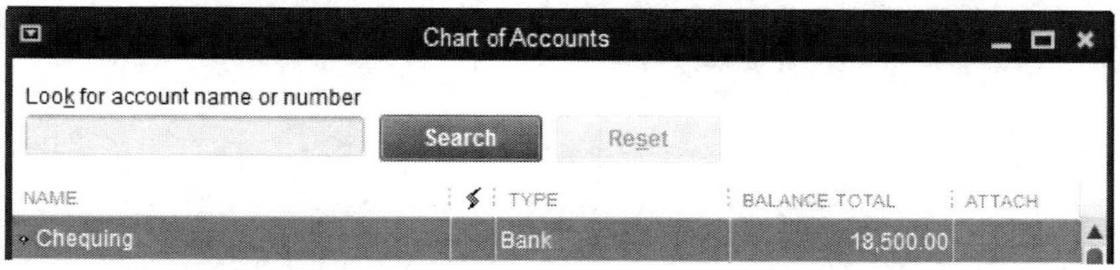

Figure 3-16: Chart of Accounts window

If you double-click the Chequing account, the Chequing register will open, as shown in Figure 3-17.

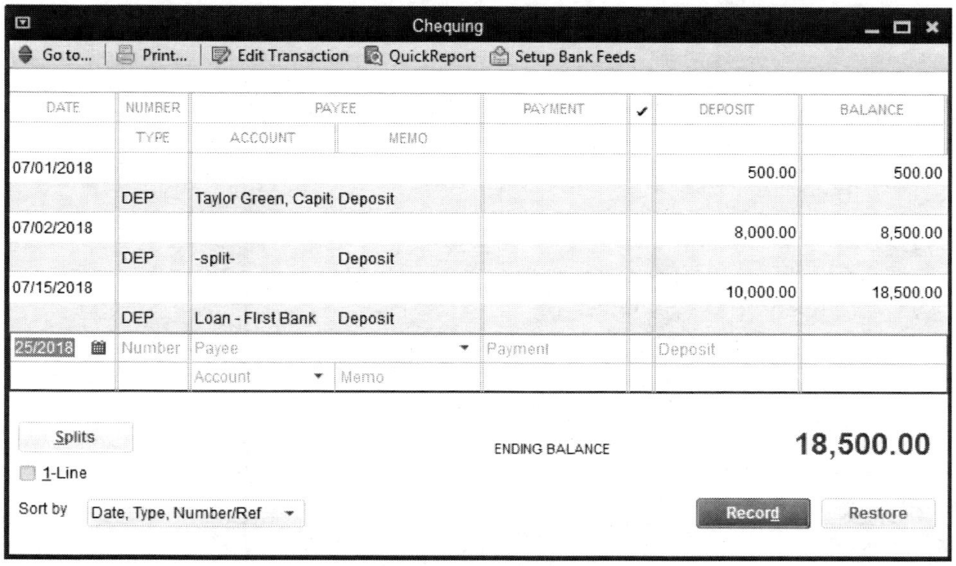

Figure 3-17: Chequing register

You can see three transactions. The DEP initials in the TYPE column refer to the transaction type—deposit. You can double-click DEP for a transaction to open the Make Deposits form for that transaction.

Note: The register shows each transaction on two lines, so the column headers also have two levels. You can specify to show each transaction on a single line by clicking the 1-Line check box at the bottom left of the register window.

Notice that the register does not display debits and credits. Instead, the column header for credits is named PAYMENT and the column header for debits is named DEPOSIT. QuickBooks consistently displays register columns for debits and credits in the reverse order of journal entries: the column for credits first and then debits. In other accounts, these two column headers are DECREASE and INCREASE and the column headers switch places depending on whether the credits or debits have the indicated effect.

Running and Modifying a QuickReport

You can also run a QuickReport to see what is in the registers (or any GL account) and locate transactions. At the bottom of the Chart of Accounts window click **Reports > QuickReport: Chequing** (Figure 3-18) to display a QuickReport for the account.

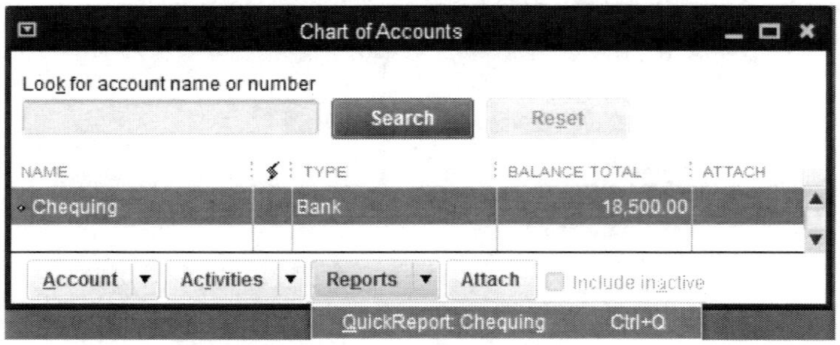

Figure 3-18: Reports > QuickReport: Chequing command sequence

The Chequing account QuickReport is shown in Figure 3-19.

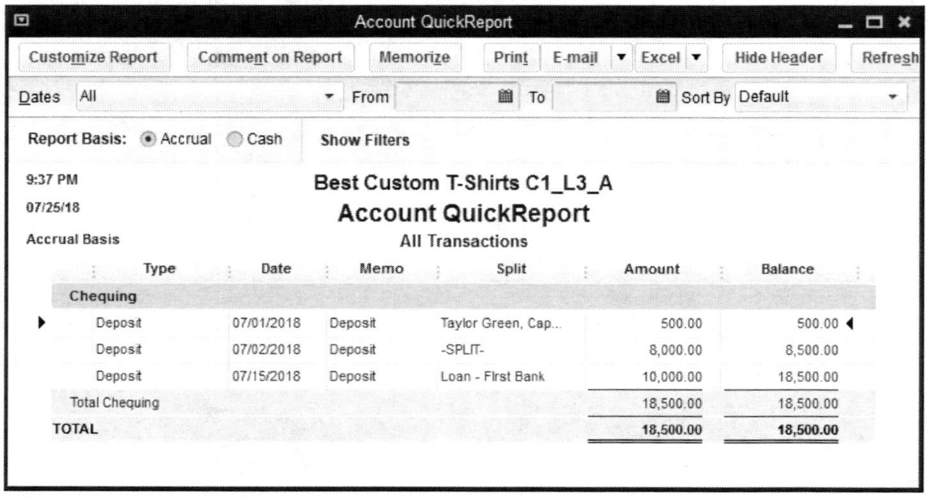

Figure 3-19: Chequing account QuickReport

We have removed several empty columns, but you can see that not all the text in the Split column appears. The Split column displays the account(s) used for the other side of the transaction. On a Make Deposits form, this is the account you chose in the FROM ACCOUNT field.

To see everything in the columns, you may need to increase the column width. You can do so by clicking and dragging the three vertical dots that separate the column headers to the left or right. You may see a message asking if you want all columns this size. In Figure 3-20, we have resized the Split column so that all the text is visible.

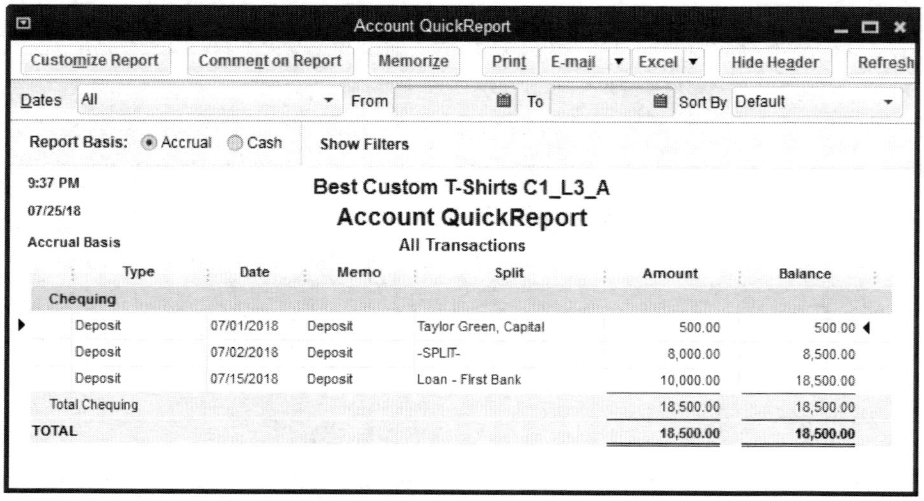

Figure 3-20: Chequing account QuickReport, Split column resized

When you print a report in QuickBooks, it will use the default column width, which may truncate many of your report's columns. If resizing the columns still does not allow you to see all the detail you need, consider exporting the report to Microsoft Excel by clicking the Excel button in the Button Bar. In Excel, you will be able to adjust the columns as you see fit; however, you may need to change your print settings within Excel to keep all the text on a single page.

Notice that this report does not show debits and credits; it displays only an Amount column. You can change the report setting to show debits and credits by clicking the Customize Report button, which will display the Modify Report dialog box shown in Figure 3-21.

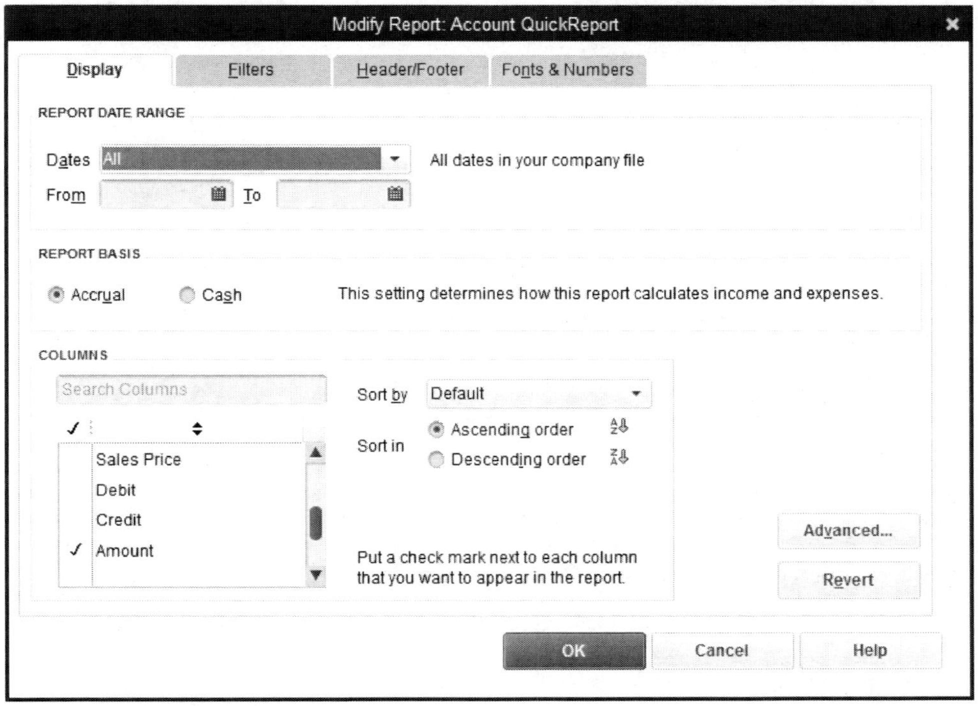

Figure 3-21: Modify Report dialog box for QuickReports, default settings

On the Display tab, in the lower left, scroll down through the column headers until you see the checkmark in front of Amount, which is the default setting for all QuickReports. To change the Amount column to Debit and Credit columns, deselect Amount and select Debit and Credit, as shown in Figure 3-22.

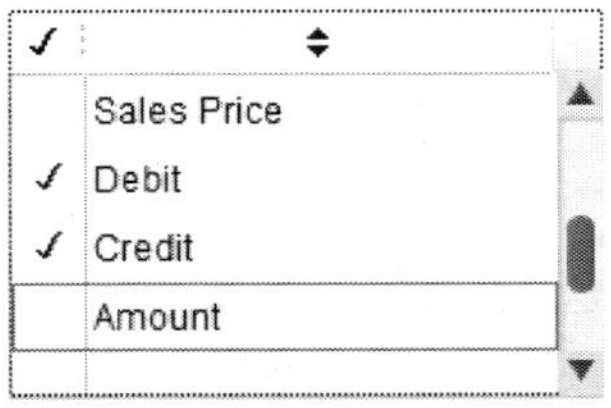

Figure 3-22: Specifying column headers

You might want to change the Amount column so that QuickBooks assigns the amount total a positive sign if the account balance is normal for its section of the accounting equation or sub-section. The report bases the definition of normal on whether a debit or credit increases the account, and if the one that increases is greater, the amount is displayed as a positive number. For example, debits increase assets. If the bank account was overdrawn and had more credits than debits, the GL Account Chequing QuickReport amount would be negative.

Figure 3-23 shows the result of the changes. Remember that you can position the mouse pointer over a debit to display the QuickZoom tool, and then double-click to open the Make Deposits form and view information about the transaction.

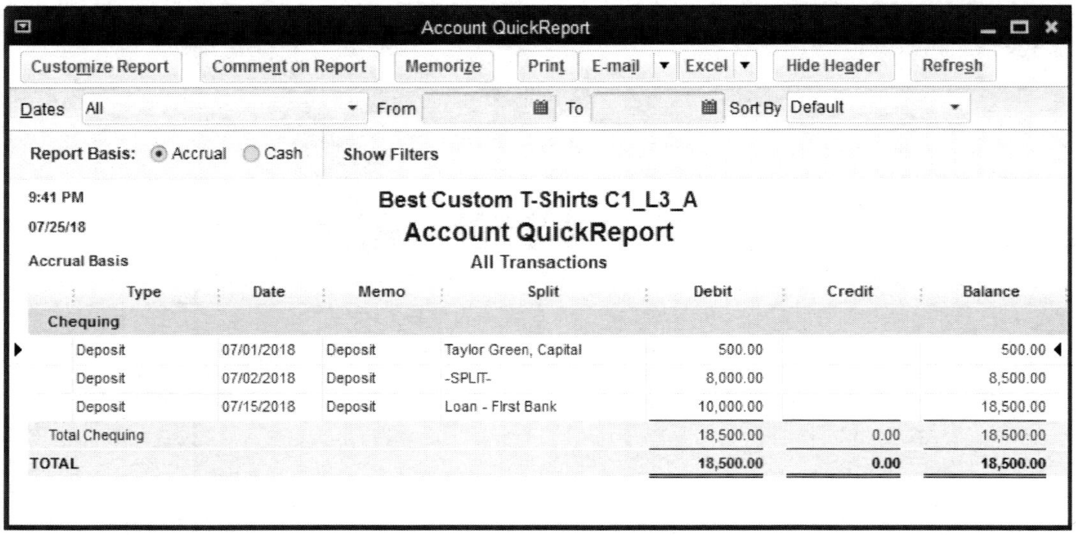

Figure 3-23: QuickReport showing Debit and Credit columns

Exercise 3.2: Opening a Register and Running a QuickReport

In this exercise, you will open a register, and run and modify a QuickReport.

Open a register.

1.   Ensure that the company file you worked on in the previous exercise is still open.

2.   Click **Lists > Chart of Accounts** to open the Chart of Accounts window.

3.   In the Chart of Accounts window, double-click **Chequing** to open the Chequing register.

4.   Resize the register window if necessary to view all three transactions, then in the *TYPE* column, double-click **DEP** to the left of the Taylor Green deposit. The Make Deposits form opens showing the deposit details.

5.   Close the Make Deposits form.

6.   Close the Chequing register.

Run a QuickReport.

7.   At the bottom of the Chart of Accounts window, click the **Reports** button, then click **QuickReport: Chequing** to open the Chequing account QuickReport.

Customize the QuickReport by changing the columns.

8.   In the Button Bar, click the **Customize Report** button to open the Modify Report dialog box.

9.   In the Display tab, in the *COLUMNS* section, click **Num** to remove the check mark. This action will remove the Num column from the report.

10. Click **OK**. Notice that the Num column no longer appears in the report.

11. Click the **Customize Report** button again.

12. In the Display tab, click the **Revert** button to change the report back to its previous state, then click **OK**. Notice that the Num column reappears in the report.

13. Close the QuickReport and close the Chart of Accounts window.

Leave the company file open for the next exercise.

Running the Balance Sheet

You can also find detailed transactions through the summary reports. In this section, we will generate a Balance Sheet for Best Custom T-Shirts. You can open the Balance Sheet by clicking **Reports > Company & Financial > Balance Sheet Standard** on the Menu Bar (Figure 3-24).

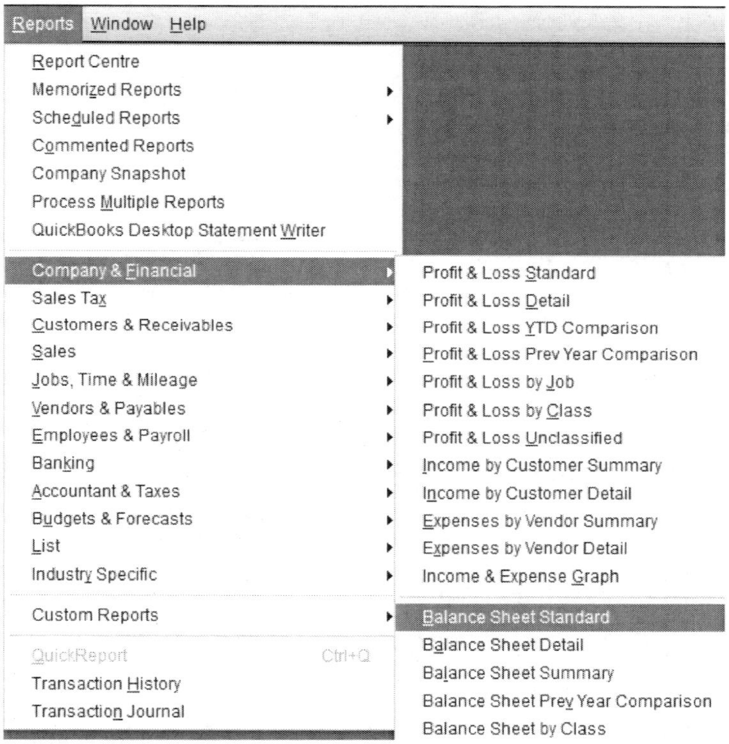

Figure 3-24: Reports > Company & Financial > Balance Sheet Standard command sequence

The Balance Sheet (Figure 3-25) displays the three sections of the accounting equation: Assets = Liabilities + Equity. The report is divided into two sections: Assets and Liabilities & Equity.

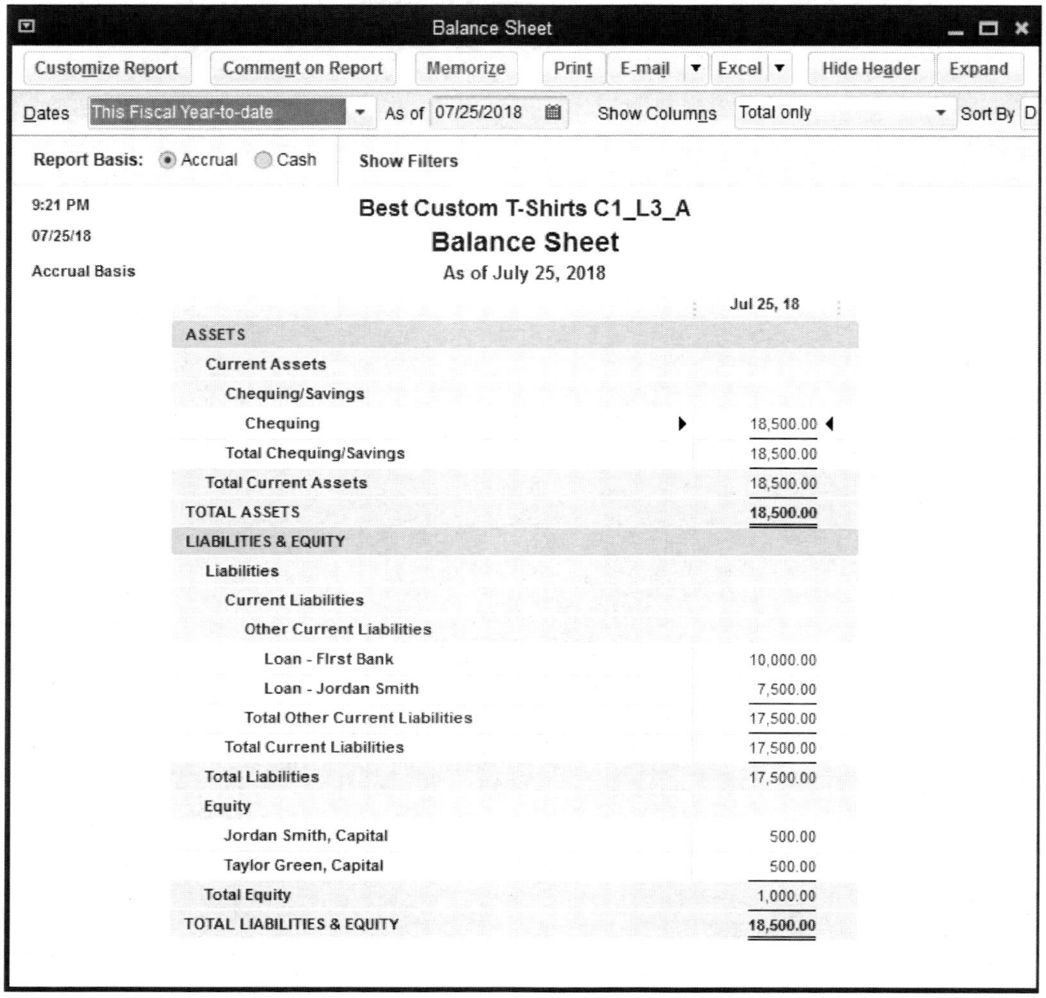

Figure 3-25: Balance Sheet

Because the business is new and has not engaged in any business activities, the Equity sub-sections, Income and Expense, do not produce any net income. Because the business is also in its first year, no prior net income has rolled into retained earnings. Only after the end of the first year of business will retained earnings show in Equity.

The funds deposited in the chequing account are what the business owns (assets). The funds loaned to the business are what the business owes (liabilities). The difference between the assets and the liabilities is the total in equity.

You may recall that each of the business owners has their own class, which is a way of categorizing all the transactions in any account. Figure 3-26 shows the same Balance Sheet as Figure 3-25, but with the amounts distributed by class. You can open a Balance Sheet by Class by clicking **Reports > Company & Financial > Balance Sheet by Class** on the Menu Bar.

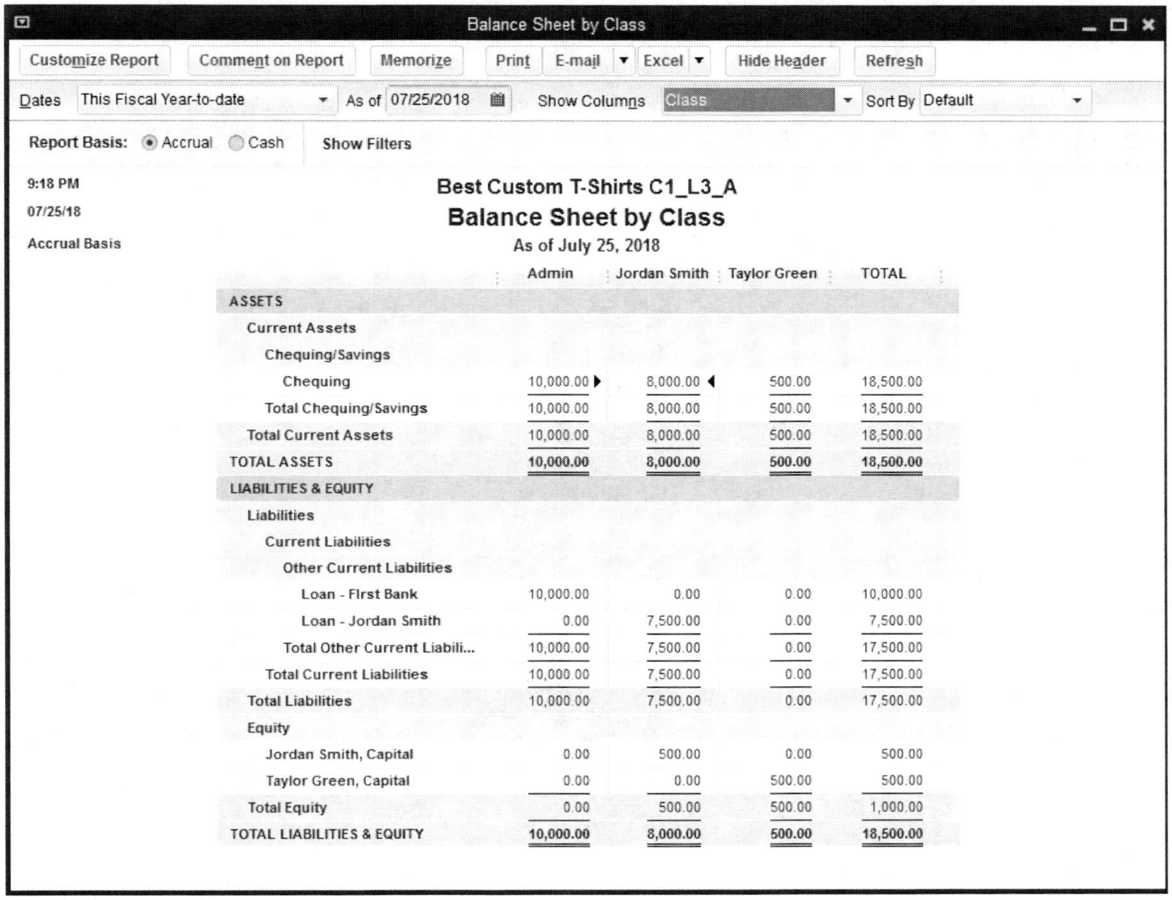

Best Custom T-Shirts C1_L3_A

Balance Sheet by Class

As of July 25, 2018

	Admin	Jordan Smith	Taylor Green	TOTAL
ASSETS				
Current Assets				
Chequing/Savings				
Chequing	10,000.00	8,000.00	500.00	18,500.00
Total Chequing/Savings	10,000.00	8,000.00	500.00	18,500.00
Total Current Assets	10,000.00	8,000.00	500.00	18,500.00
TOTAL ASSETS	10,000.00	8,000.00	500.00	18,500.00
LIABILITIES & EQUITY				
Liabilities				
Current Liabilities				
Other Current Liabilities				
Loan - First Bank	10,000.00	0.00	0.00	10,000.00
Loan - Jordan Smith	0.00	7,500.00	0.00	7,500.00
Total Other Current Liabili...	10,000.00	7,500.00	0.00	17,500.00
Total Current Liabilities	10,000.00	7,500.00	0.00	17,500.00
Total Liabilities	10,000.00	7,500.00	0.00	17,500.00
Equity				
Jordan Smith, Capital	0.00	500.00	0.00	500.00
Taylor Green, Capital	0.00	0.00	500.00	500.00
Total Equity	0.00	500.00	500.00	1,000.00
TOTAL LIABILITIES & EQUITY	10,000.00	8,000.00	500.00	18,500.00

Figure 3-26: Balance Sheet by Class

The TOTAL column displays the same information as does the TOTAL column in the Balance Sheet without classes. If a transaction was not assigned a class, the column header Unclassified would appear.

Finally, we will locate the Make Deposits transactions from the Balance Sheet. Position the mouse pointer over the figures in the chequing account to display the QuickZoom tool, then double-click to display the Transactions by Account report, shown in Figure 3-27. This report shows the Make Deposits transaction for the selected item.

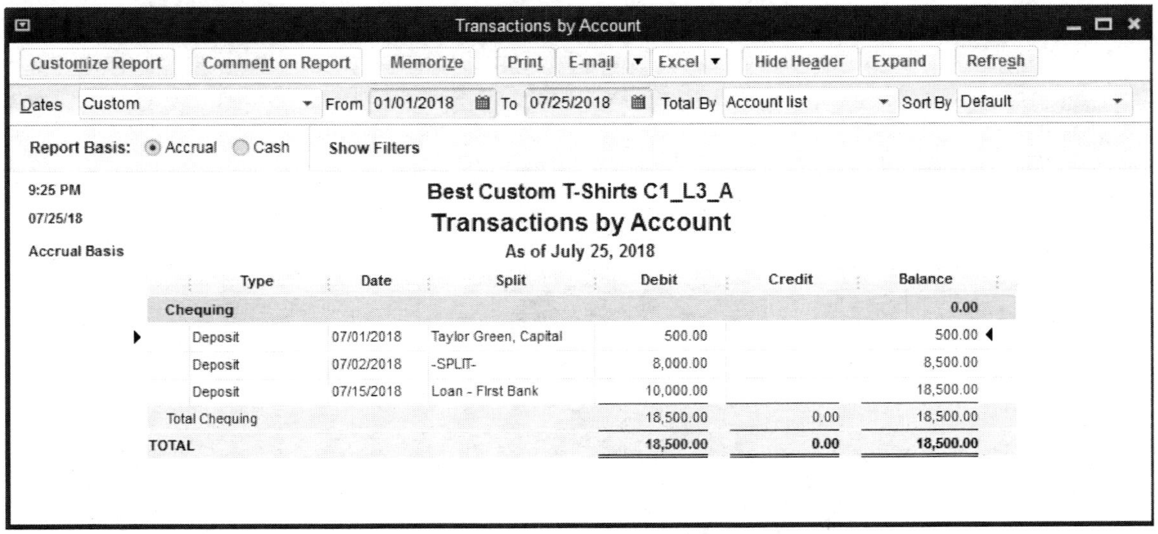

Best Custom T-Shirts C1_L3_A

Transactions by Account

As of July 25, 2018

Type	Date	Split	Debit	Credit	Balance
Chequing					0.00
Deposit	07/01/2018	Taylor Green, Capital	500.00		500.00
Deposit	07/02/2018	-SPLIT-	8,000.00		8,500.00
Deposit	07/15/2018	Loan - First Bank	10,000.00		18,500.00
Total Chequing			18,500.00	0.00	18,500.00
TOTAL			18,500.00	0.00	18,500.00

Figure 3-27: Transactions by Account report

Running the Income Statement

Because Best Custom T-Shirts has not engaged in business activities, we will use the Blue Heron Spa to look at a summary Income Statement. QuickBooks always uses the name Profit & Loss for this financial statement. You can open an Income Statement by clicking **Reports > Company & Financial > Profit & Loss (type)** on the Menu Bar. Figure 3-28 shows the Profit & Loss by Class statement to illustrate how reports display the transactions as Unclassified if no classes are used.

Notice that the Income and Expense GL accounts appear under the Ordinary Income/Expense heading. If you refer to Table 3-1, all the Equity sub-section accounts are either in this section or Other Income/Expense.

Blue Heron Spa Inc.
Profit & Loss by Class
January 1 through February 15, 2017

	Unclassified	TOTAL
Ordinary Income/Expense		
Income		
Esthetics	14,185.00	14,185.00
Massage Services	13,785.00	13,785.00
Services Income		
Body Treatments ▶	10,920.00 ◀	10,920.00
Facial Treatments	6,750.00	6,750.00
Total Services Income	17,670.00	17,670.00
Total Income	45,640.00	45,640.00
Gross Profit	45,640.00	45,640.00
Expense		
Insurance Expense	125.00	125.00
Linens and Spa Supplies	942.68	942.68
Miscellaneous Expense	58.85	58.85
Office Supplies	149.32	149.32
Payroll Expenses	14,823.27	14,823.27
Rent Expense	3,000.00	3,000.00
Telephone Expense	80.79	80.79
Utilities	302.18	302.18
Total Expense	19,482.09	19,482.09
Net Ordinary Income	26,157.91	26,157.91
Net Income	**26,157.91**	**26,157.91**

Figure 3-28: Profit & Loss by Class statement

While this Profit & Loss statement does not show all account types, you can see the total at the bottom called Net Income. Net Income is the amount in the Equity section of the Balance Sheet. These values would match if you ran the Balance Sheet for the same ending date as the Profit & Loss statement, which you can see in Figure 3-29.

Equity	
Opening Balance Equity	49,282.43
Owners Equity	-938.72
Net Income	26,157.91
Total Equity	74,501.62
TOTAL LIABILITIES & EQUITY	78,530.61

Figure 3-29: Equity section, Balance Sheet of Blue Heron Spa set to February 15, 2017 with Net Income matching the Profit & Loss

Because the GL accounts on this summary report do not have registers, use the QuickZoom tool if you want to see the transaction detail.

Note: If the Expand/Collapse button reads Expand, click it to reveal more detail in the report.

Setting the Accounting Basis

Now, bring your attention to the upper left corner of any of the reports. Directly below the date parameters are the Report Basis radio buttons: Accrual and Cash. All the transactions we've entered so far are cash, meaning that the funds moved at the same time as the event. For example, the loan was granted by the bank and the funds were transferred the same day. When a delay exists, commonly seen in the Income and Expense accounts where a sale may be made today and the money received next week, changing the basis can change the report. If you compare Figure 3-30, which shows the Balance Sheet with the Cash basis, with either Figure 3-25 or Figure 3-26, you can see that changing the basis did not change the amounts.

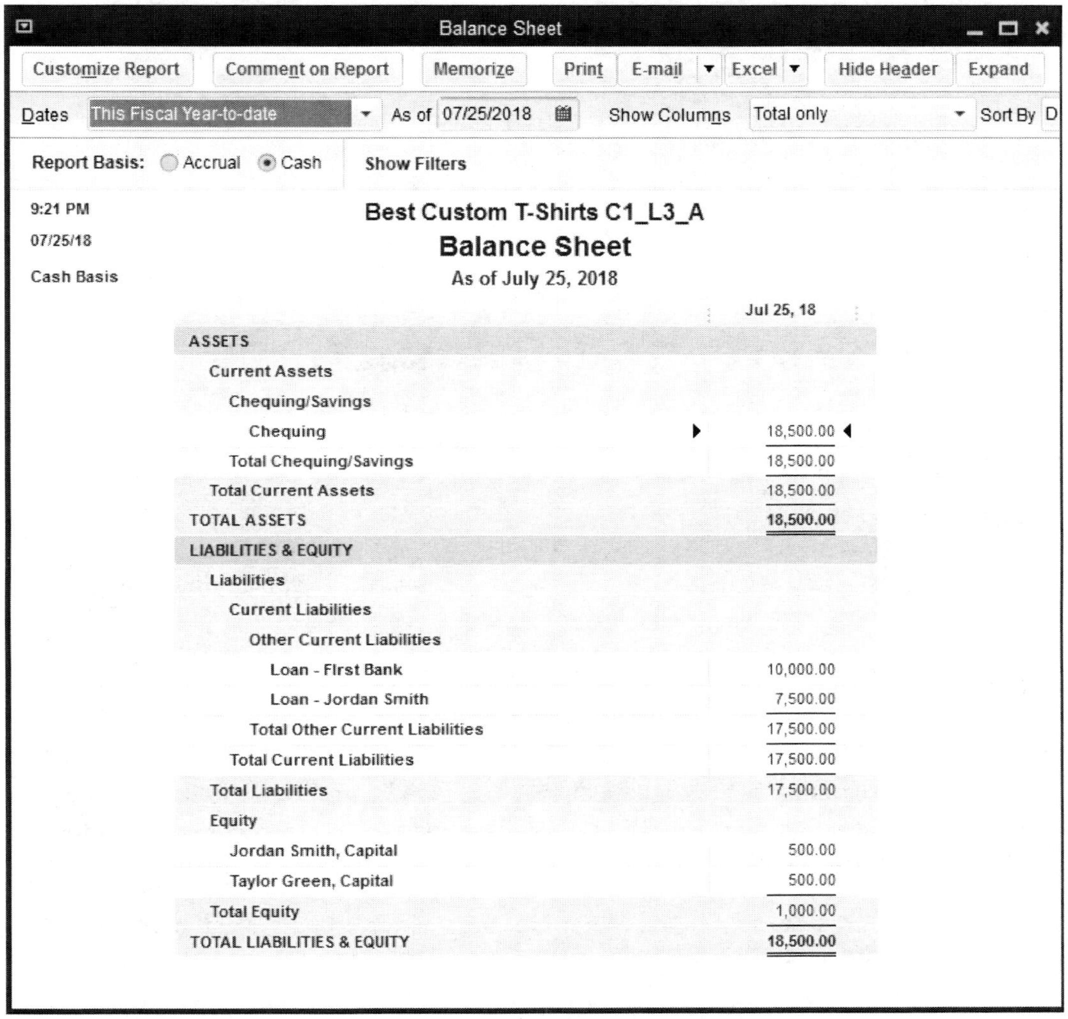

	Jul 25, 18
ASSETS	
Current Assets	
Chequing/Savings	
Chequing	18,500.00
Total Chequing/Savings	18,500.00
Total Current Assets	18,500.00
TOTAL ASSETS	18,500.00
LIABILITIES & EQUITY	
Liabilities	
Current Liabilities	
Other Current Liabilities	
Loan - First Bank	10,000.00
Loan - Jordan Smith	7,500.00
Total Other Current Liabilities	17,500.00
Total Current Liabilities	17,500.00
Total Liabilities	17,500.00
Equity	
Jordan Smith, Capital	500.00
Taylor Green, Capital	500.00
Total Equity	1,000.00
TOTAL LIABILITIES & EQUITY	18,500.00

Figure 3-30: Balance Sheet, Cash Basis

Exercise 3.3: Running Financial Reports

In this exercise, you will run Balance Sheets for Best Custom T-Shirts.

Run the Standard Balance Sheet.

1. Ensure that the company file you worked on in the previous exercise is still open.
2. Click **Reports > Company & Financial > Balance Sheet Standard**. The Balance Sheet report appears.
3. In the *As of* field, type or select **7/25/2018**, and then click the **Refresh** button.

4. In the *Report Basis* section, click the **Cash** radio button.

5. Print or Email the report according to your instructor's preference, using the appropriate buttons on the Button Bar.

Run the Balance Sheet by Class.

6. Click **Reports > Company & Financial > Balance Sheet by Class**. If the Balance Sheet by class report warning message appears informing you that you may need to enter transactions in a specific order, select the **Do not display this message in the future** check box and click **OK** to dismiss it. The Balance Sheet by Class report opens.

7. In the *As of* field, type or select **7/25/2018**, and then click the **Refresh** button.

8. In the *Report Basis* section, click the **Cash** radio button.

9. Print or Email the report according to your instructor's preference.

10. Close all open reports without memorizing them.

Leave the company file open for the next exercise.

Finding and Correcting Transactions

Objective L-3.4 Find transactions

Objective L-3.5 Correct transactions

In this section, you will learn how to locate the last transaction you made and then how to make corrections. While some accounting systems do not allow you to make corrections, QuickBooks has a process for letting you safely fix mistakes. Transactions can also be voided or deleted—you will learn about those actions in Level 2.

Finding the Last Entry

Everyone makes mistakes. For instance, while entering transactions in QuickBooks, you might accidentally save a transaction before entering all appropriate details. This type of error tends to occur if you press the ENTER key to save your transactions instead of clicking the buttons to tell a form what you want to do. While QuickBooks forms do contain optional fields, a form will not close if you do not complete the required fields.

Several types of mistakes are common. One is a drop-down menu error where you thought you made the correct selection, but instead selected the option above or below the one you intended. The date may be a week off one way or the other for the same reason—clicking above or below the target week and date in the calendar. Another problem may occur due to your QuickBooks preferences. For example, if the date preference settings specify to create a new transaction with the same date as the previous one, you may not realize that you have entered the wrong date until after you have created many transactions. Tab errors are also common, where you enter data in the wrong field, such as mistakenly entering an account number in an amount field.

QuickBooks guards against some errors. For example, if you try to enter more than two decimal points in an amount field and then TAB to the next field, a message appears telling you "This field accepts a maximum of two (2) decimal points." If you enter text in a field that only accepts numbers, a message appears stating "This field contains an invalid character."

Sometimes, when you want to find the last transaction, it may seem to have disappeared. For instance, you try looking for the transaction through a financial report because you know the GL account you meant to use, or through a register or QuickReport, but cannot find it. Perhaps the Find tool does not find the transaction. If this occurs, stop searching after the first missed attempt. The fastest way to find the transaction is to open the Journal report and set the Dates option to All. Because the report defaults to show the last transaction at the end of the report, that's where you will find it.

Of the many ways you can find a transaction, there is one method you should avoid. Remember that many forms, such as Create Invoices, contain the Find tool with two blue arrows in the ribbon (Figure 3-31).

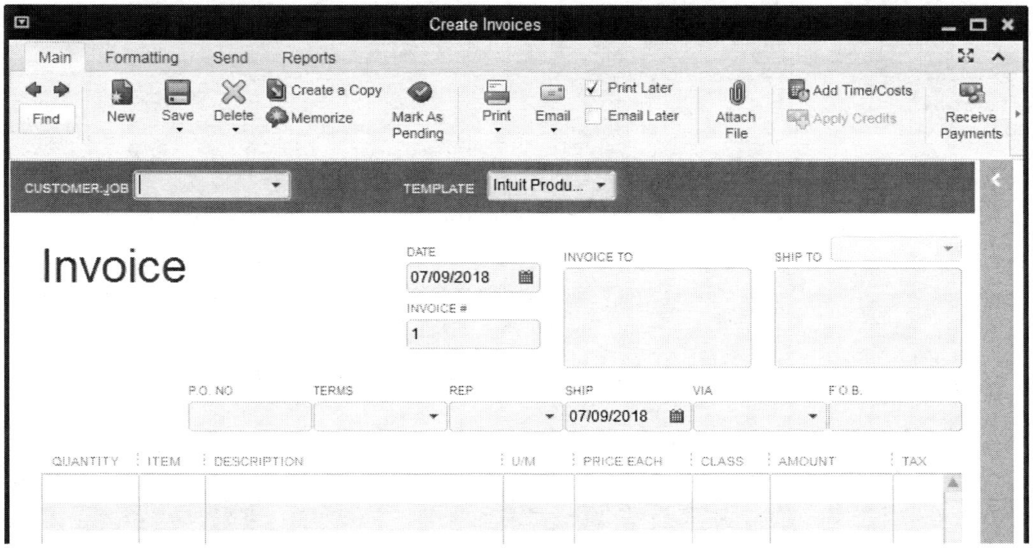

Figure 3-31: Create Invoices form

It is tempting to try using the arrows to locate your last transaction because you may think that it should appear with one click of the arrow facing to the left. However, the blue arrows do not behave that way. The arrows move among transactions based on the date shown in the form, not the date you entered the transaction. If you dated a transaction earlier than the current one, the last transaction could be far back in the list, and you could be clicking for a long time to find it. Sometimes, you may be fortunate and one click will work, but as you just learned, other options are more time-efficient.

Note: If you enter multiple transactions for the same date, the transactions may be sorted by another field, such as the customer name.

Correcting Entries

When you locate and open the entry you need to change, the original transaction form will appear. For instance, if the transaction you are changing is an invoice, the Create Invoices form will appear. QuickBooks will populate the form with the details of the transaction and, at the bottom of the form, you will see the three buttons shown in Figure 3-32.

Figure 3-32: Buttons in transaction form

The Revert button is an undo button for the changes that you have made to this form since you last saved it. If you accidentally change the wrong field, you can click the Revert button to return the transaction to the way it looked before you opened it.

When you are satisfied with your changes, click the Save & Close button to save your changes and close the form. QuickBooks gives you one more chance to change your mind about your modifications and displays the pop up message shown in Figure 3-33, which asks if you want to record your changes. Click Yes to save the transaction and close the form, click No to discard your changes and close the form, or click Cancel to return to the form and continue editing the transaction.

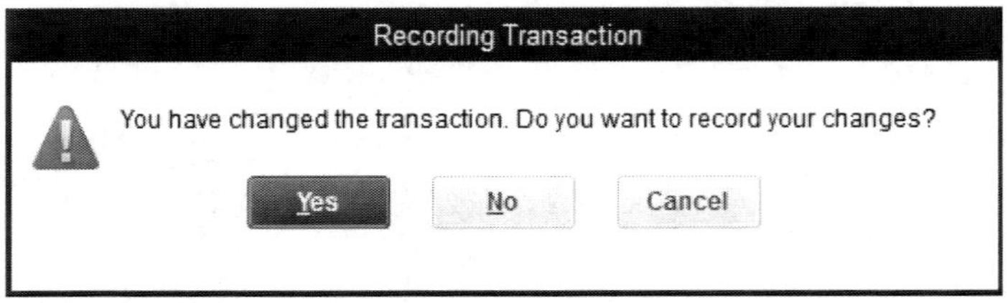

Figure 3-33: Recording Transaction pop up message

Note: If you change the amount in a transaction, you may need to click the Recalculate icon on the ribbon to update the other amounts, such as totals, that are also in the form.

Exercise 3.4: Finding and Correcting Entries

In this exercise, you will find the last entry you made, "correct" the entry, and then revert it to its previous state.

Find the last transaction.

1. Ensure that the company file you worked on in the previous exercise is still open.

2. Click **Reports > Accountant & Taxes > Journal** to display the Journal report.

3. Display the *Dates* drop-down menu and select **All**.

4. Resize the report to view all the data, then scroll to the bottom to find the last entry you made.

5. Position the mouse pointer over the last transaction (the deposit dated 07/15/2018) until the QuickZoom tool appears, and then double-click the transaction. The Make Deposits form for the transaction appears.

Correct the entry.

6. Change the value in the AMOUNT field from 10,000 to **20,000**, then press **TAB**.

Revert to the original value.

7. Click the **Revert** button to change the amount back to 10,000.

8. Close the Make Deposits form.

9. Close the Journal report without memorizing it.

Leave the company file open for the next exercise.

Reviewing Your Work

Objective L-3.6 Review your work

After completing your work for the day, taking a few minutes to review it can help uncover mistakes before they cause problems later. Two key reports allow you to see your entries for the day—the Journal report and the Audit Trail report. You may find the Journal report more helpful if you customize its settings. You can then memorize the custom report in QuickBooks to save the custom settings.

Modifying the Journal Report

If you are the only person entering data into a company file, then you can simply run the Journal report to review your daily work. Ensure that the date parameters in the report cover the full range of transaction dates you used. Remember, the date parameter in the Journal report refers to the date transactions occurred, not the date you entered the transactions in QuickBooks.

If you work in a company file set up for multiple users and you enter only one type of data, such as deposits or invoices, you can still use the Journal report, but you need to refine the criteria further. In the Modify Report dialog box, shown in Figure 3-34, you can use the Filters tab to filter the report data to show only a subset of the transactions.

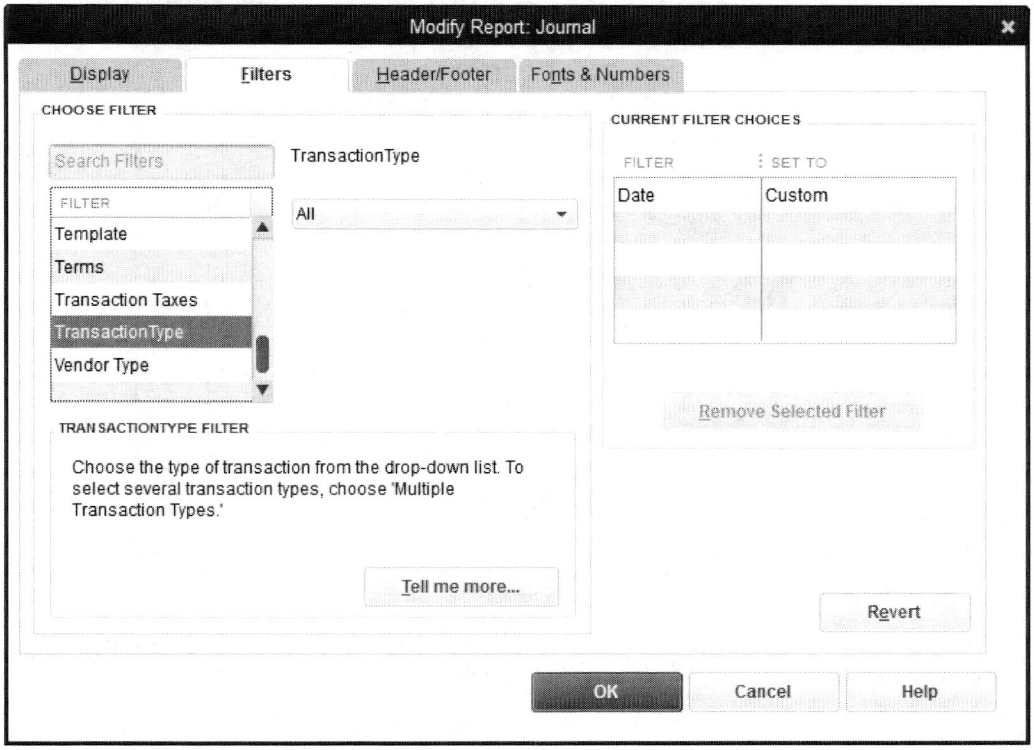

Figure 3-34: Modify Report dialog box, Filters tab

For example, to view all the deposits in a company file, you can set a filter for the Transaction Type, as shown in Figure 3-35. First, in the drop-down menu in the list on the left, select Transaction Type. Then, click the Transaction Type drop-down menu to select a transaction type.

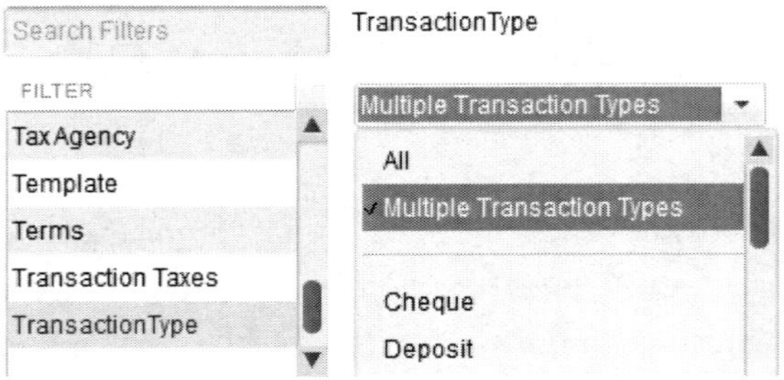

Figure 3-35: Filter transaction types

Each transaction type is the name of a form. You can also select Multiple Transaction Types if you want to include more than one type of form in the filter. Only the transaction types you select will appear in the report. When you click Multiple Transaction Types, the Select Transaction Types dialog box will appear (Figure 3-36), in which you can select the transaction types. In this example, we have chosen only the Deposit transaction type.

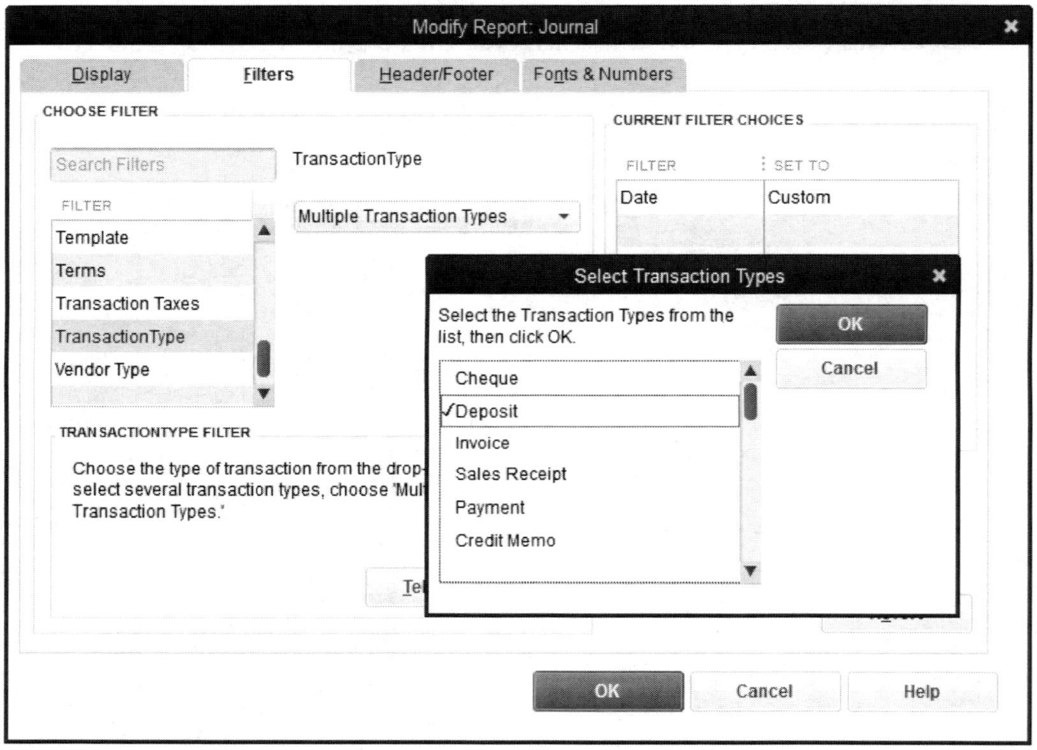

Figure 3-36: Filter is set for Deposit

Figure 3-37 shows the filter after it has been configured. Even though we selected only one type, Deposits, the type is not displayed in the filter because we specified to filter the transactions using Multiple Transaction Types. If we had selected additional types, the form would appear the same.

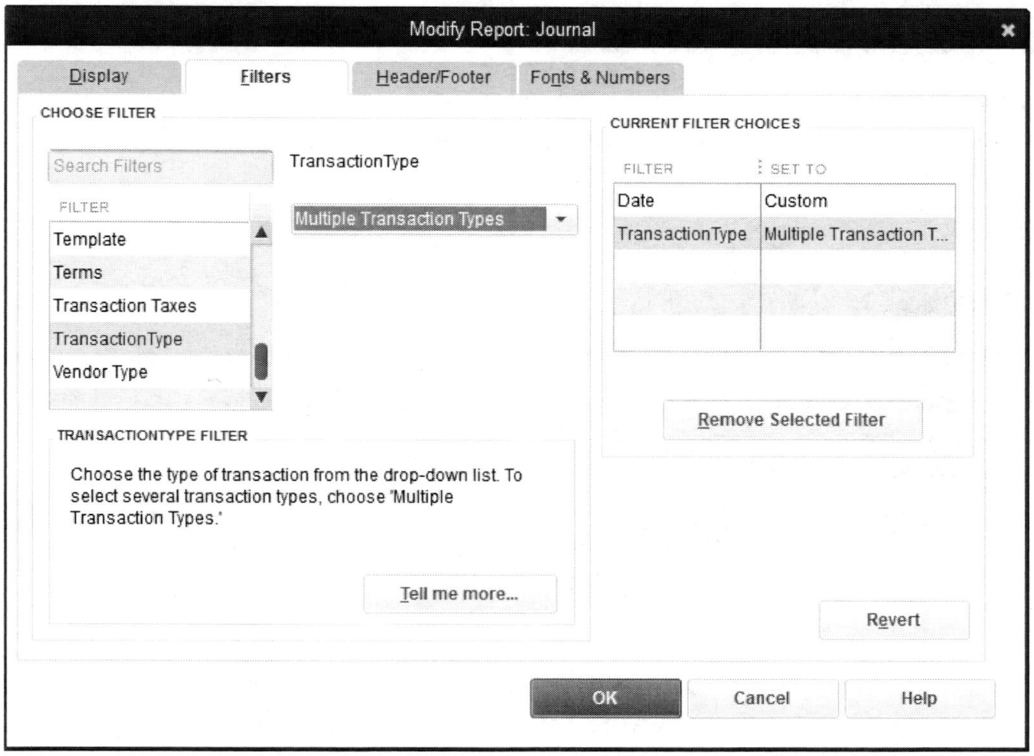

Figure 3-37: Modify Report dialog box, filter is configured

You can use the Header/Footer tab of the Modify Report dialog box (Figure 3-38) to further modify the Journal report. For instance, you can use the Report Title field, which defaults to the name of the report, to rename reports. This is useful when memorizing them, so you can distinguish one report from another.

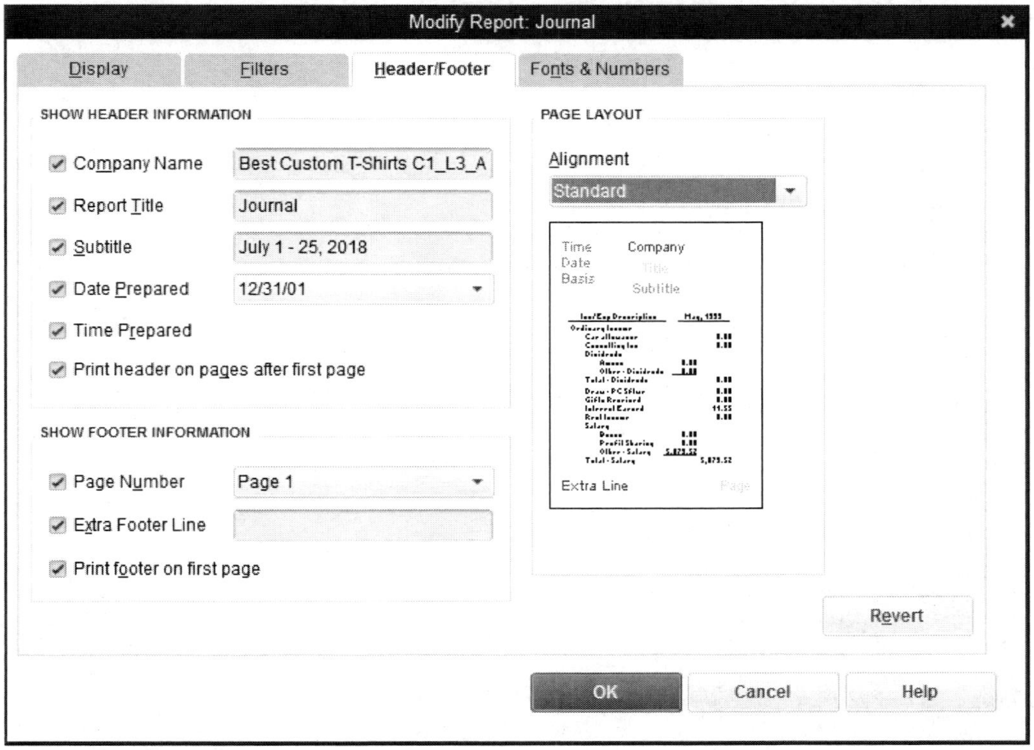

Figure 3-38: Modify Report dialog box, Header/Footer tab

Memorizing the Journal Report

Now that the filter is set on the Journal report, you can memorize it to quickly access the customized report in the future. You can click **Reports > Memorized Reports > Memorized Report List** to find memorized reports, as shown in Figure 3-39.

Figure 3-39: Reports > Memorized Reports > Memorized Report List command sequence

The Memorized Report List window will appear, which lists all your memorized reports (Figure 3-40).

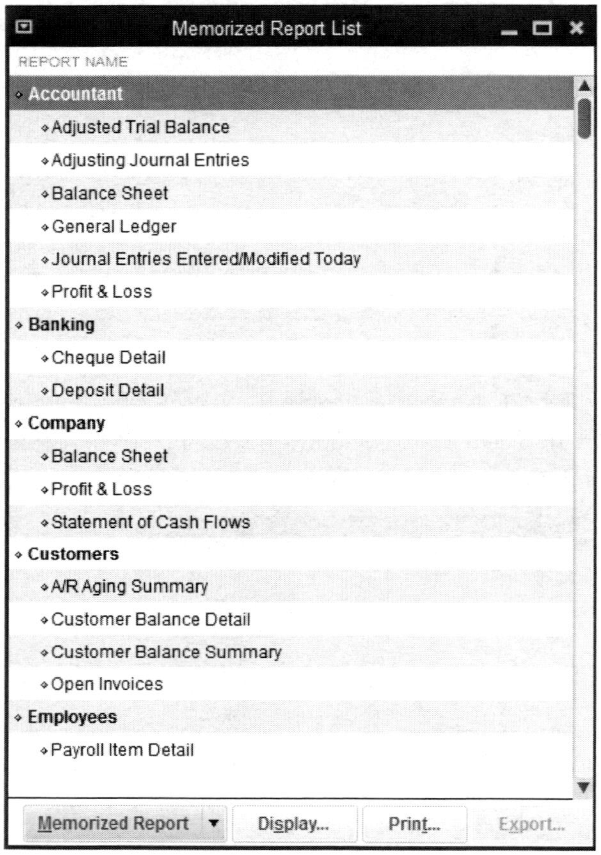

Figure 3-40: Memorized Report List window

You can also create a custom group of memorized reports. In the Memorized Report List window, display the Memorized Report drop-down menu, and then select New Group, as shown in Figure 3-41.

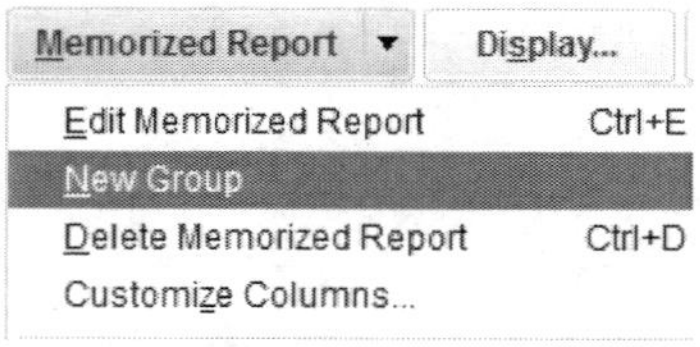

Figure 3-41: Memorized Report > New Group command sequence

Figure 3-42 shows the New Memorized Report Group window that appears, in which you can enter the name of the new group.

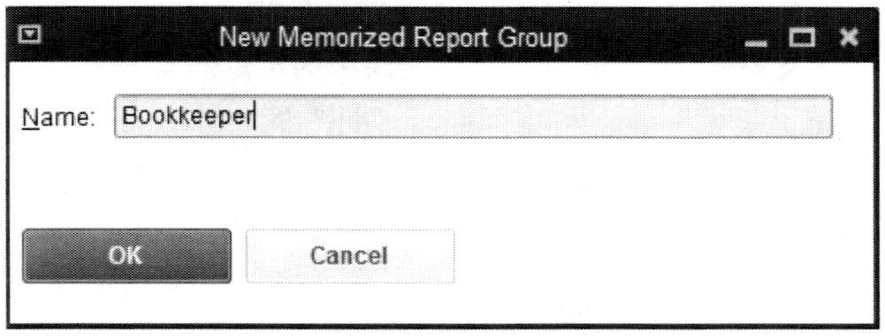

Figure 3-42: New Memorized Report Group window

Figure 3-43 shows the Memorized Report List window with the new group (selected in the figure).

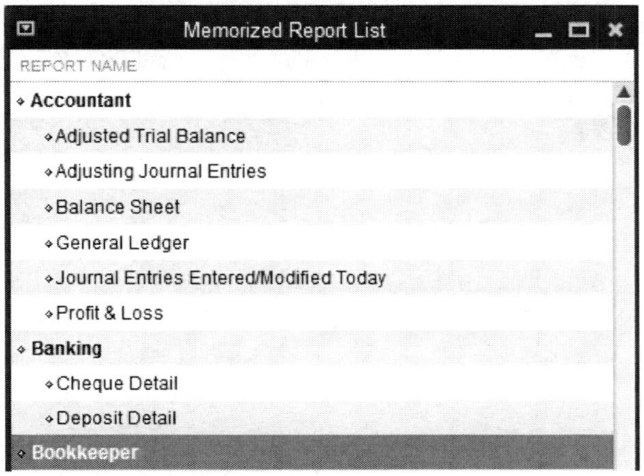

Figure 3-43: Memorized Report List window with new group

When you have the report customized the way you want it, click the Memorize button at the top of the report to display the Memorize Report dialog box (Figure 3-44). You will first want to give it a unique name.

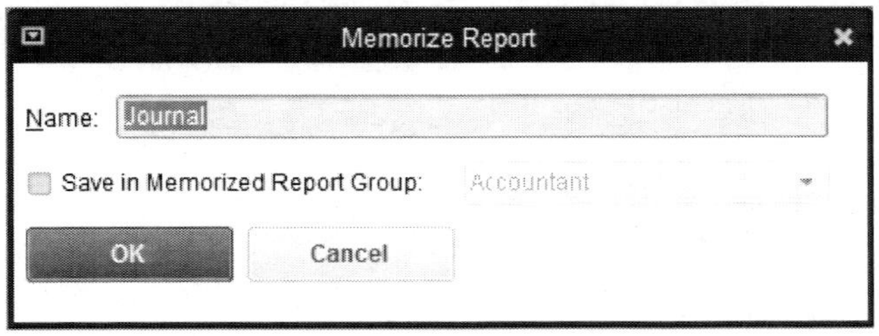

Figure 3-44: Request for location to save Memorized Report

To avoid clutter in the Memorized Report List window, use groups to organize the reports. Select the Save in Memorized Report Group check box to enable the drop-down list, and then select a group for the report.

Whenever you make changes to any report and then close the report, a Memorize Report pop up will appear asking if you want to memorize the report, as shown in Figure 3-45. While you can select the Do not display this message in the future check box, leaving it deselected is the best course of action because QuickBooks will remember your choice in this pop up and apply it in the future without prompting you. Therefore, if you click No, QuickBooks will remember this value and automatically answer No to all future instances of this message.

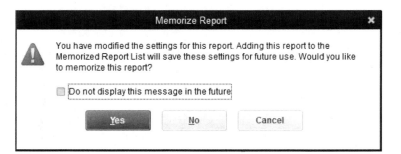

Figure 3-45: Memorize Report pop up

Exercise 3.5: Modifying and Memorizing the Journal Report

In this exercise, you will modify, rename, and memorize the Journal report.

1. Ensure that the company file you worked on in the previous exercise is still open.

2. Open the **Journal** report.

3. Set the dates, using the *From* and *To* date fields, from **07/01/2018** to **07/31/2018**. Click the **Refresh** button. The journal transactions that fall within the specified date parameters appear.

4. Click the **Customize Report** button. The Modify Report dialog box appears.

5. In the *Display* tab, scroll down in the *COLUMNS* list and select **Class**.

6. Click the **Filters** tab. Scroll down in the *FILTER* list and select **Class**.

7. Click the **All Classes** drop-down menu under the word *Class*, then select **Jordan Smith**.

8. Click the **Header/Footer** tab. In the *Report Title* field, type: **Jordan Smith.**

9. Click **OK**.

10. In the Button Bar, click the **Memorize** button. The Memorize Report dialog box appears.

11. Select the **Save in Memorized Report Group** check box and, in the drop-down menu to the right, select **Company**.

12. Click **OK**, and then close the Jordan Smith memorized Journal report.

Leave the company file open for the next exercise.

Reviewing the Audit Trail Report

Finally, the Audit Trail report allows you to see all new transactions and any changes to existing transactions that you made that day. You can also set this report to prior dates, if needed, to view changes made on a specific date. You can access the Audit Trail report by clicking **Reports > Accountant & Taxes > Audit Trail** in the Menu Bar.

The Audit Trail report provides much of the same information as the Journal report, including all the essential fields that you need to review. By default, the report shows entries made on the day you specify. Remember, this is the date you entered the transaction in QuickBooks, not the date the transaction occurred.

If multiple users create entries on the same day, the Last modified by column will show each user's QuickBooks user name. This means that you can always find out who entered a transaction and who changed it because the person responsible for the change will be listed in this report.

Figure 3-46 shows the Audit Trail report for the month of July, and shows the three transactions entered on July 11, 2018. Pay attention to the State column in this report. The State column has three possible values: Latest, Prior, and Deleted. In Figure 3-46, you can see that each transaction has the value of Latest in the State column. This indicates that no modifications have been made to the transactions.

Best Custom T-Shirts C1_L3_A

Audit Trail

Entered/Last Modified

Num	Entered/Last Modified	Last modified by	State	Date	Name	Memo	Account	Split	Debit	Credit
Transactions entered or modified by Admin										
Deposit										
	07/11/2018 23:18:25	Admin	Latest	07/01/2018		Deposit	Chequing	Taylor Green...	500.00	
6174					Green, Taylor		Taylor Green, Cap...	Chequing		500.00
Deposit										
	07/11/2018 23:23:53	Admin	Latest	07/02/2018		Deposit	Chequing	-SPLIT-	8,000.00	
8295					Smith, Jordan		Jordan Smith, Capital	Chequing		500.00
8295					Smith, Jordan		Loan - Jordan Smith	Chequing		7,500.00
Deposit										
	07/11/2018 23:25:19	Admin	Latest	07/15/2018		Deposit	Chequing	Loan - First B...	10,000.00	
					First Bank		Loan - First Bank	Chequing		10,000.00

Figure 3-46: Audit Trail report

If one of the transactions is edited, the label will change. In Figure 3-47, you can see that the State column for transaction 6174 is now labeled Prior, and the newly edited transaction, 6175, is labeled Latest. In this example, the two changes made to transaction 6175 were the cheque number and the date. QuickBooks displays these changes in bold, italic text in the latest transaction.

Best Custom T-Shirts C1_L3_A

Audit Trail

Entered/Last Modified

Num	Entered/Last Modified	Last modified by	State	Date	Name	Memo	Account	Split	Debit	Credit
Transactions entered or modified by Admin										
Deposit										
	07/26/2018 19:14:21	Admin	Latest	*07/02/2018*		Deposit	Chequing	Taylor Green ..	500.00	
6175					Green, Taylor		Taylor Green, Cap...	Chequing		500.00
	07/11/2018 23:18:25	Admin	Prior	07/01/2018		Deposit	Chequing	Taylor Green...	500.00	
6174					Green, Taylor		Taylor Green, Cap...	Chequing		500.00
Deposit										
	07/11/2018 23:23:53	Admin	Latest	07/02/2018		Deposit	Chequing	-SPLIT-	8,000.00	
8295					Smith, Jordan		Jordan Smith, Capital	Chequing		500.00
8295					Smith, Jordan		Loan - Jordan Smith	Chequing		7,500.00
Deposit										
	07/11/2018 23:25:19	Admin	Latest	07/15/2018		Deposit	Chequing	Loan - First B...	10,000.00	
					First Bank		Loan - First Bank	Chequing		10,000.00

Figure 3-47: Audit Trail report with edited transaction

Figure 3-48 shows how the Audit Trail report looks when a transaction is deleted. The third deposit in the list shows the deleted entry and the prior state. Notice that the prior state had additional details regarding the deposit information, whereas the deleted entry has no details because the transaction details were removed. If you accidentally delete a transaction, this report can help you re-enter the data.

Best Custom T-Shirts C1_L3_A
Audit Trail
Entered/Last Modified

Num	Entered/Last Modified	Last modified by	State	Date	Name	Memo	Account	Split	Debit	Credit
Transactions entered or modified by Admin										
Deposit										
	07/26/2018 19:16:28	Admin	Latest	*07/01/2018*		Deposit	Chequing	Taylor Green...	500.00	
6174					Green, Taylor		Taylor Green, Cap...	Chequing		500.00
	07/26/2018 19:14:21	Admin	Prior	*07/02/2018*		Deposit	Chequing	Taylor Green...	500.00	
6175					Green, Taylor		Taylor Green, Cap...	Chequing		500.00
	07/11/2018 23:18:25	Admin	Prior	07/01/2018		Deposit	Chequing	Taylor Green...	500.00	
6174					Green, Taylor		Taylor Green, Cap...	Chequing		500.00
Deposit										
	07/11/2018 23:23:53	Admin	Latest	07/02/2018		Deposit	Chequing	-SPLIT-	8,000.00	
8295					Smith, Jordan		Jordan Smith, Capital	Chequing		500.00
8295					Smith, Jordan		Loan - Jordan Smith	Chequing		7,500.00
Deposit										
▶	07/26/2018 19:18:40	Admin	*Deleted*						0.00	◀
	07/11/2018 23:25:19	Admin	Prior	07/15/2018		Deposit	Chequing	Loan - First B...	10,000.00	
					First Bank		Loan - First Bank	Chequing		10,000.00

Figure 3-48: Audit Trail Report after deleting a transaction

Exercise 3.6: Opening the Audit Trail Report

In this exercise, you will open and view the Audit Trail report, and then save and export your work by creating a portable version of the QuickBooks file.

Open the Audit Trail report.

1. Ensure that the company file you worked on in the previous exercise is still open.

2. Click **Reports > Accountant & Taxes > Audit Trail**. The Audit Trail report appears.

3. Set the dates, using the *From* and *To* date fields, from **07/01/2018** to **07/31/2018**. Click the **Refresh** button. The journal transactions that fall within the specified date parameters appear. Notice that Latest appears in the State column, indicating that no modifications have been made to the transactions.

4. Close the Audit Trail report without memorizing it.

Save your work as a portable company file that you can submit to your instructor.

5. Click **File > Create Copy**. The Save Copy or Backup dialog box appears.

6. Click **Portable company file**, then click **Next**. The Save Portable Company File dialog box appears.

7. Navigate to the *1767-Student-Files\Lesson 3\MyProjects* folder.

8. In the *File name* field, enter: **Best Custom T-Shirts C1_L3_<your name> (Portable)**, and then click **Save**. Respond to any message prompts that may appear.

    Note: This is the file you will turn in.

9. If you plan to perform the Practice the Skill exercise, close the company file but leave QuickBooks open; otherwise, close the company file and exit QuickBooks.

Lesson Summary

Now that you have completed this lesson, you should be able to:

☑ Match GL accounts to financial reports.   ☑ Find transactions.

☑ Produce detail and summary reports.   ☑ Correct transactions.

☑ Define cash accounting.   ☑ Review your work.

Key Terms

Term	Definition
Accounting Basis	The method by which the accounting system reports revenue and expenses.
Accrual Basis	The accounting basis used to report revenue and expenses when services or goods change hands.
Balance Sheet	A summary report showing totals for Assets, Liabilities, and Equity.
Break-Even	The point at which the debits equal the credits in the Income Statement.
Cash Basis	The accounting basis used to report revenue and expenses when payments for services or goods leave or arrive at the bank.
Financial Statements	The Balance Sheet and Income (Profit and Loss) Statement, which show the financial condition of a company in summary form.
Income Statement	A summary report showing totals for the sub-sections of Equity: Income and Expense.
Journal	A location in the company file where every detail of every transaction you enter is stored.
Journal report	The detail report that includes all transactions in the accounting records.
Loss	A financial decline in which a business has more expenses than income during a given time period.
Net Income	The total of all GL accounts in the Income Statement.
Profit	A financial gain in which a business has more income than expenses during a given time period.
Register	A QuickBooks window for viewing transaction details of GL accounts that appear on the Balance Sheet.

Activity 1: Account Types and Financials

Match the following QuickBooks account types to one of the two financial reports in GL accounts.

a.   Balance Sheet

b.   Profit & Loss

_____   Other Expense

_____   Credit Card

_____   Equity

_____   Income

_____   Other Current Asset

Activity 2: Equity Sub-sections and Net Income

Describe what happens to the two Equity sub-section GL accounts (Income and Expense) at the end of the year, and the effect on Net Income.

_____

_____

Practice the Skill

This Practice the Skill exercise is designed to reinforce the skills you have learned. In this exercise, you will create a new memorized report.

1.   If necessary, launch **QuickBooks** and restore **Best Custom T-Shirts C1_L3_B (Portable).QBM** from the *1767-Student-Files\Lesson 3\PTS* folder.

2.   Open the Jordan Smith memorized report.

     Hint: The report is located in the Company group in the Memorized Report List.

3.   Change the class to **Taylor Green**.

4.   Change the report title to **Taylor Green**.

5.   Memorize the report in the Company group in the Memorized Report List.

     Hint: You will need to replace the existing memorized report.

6.   Save the company file as a portable company file and add the letters PTS to the end of the file name (*Best Custom T-Shirts C1_L3_<your name> PTS (Portable).QBM*). Turn this file in to your instructor.

7.   Close the company file.

Course Project Exercise

In this exercise, you will run the financial statements for Blue Heron Spa. Open the Balance Sheet and Profit & Loss statement. Set the Balance Sheet date to February 28, 2017. Set the Profit & Loss dates from January 1, 2017 to February 28, 2017. Add the date you run the reports to the name of each report and memorize them. Save each report in the Company Memorized Report Group.

Filename:	Blue Heron Spa Inc 2018 C1_L3_A (Portable).QBM
Admin password:	BluSpa18
New company name:	Blue Heron Spa, Inc. L3 <your name>

Perform the following tasks:

1. Restore the portable file and change the company name as indicated in the table.

2. Open the appropriate Balance Sheet and specify the correct date parameter.

3. Memorize the Balance Sheet, add the date you run the report to the end of the report name, and save it to the Company Memorized Report Group.

4. Close the Balance Sheet.

5. Open the appropriate Profit & Loss statement and specify the correct date parameters.

6. Memorize the Profit & Loss statement, add the date you run the report to the end of the report name, and save it to the Company Memorized Report Group.

7. Close the Profit & Loss statement.

8. Create a portable file to turn in to your instructor.

9. Close the company file and exit QuickBooks.

Quiz Questions

For each question, select the best answer.

1. What statement accurately describes the location of each GL account?

    a. An Asset account is part of Equity in the Balance Sheet.

    b. An Income account is found in the Profit & Loss statement.

    c. The Expense type GL account Liabilities is in the Balance Sheet.

    d. The Bank type GL account Chequing is in the Income Statement.

2. Which report provides a summary of transactions but does not list them in detail?

    a. The register

    b. The QuickReport

    c. The Journal

    d. The Balance Sheet

3. Which statement best describes cash basis accounting?

    a. Money is kept in a drawer for emergencies.

    b. Only cash is accepted for business transactions.

    c. Revenue and expenses are recognized when the payments for services or goods leave or arrive at the bank.

    d. Revenue and expenses are recognized when services or goods change hands.

4. When you want to locate the last transaction entered, which action is fastest?

    a. Run a QuickReport from the Chart Accounts.

    b. Run the Journal report.

    c. Click the left arrow in the form's Find tool.

    d. Run the Audit Trail report.

5. Which action will *not* revise a transaction?

    a. Click the Save & New button.

    b. Press the ENTER key.

    c. Click the Revert button.

    d. Click the Save & Close button.

6. Which statement about the Audit Trail report is true?

    a. The user who last changed a transaction is shown.

    b. The user who last viewed a transaction is shown.

    c. New is one of the transaction states.

    d. Prior is the state of the changed transaction.

Lesson 4:
Purchasing with Cash or Credit

Lesson Objectives

In this lesson, you will enter cash, debit, and credit card expenses, and learn how to fund, issue, and reconcile petty cash. Upon successful completion of this lesson, you should be able to:

☐ Identify if an accrual entry is necessary in purchases.

☐ Enter credit card purchases,

☐ Enter purchases using cheques.

☐ Process petty cash reimbursements.

Reimbursing Start-up Costs and Acquiring Assets

Objective L-4.1 Identify if an accrual entry is necessary in purchases

The business now has money from loans and capital contributions to fund preparations for the business activities of buying and selling. To reach this step, the partners of Best Custom T-Shirts incurred various costs considered *start-up costs*, such as legal and accounting fees, registration fees, logo development and brochures. The business can reimburse the partners for these start-up costs and begin to purchase equipment. Often, these costs are capitalized as "Other Assets" on the Balance Sheet because they can't be expensed.

They will soon open the doors on the job training program. They can also start buying needed items using the company credit and debit cards, which were issued by the bank when they opened the chequing account and obtained the loan. For small out-of-pocket expenses, the partners also set up a Petty Cash fund.

Each of these transactions, using cash-based forms or credit cards, are shown in the Purchases Cycle in QuickBooks (Figure 4-1).

In QuickBooks, some processes are simpler to enter than others. For example, the Make Deposits form is a single form that requires only a few steps to complete. For cash purchase transactions, you will use a one-step process with a single form. Other processes are more complex, requiring the use of multiple forms in a sequence of steps or actions in one of the Cycles. For example, when a time delay exists between the purchase and movement of money, you will follow the accrual process, which will be introduced in Lesson 7. In the accrual process, all transactions use at least two forms or steps in a sequence.

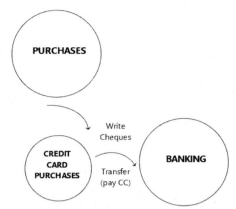

Figure 4-1: Purchases Cycle and Credit Card Purchases Cycle Intersecting Banking Cycle

All purchase transactions, except for credit card purchases, use the Write Cheques form. The three types of cash purchases we will cover in this lesson are:

- Payment with cheque
- Payment with debit card
- Payment with petty cash

Another type of form to make purchases is the Enter Credit Card Charges form. In Canada, credit cards are different instruments than debit cards. Although your card is associated with your bank, it is issued and managed by the credit card company (Visa, Mastercard, American Express, and so on). With credit card purchases, a delay occurs from the time you make your purchase until you pay the charge on the statement. Once you make a purchase with a credit card, it immediately affects the credit card balance and the amount of credit still available. The liability account that is set up in the GL increases and the expense paid for or asset purchased increases similarly. This is a transaction based on accrual accounting, which we will cover later in the course. However, we will cover the use of the Enter Credit Card Charges form in this lesson.

Best Custom T-Shirts is already registered with the taxing authorities, which means that its taxable start-up costs are eligible for tax credits. Since it is in British Columbia, both the national **GST** (Goods and Services Tax) and **PST** (Provincial Sales Tax) may apply to some purchases. Some taxes the business collects from customers may be offset by taxes the business previously paid.

Acquiring an Asset – The Write Cheques Form

Objective L-4.2 Enter cash purchases using cheques

The owners of Best Custom T-Shirts need a new dryer for the screen-printing operation to dry t-shirts after they've been printed. They locate a dryer for $2,500. Your task is to enter the transaction in QuickBooks and print the cheque for the partners to deliver when they pick up the dryer.

First, however, we need to discuss how assets are categorized.

Categorizing Assets Versus Expenses

We need to determine whether the purchase is a capital expenditure or an operating expense. **Capital** is money or assets available for starting or investing in a business. However, the meaning of capital can change slightly when combined with other words. For example, capital already invested or borrowed can be used to acquire an asset, known as a **capital expenditure**. Equipment that is not consumed during business activities and is expected to last more than one year becomes an asset of the business. As assets eventually wear out, the portion used each year becomes an expense. This means the asset is **depreciable property**.

In general, depreciation is calculated by estimating the life of the asset as well as its potential salvage value at the end of its useful contribution, and then amortizing that net value over the number of years estimated. Two common methods are used as systems of amortization: declining balance and straight line. Conceptually, the residual balance of the asset when added to the costs of repair and maintenance should be constant. That means that as value decreases, repair and maintenance will increase.

The cost of the asset converts to an expense over the life of the asset through **depreciation**. This is an amount entered every year that decreases the asset value in the accounting records and increases expenses. Another way to describe this process is to **capitalize** the asset and then spread the cost over the life of the asset. Depreciation is a measure of utility over time.

Depreciation should not be confused with **capital cost allowance**. Capital cost allowance is a government incentive to purchase capital equipment by providing tax relief, often at a rate greater than the asset depreciates on the books. Both schedules are prepared with similar systems. Every time the financial statements to be submitted with a tax return are prepared, a reconciliation between depreciation and capital cost allowance must also be prepared. This allows for the proper calculation of taxable income.

About the Write Cheques Form

Once we have determined how to categorize an asset, we can use the Write Cheques form to enter a cash-based purchase. You can access the Write Cheques form by clicking the Write Cheques icon in the BANKING section of the Home page or by clicking **Banking > Write Cheques** in the Menu Bar.

Because the Write Cheques form is used to withdraw money from the bank account, it has the opposite effect of using the Make Deposits form. The two forms have many similar elements because every transaction you enter needs the essential parts of a journal entry, but the layouts are different. Figure 4-2 shows the Write Cheques form with the information for the dryer purchase filled in.

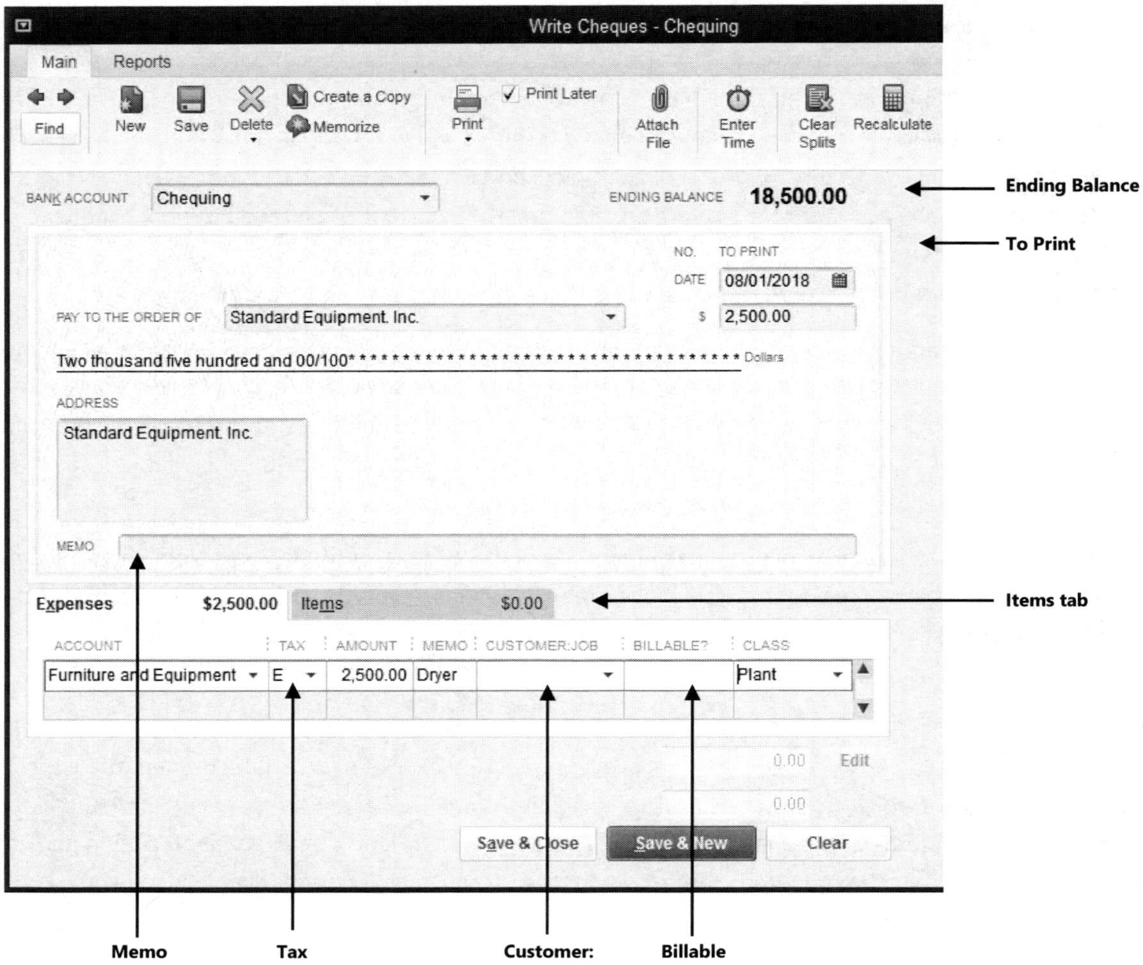

Figure 4-2: Write Cheques form completed for asset purchase and ready for printing

Instead of a grid-like detail area, the Write Cheques form displays a cheque image for some of the fields. While the Make Deposits form has the button bar, the Write Cheques form has the ribbon you saw in the Bill and Invoice forms in Lesson 1. Like all the form ribbons, the icons in the left-most section are alike. Icons specific to this form are labeled in Figure 4-2.

Note: When introducing new forms, we will draw attention only to the new or distinctive elements, because each form builds on the similarities previously described.

Each entry you make with this form debits (increases) the GL account entered in the detail area below the cheque and credits (decreases) the bank account. If this cheque were for an expense, the debit would increase expenses in the Profit & Loss statement. For this transaction, only the Balance Sheet figures are affected because the debit increases an asset section account, instead of posting to the equity sub-section expense accounts.

Write Cheques Form Elements

The Write Cheques form includes the following elements:

- **Print Later** – Not all Write Cheques forms need to be printed. When this check box is selected, the cheque goes through the print queue and the cheque number becomes part of the entry. If this check box is not selected, then a field for entering a cheque number or other memo appears. (You can see how this looks in Figure 4-5: Write Cheques form used for debit card purchase.)

- **NO.** – Figure 4-2 shows "TO PRINT" when a cheque will be printed later. A data entry field in which to enter the cheque number appears when the *Print Later* check box is not selected.

- **ENDING BALANCE** – The amount shown here is the chequing account balance as of the date of the cheque before entering the cheque amount.

- **MEMO** – On the cheque image, this is an optional field that appears only in the printed cheque's memo section. The MEMO field in the detail area of any form is part of the journal entry and appears in the accounting records.

- **TAX** – Depending on the transaction, various taxes may be applied. This asset purchase does not have tax charged, so the choice for tax is *E* (for *exempt* from tax).

- **CUSTOMER: JOB** and **BILLABLE** – This pair of optional fields receives further attention in later lessons. When used, you can enter purchase amounts on invoices to customers.

- **Items** – The Items tab appears on many forms. You may have noticed this on the Bill and Invoice forms in Lesson 1. *Items* in QuickBooks provide a way to associate the name or description of an expense or income with a GL account. You will use items in Lesson 5.

After you have entered all the required information in the Write Cheques form, you can print the cheque. QuickBooks offers multiple ways to print a cheque. If you click the Print icon in the form ribbon, QuickBooks saves the transaction and displays the Print Cheque dialog box in which to enter the cheque number (Figure 4-3).

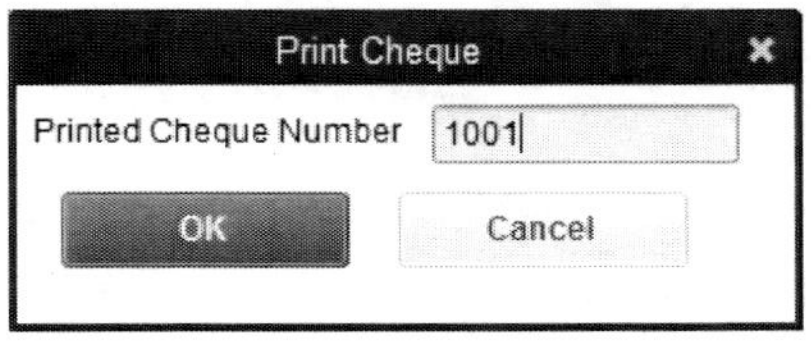

Figure 4-3: Print Cheque dialog box

Alternatively, you can click **File > Print Cheque** in the Menu Bar to print a single check, or **File > Print Forms > Cheques** to print one or more cheques. We will discuss the Print Forms option in more detail in Lesson 7.

Figure 4-4 shows the Cheque Register after the cheque for the dryer prints and receives the cheque number.

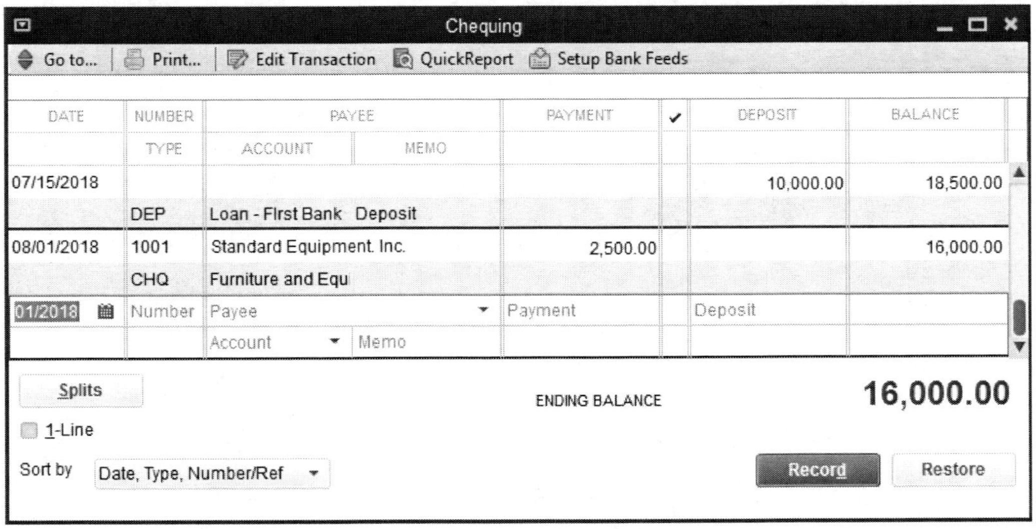

Figure 4-4: Cheque Register

Spending Money – Using the Debit Card

One of the partners, Taylor Green, used the new debit card for several purchases and gave you a packet of receipts. Because each purchase appears as a separate item in the bank statements, you need to enter each receipt individually. The purchase costs appear in the Balance Sheet as assets because they are start-up costs. Like assets such as equipment, some start-up costs become expenses over the life of the asset using the same process as depreciation, but this process is known as **amortization**.

Other Assets can be split into Intangible Assets which are never amortized and some tangible assets we'll call Start-up Costs, which can be amortized. As an example, incorporation fees will last the life of the company, so they are not amortized. Brochures prepared prior to operations commencement will be amortized over the time they will last. A patent, which many will think of as intangible, can be amortized because it has a fixed life.

The two expense receipts that Taylor Green gave you took care of the initial $150.00 for the website cost and domain name registration (www.bestcustomtshirt.com), and the $250.00 filing fee to pay for the incorporation of the business. The company became a limited liability corporation through BC Registries and Online Services, then later used a DBA to name the business Best Custom T-Shirts. The second entry is shown in Figure 4-5. Neither of these transactions are taxable.

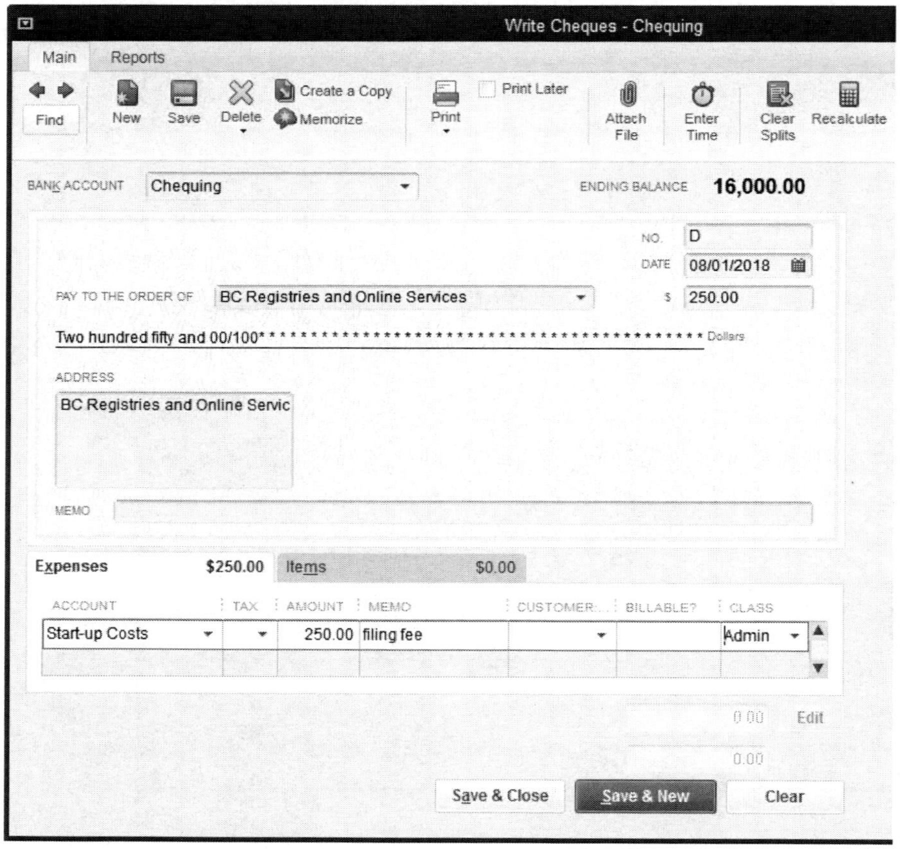

Figure 4-5: Write Cheques form used for debit card purchase

Because using a debit card is exactly like writing a cheque from the chequing account, you use the Write Cheques form for both types of transactions. As shown in Figure 4-5, the Print Later check box is not selected and the NO. field, which allows data entry, displays a D (for debit). The exact text entered in the NO. field matters less than using the same abbreviation consistently or making sure you use what the client prefers.

As you learned previously, you should check your work by running the Balance Sheet to show the results of your entries in the Start-up Costs account in the Assets section (Figure 4-6).

Best Custom T-Shirts C1_L4_A
Balance Sheet
As of August 1, 2018

		Aug 1, 18
ASSETS		
Current Assets		
Chequing/Savings		
Chequing	▶	15,600.00 ◀
Total Chequing/Savings		15,600.00
Total Current Assets		15,600.00
Fixed Assets		
Furniture and Equipment		2,500.00
Total Fixed Assets		2,500.00
Other Assets		
Start-up Costs		400.00
Total Other Assets		400.00
TOTAL ASSETS		18,500.00

Figure 4-6: Balance Sheet on August 1, 2018

If, for some reason, you need to process a refund for the debit card, use the Make Deposits form to process the refund.

Exercise 4.1: Entering Transactions Using the Write Cheques Form

In this exercise, you will restore the portable file *Best Custom T-Shirts C1_L4_A (Portable).QBM* and enter transactions from Taylor Green using the Write Cheques form.

Taylor Green paid $125 (*E* tax code) out of her personal funds for website hosting, which is not a start-up cost. It should post to the Computer and Internet Expenses account using the Admin Class. She also paid $98.21 (*S* tax code) for ten protective aprons from Hardware Central using the debit card. The aprons should post to the Production Supplies:Misc. GL account using the Training class.

1. Launch **QuickBooks** and restore the portable file **Best Custom T-Shirts C1_L4_A (Portable).QBM** from the *1767-Student-Files\Lesson 4\StarterFiles* folder.

2. Save the company file as **Best Custom T-Shirts C1_L4_<your name>** in the *1767-Student-Files\Lesson 4\MyProjects* folder.

3. Change the company name to **Best Custom T-Shirts C1_L4_<your name>**.

Open the Write Cheques form and enter the first transaction.

4. Click **Banking > Write Cheques**. The Write Cheques form appears.

5. On the *ribbon*, click the **Print Later** check box to select it.

6. In the *PAY TO THE ORDER OF* drop-down menu, select **Green, Taylor**.

7. Set the *DATE* to **08/05/2018**.

8. In the *Expenses* tab, in the *ACCOUNT* drop-down menu, select the expense account **Computer and Internet Expenses**.

9. In the *TAX* drop-down menu, select the tax code **E**, which represents tax exempt status.

10. In the *AMOUNT* field, type: **125.00**.

11. In the *MEMO* field, type: **host website**.

12. In the *CLASS* drop-down menu, select **Admin**.

13. Click the **Save & New** button. A blank Write Cheques form appears.

Enter the second transaction.

14. On the *ribbon*, deselect the **Print Later** check box.

15. In the *NO.* field, type: **D**, which we will use to indicate the purchase was made with a debit card instead of a paper cheque.

16. Set the *DATE* to **08/05/2018**, if necessary.

17. In the *PAY TO THE ORDER OF* drop-down menu, select **Hardware Central**.

18. In the *Expenses* tab, in the *ACCOUNT* drop-down menu, select the expense account **Production Supplies:Misc**. (To select this account, click the line that contains the text *Misc*.)

19. In the *TAX* drop-down menu, select the tax code **S**, which represents standard tax status.

20. In the *AMOUNT* field, type: **98.21** and press **TAB**. Notice that QuickBooks automatically populates the tax fields at the bottom of the form and updates the cheque amount in the cheque portion of the form so that it includes the appropriate taxes.

21. In the *CLASS* drop-down menu, select **Training**.

22. Click the **Save & Close** button.

Check your work and print the cheque for the first transaction.

23. Click **Lists > Chart of Accounts** to display the Chart of Accounts, then double-click the **Chequing** GL account. The Cheque Register appears.

24. Scroll to the *Green, Taylor* entry (dated *8/5/2018*) at the bottom of the form. The NUMBER field should display *To Print*. Double-click the form abbreviation letters **CHQ**. The Write Cheques form appears.

25. On the *ribbon,* click the **Print** icon drop-down menu, and then select **Cheque**. The Print Cheque dialog box appears.

26. In the *Printed Cheque Number* field, type: **1004**, and then click **OK**. The Print Cheques dialog box appears.

27. Select a printer from the *Printer name* drop-down menu.

    Note: Printing in the classroom is at your instructor's discretion. You may be directed to send your printed output to a file.

28. Click the **Print** button. A Print Cheques Confirmation dialog box appears. If your cheque printed correctly, Click **OK**. (If it did not print correctly, return to Step 25 and try again.)

29. Click the **Save & Close** button to close the Write Cheques form, then close the Cheque Register and the Chart of Accounts window.

30. Click **Reports > Company & Financial > Profit & Loss Standard.** The Profit & Loss window appears.

31. Set the *From* and *To* dates to **08/05/2018**, and refresh the report if necessary.

32. Position the mouse pointer over the number **125.00** to the right of *Computer and Internet Expenses.* When the QuickZoom tool appears, double-click the number. The Transaction Detail By Account window appears.

33. Position the QuickZoom tool anywhere over the transaction and double-click. The Write Cheques window for check NO. 1004 appears. You can trace the report data back to the source documents.

34. Close the Write Cheques window and the Transaction Detail By Account window.

35. Close the Profit & Loss window and do not memorize the report.

36. Click **Home** in the My Shortcuts pane if necessary to return to the Home page.

Leave the company file open for the next exercise.

Using Credit – Recording Credit Card Liabilities

Objective L-4.3 Enter credit card purchases

As with debit card transactions, each receipt on a credit card statement is a separate line item that you must enter separately. Otherwise, numbers in the accounting system will not match the credit card statement.

Note: You should not summarize your transactions before entering them into the accounting records. You should not enter a *net* number, or the difference between a cash inflow and outflow, such as a purchase and a refund. Net numbers cannot be traced to unique source documents, so it is best to avoid them.

You can display the Enter Credit Card Charges form (Figure 4-7) by clicking the Enter Credit Card Charges icon in the BANKING section of the Home page or by clicking **Banking > Enter Credit Card Charges** in the Menu Bar.

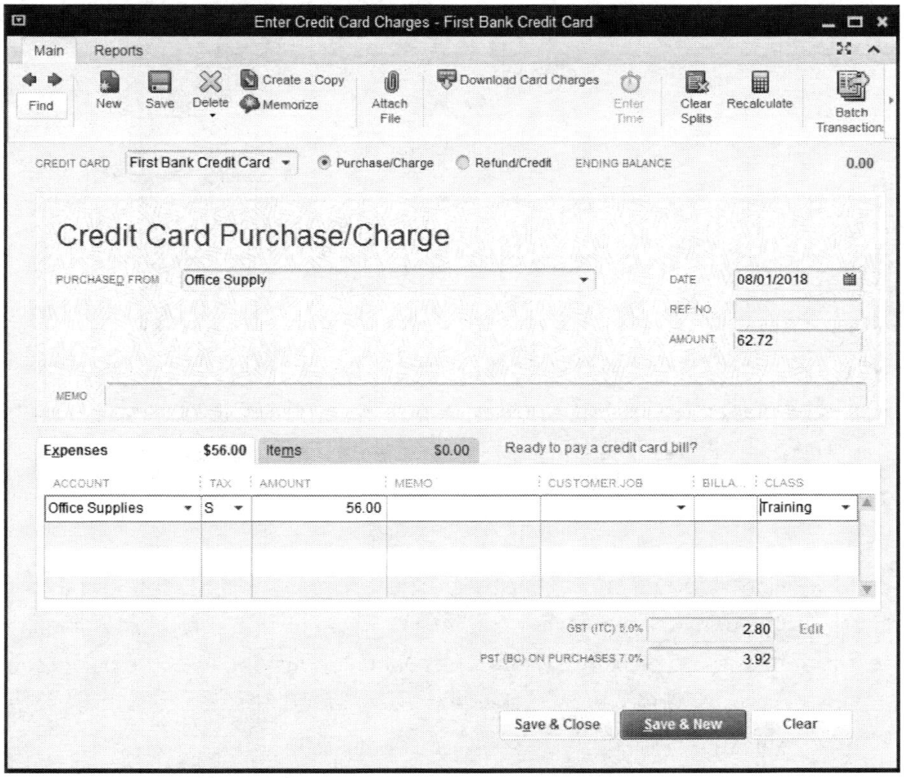

Figure 4-7 Enter Credit Card Charges form – Credit Card Purchase/Charge

The Enter Credit Card Charges form is similar to the Write Cheques form; however, each form affects GL accounts differently. While writing a cheque or using a debit card decreases the bank account balance, using a credit card increases what the business owes, creating a liability and crediting the credit card's GL account. The other side of the transaction debits an expense account or an asset account, such as start-up costs. When entering a refund, the opposite occurs – the credit card GL account receives the debit and decreases what is owed, while the expense GL account receives the credit and also decreases.

The two key differences you will find on this form are the radio buttons to the right of the CREDIT CARD drop-down menu, and the REF NO. field (reference number), which appears in place of the (cheque) NO. field in the Write Cheques form. You can use the radio buttons to specify that the form be used for credit card purchases/charges (Figure 4-7) or credit card refunds/credits (Figure 4-8).

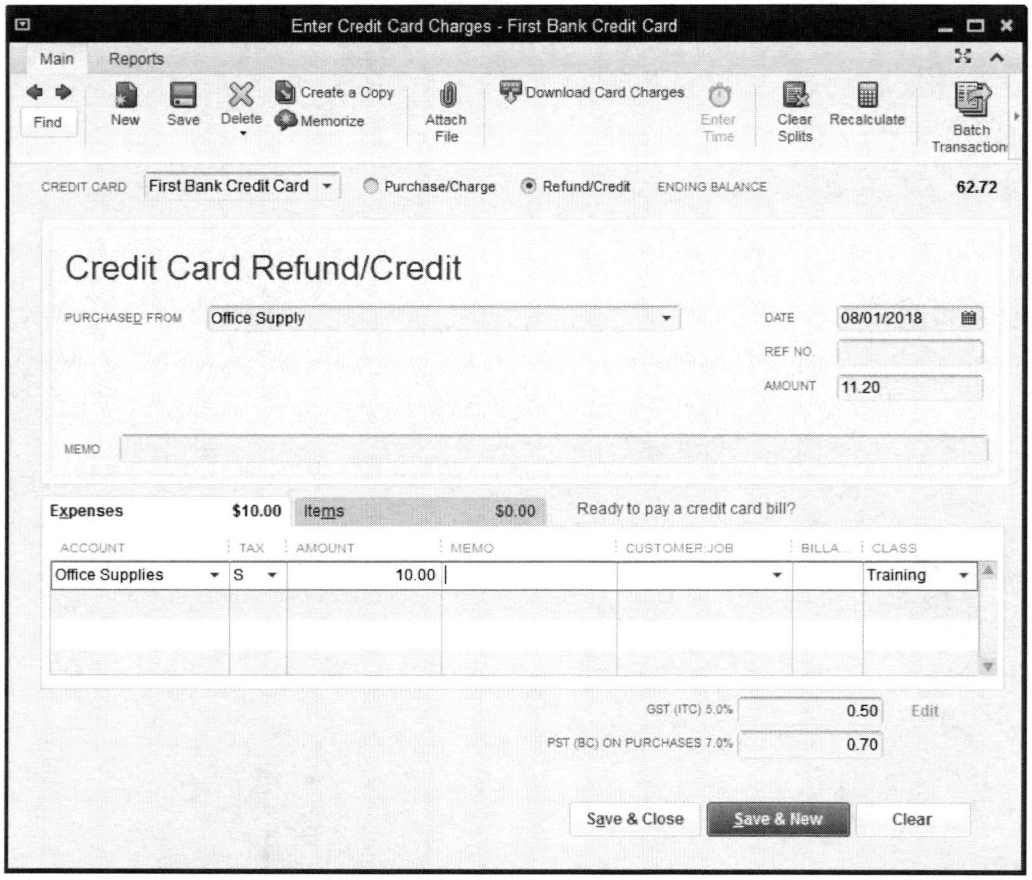

Figure 4-8: Enter Credit Card Charges form – Credit Card Refund/Credit

Also notice the ending balance in the credit card GL account that appears in the upper right corner below the ribbon. Because the transaction in Figure 4-7 is the first charge, the previous balance is zero. The balance from the entry of the transaction in Figure 4-7 ($62.72) appears in the refund transaction not yet saved in Figure 4-8.

Note: Recall that in Lesson 2, we learned about the reverse language between accounting for a business and accounting for a bank. The same principle applies for credit cards. Credits in the credit card liability GL account increase what the business owes to the credit card holder, while debits decrease the balance. When the credit card company decreases what you owe, such as with a refund, the debits in the accounting records become credits for the credit card company's account.

Paying the Credit Card Statement

When the credit card statement arrives for reconciliation, you need to make the payment for the credit card charges. Often you will do this online, without mailing a cheque, so you can use the Write Cheques form in the same way you would for a debit card transaction.

Note: You will reconcile credit card statements in a later lesson.

Exercise 4.2: Entering Credit Card Transactions

In this exercise, you will enter credit card transactions. Jordan Smith purchased some basic office supplies for the training program and has given you the receipts. He also returned one item, so one receipt is a credit card refund. Smith's transactions included taxes.

Enter the credit card purchase.

1. Ensure that the company file you worked on in the previous exercise is still open.

2. Click **Banking > Enter Credit Card Charges**. The Enter Credit Card Charges form appears.

3. Ensure that the **Purchase/Charge** radio button is selected.

4. If necessary, in the *CREDIT CARD* drop-down menu, select **First Bank Credit Card**.

5. In the *DATE* field, type: **08/01/2018**.

6. In the *PURCHASED FROM* drop-down menu, select **Office Supply**.

7. In the *Expenses* tab, in the *ACCOUNT* drop-down menu, select **Office Supplies** if necessary.

8. In the *TAX* drop-down menu, select **S** if necessary. This will auto-fill the tax fields at the bottom of the form after you enter the amount of the purchase.

9. In the *AMOUNT* field, type: **56.00**.

10. In the *CLASS* drop-down menu, select **Training**.

11. Click the **Save & New** button to save the credit card purchase. A blank Enter Credit Card Charges form appears.

Enter the refund.

12. Click the **Refund/Credit** radio button to use the form for credit card refunds/credits.

13. To process the refund, ensure that the *CREDIT CARD* is still **First Bank Credit Card**.

14. In the *DATE* field, type: **08/01/2018** if necessary.

15. In the *Expenses* tab, in the *ACCOUNT* drop-down menu, select **Office Supplies**.

16. In the *TAX* drop-down menu, select **S** if necessary.

17. Enter the refund amount: **10.00** in the *AMOUNT* field and press **TAB**. Notice that the Amount field in the top half of the form reflects the refund amount plus the tax ($11.20). QuickBooks also auto-filled the tax fields (GST and PST) at the bottom of the form with the correct amounts, and selected the correct (only) vendor for this expense.

18. In the *CLASS* drop-down menu, select **Training**.

19. Click the **Save & Close** button to save the refund and return to the Home page.

Leave the company file open for the next exercise.

Processing Petty Cash Reimbursements

Objective L-4.4 Process petty cash reimbursements

Setting up a Petty Cash fund is simple. However, accurately tracking petty cash expenses and reimbursements can become time-consuming, unless you follow clear procedures. Once the Petty Cash GL account is funded, the amount never changes unless the funds are increased or returned to the bank in whole or in part. Until reconciliation, when the receipts for expenses are added and the balance in the petty cash fund is counted, petty cash does not become part of the accounting records. You still need to keep your receipts for purchases though, because that is how you will account for the use of the petty cash funds. However, you will not enter every transaction immediately like you did with the other accounts, such as credit or debit cards.

Ideally, when you reconcile the Petty Cash account, the receipts you have kept, plus the balance of the cash, equals the starting amount. If not, the difference between the amounts becomes income or an expense. If you have more cash in the Petty Cash account than when you began, you record the surplus as income and deposit it in the bank using the Make Deposits form. If you have less cash in the Petty Cash account than when you started, you would write a cheque to withdraw cash to fund the account back to the starting amount. For example, you could use the Write Cheques form to create a cheque for $100, payable to Taylor Green, dated August 1, 2018, for the GL account Petty Cash.

Funding Petty Cash

The first step is to complete and print a Write Cheques form. The GL account is a new GL bank account type named Petty Cash. The transaction credits and reduces the chequing account and debits and increases the Petty Cash account. The actual money may simply be kept in an envelope in a drawer or a business may have a small box kept for this purpose. The cheque may be made out to the person taking it to the bank to cash. This is safer than making a cheque out to *Cash* because, if the cheque is lost, anyone could cash it.

Issuing Petty Cash

Often petty cash is handled informally on-site by an administrative person, unless the business has a full-time bookkeeper. The partners of Best Custom T-Shirts plan to keep the Petty Cash fund at their office. Larger businesses usually have an official receipt book, but petty cash is often handled informally in small businesses. Because keeping exact change in the fund to reimburse people for small purchases can be difficult, authorized people may take the cash they need and bring back receipts and change.

Reconciling Petty Cash

Reconciliation of the Petty Cash fund should occur at regular intervals or when the amount in petty cash runs low, before replenishing the fund. The remaining money, plus the receipts, should equal the amount of the fund. If a discrepancy exists, then the amount can be posted to a Miscellaneous or Over/Under Cash expense account. A discrepancy between the actual cash on hand and the value of the fund can easily occur if some of the change goes into a parking meter or if the change is mixed with an employee's individual money. These occurrences are common, so knowing how to enter these types of discrepancies will be valuable.

The Petty Cash equation helps you determine if you need an adjustment, and how much of an adjustment to make. The equation is: Petty Cash fund - money leftover - receipts = 0. If the equation is not equal to zero, then it needs an adjustment. The amount subtracted or added to reach zero is the amount to adjust. If the equation result is less than zero, then too much change came back and the replenishment amount is the receipt total minus the difference, and the Over/Under GL account receives a credit. If the equation result is greater than zero, then not enough change came back, and the replenishment amount is the receipt total plus the difference, and the Over/Under GL account receives a debit. Always enter the full amounts of the receipts.

Note: On rare occasions, you will need to enter a negative amount to turn the debit or credit the form automatically enters into the opposite. To credit the Over/Under GL account for a cash overage (the equation result is less than zero), enter the receipts in their GL accounts and then enter the overage as a negative number in the Over/Under GL account.

After you know the amount needed to restore Petty Cash to the original amount, complete another Write Cheques form. Each type of receipt can be entered on one line. For example, if two receipts both go into the same GL account, they can be summed together. Any discrepancy becomes part of the Over/Under GL account, which is usually an expense account.

Following this process means that the total in the Petty Cash fund GL account does not increase or decrease, but the cash remains available for use and the expenses are posted. Figure 4-9 shows the Write Cheques form filled out to replenish the Petty Cash fund.

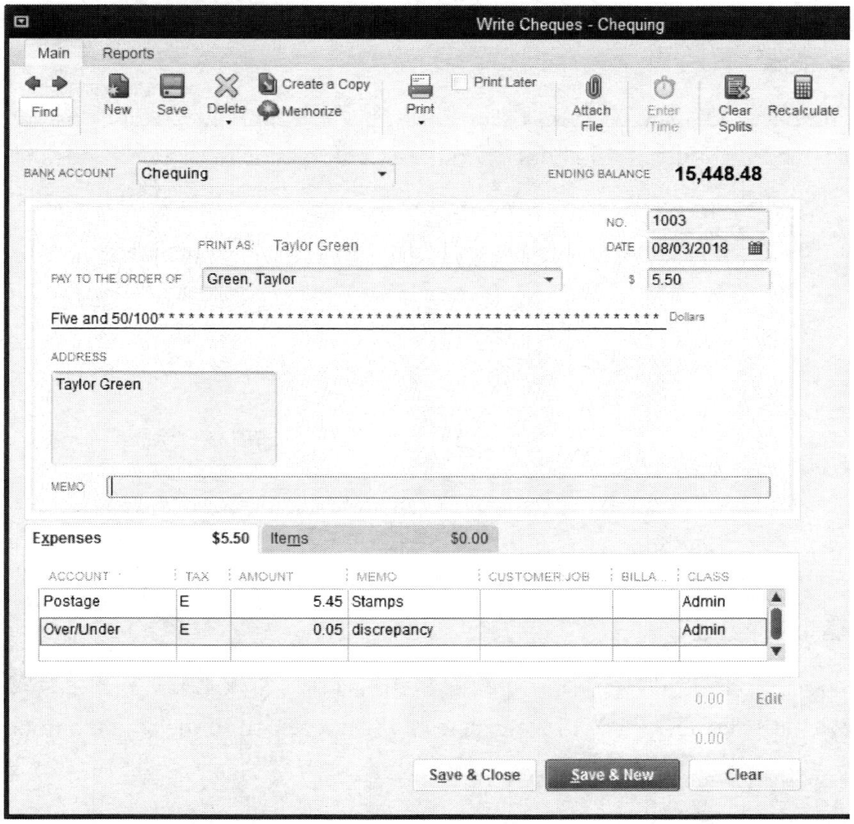

Figure 4-9: Write Cheques form to replenish the Petty Cash fund

In Figure 4-9, the Petty Cash equation resulted in an amount that is $0.05 short. Taylor Green took $10 from the fund, spent $5.45 on stamps, but only brought back $4.50 instead of $4.55. If she had brought back $4.60, then the Over/Under amount would be a negative $0.05.

Exercise 4.3: Entering Petty Cash

In this exercise, you will fund and reconcile the Petty Cash account. You will fund Petty Cash with the Amount of $100.00. You will use the Write Cheques form and make the cheque out to Taylor Green on August 1, 2018, who will be cashing the cheque for the fund. You will then reconcile the Petty Cash account using a receipt presented to you from Jordan Smith, who took $20.00 to mail a package. He spent $15.45, but only brought back $4.50. The account is five cents short.

Fund the Petty Cash account.

1.   Ensure that the company file you worked on in the previous exercise is still open.

2.   Click **Banking > Write Cheques**. The Write Cheques form appears.

3.   In the *BANK ACCOUNT* drop-down menu, select **Chequing** if necessary.

4.   In the *NO.* field, type: **1005**.

5.   In the *DATE* field, type: **08/01/2018** if necessary.

6.   In the *PAY TO THE ORDER OF* drop-down menu, select **Green, Taylor**.

7.   In the *$* field, type: **100.00**.

8.   In the *Expenses* tab, in the *ACCOUNT* drop-down menu, select **Petty Cash**.

9.   In the *CLASS* field, select **Admin**.

10. Click **Print**. The Print Cheque dialog box appears.

11. Make sure the cheque number (1005) is correct and click **OK** to display the Print Cheques dialog box. Select the printer and click the **Print** button. The Print Cheques – Confirmation dialog box appears. Click **OK** if your cheque printed correctly.

12. Click the **Save & New** button to save the transaction and open a new Write Cheques form.

Reconcile the Petty Cash account.

13. In the new Write Cheques form, ensure that the *BANK ACCOUNT* field is set to **Chequing**.

14. Ensure that the *NO.* field is set to **1006**.

15. Ensure that the *DATE* field is set to **08/01/2018**.

16. Select **Smith, Jordan** from the *PAY TO THE ORDER OF* drop-down menu.

17. In the *Expenses* tab, in the *ACCOUNT* drop-down menu, select **Postage**.

18. In the *TAX* drop-down menu, select **E**.

   Note: Postage in Canada is subject to sales tax, so you would normally use S (standard tax). However, to simplify the exercise, we have chosen to use E so that sales tax is not added to the stated amounts.

19. In the *AMOUNT* field, type: **15.45**.

20. In the *MEMO* field (in the *Expenses* tab), type: **Postage**.

21. In the *CLASS* drop-down menu, select **Admin**.

22. On the second line, in the *ACCOUNT* drop-down menu, select **Over/Under**.

23. In the *TAX* drop-down menu, select **E**.

24. In the *AMOUNT* field, type: **0.05**. The $ amount in the top half of the form will change to $15.50 after you move to the next field.

25. In the *MEMO* field (in the *Expenses* tab), type: **discrepancy**.

26. In the *CLASS* drop-down menu, select **Admin**.

27. Click **Print**. The Print Cheque dialog box appears.

28. Make sure the cheque number (1006) is correct and click **OK** to display the Print Cheques dialog box. Select the printer and click the **Print** button. The Print Cheques – Confirmation dialog box appears. Click **OK** if your cheque printed correctly.

29. Click the **Save & Close** button.

Create a portable file to turn in as part of this lesson's assignments.

30. Save the company file as a portable file in the *1767-Student-Files\Lesson 4\MyProjects* folder.

    Note: This is the file you will turn in.

31. If you plan to perform the Practice the Skill exercise, close the company file but leave QuickBooks open; otherwise, close the company file and exit QuickBooks.

Lesson Summary

Now that you have completed this lesson, you should be able to:

☑ Identify if an accrual entry is necessary in purchases. ☑ Enter credit card purchases.

☑ Enter cash purchases using cheques. ☑ Process petty cash reimbursements.

Key Terms

Term	Definition
Amortization	Transferring annual amounts from the Balance Sheet to the Profit and Loss statement through amortization expense.
Capital	Money or assets available for starting or investing in a business.
Capital Cost Allowance	A government incentive to purchase capital equipment by providing tax relief, often at a rate greater than the asset depreciates on the books.
Capital Expenditure	The purchase of an asset.
Capitalized	An item that it is purchased as an asset rather than as an expenditure. It appears in the Balance Sheet rather than in the Profit & Loss statement.
Depreciable Property	Property expected to last more than one year, which therefore needs to be expensed over its lifetime.
Depreciation	The loss in value of an asset due to devaluation from use. This is also a measure of utility over time.

Term	Definition
GST	Goods and Services Tax – the Canadian national tax.
Items	QuickBooks term for the pairing of the name of an income or expense with a GL account.
Net	The difference between two numbers, such as a debit and a credit.
PST	Provincial Sales Tax.
Start-up Costs	Costs owners pay before business activities begin.

Activity 1: Choosing the Correct Form

If the owners make a purchase online using the company debit card, which choice is the correct form to use to record the transaction and why?

    a)   Write Cheques

    b)   Enter Credit Card Charge

Activity 2: Knowing How the Form Affects GL Accounts

When using the company credit card for purchasing an item that is an expense, what pair of phrases describes the correct effect on the accounting records?

    a)   The Chequing GL asset decreases and Credit Card liability GL account increases.

    b)   The Credit Card liability GL account decreases and an expense GL account increases.

    c)   The Credit Card liability GL account increases and an expense GL account increases.

Activity 3: Determining the Correct Petty Cash Process

Which is the correct choice for processing petty cash requests to replenish petty cash?

    a)   Count the remaining cash, tally the receipts, find the difference between the Petty Cash balance and the total cash and receipts, and issue a cheque from the Chequing GL for the difference, posting the difference to the Petty Cash GL.

    b)   Count the remaining cash, subtract the total from the Petty Cash fund balance, then subtract the receipts. Add or subtract any difference to reach zero and issue a cheque from the Chequing GL account against the correct GL expense accounts for the receipts and difference.

    c)   Tally the receipts and issue a cheque from the Chequing GL account for the total, making sure the expenses are in the correct GL accounts.

    d)   Enter a Write Cheques form for the total receipts and the difference between the total of the receipts and the Petty Cash fund balance using the Petty Cash fund GL account instead of the expense GL accounts.

Practice the Skill

This Practice the Skill exercise is designed to reinforce the skills you have learned. In this exercise, you will enter cash and credit card transactions.

Jordan Smith presents you with receipts paid by credit and debit card. He purchased ink for the screen-printing press and needed to return one item. Both receipts are dated August 10, 2018. Taylor Green also took care of the $250.00 filing fee for the business. This transaction is not taxable.

1. If necessary, launch **QuickBooks** and open **Best Custom T-Shirts C1_L4_B (Portable).QBM** from the *1767-Student-Files\Lesson 4\PTS* folder.

2. For Jordan Smith's purchase, open the Enter Credit Card Charges form. Use the following information to record the credit card purchase and the refund.
    - The vendor is Ink Suppliers.
    - The date is August 10, 2018.
    - The GL account is Production Supplies:Ink. Because the company will use the ink only for training and not to produce items for sale, the account is in the expense section under Production Supplies.
    - The Tax code is S.
    - Jordan purchased $75 of ink, not including tax, and returned $15 worth of ink.
    - The Class is Training.

3. Save your work.

4. For Taylor Green's purchase, open the Write Cheques form. Fill in the form using the following information:
    - The bank account is Chequing.
    - The No. is D for debit card.
    - The date is August 10, 2018.
    - The vendor is BC Registries and Online Services.
    - The GL account is Start-up Costs.
    - The Memo field should display the word "Fee."
    - The Class is Admin.

5. Save your work.

6. Save the company file as a portable company file and add the letters PTS to the end of the file name (*Best Custom T-Shirts C1_L4 <your name> PTS (Portable).QBM*). Turn this file in to your instructor.

7. Close the company file.

Course Project Exercise

On August 7, 2017, Arlene Stohl, the new partner in Blue Heron Spa, paid the janitor's fee out-of-pocket and needed to be reimbursed $45.00. On the same day, Blue Heron Spa ordered supplies online from SpaSupplies.com for $111.81 pre-tax (S) using their Bank One credit card. One item needed to be returned. On August 10, 2017, SpaSupplies.com issued a refund of $12.00 pre-tax (S) on the credit card. The account for both transactions is Linen and Spa Supplies. Fill out the necessary forms to record these transactions. When you are finished, save your work.

Filename:	Blue Heron Spa Inc 2018 C1_L4_A (Portable).QBM
Admin password:	BluSpa18
New company name:	Blue Heron Spa Inc. L4 <your name>

Perform the following tasks:

1. Restore the portable file and change the company name as indicated in the table above.

2. Write a reimbursement check to Arlene Stohl for $45.00 dated 8/7/2017. Ensure that you specify the correct customer, GL account, tax code, and appropriate memo text.

3. Print the cheque, and then save and close the transaction form.

4. Create the appropriate credit card purchase transaction for the supplies purchased by Blue Heron Spa on 8/7/2017. Ensure that you specify the correct credit card, vendor, purchase amount, GL account, tax code, and appropriate memo text.

5. Save the credit card purchase transaction and prepare to create the appropriate refund transaction for the returned item.

6. Ensure that you specify the correct credit card, vendor, refund amount, GL account, tax code, and appropriate memo text.

7. Save and close the refund transaction.

8. Create a portable file to turn in to your instructor.

9. Close the company file.

Quiz Questions

For each question, select the best answer.

1. Which one of the following expense-related transactions does not use a cash-based payment form?

    a. You received a bill from a vendor for supplies that were ordered and delivered last week.

    b. You wrote a cheque to reimburse an employee for hardware supplies purchased yesterday.

    c. You used a debit card to order office supplies online, and the supplies will arrive in two days.

    d. You used a debit card to pay government-related fees.

2. Which choice describes why you would use the Write Cheques form for a debit card purchase?

   a. The Write Cheques form automatically selects the correct debit account to expense.

   b. The Write Cheques form works for debit and credit cards.

   c. Using a debit card has the same effect on the chequing account as writing a cheque.

   d. The journal entry created by the Write Cheques form debits the chequing account.

3. Which choice describes the steps you should take to process a refund for a credit card purchase?

   a. Open the Enter Credit Card Charges form, specify Refund/Credit, and specify the Credit Card company in the *PURCHASED FROM* field because they refunded the amount.

   b. Open the Enter Credit Card Charges form, specify Refund/Credit, and use the Credit Card GL account for the refund because the balance will be reduced.

   c. Open the Enter Credit Card Charges form, specify Purchase/Charge, and use a negative number for the same GL account as the purchase.

   d. Open the Enter Credit Card Charges form, specify Refund/Credit, and use the same GL account for the expense as you do for the purchase.

4. After the Petty Cash Reconciliation process is complete, and a cheque written and cashed, what is the balance in the Petty Cash fund GL account?

   a. The Petty Cash fund GL balance decreases by the amount spent.

   b. The Petty Cash fund GL balance is the same as it was before any money was moved in or out of the fund.

   c. The Petty Cash fund GL balance increases by the difference between the receipts and remaining cash.

   d. The Petty Cash fund GL balance is the same as the remaining cash plus receipts.

Lesson 5: Receiving Cash Sales

Lesson Objectives

In this lesson, you will enter and identify cash sales and make deposits. Upon successful completion of this lesson, you should be able to:

☐ Identify when an accrual is required as opposed to a cash-based sale.

☐ Enter sales receipts.

☐ Make deposits.

☐ Issue cash refunds.

Beginning Business Activities

Objective L-5.1 Identify when an accrual is required as opposed to a cash-based sale

Best Custom T-Shirts needs workers for their screen-printing facility. The city agrees to sponsor vocational training when interested applicants meet certain criteria. The company will offset costs if applicants qualify and agree to pay some of the cost. For successful completion of the program, trainees may earn employment or rebates on the training.

The first training session begins this week and enrollment fees are arriving with various payment types. Because the retail store has not yet opened, the training income is the first income from business activities. The company has set up both an online account to accept payments via the website and a merchant account to accept credit card payments directly. As the bookkeeper, you will process these first sales transactions.

These initial sales for vocational training are tax exempt, while sales of other services and merchandise are taxable. You will learn more about taxes in Lesson 8.

Cash-Based Sales

QuickBooks handles sales several ways, depending on the timing. If there is a delay between the time the customer receives services or goods and the time they pay for them, then an accrual is required. This decision is more critical with the advent of computerized accounting, because a financial statement can be run at any moment rather than at the end of a specific period. Previously, you might have closed the sales journal at the end of the month and determined what needed to be accrued or set up as a prepaid; now, you make this decision at the time of each transaction. We will cover the accrual basis sales process in Lesson 8.

You can see the location of sales in the QuickBooks Cycles in Figure 5-1.

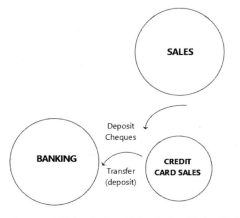

Figure 5-1: Sales Cycle and Credit Card Sales Cycle intersect the Banking Cycle

The sales covered in this lesson do not require an accrual. Future sales from the retail store or the website will also not require an accrual. No delay occurs in those sales because either the customers pay in full at the store or they pay by credit card online, which means the balance changes immediately. Even though a small delay occurs between the time a customer pays online through the website and the time the merchandise arrives by delivery service, placing an order online is the same as buying in the store for accounting purposes.

Credit card sales usually involve a processing fee that the business must pay, whether the credit card processor keeps the fee from the sale at the time they process the transaction or charges the company later.

The type of payment determines the process for entering the sale. Here is the list of payment types covered in this lesson:

- Payment with cheque
- Payment online, fee kept by the processor
- Payment with a credit card, fee charged later by the processor

Additionally, because customers sometimes change their minds about a sale, this lesson also covers simple refunds of cash and credit sales for the training program.

Receiving Payment for Sales

Objective L-5.2 Enter sales receipts

Objective L-5.3 Make deposits

The first cheque arrives for the training program. The QuickBooks file you will be using already has an income account set up for training. Additionally, the Class, *Training,* already exists so that you can properly categorize the sale.

Cash sales use only one form – the Enter Sales Receipts form. This form can directly affect the chequing GL balance, depending on the Payment Preferences set for the company file.

Unlike the forms for expenses that include two tabs (one for GL accounts and the other for Items), the Enter Sales Receipts form allows you to specify only items.

You enter sales by specifying items associated with a particular GL account (this allows QuickBooks to perform any actions necessary for tracking **inventory**). We have already created the item for Training in QuickBooks for your use.

To open the Enter Sales Receipts form, click **Customers > Enter Sales Receipts**, or on the Home page, in the CUSTOMERS section, click the Create Sales Receipts icon.

The Enter Sales Receipts form combines some of the features of the Make Deposits form with the elements needed for entering a sale. It enables the direct deposit of the transaction into the chequing GL account; however, you can decide to group several sales transactions before making a deposit. What drives the decision to group transactions is whether the payments are deposited individually in the bank account. If the numbers posted to the chequing GL account match what appears on the **bank statement,** then reconciliations are much easier.

Enter Sales Receipts Form Elements

Figure 5-2 shows a sales receipt for a cheque received for the training program. The unique elements on the Enter Sales Receipts form are labeled. One fundamental difference between entering a sales receipt and using the Make Deposits form or the Write Cheques form is that, while it is possible to complete a deposit or write a cheque using the name of any entity in QuickBooks, whether a customer or a vendor, the Enter Sales Receipts form accepts only customers.

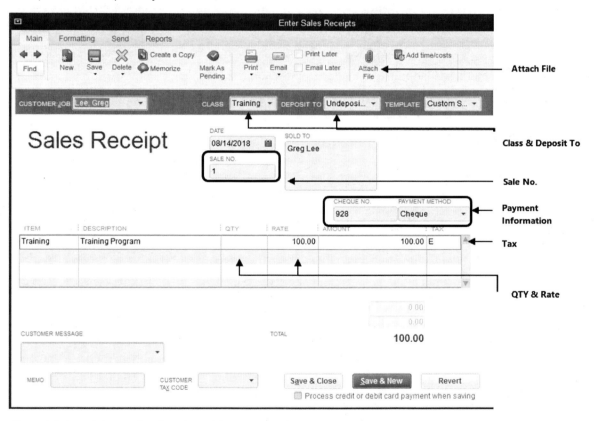

Figure 5-2: Enter Sales Receipts form for training program cheque

The Enter Sales Receipts form includes the following elements:

- **CLASS** – The CLASS field is at the top of the form, not on each line. Every item on the Sales Receipt goes into the same class.

- **DEPOSIT TO** – use this field to specify the GL account into which the funds will be deposited. Funds can either go directly into the Chequing GL account or into a **suspense account** for grouping. The Undeposited Funds GL account appears in the drop-down list for this field. You will learn more about the Undeposited Funds GL account later in this lesson.

- **Attach File** – Click the paperclip icon to attach a file or scanned document to the Sales Receipt.
- **SALE NO.** – Sale Number. QuickBooks automatically increments this field, or you can enter a number manually.
- **Payment information fields** – You can select a payment method from the PAYMENT METHOD drop-down menu. If the payment is via cheque, you can enter the cheque number in the CHEQUE NO. field.
- **TAX** – You can specify a tax code for each item.
- **QTY** and **RATE** – You can use this pair of fields together to calculate the Amount. QTY is the number sold and RATE is the price per item. Alternatively, you can enter an Amount without using the QTY and RATE fields.

Receiving Online Payment for Sales

Online payments for sales often have processor or *merchant fees* removed, or "netted out," of the total amount of the sale. The amount of the fee assessed depends on the payment processor and the payment method used. Some payment processors offer certain transaction types without charging a merchant fee.

For this lesson, the payment processor of the online transaction retains the fee from each purchase, thereby reducing the total payment the business receives by a few percentage points.

It is important to enter the total amount of the sale, separate from the merchant fee, as shown in Figure 5-3. The sale and the merchant fee can be included in the same transaction as long as each posts to its own GL account. Assigning these amounts to separate GL accounts will allow the business to see the total amount of sales and the costs of using the payment processor.

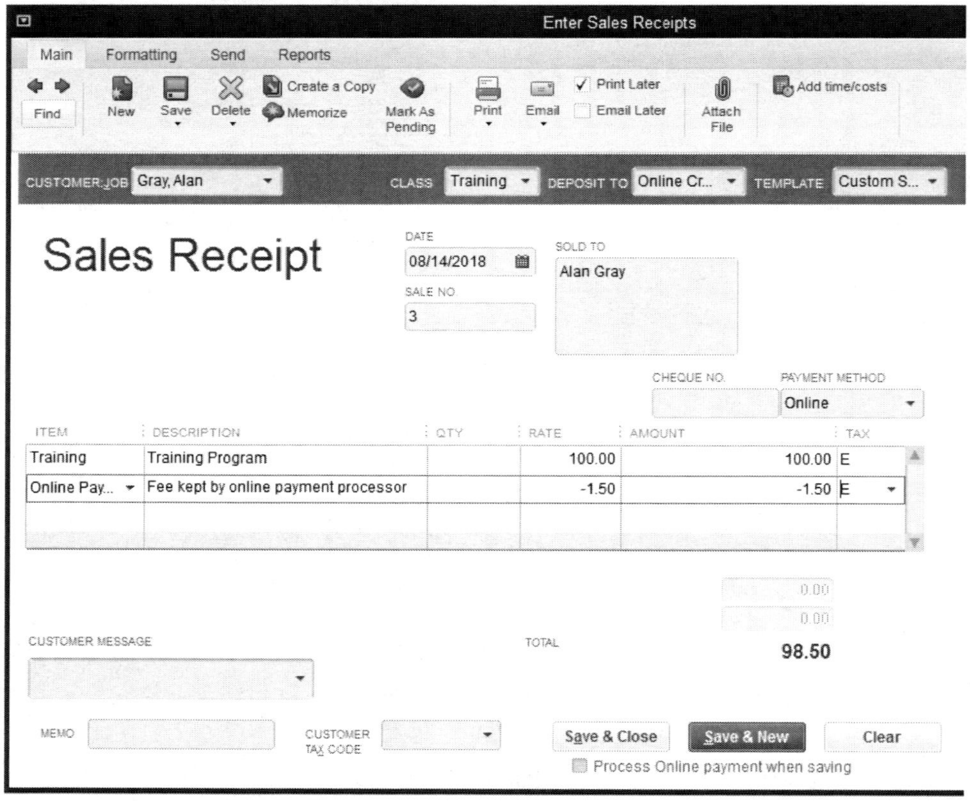

Figure 5-3: Sales Receipt for training program paid online

The merchant fee is a special type of item in QuickBooks that reduces the amount on the Sales Receipt and posts the merchant fee to the account number assigned in the item, which in this case is the Credit Card Fee expense account (see the second line in Figure 5-3).

Figure 5-4 shows the Sales Receipt as a journal entry, so you can see the items translated into the GL accounts.

Best Custom T-Shirts C1_L5_A
Journal
August 2018

Trans #	Type	Date	Num	Adj	Name	Memo	Account	Debit	Credit
18	Sales Rece...	08/14/2018	3		Gray, Alan		Online Credit Card	98.50	
					Gray, Alan	Training Program	Training		100.00
					Gray, Alan	Fee kept by online payment processor	Credit Card Fees	1.50	
								100.00	100.00

Figure 5-4: Sales Receipt as a journal entry in the journal report

Notice that for this online payment, the *DEPOSIT TO* field (in Figure 5-3) is set to a different account. The full GL name is Online Credit Card, which is a bank type GL account. This account is a suspense account for the online credit card processor.

In Figure 5-4 you can see that the Sales Receipt:

- Debited (increased) the Online Credit Card account (asset, bank type GL account),
- Credited (increased) the Training account (income GL account), and
- Debited (increased) the Credit Card Fees account (expense GL account).

Receiving Credit Card Payment for Sales

For credit card sales at a business location, the processor usually remits the total amount collected. Some credit card processors take the merchant fee out first. If the processor does not take the merchant fee out, it later deducts the merchant fee, sometimes called the ***discount*** on the sale, from the bank account.

The Sales Receipt shown in Figure 5-5 looks very similar to the Sales Receipt for the cheque payment shown in Figure 5-2, except for the type of payment, the lack of a cheque number, and the Deposit To GL account is set to the Merchant Credit Card GL. No payment fee is deducted because the credit card processor charges for it later. How much later will determine whether an accrual for the liability should be set up. Also, the volume of transactions will dictate if an accrual is necessary based on the principle of materiality.

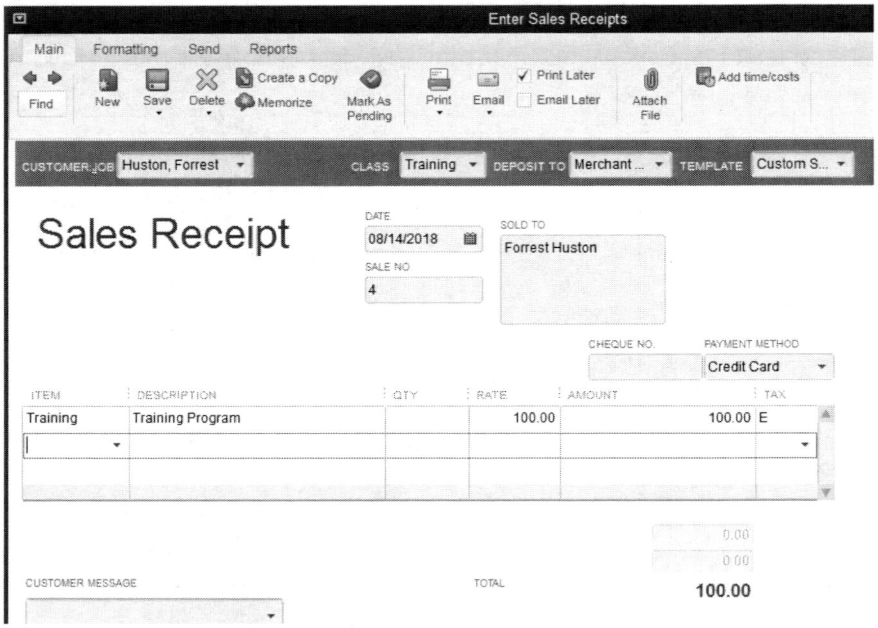

Figure 5-5: Sales Receipt for training program paid with a credit card

About the Undeposited Funds GL Account

For deposits, the payment type matters. Only payments of cash or cheques can go directly into the chequing GL account. However, unless the cash or cheque amounts for every sales receipt are listed separately on the bank statement, all sales receipts for these payment types need to go through a suspense account.

There is a preference setting in the Payments Company Preferences (Figure 5-6) that specifies to use the QuickBooks suspense GL account called *Undeposited Funds* as a default deposit to account. This setting is selected by default.

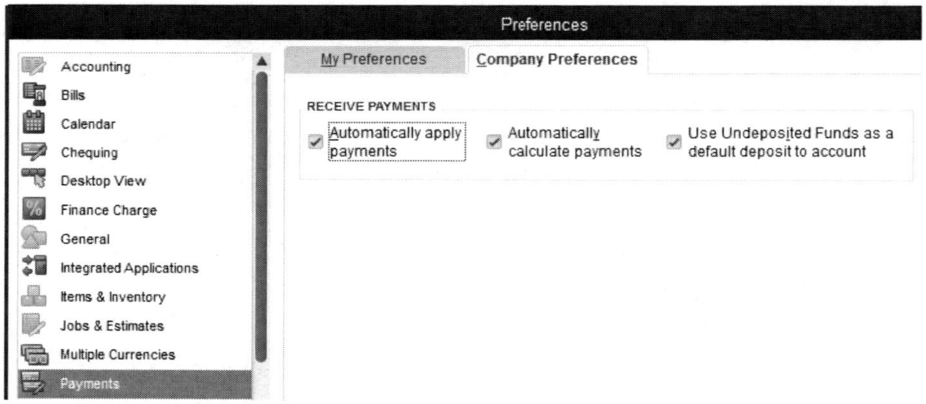

Figure 5-6: Payments Company Preferences with Use Undeposited Funds as a default deposit to account option selected

Undeposited Funds is a special GL account that holds the Sales Receipts you have entered until you choose to group them into a deposit. This account is convenient if cheques arrive daily for a weekly deposit because the bookkeeping can be completed up to the deposit step.

However, when this preference is in effect, the Deposit To field does not display in the Enter Sales Receipts form, and you cannot specify a Deposit To GL account.

If the company uses credit card processors and needs to use multiple suspense accounts, you should turn off this preference setting by deselecting the **Use Undeposited Funds as a default deposit to account** check box. Then the Deposit To field will be available in the Enter Sales Receipts form and you can specify the appropriate Deposit To account each time.

Note: In the company file used in this lesson, the Use Undeposited Funds as a default deposit to account setting has been turned off.

Exercise 5.1: Entering Sales Receipts for Cheques

In this exercise, you will launch QuickBooks, restore the Best Custom T-Shirts C1_L5_A (Portable).QBM file, and enter two sales receipts. When you complete this exercise, you will be able to enter sales receipts for cheques.

1. Launch **QuickBooks** and restore **Best Custom T-Shirts C1_L5_A (Portable).QBM** from the *1767-Student-Files\Lesson 5\StarterFiles* folder. Save the restored company file as **Best Custom T-Shirts C1_L5_<your name>.QBW** in the *1767-Student-Files\Lesson 5\MyProjects* folder.

   Note: This process may take a few minutes.

2. If the QuickBooks Desktop Login dialog box appears, ensure that **Admin** displays in the *User Name* field, then click **OK** to log in as the Admin. Click **OK** again to close the message box informing you that the portable company file has been opened successfully.

3. Change the Company Name to **Best Custom T-Shirts C1_L5_<your name>**.

Open a new Enter Sales Receipts form.

4. Click **Customers > Enter Sales Receipts** or click the **Create Sales Receipts** icon on the Home page.

5. Ensure that the **Print Later** check box is selected in the ribbon at the top of the form.

The first cheque is from Michael Black. He will not appear in the Customer list because he is a new customer, so you will need to add him.

6. Click the drop-down arrow for the *CUSTOMER: JOB* field and click **<Add New>**. The New Customer dialog box appears.

7. In the *CUSTOMER NAME* field, type: **Black, Michael**, then click **OK** to add the new customer and close the New Customer dialog box.

8. In the *CLASS* drop-down menu, select **Training**.

9. In the *DEPOSIT TO* drop-down menu, select **Undeposited Funds**.

10. Change the date to **08/16/2018**.

11. In the *SOLD TO* field, type: **Michael Black**.

12. In the *CHEQUE NO.* field, type: **604**.

13. In the *PAYMENT METHOD* drop-down menu, select **Cheque**.

14. In the *ITEM* drop-down menu, select **Training**. This auto-fills the DESCRIPTION and TAX fields as well.

15. Skip the QTY and RATE fields, and in the *AMOUNT* field, type: **100.00**.

Note: When you click in the RATE field or enter a value in the AMOUNT field, a drop-down arrow appears. This is a convenience feature you can use when you have set up standardized rates. We have not set these up, so if you click the arrow now a pop up appears telling you that you have not created any price levels. If this happens, click OK to dismiss the pop up.

16. When the form is complete, click the **Save & New** button. If the Information Changed pop up appears, click **Yes**. A blank Enter Sales Receipts form appears.

Enter the second cheque.

17. Ensure that **Print Later** is still selected in the ribbon at the top of the form.

18. The second cheque is also from Michael Black, so select his name from the *CUSTOMER: JOB* drop-down list.

19. In the *CLASS* drop-down menu, select **Training**.

20. In the *DEPOSIT TO* field, ensure **Undeposited Funds** is selected.

21. Ensure the date is still set to **08/16/2018**.

22. In the *CHEQUE NO.* field, type: **865**, and in the *PAYMENT METHOD* drop-down menu, select **Cheque**.

23. In the *ITEM* drop-down menu, select **Training**. This auto-fills the DESCRIPTION and TAX fields as well.

24. In the *AMOUNT* field, type: **100.00**.

25. When the form is complete, click the **Save & Close** button. Notice the red number *2* that appears on the Record Deposits icon in the BANKING section of the Home page. This indicates that you have recorded two customer payments.

Leave the company file open for the next exercise.

Depositing Payments

Objective L-5.3 Make deposits

Unless you specified the Chequing GL account as the *Deposit To* account on the Sales Receipt (which sends the money directly to the chequing account), you must perform a second step to deposit the payments you receive.

The bookkeeper may be involved in preparing the physical deposits, or may enter them in QuickBooks only after someone else prepares them and makes the physical deposit at the bank. Because most cheques are scanned and can be viewed online, making copies of cheques is less critical than it was in the past. However, information on the cheques or cheque stubs, such as the **remittance advice,** may still be needed by the bookkeeper that may not otherwise be available.

Note: QuickBooks allows you to attach documents to forms by using the paperclip icon on the ribbon. This would be an excellent place to store cheque scans.

Now, let's look at how to deposit the sales receipts that are waiting in the Undeposited Funds account.

After entering all the sales receipts, depending on the timing, you will need to either enter the deposit and prepare it for the bank or only enter it in QuickBooks. The key to this part of the process is making sure that the sales receipts included in one (physical) bank deposit are also grouped in the deposit in QuickBooks. Otherwise, it will be very difficult to reconcile the QuickBooks accounting records against the bank statement.

Before making any deposits, let's see how the Balance Sheet (Figure 5-7) appears after the sales receipts described in the *Receiving Payment for Sales* section of this lesson have been recorded. The two $100 payments made with cheques appear in Undeposited Funds. The online payment is in the Online Credit Card GL account (it shows the net payment, after merchant fees that were kept by the payment processor), and the credit card payment is in the Merchant Credit Card GL account.

Best Custom T-Shirts C1_L5_A
Balance Sheet
As of August 14, 2018

	Aug 14, 18
ASSETS	
Current Assets	
Chequing/Savings	
Chequing	15,207.99
Merchant Credit Card	100.00
Online Credit Card	98.50
Petty Cash	100.00
Total Chequing/Savings	15,506.49
Other Current Assets	
Undeposited Funds	200.00
Total Other Current Assets	200.00
Total Current Assets	15,706.49

Figure 5-7: Balance Sheet after four training payments entered but before deposit

The Home page also shows the two cheques waiting in Undeposited Funds on the Record Deposits icon, as shown in Figure 5-8.

Figure 5-8: Number of cheques to deposit shown on Record Deposits icon

Depositing Cheque Payments

Now that you have performed Exercise 5.1 and have two cheques ready to deposit, you can either click the **Record Deposits** icon on the Home page or click **Banking > Make Deposits**. Either action simultaneously opens the Payments to Deposit dialog box and the Make Deposits form.

First, in the Payments to Deposit dialog box, you select the sales receipts that belong in the deposit you want to make. Click to the left of each desired sales receipt to display a check mark, as shown in Figure 5-9.

Payments to Deposit

SELECT VIEW

View payment method type   All types   What are payment method views?

Sort payments by   Payment Method

SELECT PAYMENTS TO DEPOSIT

✓	DATE	TIME	TYPE	NO.	PAYMENT METH.	NAME	AMOUNT
✓	08/14/2018		RCPT	1	Cheque	Lee, Greg	100.00
✓	08/14/2018		RCPT	2	Cheque	Tanner, Amy	100.00

Figure 5-9: Payments to Deposit dialog box with receipts checked

When you have selected the sales receipts you want to include, click OK. This action transfers the cheques to the Make Deposits form, as shown in Figure 5-10.

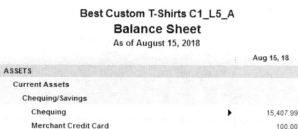

Figure 5-10: Make Deposits form

Let's assume that the deposit will go to the bank the day after you entered the sales receipts. In our example, the Balance Sheet contains information as of August 14, 2018, so on the Make Deposits form, change the date to 08/15/2018. After you click Save & Close, the deposit is made.

Figure 5-11 shows the Balance Sheet after the deposit transaction. Undeposited Funds is now zero and does not appear in the report, and the Chequing GL account is now increased by the $200 that was previously in the Undeposited Funds GL account.

Best Custom T-Shirts C1_L5_A
Balance Sheet
As of August 15, 2018

	Aug 15, 18
ASSETS	
Current Assets	
Chequing/Savings	
Chequing	15,407.99
Merchant Credit Card	100.00
Online Credit Card	98.50
Petty Cash	100.00
Total Chequing/Savings	15,706.49
Total Current Assets	15,706.49

Figure 5-11: Balance Sheet after deposit

Exercise 5.2: Depositing Cheque Payments

In this exercise, you will continue with the file from Exercise 5.1, open the Make Deposits form, find the sales receipts you filled out in the previous exercise, and save the deposit.

1. Ensure that the company file you worked on in the previous exercise is still open.

2. Click **Banking > Make Deposits** (or on the Home page, in the BANKING section, click the **Record Deposits** icon, now showing a red **2** for the two Sales Receipts waiting to be deposited).

3. In the Payments to Deposit dialog box, click to the left of both payments so that a checkmark appears in front of each. Then click **OK**. The Payments to Deposit dialog box closes and the two payments automatically appear in the Make Deposits form.

4. In the Make Deposits form, change the date to **August 17, 2018**, the date the deposit will go to the bank. Click the **Save & Close** button. Notice that the Record Deposits icon on the Home page no longer displays a red 2.

You can check your work by looking at the balance sheet for the date of the deposit.

5. Click **Reports > Company & Financial > Balance Sheet Standard**. When the Balance Sheet opens, change the *As of* (date) field to **August 16, 2018**, and then press **TAB**. Notice that the Undeposited Funds have not been deposited into the Chequing account.

6. Change the *As of* (date) field again to **August 17, 2018**, and then press **TAB**. Notice that the funds have now been deposited into the Chequing account and the Undeposited Funds account is no longer listed.

7. Close the Balance Sheet.

   Note: If the Memorize Report dialog box opens, click **No** to dismiss it.

Leave the company file open for the next exercise.

About Depositing Credit Card Payments

Credit card transactions, whether instore or online, go through a credit card processor before reaching a bank account. Because of this, each credit card processor needs its own GL account of the bank type. When entering sales receipts for credit card payments, they should be deposited individually to the correct credit card processor GL account by selecting that account in the *Deposit To* drop-down list in the Make Deposits form.

If the credit card sales receipts went directly into the chequing GL account, this account could become flooded with individual transactions in amounts that do not appear on the bank statement. The individual transaction amounts on the sales receipts are contained within the larger amounts batched by the credit card processor that *do* appear on the bank statement.

Payments made with credit cards or online come through a credit card processor in a **batch** or group of transactions. The word *batch* can also refer to transmitting the transactions from the business credit card terminal singly or in a group for processing at the end of the day. Although many transactions now instantly go through the credit card processor and appear on the purchaser's credit card or bank account, the credit card processor usually remits to the business the amount of multiple transactions at one time. You may also use the Enter Sales Receipts form to summarize an entire batch of sales if they are recorded in a different system, such as a cash register.

The additional bank GL accounts for each credit card processor function as suspense accounts until the information about the transactions becomes available from the credit card processors. The information could be in the form of a paper document or electronic download. This information can also include the type of credit card used, which can affect the grouping of the transactions deposited into the chequing account. Then, the sales can be matched to the credit card processor records and the batch amount transferred to the chequing account.

Refunding Cash Sales

Objective L-5.4 Issue cash refunds

If the payment for a sale is by cash or cheque, then you use the Write Cheques form in QuickBooks to send the customer a refund. In the form, use the same item for the refund that you used for the sale on the Enter Sales Receipts form. If the payment for the sale is an online or credit card payment, the refund amount goes back to the customer through the credit card processor.

Exercise 5.3: Refunding Cash Sales

In this exercise, you will return a payment to Michael Black for one of the Training classes because he accidentally paid twice. You will continue with the file from Exercise 5.2. You will open the Write Cheques form and enter the necessary information to refund cheque 865 for $100.00. Don't forget that the item must be the same on the refund as it was on the sales receipt, in this case, Training.

1. Ensure that the company file you worked on in the previous exercise is still open.

2. Click **Banking > Write Cheques**. The Write Cheques form appears.

3. Ensure the *BANK ACCOUNT* has **Chequing** selected. You can allow QuickBooks to assign the check number in the NO. field.

4. In the *DATE* field, select or type: **08/17/2018**, if necessary.

5. In the *PAY TO THE ORDER OF* field, select **Black, Michael**.

6. Click the **Items** tab, then in the *ITEM* drop-down menu, select **Training**. A pop up message appears telling you that this item is associated with an income account and asks if you want to continue. Click **OK**.

7. In the *AMOUNT* field, type: **100.00**, then press **TAB**. A pop up message appears warning you that you are changing the cost of this Item. Click **Yes**.

8. In the *CLASS* drop-down menu, select **Training**.

9. Click **Save & Close**.

10. In the *BANKING* section of the Home page, click the **Cheque Register** icon. The Use Register dialog box appears.

11. Ensure that **Chequing** displays in the Select Account field, then click **OK** to open the Chequing Register.

12. Locate the cheque you just created and double-click it. The Write Cheques form appears.

13. Click **Print** in the ribbon at the top of the form. The Print Cheque dialog box appears.

14. Type the cheque number you want to use if it did not auto-fill and click **OK**. The Print Cheques dialog box appears.

15. Select the printer and click the **Print** button. The cheque will print to the selected printer. The Print Cheques - Confirmation dialog box appears when the print process ends. Click **OK** if your cheque printed correctly.

   Note: Printing in the classroom is at your instructor's discretion. You may be directed to send your printed output to a file.

16. Close the Write Cheques form and the Chequing Register.

Create a portable file to turn in as part of this lesson's assignments.

17. Save the company file as a portable file in the *1767-Student-Files\Lesson 5\MyProjects* folder.

    Note: This is the file you will turn in.

18. If you plan to perform the Practice the Skill exercise, close the company file but leave QuickBooks open; otherwise, close the company file and exit QuickBooks.

Lesson Summary

Now that you have completed this lesson, you should be able to:

☑ Identify when an accrual is required as opposed to a cash-based sale.

☑ Enter sales receipts.

☑ Make deposits.

☑ Issue cash refunds.

Key Terms

Term	Definition
Bank Statement	A monthly summary from the bank showing the prior month's ending balance, all withdrawals and deposits the bank processed or cleared, and the current month's ending balance.
Batch	A group of credit card transactions transmitted for processing.
Discount	A reduction in the sale amount for merchant accounts, often for credit card fees.
Inventory	Products stocked for sale.
Merchant Fees	Fees that the payment processor, such as a credit card provider, charges a business for the ability to accept payment using their credit card.
Remittance Advice	Information about what a cheque payment is for. It is usually located on a removable section of the cheque or on an attachment, or it may appear only in the memo section of a cheque.
Suspense Account	A GL account that serves as a temporary holding place for transactions until they can be posted.

Activity 1: Processing Cheque and Credit Card Payments

Indicate which statement is true about cheque and credit card payments, and which statement is false.

_____ Cheque payments always go through processing by the bookkeeper before being deposited in the chequing account.

_____ Credit card payments go through a credit card processor before being deposited in the chequing account.

Activity 2: Making Deposits Correctly

You have ten cash-based Sales Receipts to enter for the same date, each for $100. Cheques were used to pay for three of them and go to the bank together as one deposit, two were paid online, and the remaining five were paid by credit card. What is the correct amount to deposit in the Chequing GL account?

a) $1,000

b) $ 300

c) $ 100

d) $ 500

e) $ 200

Practice the Skill

This Practice the Skill exercise is designed to reinforce the skills you have learned. In this exercise, you will refund training fees for Best Custom T-Shirts. They have one student who paid previously by cheque but decided not to take the training. You need to refund his training fee.

1. If necessary, launch **QuickBooks** and open **Best Custom T-Shirts C1_L5_B (Portable).QBM** from the *1767-Student-Files\Lesson 5\PTS* folder.

2. To refund the training fee to Greg Lee, open the Write Cheques form and fill it in using the following information:

    – The cheque number is 1005.

    – The date is August 20, 2018.

    – The Item (in the Items tab) is Training. If you receive a warning message reminding you this item is associated with an income account, click OK.

    – The cheque amount is $100. If you receive a message asking you if you want to change the cost of the item, click the No button.

    – The class is Training.

    – Print the cheque.

3. Save your work.

4. Open the Profit & Loss report and set the dates to the month of August, 2018. Position the mouse pointer over the income figure until the QuickZoom tool appears, then double-click. You can see the result of your entries in the detailed report.

5. Save the company file as a portable company file and add the letters PTS to the end of the file name (*Best Custom T-Shirts C1_L5<your name> PTS (Portable).QBM*). Turn this file in to your instructor.

6. Close the company file.

Course Project Exercise

The Blue Heron Spa needs the bookkeeping done for their weekly sales. Start a new Sales Receipt for the customer, Weekly Sales, for the week ending August 17, 2018. These sales are paid by credit card. The total amount will be deposited to Merchant Credit Card. The items already have the tax codes assigned. Here are the items to enter on the Sales Receipt. Be sure to use only the QTY field to create the amount.

ITEM	QTY
Body Treatments: Body Wrap	1
Esthetics: Gel Nails	4
Esthetics: Manicure	7
Esthetics: Pedicure	5
Facials: Blue Heron Special	3
Massage: Hot Stone Massage	2
Massage: Reflexology	4
Massage: Relaxation Massage	8

Filename:	Blue Heron Spa Inc 2018 C1_L5_A (Portable).QBM
Admin password:	BluSpa18
New company name:	Blue Heron Spa, Inc. L5 <your name>

Perform the following tasks:

1. Restore the portable file and change the company name as indicated in the second table.

2. Create a new Sales Receipt and enter the appropriate information for the Weekly Sales customer. Specify the correct date, Deposit To account, and then enter the items and quantities specified in the first table.

3. Save and close the transaction form.

4. Create a portable file to turn in to your instructor.

5. Close the company file.

Quiz Questions

For each question, select the best answer.

1. Which choice best describes cash-based sales?

    a. Only sales at a store qualify because the customer leaves with their purchase.

    b. The sale and movement of money are simultaneous for accounting purposes.

    c. The sale and movement of money in the account occur within two days of each other.

    d. The sale is made using cash.

2. Which of the following statements is true about entering sales receipts in QuickBooks?

    a. Cash sales use only one form – the Make Deposits form.

    b. If you use the Enter Sales Receipt form to enter sales receipts in QuickBooks, you must enter the receipts individually.

    c. For credit card sales at a business location, the processor always remits the total amount collected.

    d. For online payments, you should enter the total amount of the sale, separate from the merchant fee.

3. Which choice describes one key point about making a deposit?

    a. Making deposits always requires the use of the Make Deposits form.

    b. Every sales receipt must go in the Chequing GL account individually.

    c. The deposit total in QuickBooks should match the deposit amount on the bank statement.

    d. The *Deposit To* choice in the Make Deposits form must be the Chequing account.

4. What is the effect of a cash refund on the accounting records?

    a. The Write Cheques form credits the Chequing GL account and debits Income.

    b. The Write Cheques form credits Credit Card fee expense and debits Chequing.

    c. The Write Cheques form debits the Income GL account and credits Undeposited Funds.

    d. The Write Cheques form credits income and debits the Chequing account.

Lesson 6: Entering and Exporting Business Names and Lists

Lesson Objectives

In this lesson, you will inspect business name and list management systems in QuickBooks, discover how to add new names and lists, edit existing ones, continue to practice with report settings, and export reports. Upon successful completion of this lesson, you should be able to:

☐   Navigate Centres.

☐   Create vendor name records.

☐   Create customer name records.

☐   Edit name records.

☐   Access and update related lists.

☐   Memorize and export reports.

Business Names and Information

The practice of bookkeeping requires more than just entering numbers. Often, you need to combine the numbers with information from documents to determine their meaning. The information you need can be anything from the document date and/or number, to what the business purchases and sells, when payments must be made, and the business names and contact details of buyers and sellers. When you enter information correctly, finding what you need is easy. Organizing the information efficiently makes your job easier and ensures that funds go where they should.

This lesson covers the second Administrative Cycle, Lists. You have already encountered lists when entering names, payment types, classes, items, and GL accounts. This lesson focuses mainly on lists for names and the attributes associated with names. Because items and GL accounts control where the numbers belong in the accounting records, each of these lists receives attention in later lessons.

The two main lists of names are Vendors and Customers. Each list appears in a dashboard called a Centre. In this lesson, you will learn where to find lists and how to update them.

While QuickBooks provides easy-to-use methods for storing and accessing the information you need, how you enter that information requires attention and care. When a business is new with only a few entities in the accounting records, finding names is easy. As the business grows, relationships with entities, suppliers, vendors, and customers increase. So, you must ensure that you can continue to locate records by entering them consistently and in a way that people can remember.

At times, you may want to review a list in a spreadsheet or convert it to a mailing list for promotions. We will show you how to export lists as reports to Excel and discuss special exporting features and additional points about memorizing reports.

Entering QuickBooks Names

Objective L-6.1 Navigating Centres

Objective L-6.2 Create vendor name records

Objective L-6.3 Create customer name records

Every entity with a relationship to the business falls into one of four categories (types): Vendor, Customer, Employee, or Other. The Vendors, Customers, and Employees each have a Centre. The *Other* category serves as a miscellaneous or suspense designation. Even though each category or type appears only in its own Centre, QuickBooks stores all entities in one list.

Each name type in QuickBooks has a specific role defined by its relationship to the business. For example, you can select only vendors in the drop-down lists in the forms for vendors, such as the Enter Bills form. Customer names do not appear in the drop-down lists for those forms. Conversely, you can select only customer names in the customer forms, such as the Enter Sales Receipts or Create Invoices forms. All banking forms introduced in previous lessons (the Make Deposits, Write Cheques, and Credit Card forms), allow you to select any name type.

Note: You need to set up the Employee Centre only when using the QuickBooks payroll service. This service is not covered in this course, although payroll posting is part of the Level 2 course.

The Other type is useful for one-time transactions involving the banking forms. For example, if a new delivery service arrives at the last minute and requires payment, you might use the Other name type to record the payment. Since they are new, and no on-going relationship exists, a simple cash transaction is sufficient. You can use the Write Cheques form without entering the delivery service as a vendor. If a vendor sends a refund cheque, you can complete the Make Deposits form without entering the vendor as a customer because the vendor isn't buying anything. If the entity later develops a relationship with the business, you can change the Other name type permanently (and irreversibly) to either a customer or vendor. Using the Other name type limits what you can do with that name, because you cannot use it on name-type-specific forms. You will use the Other type only rarely, because you can usually assign a name to either a vendor or customer type.

Each name has many kinds of available information attributes. The attributes relate mostly to contact information, but you can also add settings for payments, sales tax, and you can define custom attributes. Some of the attributes are tied to a particular name type. In most cases, the standard fields offered will be sufficient because QuickBooks offers coverage for a wide variety of user needs, but you can add custom fields if needed.

The lists of names and their attributes can be accessed in multiple places: From the Reports command in the Menu Bar, from the Home page, from the My Shortcuts sidebar, or from within each Centre.

About the Customer and Vendor Centres

The Customer and Vendor Centres each have the same layout. Figure 6-1a shows the Customer Centre when you first open it.

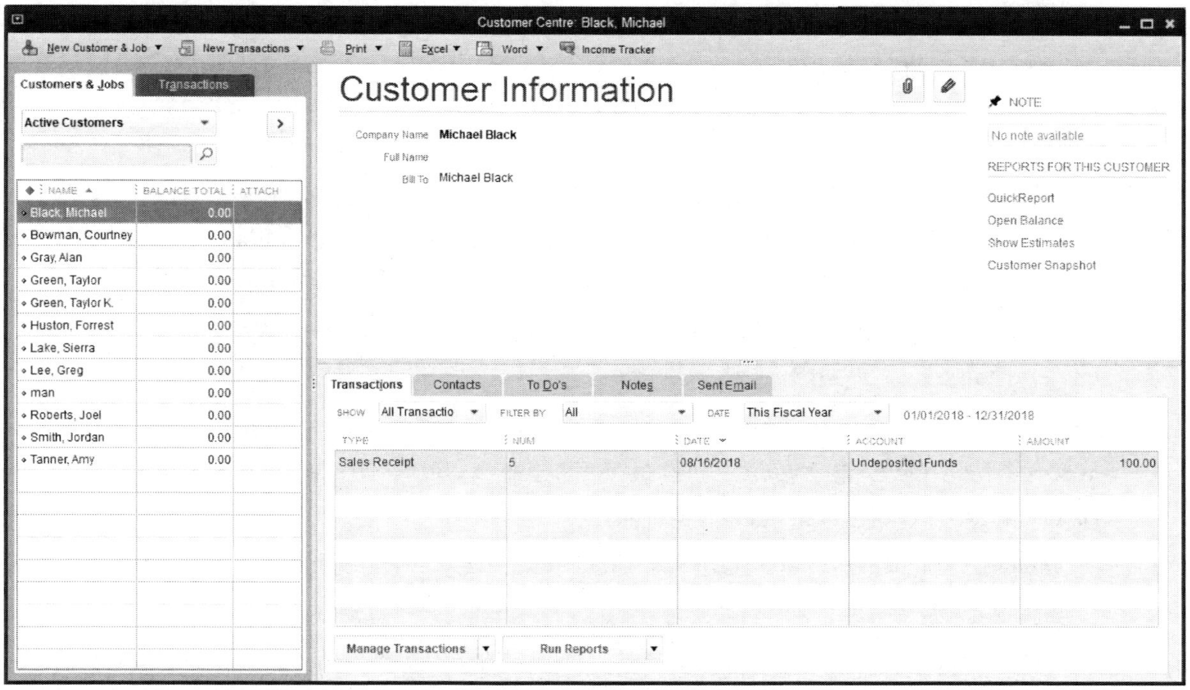

Figure 6-1a: Customer Centre

Figure 6-1b shows the Vendor Centre when you first open it.

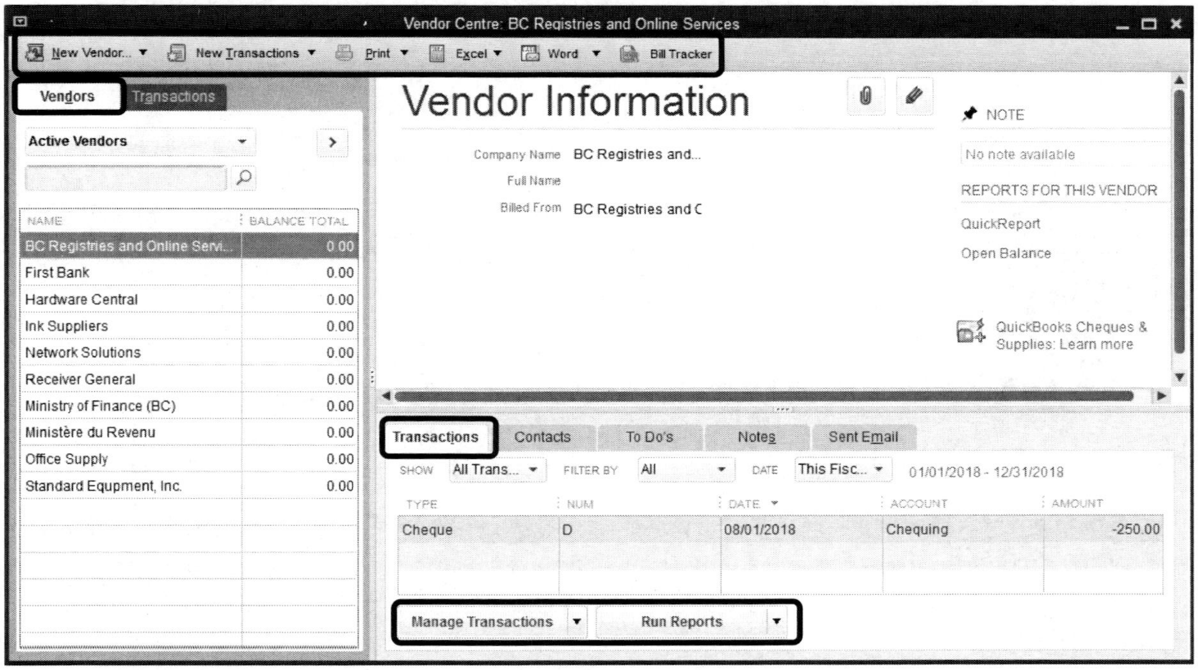

Figure 6-1b: Vendor Centre

The Centres have two main sections. In the left section, two tabs offer choices for the desired view that will appear in the right section. In the Customer Centre, the Customers tab provides summary information about the selected customer at the top right (as shown in Figure 6-1a). Below, additional tabs for that customer manage other information. The Transactions tab lists customer transactions by type on the right for all customers. You can select the type of transaction that appears (for example, estimates, sales orders, invoices, and so on) or view all of them.

In the Vendor Centre, the Vendors tab provides summary information about the selected vendor at the top right (as shown in Figure 6-1b). Below, additional tabs for that vendor manage other information. The Transactions tab lists vendor transactions by type on the right for all vendors. You can select the type of transaction that appears (for example, bills, payments, credit card activities and so on) or view all of them.

As the Centres are so similar in layout and function, we will focus primarily on the Vendor Centre for the remainder of this section. In the Button Bar at the top of the window, you will find buttons to initiate various actions:

- **New Vendor** – allows you to add a new vendor or multiple vendors.
- **New Transactions** – allows you to open forms to enter bills or pay bills.
- **Print** – allows you to print the vendor list, information about one vendor, or the vendor transaction list.
- **Excel** – allows you to export vendor information and lists, and import data from Excel.
- **Word** – provides choices for sending letters.
- **Bill Tracker** – opens a dashboard that provides an overview of open and overdue transactions, as well as a history of vendor transactions.

At the bottom of the right section, there are two additional buttons, Manage Transactions and Run Reports, that offer duplicate access to transaction and report actions. For any name selected in the Vendor and Customer Centres, if you open any form that uses that name type, the form auto-fills with the name.

While the standard column layout in the Centres serves most purposes, you can specify which columns to display in the left and bottom-right sections. Click **View > Customize Columns** in the Menu Bar to specify the vendor attributes to display in the left section. Click **View > Customize Transaction List Columns** to specify the columns to display in the lower-right section.

The other tabs in the lower-right section offer other types of informational data storage:

- **Contacts** – lists people associated with the business entity other than the business owner. For example, you may want to list the name and number of the shipping manager or the accounts receivable person.
- **To Do's** – acts as a reminder list.
- **Notes** – contains additional information you may need to access.
- **Sent Email** – keeps a record of emails you sent to vendors through QuickBooks.

Entering Names in Lists

To avoid common problems, we will now present a few guidelines for entering names. Whenever possible, you should consider the way people look for needed information. Even though QuickBooks has a robust search feature in both the Vendor Centre and the Customer Centre, inconsistent list entries can be challenging to find.

In all lists, each entry must be unique. For most lists this is not a problem. However, certain situations require special knowledge because QuickBooks effectively stores all names in one list. How would you enter names:

- If one person has two relationships with the business, as both a vendor and a customer?
- If you have two customers with the exact same name?

QuickBooks offers a special feature in the names list to handle duplicates within each main list or between them by providing text entry fields for both an ***internal name*** and ***legal name*** for each entity. An internal name means that the name shows only in documents that stay inside the company, such as reports or lists. The internal name is a subset of the legal name and must be unique. The legal name is the official entity name, or the way you want it to appear in documents such as cheques or statements. QuickBooks allows duplicate legal names because they can be differentiated by their subsets (the internal name). Because some businesses may have the same name but multiple locations, this is a helpful feature. If the entity is a business, then the internal and legal names could be the same, or the internal name could be abbreviated or entered with key initials or could include a location reference. First, we'll demonstrate what to do with duplicates within a type, then between the customer and vendor types.

Creating Duplicate Names within a Type

Figure 6-2 shows a section of the Edit Customer form. Note the two boxed fields. Best Custom T-Shirts already has a customer named Taylor Green, one of the partners. Her internal name is entered following the *last name, first name* protocol in the Customer Name field. Then, her legal name is entered in the Company Name field. Notice that her name appears as required for printing on cheques or for mailing a letter as *first name, last name*.

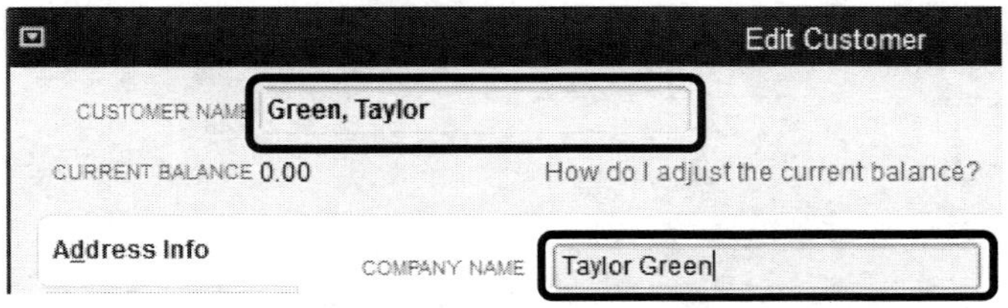

Figure 6-2: Edit Customer form, existing customer

If you need to add another customer named Taylor Green, you need to create a unique version of the internal name. In Figure 6-3, adding the middle initial for the second Taylor Green in the CUSTOMER NAME field in a new customer record allows both names to exist as customers using the same legal, or company, name.

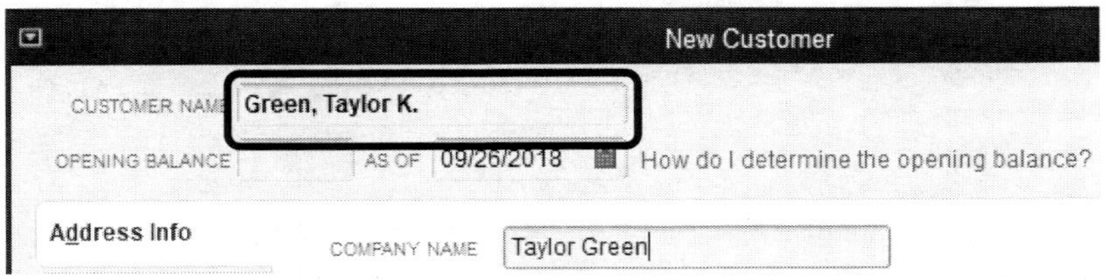

Figure 6-3: New customer with the same name

At a minimum, you must enter a name in the Customer Name field to add a new customer. QuickBooks allows you to create a new record using only this internal name even while in the middle of entering a transaction.

Using the Quick Add Feature

Generally, when an exercise directs you to select a name, you will use a drop-down menu. However, you can also start typing the first few letters of a name and an auto-fill feature completes it. If no match exists, the entire drop-down list of names appears so you can select a name. If you then realize you need to enter a new name, you could press TAB to use the Quick Add feature.

For example, suppose you want to specify the name *Liz Manning* in the PAY TO THE ORDER OF field in the Write Cheques form, but typing *man* does not bring up the name. If you press TAB, the Name Not Found pop up message (Figure 6-4) appears.

Figure 6-4: Name Not Found pop up message

If you click the Quick Add button, the available name types appear in the Select Name Type dialog box (Figure 6-5).

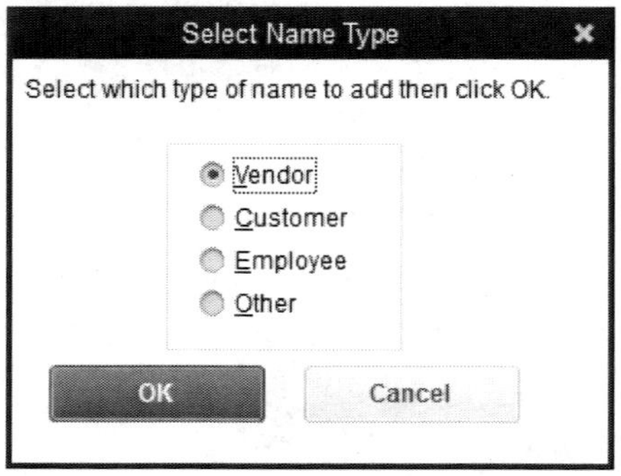

Figure 6-5: Select Name Type dialog box

At this point, selecting the Customer radio button and clicking OK accepts whatever you typed in the form (in this case, "man"), whether it is correct or not, and creates a new name record.

While the Quick Add feature can be helpful, in this case QuickBooks creates a record for a customer named man. The incorrect customer record needs to be corrected (Figure 6-6).

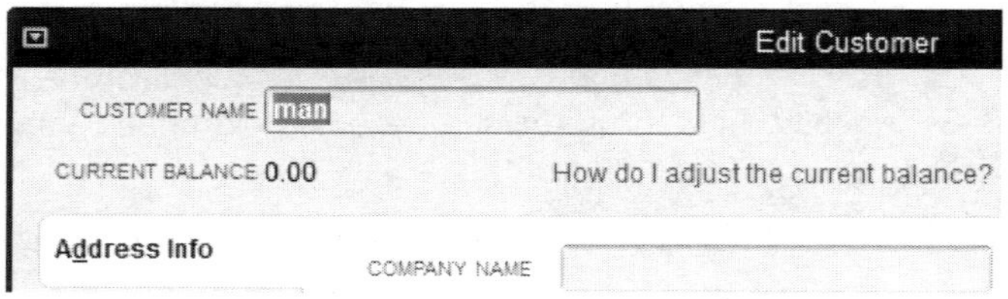

Figure 6-6: Customer name record needs editing

To prevent an extra editing step, click the Set Up button in the Name Not Found pop up message (Figure 6-4) instead of the Quick Add button. This displays the full Edit Customer form where you can enter both the internal and legal names. If you ever intend to send an external document to the entity, such as a cheque, the legal name must be entered, or no name will print on the cheque.

Note: Another way to avoid an extra editing step is to click Cancel in the Name Not Found pop up, type the correct internal name in the form, and then use the Quick Add feature to create the new record.

Creating Duplicate Names across Types

Let's consider now how to add customer Taylor K. Green as a vendor. When we create a new vendor record for her, we can add a *V* to the last name in the internal Vendor Name field, as shown in Figure 6-7.

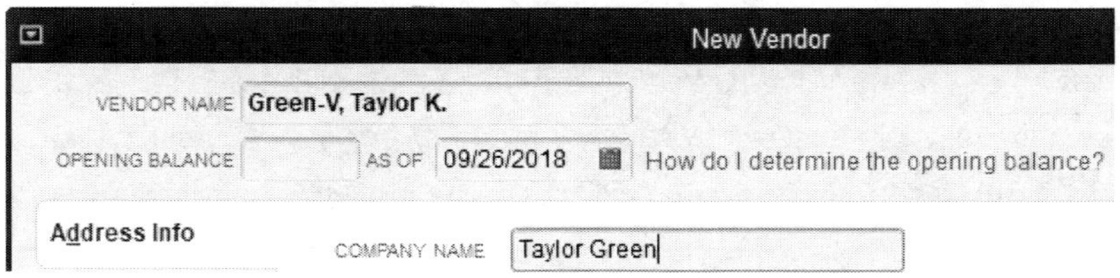

Figure 6-7: Adding customer as vendor

In the reverse case, if Taylor K. Green already had a Vendor record and needed to be added as a Customer, you could add a *C* to the Customer record.

The Importance of Using Consistent Naming Conventions

Because QuickBooks accepts only unique names, the problems you find with inconsistent naming are apparent. Let's say the business protocol is to enter names *last name, first name*. If someone entered Taylor Green's name in the internal Customer Name field following the *first name, last name* protocol instead, then someone else using the file could think the name still needed to be entered. Even one additional space or period in the name makes it unique.

Adding Vendor and Customer Names

In the Vendor Centre, you can click **New Vendor > New Vendor** to display the New Vendor form to add a new vendor. (Similarly, in the Customer Centre, you can click **New Customer & Job > New Customer** to display the New Customer form to add a new customer.)

Figure 6-8 shows new vendor information being added in the Address Info tab of the New Vendor form.

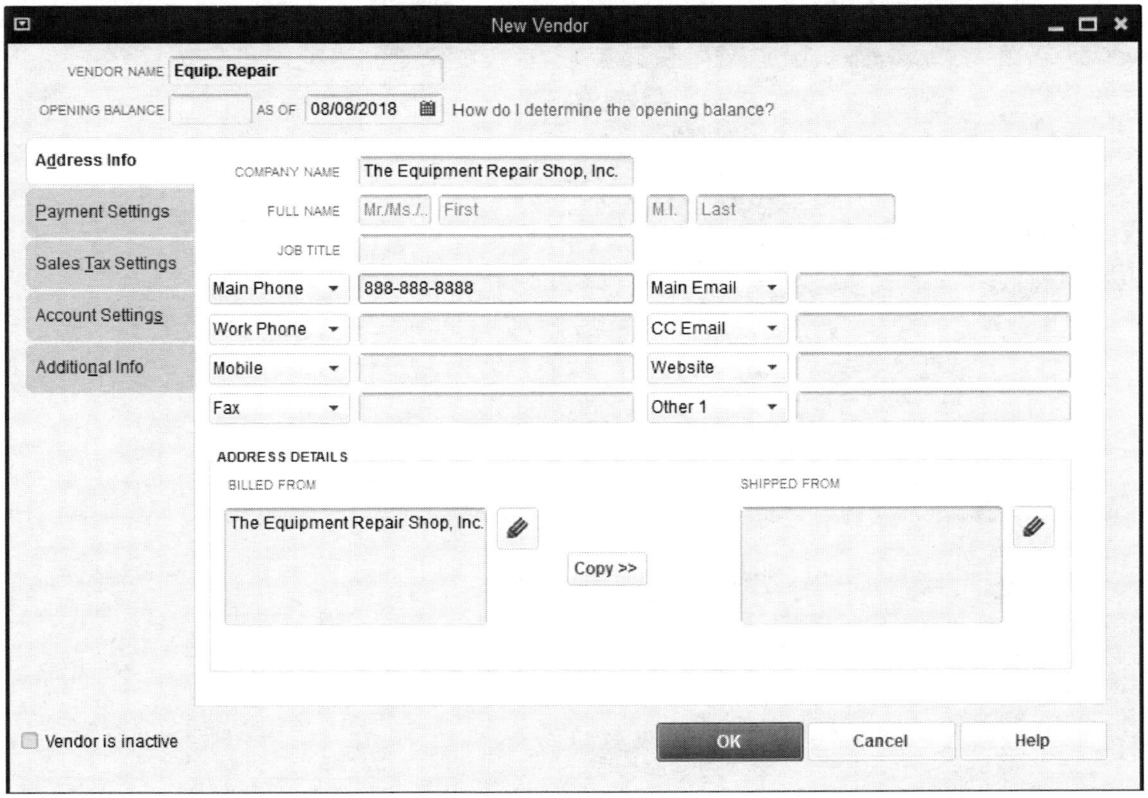

Figure 6-8: New Vendor form

So far, the user has entered the internal vendor name (in the VENDOR NAME field), the legal company name (in the COMPANY NAME field), and a phone number. Notice that the legal name also appears in the Billed From address block. QuickBooks auto-fills this field with the legal name as soon as the cursor leaves the Company Name field. If you notice a mistake in the company name later, the mistake must also be corrected in the Billed From field.

It is important to remember that the internal name, legal name, and address block have character limits, so you may need to abbreviate entries. After the address block auto-fills with the company name, the rest of the address can be entered as shown in Figure 6-9. In this field, using the ENTER key will not save the entry, but moves the cursor to the next line. If needed, you can click the Copy button to copy the address to the Shipped From address block, which ensures both address blocks contain the correct information.

ADDRESS DETAILS

BILLED FROM

The Equipment Repair Shop, Inc
10 North Main Street.
Vancouver, BC V7H 2G1

Copy >>

SHIPPED FROM

Figure 6-9: Address block

You can add as much information as necessary in the contact detail fields. Each of the text fields has a drop-down menu that offers choices related to what appears on the button label. The drop-down menu for each field has the same set of choices ranging from internet phone numbers to social media accounts.

In the New Vendor and New Customer forms, the choices in the Additional Info tab are very similar. Figure 6-10a and Figure 6-10b show the Additional Info tab in each form.

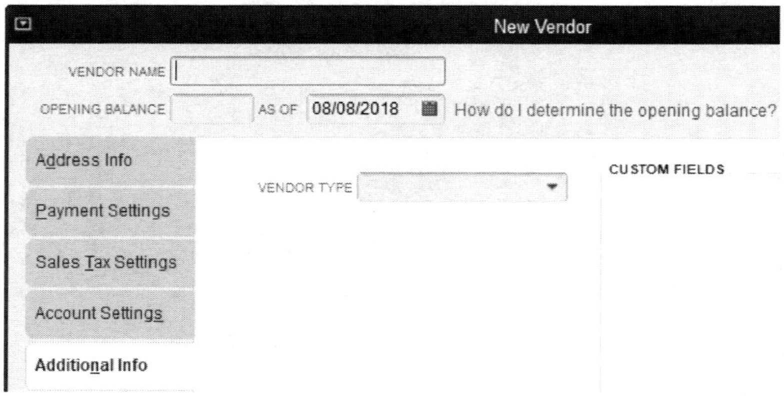

New Vendor

VENDOR NAME

OPENING BALANCE   AS OF 08/08/2018 📅 How do I determine the opening balance?

Address Info

Payment Settings   VENDOR TYPE

Sales Tax Settings

Account Settings

Additional Info

CUSTOM FIELDS

Figure 6-10a: New Vendor form, Additional Info tab

New Customer

CUSTOMER NAME

OPENING BALANCE   AS OF 08/08/2018 📅 How do I determine the opening balance?

Address Info

Payment Settings   CUSTOMER TYPE

Sales Tax Settings   REP

Additional Info

CUSTOM FIELDS

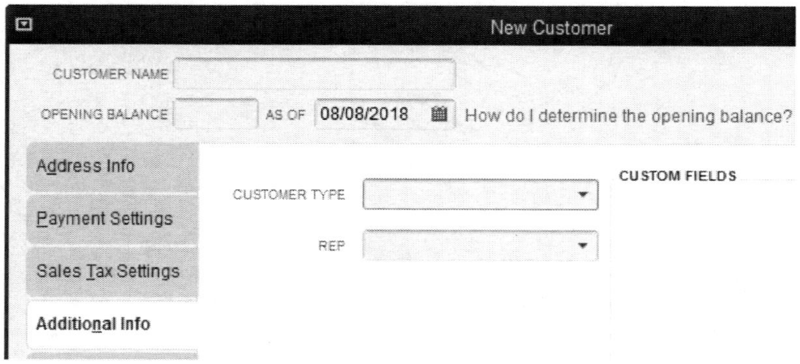

Figure 6-10b: New Customer form, Additional Info tab

The Vendor Type and Customer Type drop-down menus are two of the attribute lists. The key point of these two types is that, as a business grows, locating sub-sections of customers and vendors can be easier if they are categorized. QuickBooks suggests classifying customers according to where they heard about the business, by their industry type, or by their entity type (individual or business). Classifying vendors as suppliers or consultants might be helpful.

Note: The *Examining Other Lists* section of this lesson covers how to change attribute lists.

In Figure 6-10b above, notice the REP field that appears in the Additional Info tab of the New Customer form. If the business employs people who help bring in customers and their business, then often these sales representatives, who are entered as vendors, receive commissions. Knowing which customer is associated with which sales rep can be very important.

Finally, in case you need to retain additional pieces of information, you can set up custom fields. If you click the Define Fields button in the Custom Fields section, the Set up Custom Fields for Names dialog box appears (Figure 6-11). Once you create a custom field and use it, the field can be modified but not deleted.

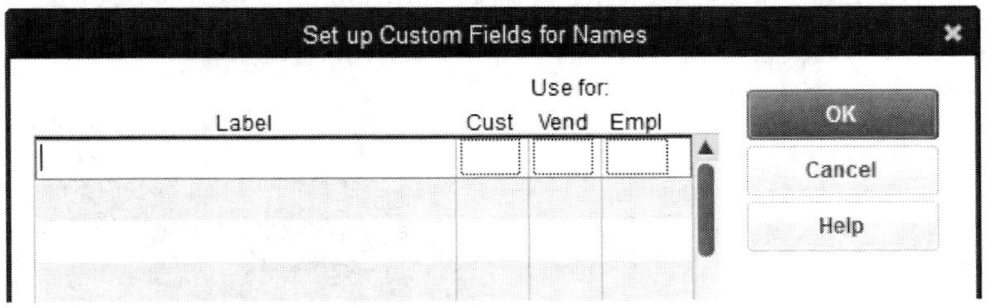

Figure 6-11: Set up Custom Fields for Names dialog box

Adding Vendor-specific Names

Vendors have fields specific to their type, as shown in the Payment Settings tab of the Edit Vendor form (Figure 6-12).

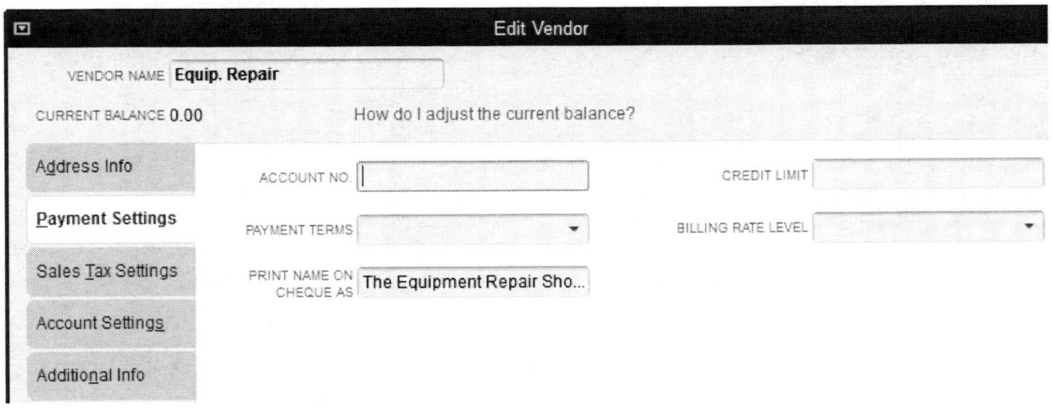

Figure 6-12: Edit Vendor form, Payment Settings

There are five fields in the Payment Settings tab:

- **ACCOUNT NO.** – stores the business account number with the vendor. However, a more useful place for this can be in the memo that prints on cheques or purchase documents for the vendor.

- **PAYMENT TERMS** – This is a drop-down menu selection for the length of time credit is extended from the date on the bill (vendor invoice) to the date the bill should be paid. Payment terms will also indicate whether a discount is available for early payment and, if so, when it must be paid. Any penalty for late payment will also appear here. Lessons 7 and 10 cover this in more depth.

- **PRINT NAME ON CHEQUE AS** – This is the legal name that auto-fills after you enter it in the New Vendor form, but you can modify it if needed.

- **CREDIT LIMIT** – Some vendors may have a limit on how much, in dollars, the business can order from them, just as a credit card usually has a limit.

- **BILLING RATE LEVEL** – This is an advanced feature not covered in this course.

The Account Settings tab allows you to specify auto-fill options that can fill in account information when you enter bills for a vendor.

Adding Customer-specific Names

For customers, the Job Info tab (in the New Customer and Edit Customer forms) is used only when one customer has multiple jobs. In QuickBooks, a *job* could be one of several projects you perform for a customer. Entering information for specific jobs allows you to track your income and expenses on a job-by-job basis.

The Payment Settings for customers and vendors have some fields in common, but there are many more options for customers because of the additional credit card information fields. QuickBooks offers an integrated credit card processing system with good information security.

Customers have fields specific to their type, as shown in the Payment Settings tab of the New Customer form (Figure 6-13).

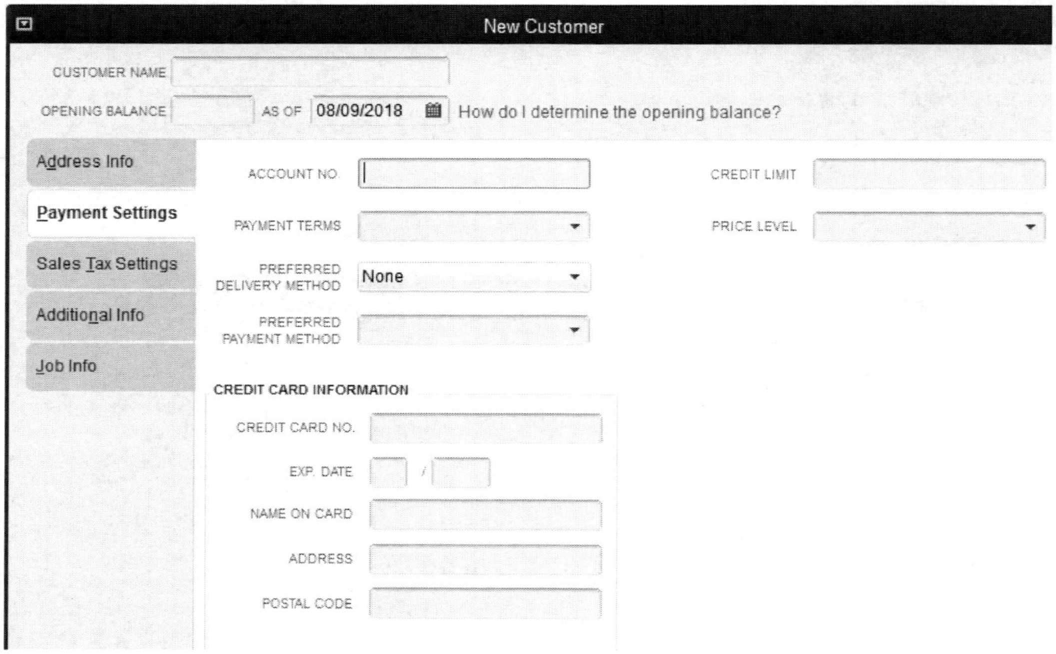

Figure 6-13: New Customer form, Payment Settings

There are six fields in the Payment Settings tab, three of which also appear for vendors:

- **ACCOUNT NO.** – Each customer usually has a number for the business that you can enter in this form.

- **PAYMENT TERMS** – This drop-down menu provides options that state the length of time the business extends credit to the customer. Payment terms will also state when the customer is entitled to a discount for early payment and when there will be a penalty for late payment. Lessons 8 and 10 cover this in more depth.

- **CREDIT LIMIT** – If the business places a credit limit on the customer, you enter it in this field.

- **PRICE LEVEL** – This is an advanced feature not covered in this course.
- **PREFERRED DELIVERY METHOD** – Specify how to deliver paperwork to the customer, by mail or email.
- **PREFERRED PAYMENT METHOD** – This is the same list as the Payment Terms that are available in forms and includes credit cards, cheques, and EFTs.

Editing Vendor and Customer Names

Objective L-6.4 Edit name records

Once a vendor or customer record exists, making changes simply requires opening the Edit Vendor or Edit Customer form from within their respective Centres. Double-click the name you want to edit, and the form appears.

Exercise 6.1: Adding and Editing Names

In this exercise, you will add a name, correct an existing name using the Quick Add feature, and add a customer as a vendor.

1. Launch **QuickBooks** if necessary, and restore **Best Custom T-Shirts C1_L6_A (Portable).QBM** from the *1767-Student-Files\Lesson 6\StarterFiles* folder. Save the restored company file as **Best Custom T-Shirts C1_L6_,your name>.QBW** in the *1767-Student-Files\Lesson 6\My Projects* folder.

2. Change the Company Name to **Best Custom T-Shirts C1_L6_<your name>**.

Add a new customer.

3. Click **Customers > Customer Centre**. The Customer Centre appears.

4. In the *New Customer & Job* drop-down menu, select **New Customer**. The New Customer form appears.

5. In the *CUSTOMER NAME* field, type: **Novak, Janice**.

6. In the *COMPANY NAME* field, type: **Janice Novak**.

7. Click the **Additional Info** tab and, in the *CUSTOMER TYPE* drop-down menu, select **Retail**.

8. Click **OK** to add Janice Novak as a customer.

Modify an existing customer.

9. In the *Customers & Jobs* tab, double-click the customer **man.** The Edit Customer form appears.

10. In the *CUSTOMER NAME* field, delete or select the text **man**, and then type: **Manning, Liz**.

11. In the *COMPANY NAME* field, type: **Liz Manning**.

12. Copy what you just typed in the *COMPANY NAME* field and paste it over the text **man** in the INVOICE/Bill to address block.

13. Click **OK**. *Manning, Liz* replaces *man* in the Customers & Jobs tab.

14. Close the Customer Centre.

Add a customer as a vendor.

15. Click **Vendors > Vendor Centre**. The Vendor Centre appears.

---

16. In the *New Vendor* drop-down menu, select **New Vendor**. The New Vendor form appears.

17. In the *VENDOR NAME* field, type: **Novak-V, Janice**.

18. In the *COMPANY NAME* field, type: **Janice Novak**.

19. Click **OK** to add Janice Novak as a new vendor.

20. Close the Vendor Centre.

Leave the company file open for the next exercise.

Examining Other Lists

Objective L-6.5 Access and update related lists

You can access the lists related to names by clicking **Lists > Customer & Vendor Profile Lists** in the Menu Bar, as shown in Figure 6-14.

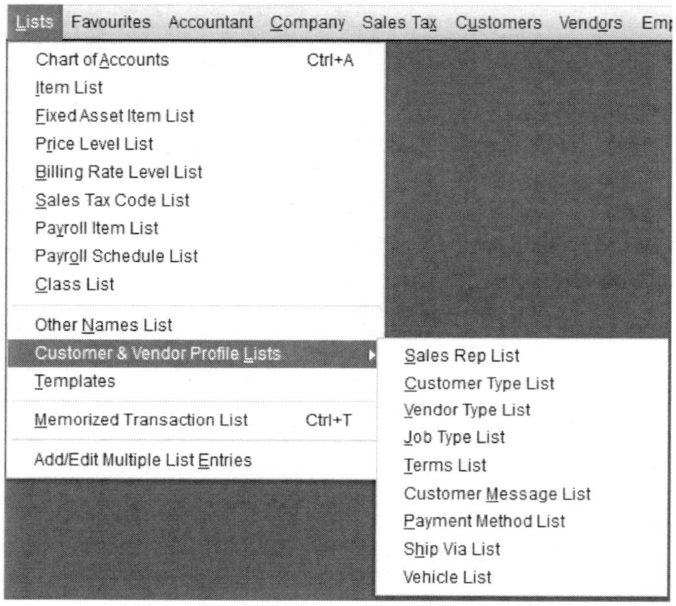

Figure 6-14: Accessing customer and vendor lists from the Menu Bar

Notice the variety of name lists.

We'll look at the Payment Method List to see how to add or edit entries in the list, and then at the Sales Rep List. In the Vendor Type List, we'll look at an important QuickBooks feature available in many lists—the creation of sub-types that groups list items into a hierarchy.

Figure 6-15 shows the Payment Method List and the Payment Method drop-down menu.

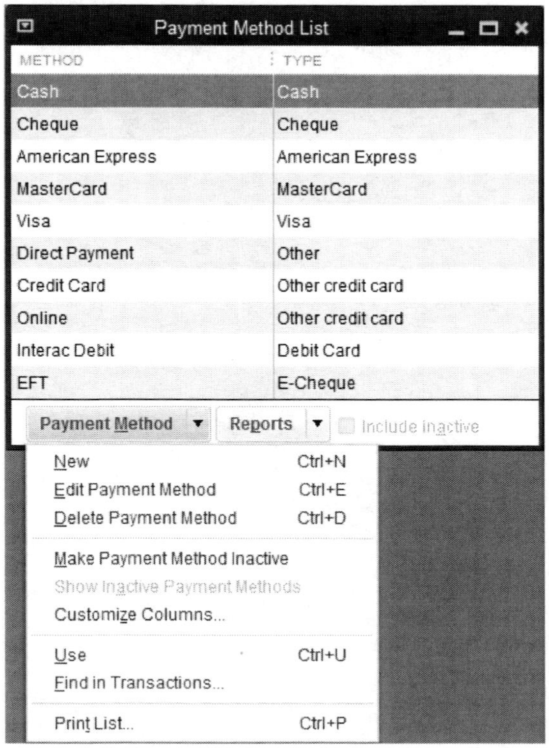

Figure 6-15: Payment Method List

Note: The Payment Method drop-down menu, while specific to this list, is also **QB Global**. All lists use the same actions to create new entries. You can also access these actions from the Edit command in the Menu Bar when the list window is open. Also, creating a hierarchy through sub-types operates in the same manner in each list that offers it. Usually, all lists provide multiple options for deactivating an entry, which hides it from view in the list. No list entry can be deleted if it is used in any transaction.

Selecting New in the Payment Method drop-down menu, or pressing CTRL+N, opens the New Payment Method window, shown in Figure 6-16. Selecting Edit Payment Method or pressing CTRL+E opens the Edit Payment Method window, in which you can edit an existing entry. You can edit all list entries even when they are used in transactions.

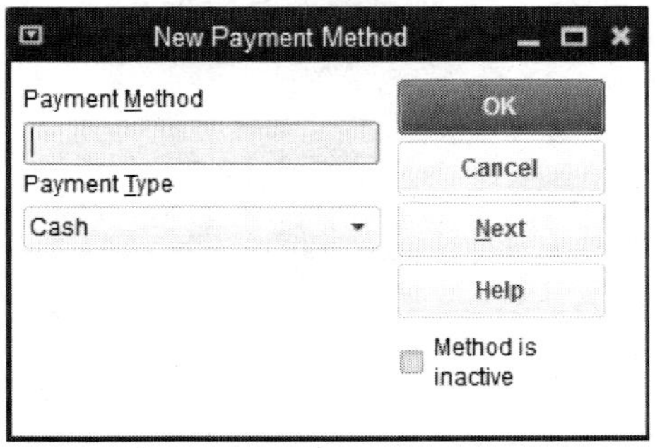

Figure 6-16: New Payment Method window

You can use the New Payment Method window to add a new payment method and specify the payment type. The existing options in the Payment Type drop-down menu are an extended list of the payment methods. Later, if you no longer need the payment method, you can select the Method is inactive check box.

Figure 6-17 shows the Sales Rep List and the New Sales Rep window, in which you can add a new sales rep.

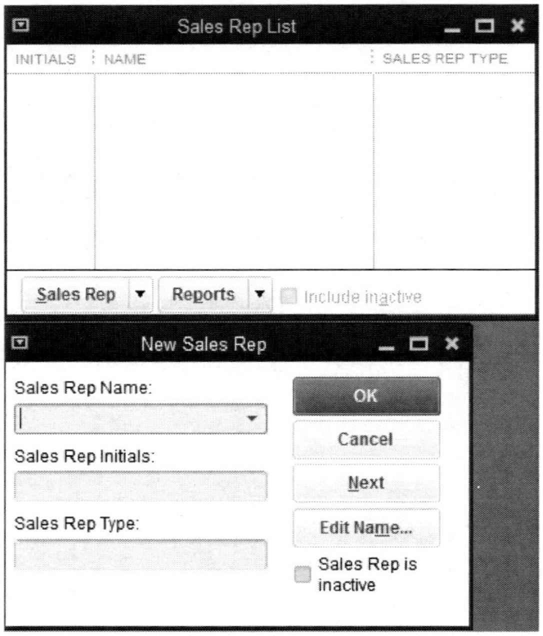

Figure 6-17: Sales Rep List and New Sales Rep window

In the New Sales Rep window, the sales rep must exist as a vendor in order to appear in the Sales Rep Name drop-down menu. After choosing the vendor, the Sales Rep Initials field will auto-fill with several letters, usually the first initial of the first name followed by the first initial of the last name—this can be modified to include up to five letters in case of duplicates or for clarity.

Figure 6-18a shows the Vendor Type List and the New Vendor Type window.

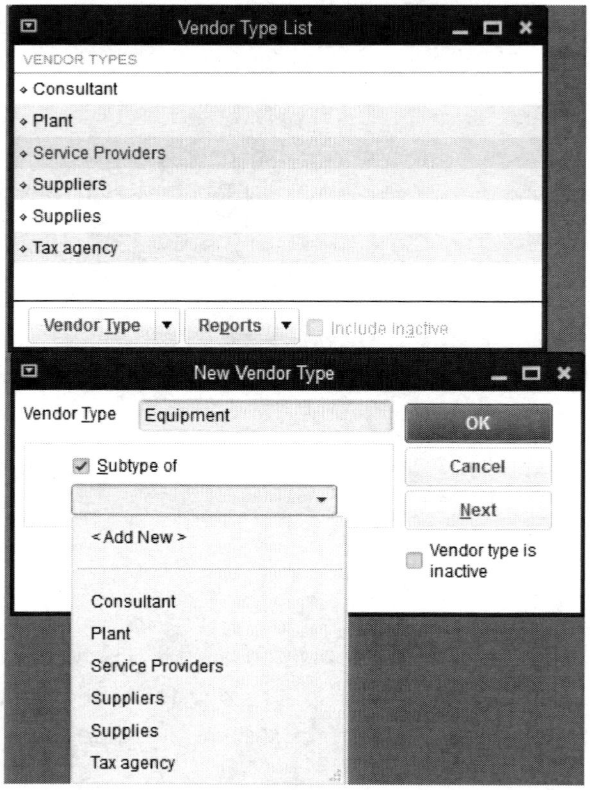

Figure 6-18a: Vendor Type List and New Vendor Type window

Notice that the Subtype of check box is selected for the new Vendor Type, *Equipment*. The Subtype of drop-down menu displays the existing vendor types. You can use the Subtype of drop-down menu to specify the parent vendor of the new vendor you are adding, thereby creating a hierarchy.

Note: The process of creating hierarchy in QuickBooks is another **QB Global** action. This works the same way in all lists. When the new entry needs to be shown on one line, then a colon separates the header or highest level of hierarchy from the sub-type; for example, Plant: Equipment.

Figure 6-18b shows the Vendor Type List after assigning the new vendor you created, *Equipment*, as a sub-type of the existing vendor, *Plant*. Plant is now the parent vendor of Equipment in the hierarchy.

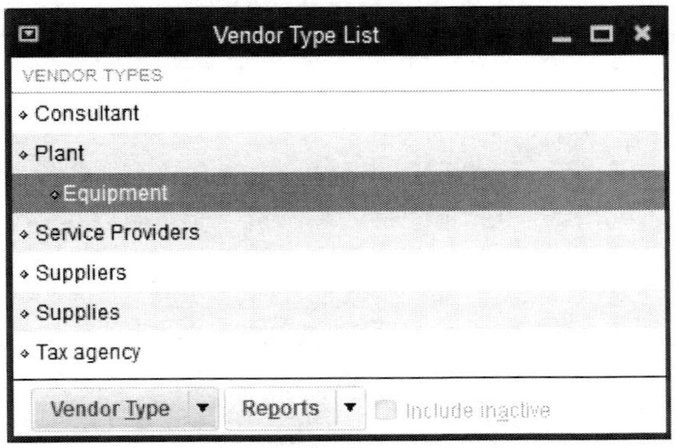

Figure 6-18b: Plant sub-type—Equipment

Figure 6-18c shows the Edit Vendor Type window, in which you can edit an existing vendor.

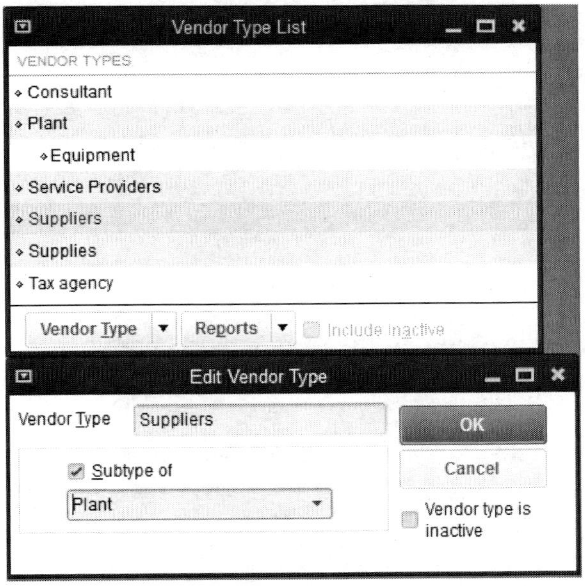

Figure 6-18c: Edit Vendor Type window

Figure 6-18d shows the Vendor Type List after assigning an existing vendor, *Suppliers*, as a sub-type of the existing vendor, *Plant*. Plant is now the parent vendor of Equipment and Suppliers in the hierarchy.

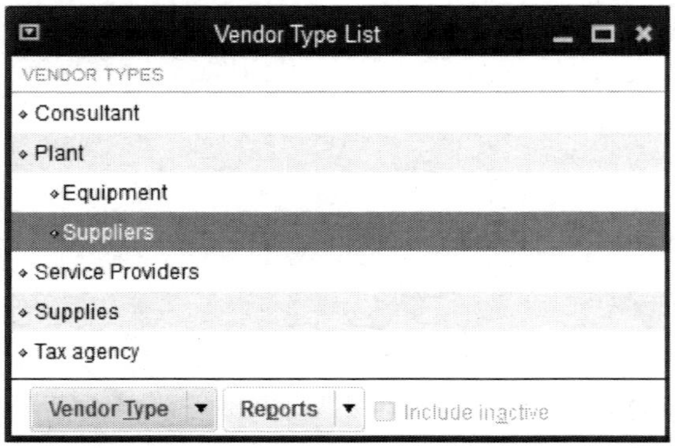

Figure 6-18d: Plant sub-types—Equipment and Suppliers

Exercise 6.2: Modifying Lists

In this exercise, you will open and modify the Payment Method List, the Sales Rep List, and the Vendor Type List.

Add a new payment type to the Payment Type List.

1. Ensure that the company file you worked on in the previous exercise is still open.

2. Click **Lists > Customer & Vendor Profile Lists > Payment Method List**. The Payment Method List appears.

3. Click the **Payment Method** drop-down menu and select **New**. The New Payment Method window appears.

4. In the *Payment Method* field, type: **Discover Card**.

5. In the *Payment Type* drop-down menu, select **Other credit card**, then click **OK**. Your new payment method appears in the Payment Method List.

6. Close the Payment Method List.

Add a new sales rep to the Sales Rep List.

7. Click **Lists > Customer & Vendor Profile Lists > Sales Rep List**. The Sales Rep List appears.

8. Click the **Sales Rep** drop-own menu and select **New**. The New Sales Rep window appears.

9. In the *Sales Rep Name* drop-down menu, select **Novak-V, Janice**. The *Sales Rep Initials* and *Sales Rep Type* fields should auto-fill with the new sales rep's information because she is an existing vendor.

10. If necessary, in the *Sales Rep Initials* field, type: **JN**.

11. If necessary, in the *Sales Rep Type* field, type: **Vendor**.

12. Click **OK** to add the new sales rep to the Sales Rep List.

13. Close the Sales Rep List.

Add a new vendor type to the Vendor Type List.

14. Click **Lists > Customer & Vendor Profile Lists > Vendor Type List**. The Vendor Type List appears.

15. Click the **Vendor Type** drop-down menu and select **New**. The New Vendor Type window appears.

16. In the *Vendor Type* field, type: **Plant**.

17. Click **OK**. The new vendor type appears in the Vendor Type List.

Add a new vendor sub-type to the Vendor Type List.

18. In the Vendor Type List, click the **Vendor Type** drop-down menu and select **New**. The New Vendor Type window appears.

19. In the *Vendor Type* field, type: **Equipment**.

20. Select the **Subtype of** check box, display the drop-down menu below it, and then select **Plant**.

21. Click **OK**. Notice that *Equipment* now appears in the Vendor Type List as a sub-type of *Plant*.

22. Close the Vendor Type List.

Leave the company file open for the next exercise.

Exporting Memorized Reports and Lists

Objective L-6.6 Memorize and export reports

You will not export lists as often as reports, but knowing how to create a list with the information you need is important. You can also specify multiple Excel options that work the same way for reports and lists.

To access the Customer Contact List (Figure 6-19), click **Reports > Customers & Receivables > Customer Contact List** in the Menu Bar.

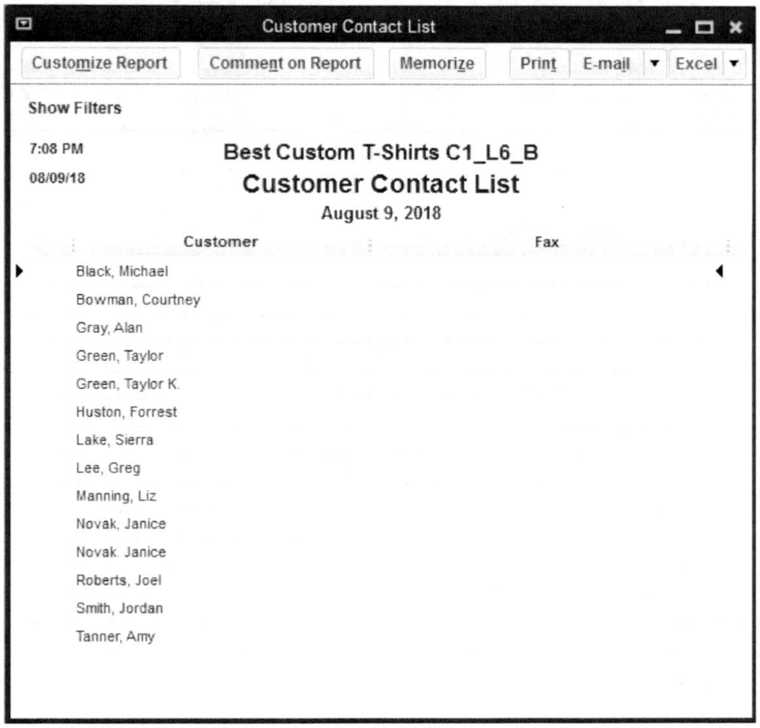

Figure 6-19: Customer Contact List

You can click the Customize Report button to customize the Customer Contact List by specifying the columns of information you want to display. Figure 6-19 shows the list with only the Customer and Fax columns. If you specify to display all columns of information, you can see what data the system currently contains and what relationships exist among the column selections and the data entry fields.

You can memorize the customer list by clicking the Memorize button or pressing CTRL+M. You can also save the memorized report in a Report Group, change the report title, and open the memorized report to make a change. To change the report title, click the Customize Report button and enter a new name in the Report Title field in the Header/Footer tab, as shown in Figure 6-20.

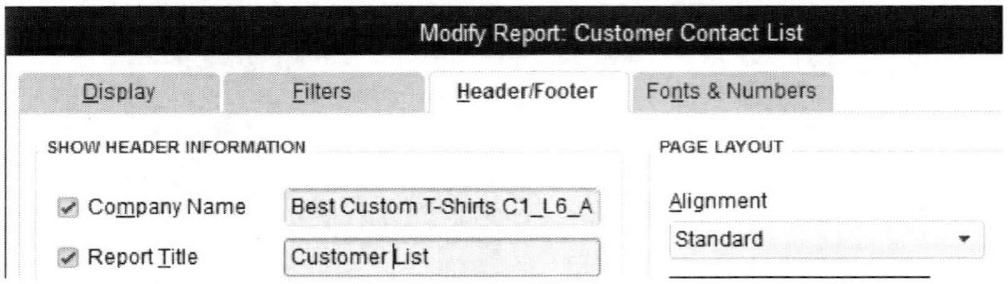

Figure 6-20: Modify report title

When you close a memorized report, the Memorize Report message shown in Figure 6-21 appears, asking if you want to memorize the custom report.

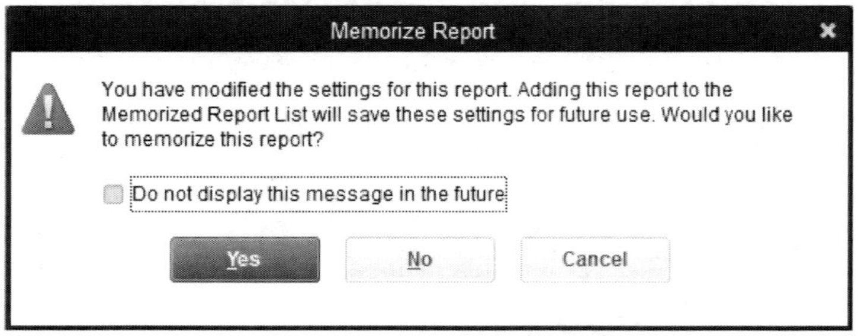

Figure 6-21: Memorize Report message

It is best to leave the Do not display this message in the future check box deselected so that the message will continue to appear. If you click the No button, the report will not be saved. If you click the Yes button, the message in Figure 6-22 appears.

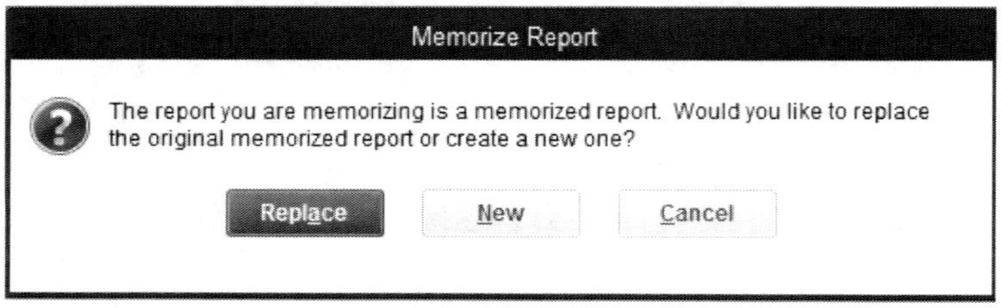

Figure 6-22: Memorize Report—Replace or New

Clicking the Replace button substitutes the current changes for any prior changes. Clicking the New button takes you back to the window that allows you to create a new memorized report.

Another feature of memorized reports is that you can run multiple reports at the same time. This is especially helpful if you routinely run the same set of reports—you can process the entire set at once and make sure you do not overlook any. Click **Reports > Memorized Reports > Memorized Report List** in the Menu Bar to display the Memorized Report List window, shown in Figure 6-23.

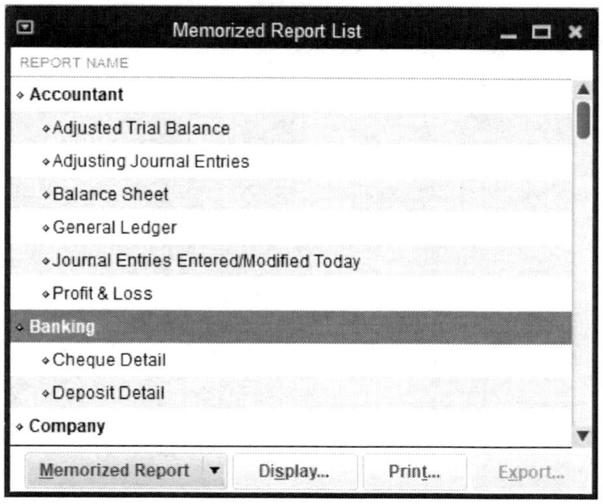

Figure 6-23: Memorized Report List window

You can either double-click one of the group headers (such as *Banking*) or click the Print button to display the Process Multiple Reports dialog box, shown in Figure 6-24.

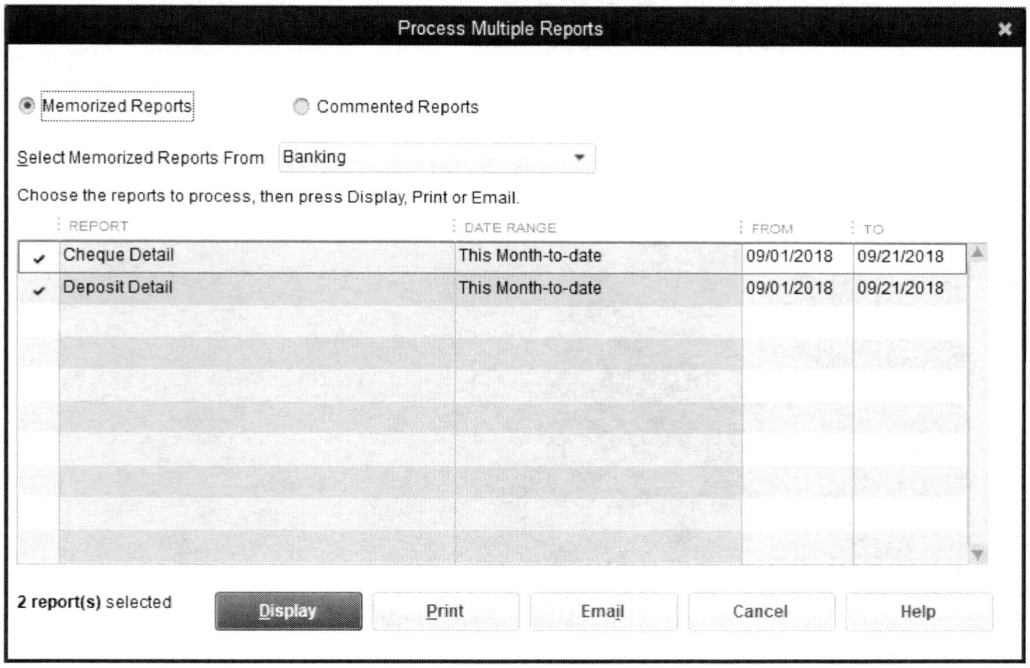

Figure 6-24: Process Multiple Reports dialog box

You can use the Process Multiple Reports dialog box to specify the report parameters. You can click Display to open the selected reports so you can check them prior to exporting them.

After you display a report or a list, you can click the Excel drop-down button (Figure 6-25) to create a new worksheet or update an existing worksheet.

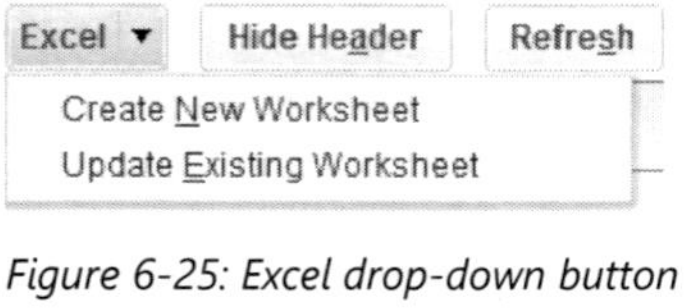

Figure 6-25: Excel drop-down button

Selecting Create New Worksheet displays the Send Report to Excel dialog box, shown in Figure 6-26.

Figure 6-26: Send Report to Excel dialog box

For now, we will focus on the top three radio buttons. Clicking the Create new worksheet radio button displays the *in new workbook* and *in existing workbook* radio buttons. If you click the *in new workbook* radio button and then click Export, the report or list will open in a new Excel workbook, as shown in Figure 6-27.

A	B	C	D	E	F	G	H
		Customer		Fax			
		Black, Michael					
		Bowman, Courtney					
		Gray, Alan					
		Green, Taylor					
		Green, Taylor K.					
		Huston, Forrest					
		Lake, Sierra					
		Lee, Greg					
		Manning, Liz					
		Novak, Janice					
		Novak. Janice					
		Roberts, Joel					
		Smith, Jordan					
		Tanner, Amy					

QuickBooks Desktop Export Tips   Sheet1

Figure 6-27: Excel—new workbook

Notice the QuickBooks Desktop Export Tips worksheet that appears to the left of the exported report. This worksheet provides tips for updating the Excel report with new QuickBooks data.

If you click the *in existing workbook* radio button in the Send Report to Excel dialog box, the options in the dialog box will change, as shown in Figure 6-28.

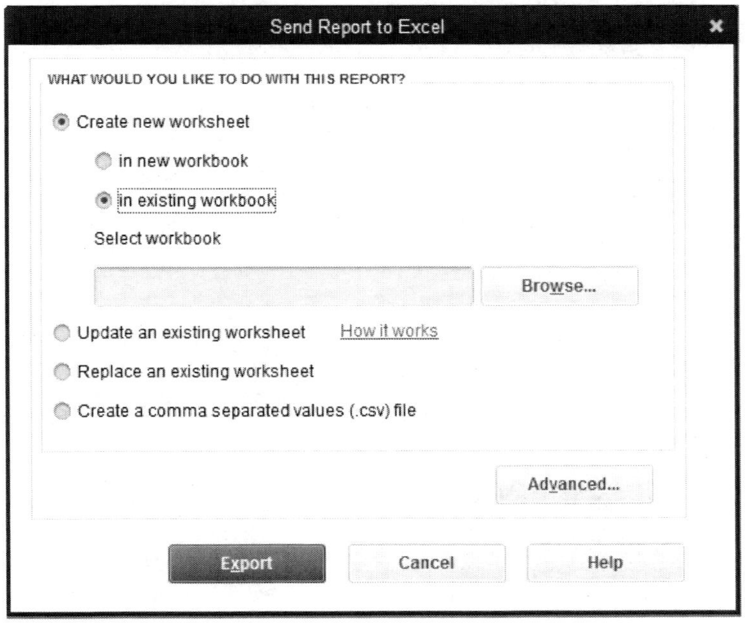

Figure 6-28: Send Report to Excel dialog box—in existing workbook

If you previously used the *in existing workbook* radio button, an existing workbook file and location may appear in the Select workbook field. Because it may be difficult to read the full file path, and because the file that appears may not be the correct one or may not be in the correct location, it is a good idea to use the Browse button to confirm the file name and location. This is a good practice before clicking the Export button and adding a worksheet to an existing file. Because the export is not final until you save the Excel file, you can close the Excel file and try again if you make a mistake.

If you send a memorized report to the same file name and location on your computer more than once, QuickBooks will display the file and its location in the Send Report to Excel dialog box each time you open it.

Finally, if you click the Advanced button, the Advanced Excel Options dialog box appears, as shown in Figure 6-29 with the default selections. The first four check boxes in the QuickBooks Options section govern how reports will look in Excel. Unless you need no space between columns, keeping these check boxes selected will produce Excel reports that are easy to read when printed.

Recall the QuickBooks Desktop Export Tips worksheet shown in Figure 6-27. If you don't want this worksheet to appear in the Excel file, deselect the Include QuickBooks Export Guide worksheet with helpful advice check box.

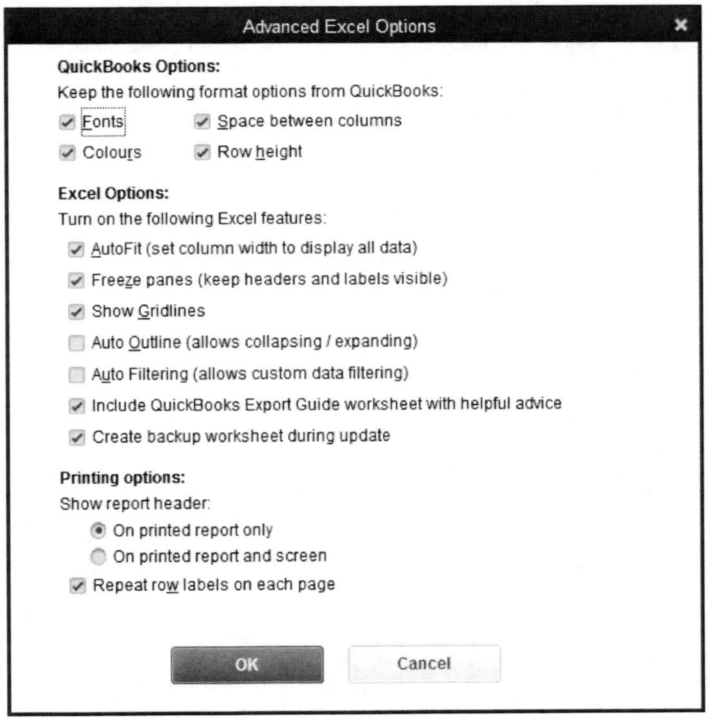

Figure 6-29: Advanced Excel Options dialog box

Exercise 6.3: Exporting Memorized Reports and Lists

Note: Steps 19-30 of this exercise require Microsoft Excel. If Excel is not installed, skip these steps.

In this exercise, you will customize, memorize, and export the customer contact list to Excel.

Customize the Customer Contact List.

1. Ensure that the company file you worked on in the previous exercise is still open.

2. Click **Reports > Customers & Receivables > Customer Contact List**. The Customer Contact List appears.

3. Click the **Customize Report** button, and then select **Customer** in the COLUMNS list (if necessary) to ensure the customer name will appear in the list. Deselect all other columns that are selected to narrow your list to customer names only.

4. Change the title of the report by clicking the **Header/Footer** tab and, in the *Report Title* field, type your name after *Customer Contact List*.

5. Filter the list by clicking the **Filters** tab, select **Customer Type** in the *CHOOSE FILTER* list, and then select **Retail** in the *Customer Type* drop-down menu.

6. Click **OK**. The contact list with a single column of customer names and new title will appear. The list should contain one item—*Novak, Janice*.

Memorize the report.

7. Click the **Memorize** button to display the Memorize Report dialog box.

8. In the *Name* field, type: **Customer Contact List - <name>** if it did not auto-fill.

9. Select the **Save in Memorized Report Group** check box and select **Customers** in the drop-down menu.

10. Click **OK** to save the memorized Customer Contact List to the Customers Report Group.

11. Close the memorized Customer Contact List.

12. Click **Reports > Memorized Reports > Memorized Report List**. The Memorized Report List window appears.

13. Scroll to view the *Customers* heading in the Memorized Report List window to see that your new memorized report appears in the Customers group.

14. In the Memorized Report List window, scroll up and then double-click **Banking** to display the Process Multiple Reports dialog box for the Banking group.

15. Ensure that the **Memorized Reports** radio button is selected, and that **Banking** appears in the *Select Memorized Reports From* drop-down menu.

16. Ensure that **Cheque Detail** and **Deposit Detail** are selected in the *REPORT* column (each report should display a check mark to the left of the report name).

17. Change the *FROM* and *TO* dates for both reports to **08/01/2018** and **08/31/2018** respectively. The Process Multiple Reports dialog box should appear as shown below.

18. Click the **Display** button to examine the reports.

Export the report.

19. In the Cheque Detail report, click the **Excel** drop-down button and select **Create New Worksheet**.

20. Ensure that the **Create new worksheet** and **in new workbook** radio buttons are selected.

21. Click the **Export** button to open the Cheque Detail report in Excel.

22. In Excel, click **File > Save As**, navigate to the *1767-Student-Files\Lesson 6\MyProjects* folder, select the text in the *File name* field and type: **<your name> Lesson 6 Cheque**, then click the **Save** button. A message appears because the QuickBooks Desktop Export Tips worksheet includes macros. You can save the file without the macros, or specify to save it as a macro-enabled workbook.

23. Click **Yes** in the message box to save the file as a macro-free workbook.

24. Close the Excel application window, and then close the Cheque Detail report.

25. Repeat Steps 19 and 20 for the Deposit Detail report.

26. In the Send Report to Excel dialog box, click the **Advanced** button to open the Advanced Excel Options dialog box.

27. Deselect the **Include QuickBooks Export Guide worksheet with helpful advice** check box, then click **OK**.

28. Click the **Export** button to open the Deposit Detail report in Excel. Notice that the report includes only one tab.

29. In Excel, click **File > Save As**, navigate to the *1767-Student-Files\Lesson 6\MyProjects* folder, select the text in the *File name* field and type: **<your name> Lesson 6 Deposit**, then click the **Save** button. Notice that no message box displays because there are no macros in the workbook.

30. Close the Excel application window, and then close the Deposit Detail report.

31. Close the Memorized Report List window.

Create a portable file to turn in as part of this lesson's assignments.

32. Save the company file as a portable file in the *1767-Student-Files\Lesson 6\MyProjects* folder.

    Note: This is the file you will turn in.

33. If you plan to perform the Practice the Skill exercise, close the company file but leave QuickBooks open; otherwise, close the company file and exit QuickBooks.

Lesson Summary

Now that you have completed this lesson, you should be able to:

☑ Navigate Centres.   ☑ Edit name records.

☑ Create vendor name records.   ☑ Access and update related lists.

☑ Create customer name records.   ☑ Memorize and export reports.

Key Terms

Term	Definition
Internal Name	An entity name that shows only on documents that stay inside the company. The internal name is a subset of the legal name and must be unique.
Job	A specific project that you perform for a customer that you want to track.
Legal Name	The official entity name as it appears in documents such as cheques or statements.

Activity 1: Matching Name Types to Forms

Match the two name types, Vendor and Customer, using *V* or *C*, to the forms you can use them with. Each form has two entry lines because some forms allow more than one entry.

_____ _____   Sales Receipts

_____ _____   Make Deposits

_____ _____   Invoice

_____ _____   Write Cheques

_____ _____   Bill

Activity 2: Entering Names

If the following name already exists as a Vendor type, how would you enter the name as a Customer in the Customer Name fields of various forms?

Vendor Name: Brown, Alvin

Practice the Skill

This Practice the Skill exercise is designed to reinforce the skills you have learned. Best Custom T-Shirts needs computers for their design team and office staff. They plan to purchase these items from a local supplier, Computer Supplies. They also need an IT contractor to set up their office and plant network; Jamie Lee made a successful proposal for the work. Add these two vendors using the Vendor Centre. Jamie Lee offers a refund if certain conditions are met, so he also needs to be entered as a customer.

1. If necessary, launch **QuickBooks** and open **Best Custom T-Shirts C1_L6_B (Portable).QBM** from the *1767-Student-Files\Lesson 6\PTS* folder.

2. Create new vendor entries for *Computer Supplies* and *Jamie Lee*. Assign the *Plant:Equipment* vendor type to Computer Supplies, and the *Consultant* vendor type to Jamie Lee.

    Hint: Enter Jamie Lee's vendor name as *Lee, Jamie*.

3. Create a new customer entry for *Jamie Lee*.

4. Open the Vendor Contact List (*Reports > Vendors & Payables > Vendor Contact List*) and create a custom Vendor List that displays only the Vendor and Vendor Type columns.

5. Memorize the report in the Vendors group.

6. Edit the report so that the header reads *Vendor Type List*. Replace the previous memorized report when you memorize the new one.

7. Export the report to a new Excel workbook, and include the QuickBooks Desktop Export Tips worksheet.

8. Save the workbook in the *Lesson 6\MyProjects* folder as a macro-free workbook named **<your name> Lesson 6 Vendors**. Close the workbook, then close the memorized report.

9. Save the company file as a portable company file and add the letters PTS to the end of the file name (*Best Custom T-Shirts C1_L6_<your name> PTS (Portable).QBM*). Turn this file in to your instructor

10. Close the company file.

Course Project Exercise

Blue Heron Spa just advertised specials through a website promotion and two new customers scheduled appointments: Lily Thomas and Ginny Free. You need to enter these customers using the *first name, last name* protocol. You also need to create a new customer type named *Web Promotion*, which should be the customer type for the two new customers. The owners want to see the results of the promotion. You need to use the Customer Contact List and remove all columns except *Customer* and *Customer Type*. Filter the report to show only the *Web Promotion* customer type. Change the title of the report to *Web Promotion* and memorize it in the *Customers* group. Export the report to Excel and save it as a macro-free workbook named *<your name> Lesson 6 Web Promotion*.

Filename:	Blue Heron Spa Inc 2018 C1_L6_A (Portable).QBM
Admin password:	BluSpa18
New company name:	Blue Heron Spa, Inc. L6 <your name>

Perform the following tasks:

1. Restore the portable file and change the company name as indicated in the table.

2. Enter a new Customer Type named Web Promotion.

3. Enter the two new customers, Lily Thomas and Ginny Free, and specify the Web Promotion customer type for each one.

4. Run a report for the Customer Contact List that displays only the Customer and Customer Type columns.

5. Modify and filter the report as directed in the introductory paragraph.

6. Memorize the report.

7. Export the report to Excel (including the QuickBooks Desktop Export Tips worksheet), and save it as directed in the introductory paragraph.

8. Create a portable file to turn in to your instructor.

9. Close the company file.

Quiz Questions

For each question, select the best answer.

1. If you want to see only the transactions for a selected customer or vendor, what action do you take?

   a. Double-click any name on the left side of the appropriate Centre, and then click the Transactions tab on the right side.

   b. Click any name on the left side of the appropriate Centre, and then click the Transactions tab on the right side.

   c. Click the Transactions tab on the left side of the appropriate Centre.

   d. Click the name on the right side of the appropriate Centre, and then click the Transactions tab on the left side.

2. Which fields auto-fill after entering the vendor Company Name?

   a. Line #1 of the SHIPPED FROM address block and VENDOR TYPE.

   b. VENDOR NAME and CREDIT LIMIT.

   c. FULL NAME and Line #1 of the BILLED FROM address block.

   d. Line #1 of the BILLED FROM address block and PRINT NAME ON CHEQUE AS.

3. Which pair of fields must contain unique values for every name entry?

   a. CUSTOMER TYPE and COMPANY NAME.

   b. VENDOR TYPE and FULL NAME.

   c. CUSTOMER NAME and VENDOR NAME.

   d. COMPANY NAME and FULL NAME.

4. Which of the following is not an option when editing a name record?

   a. Changing the name type

   b. Changing the payment type

   c. Changing the company name

   d. Changing the PRINT NAME ON CHEQUE AS field.

5. What can you not do if a list entry has ever been used in a transaction?

   a. Make the list entry a sub-entry.

   b. Deactivate the list entry.

   c. Edit the list entry.

   d. Delete the list entry.

6. Which set of actions changes the header in an open memorized report and saves it with the same name?

   a. Select the Header/Footer tab, edit the *Report Title* field, click OK, close report, click the Replace button, then choose the location for the memorized report.

   b. Click the Customize Report button, select the Header/Footer tab, edit the *Report Title* field, click OK, click Yes in the Memorize Report message, close the report, and then click the Replace button.

   c. Click the Customize Report button, select the Header/Footer tab, edit the *Report Title* field, click OK, click Yes in the Memorize Report message, close the report, and then click the New button.

   d. Click Reports > Memorized Reports, select the report, click the Customize Report button, click the Header/Footer tab, edit the *Report Title* field, click OK, click Yes in the Memorize Report message, close the report, and then click the New button.

7. Which sequence of actions will open the Process Multiple Reports dialog box and allow you to select multiple reports for printing?

   a. Click the Print button in the Memorized Report List window.

   b. Click the Multiple Reports button in any report window.

   c. Click Reports > Multiple Reports > Process All in the Menu Bar.

   d. Any of these sequences will open the Process Multiple Reports dialog box.

8. If you are exporting a report to Excel, how can you specify to NOT include the QuickBooks Desktop Export Tips worksheet in the Excel file?

   a. Click the Excel drop-down button in the report window, then click Create New Worksheet Data Only.

   b. Select the Data Only radio button in the Send Report to Excel dialog box.

   c. Click the Advanced button in the Send Report to Excel dialog box, and then select the Data Only radio button in the Advanced Excel Options dialog box.

   d. Click the Advanced button in the Send Report to Excel dialog box, and then deselect the Include QuickBooks Export Guide worksheet with helpful advice check box in the Advanced Excel Options dialog box.

Lesson 7: Credit Purchasing Transactions

Lesson Objectives

In this lesson, you will learn about credit purchasing transactions. Upon successful completion of this lesson, you should be able to:

☐ Understand how customer and vendor credit transactions differ in QuickBooks.

☐ Enter credit purchases.

☐ Understand how credit purchases affect reports.

Accrual Accounting and Payment Terms

Objective L-7.1 Understand how customer and vendor credit transactions differ in QuickBooks

In this lesson, you will enter credit transactions for Best Custom T-Shirts. Understanding accrual accounting means you understand the effect of entering credit transactions using the Enter Bills and Create Invoices forms to enter them into the accounting system. Essentially an entry is made to record a sale or purchase, with a different form being used depending on whether credit is involved.

If a sale is made and paid for, then a sales receipt is issued by the business and becomes the document of original entry. If a sale is made on credit, then an invoice is used by the business. If a purchase is made and paid for, the vendor issues a sales receipt, and this becomes the business document of original entry. The recording of such a purchase is made through a form detailing the method of payment. If a purchase is made on credit, then the vendor issues an invoice and the business records it in an Enter Bills form.

Note: Very few types of businesses in Canada can use the cash accounting basis for tax reporting to defer reporting revenue, and most are required to use the accrual basis. Only accrual accounting conforms to International Financial Reporting Standards (IFRS) guidelines. Only accrual accounting is recognized in Canada by financial institutions. Following IFRS provides businesses with accurate information about their financial well-being and allows investors to accurately compare one business to another. QuickBooks offers the capability to switch reports from accrual to cash basis accounting as needed, but we encourage you never to use it.

Accrual accounting implements two key IFRS principles: the matching principle and the recognition principle.

The *matching principle* means posting costs in the same reporting period as the revenue the costs generate. The period is either the same date for some transactions or within one month or one year for others.

The revenue **recognition principle** means posting transactions on the date services or products change hands, not when the money moves. Because these two events can happen at different times, the delay means the transaction date and payment date may be different. Accrual financial reports rely upon the transaction dates, not the payment dates.

Businesses define the details of a delayed payment by using **payment terms**. Payment terms are agreements between businesses that determine when an invoice must be paid. Payment terms also specify deductions from amounts owed if entities pay more quickly than the payment due date.

The accounting system manages the delay and produces the reports by using two special GL accounts in the Balance Sheet. Each of these GL accounts is like a suspense account. Amounts the customers owe the business are held in the Accounts Receivable (A/R) GL account, in the Asset section of the Chart of Accounts until they are paid. Amounts the business owes to others are held in the Accounts Payable (A/P) GL account, in the Liability section of the Chart of Accounts until they are paid. When you enter a sale or purchase, the amount remains in A/R or A/P until you receive or make the payment for the transaction. When you enter the payment, only the A/R or A/P account and the Chequing GL account change. The payment step in the QuickBooks Cycle will be covered in a later lesson.

Business Documents and Payment Terms

Reviewing how to approach business documents and what they mean prepares you for processing them into the accounting records.

The business has relationships with customers and vendors. In turn, the business is the vendor of the customers, and the customer of the vendors. If the business allows customers to buy now and pay later, without using credit cards, you enter the transaction in the Create Invoices form, not the Sales Receipts form. If the business has permission to buy from vendors now and pay later, you enter the transaction on an Enter Bills form, not a Write Cheques form or Credit Card Purchase/Charge form.

QuickBooks uses the two different names for transaction forms to clarify which entity is selling and which is buying from the perspective of the business. Only customers can be entered in a QuickBooks Create Invoices form and only vendors on an Enter Bills form; however, they are all invoices. The word *bill* does not appear on any business document, although the term **billing** describes the activity of sending invoices to customers. In accounting, being *billed* means receiving invoices from a vendor. Businesses send the customers invoices and receive invoices from vendors. Other accounting systems may use the term *purchase invoice* for an invoice associated with a vendor and *sales invoice* for a customer invoice.

While many business documents function like contracts, not all agreements can be legally enforced. Businesses still depend on the information in documents for decisions about when to make payments. Retaining all documents for transactions, in either hardcopy or scanned form, is customary and required for the standard period of seven years. These could be needed later for audits to prove that no mistakes occurred when transactions were entered or payments were made.

You must take great care when entering each document into the accounting records. You must first check the name of the document and ensure you are looking at an invoice. Then, you need to enter the exact names, document numbers, amounts, and dates in the required form fields. The data you enter must match the document information. Otherwise, accounting reports will be incorrect and costly errors, such as making payments too soon or too late, may result. The date you enter may also be necessary to determine when merchandise legally changed hands.

In QuickBooks, the vendor or customer name and the document or reference number creates a unique entry in the accounting records when you complete the Enter Bills or Create Invoices forms. QuickBooks ignores everything else on the form when deciding if you are trying to enter a transaction more than once. If you accidentally enter a transaction with a name and number that matches one already in the system, a warning message will appear when you try to save the form. You can dismiss the message and save the transaction only after you determine why the program warned you or with approval from a supervisor, who can determine if the transaction was recorded correctly.

Certain documents, such as routine, monthly, general and administrative **overhead** costs, like phone bills, may lack unique numbers. You need a system for creating unique numbers, such as a month and year combination. If you start working in an existing company file, check the references used in the REF. NO. field in prior bills to help with consistency by using the same system. Duplicating bills, which is covered later in this lesson, is another method you can use to maintain consistency.

Be very careful with any document called a **statement**. Statements often only summarize unpaid, outstanding invoices, and any over-due invoices. Enter only transactions from individual invoices unless you are certain that the vendors send documents called statements rather than invoices.

You may see other documents such as packing slips, but usually they list only products, not amounts. The arrival of a packing slip or a **bill of lading** is proof the product either shipped or arrived. You should retain these documents and make payments only with proof of receipt.

Payment Terms

Payment terms tell the business receiving an invoice how long they have until the invoice must be paid. Payment terms can include one or two elements. The first element is how much time you have before you are required to make the payment. The optional second element has two parts; the first part specifies whether the payor can reduce what they owe if they pay early, and the second part specifies how much of a reduction they can take.

The reduction is called a discount. It is usually a percentage of the total amount owed. A discount may also refer to the amount credit card merchants retain from sales, as described in an earlier lesson. The meaning of *discount* can change according to the situation. Figure 7-1 shows the Terms List for Best Custom T-Shirts.

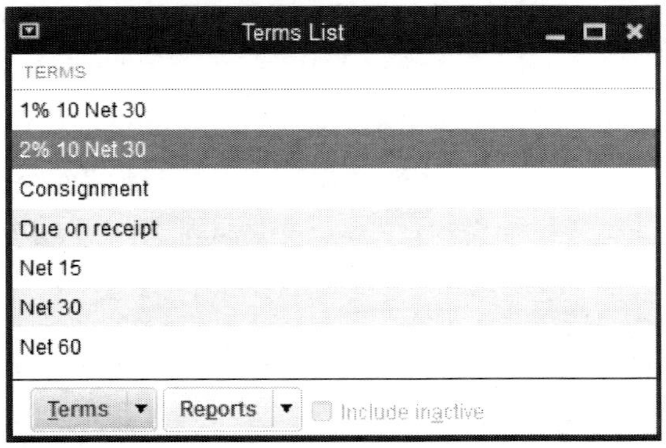

Figure 7-1: Terms List

After two entities agree on the payment terms, you enter them in the customer or vendor name PAYMENT TERMS drop-down menu, as shown in Figure 7-2.

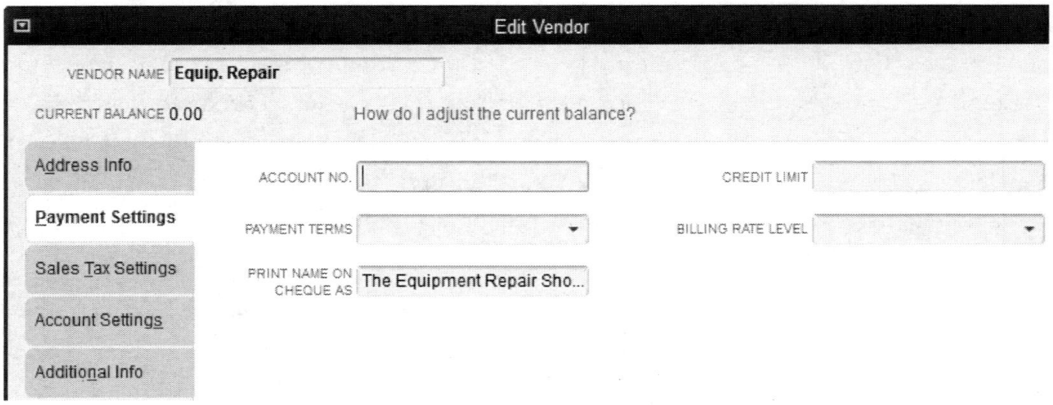

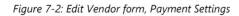

Figure 7-2: Edit Vendor form, Payment Settings

Vendor and customer name records each have a *Payment Settings* tab where you select the payment terms. Usually, businesses print standard payment terms on the invoice, but sometimes special payment terms exist. This can be true regardless of the due date printed on the invoice. If payment terms in QuickBooks do not match the terms printed on an invoice, check with your supervisor before making any changes.

While some discount amounts may be minor, very large invoices could have a substantial discount. If the payment does not arrive within the term time frame, a payor who takes a discount to reduce what they pay may still have to repay the discount if the payment arrives late.

The invoice date starts the clock on the payment terms. Both the Enter Bills and Create Invoices forms in QuickBooks check the payment terms to determine and auto-fill the due date. In some cases, you may need to check the auto-filled fields for accuracy.

The typical term notation looks cryptic, but deciphering the meaning is simple. For the payment terms *2% 10 Net 30*, the optional element, *2% 10* comes first. *2%* refers to the percentage of the total to deduct and may sometimes be noted without the % symbol. But the deduction is allowed only if paid within the number of days specified next, *10*. The required element is *Net 30*. This means that if the payor does not pay early, the entire amount is due within thirty days, or the business may charge interest on the amount that is owed. If the payment terms simply read *Net 30,* then no discount is given.

While *2% 10 Net 30* is common, both elements can differ for different business entities. You may have to choose between many different entries in the Terms List to find the one on the invoice. Discounts on incoming payments from customers occur more often than on outgoing payments to vendors. Each has a GL account to track the total discounts taken.

Other payment terms may also be listed. *Due upon receipt* means exactly that, the due date is the same date as the invoice date. *Prepaid* could mean that merchandise will not be sent until payment arrives. *Cash on Delivery (COD)* means payment must be made when the delivery arrives.

Best Custom T-Shirts wants to offer customers several options. Figure 7-3 displays the payment terms 1% 7 Net 30.

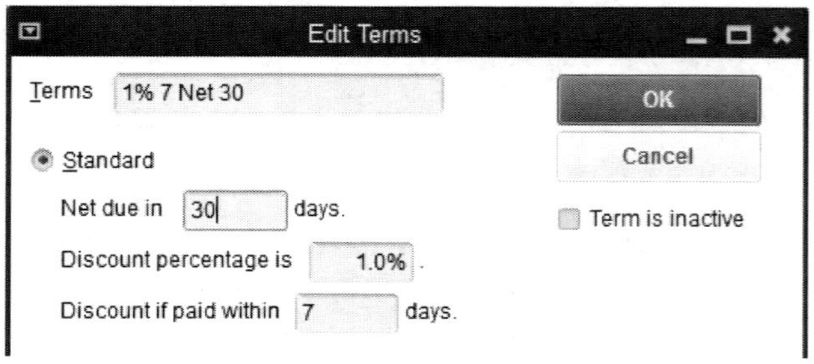

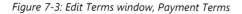

Figure 7-3: Edit Terms window, Payment Terms

Exercise 7.1: Entering a New Payment Term

In this exercise, you will enter a new payment term for Best Custom T-Shirts.

1. Launch **QuickBooks** if necessary, and restore **Best Custom T-Shirts C1_L7_A (Portable).QBM** from the *1767-Student-Files\Lesson 7\StarterFiles* folder. Save the restored company file as **Best Custom T-Shirts C1_L7_<your name>.QBW** in the *1767-Student-Files\Lesson 7\MyProjects* folder.

2. Change the Company Name to **Best Custom T-Shirts C1_L7_<your name>**.

3. Click **Edit > Preferences**, and then click **Reports & Graphs**. Click the **Company Preferences** tab, ensure that the default radio button, **Accrual**, is selected, and then click **OK**.

4. Click **Lists > Customer & Vendor Profile Lists > Terms List**. The Terms List appears.

5. Press **CTRL+N** or click **Terms > New** to display the New Terms window.

6. In the *Terms* field, type: **2% 10 Net 21**.

7. Ensure that the default radio button, **Standard**, is selected.

8. In the *Net Due in* field, type: **21**.

9. In the *Discount percentage is* field, type: **2.0**.

10. In the *Discount if paid within* field, type: **21**, then click **OK**. Notice that the new payment term appears in the Terms List.

11. Close the **Terms List**.

Leave the company file open for the next exercise.

Reporting Purchase Transactions

Objective L-7.2 Understand how credit purchases affect reports

Objective L-7.3 Enter credit purchases

After you start entering Enter Bills forms in the accounting system, the document dates from the forms combine with the payment terms to categorize the bills by due date. The bills and due dates together are used to create the A/P Aging Summary report, shown in Figure 7-4.

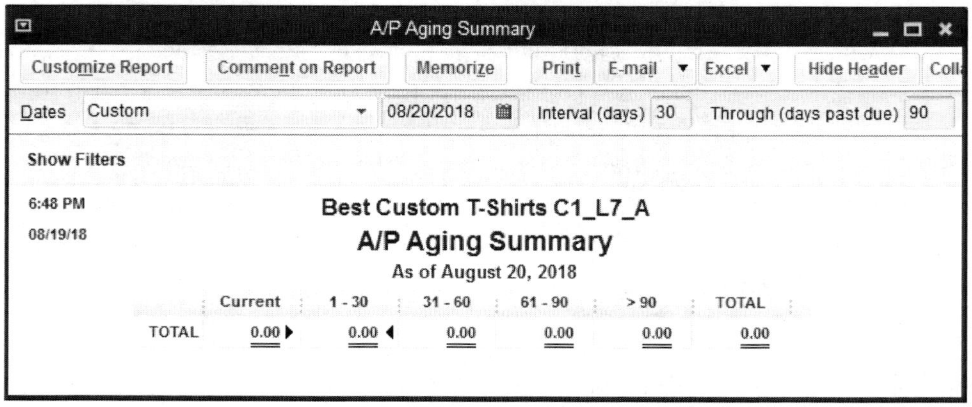

Figure 7-4: A/P Aging Summary report

Bills appear in the *Current* column unless they are overdue. The remaining columns detail the amount of time payments are overdue: 30 days, 60 days, 90 days, or more than 90 days. The relationship between the dates in forms and the exact category in the report can be imprecise because some months don't have 30 days. Figure 7-4 shows the A/P Aging Summary report without any transactions. Before we can look at the report in detail, we need to enter at least one bill.

Entering a Credit Transaction

To illustrate how reports change after credit transactions begin, we will describe how to enter the first bill for Best Custom T-Shirts, as shown in Figure 7-5.

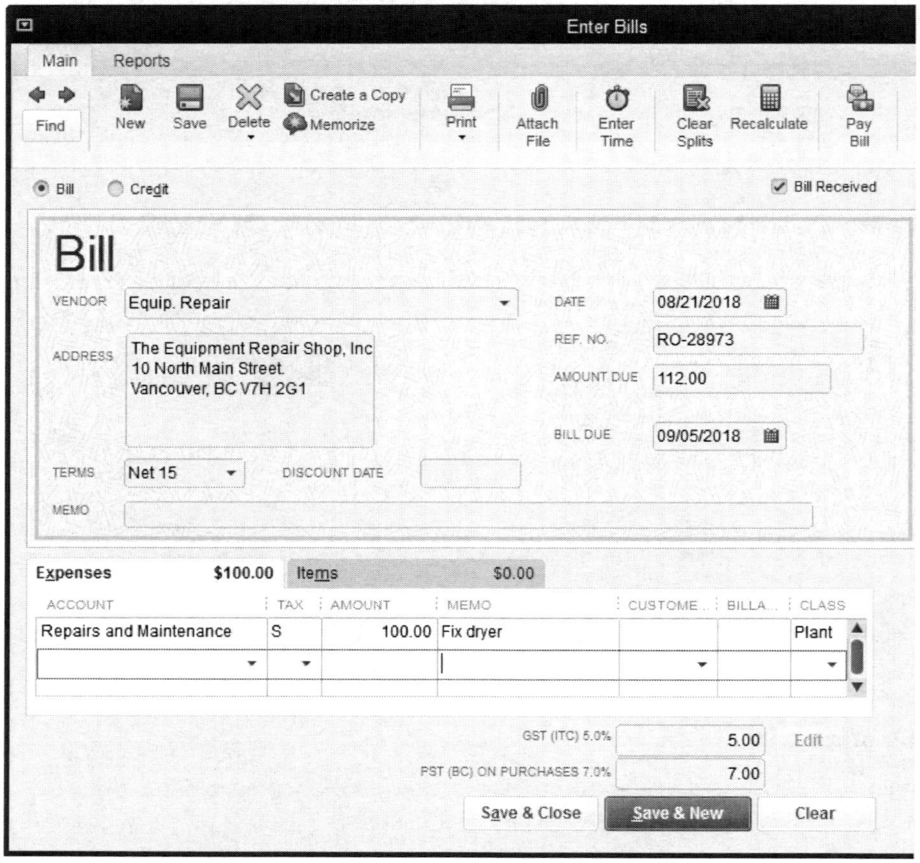

Figure 7-5: Entering a bill from The Equipment Repair Shop, Inc.

The partners arranged payment terms with The Equipment Repair Shop, Inc., allowing them to pay within 15 days after repairs. After entering the payment terms for the vendor, *Net 15*, open a new Enter Bills form and select the vendor in the VENDOR drop-down menu. The fields auto-populate with the name and payment terms completed. Then, you enter the date *8/21/2018*, document number (Ref. No.) *RO-28973*, amount *$100*, memo *Fix dryer*, and class *Plant*. The Bill Due date auto-fills with *09/05/2018* by adding 15 days to the bill date of 8/21/2018. If Best Custom T-Shirts had an account number with The Equipment Repair Shop, Inc., you could enter the number in the *Memo* field and it would print on the cheque.

Note: We will cover posting taxes in a later lesson.

After you save the transaction, the bill debits Repairs and Maintenance and credits Accounts Payable. Figure 7-6 shows the effect of entering the bill: the creation of a journal entry.

Best Custom T-Shirts C1_L7_A
Journal
August 21, 2018

Trans #	Type	Date	Num	Adj	Name	Memo	Account	Debit	Credit
27	Bill	08/21/2018	RO-28973		Equip. Repair		Accounts Payable		112.00 ◀
					Equip. Repair	Fix dryer	Repairs and Maintenance	107.00	
					Receiver General	GST on purchases (Input Tax Credit)	GST/HST Payable	5.00	
					Ministry of Finance...	PST (BC) on purchases		0.00	
								112.00	112.00
TOTAL								**112.00**	**112.00**

Figure 7-6: Journal entry created by Enter Bills form

Examining a Credit Transaction in the Financial Reports

Next, we'll look at the credit transaction in financial reports. Figure 7-7 shows the Profit & Loss set to the accrual basis.

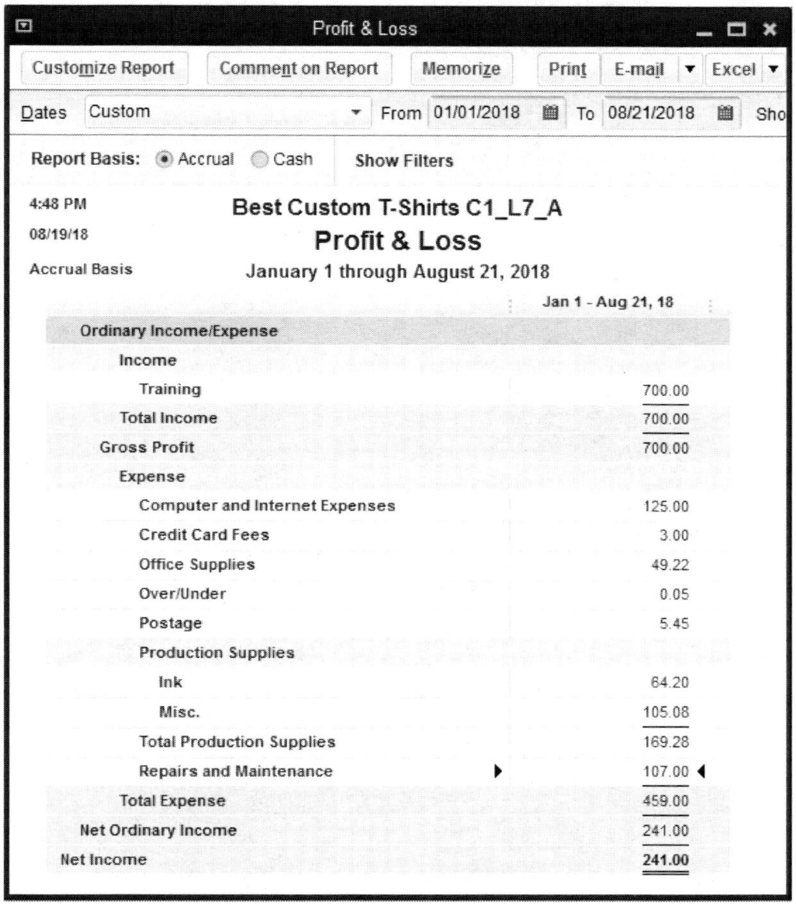

Best Custom T-Shirts C1_L7_A
Profit & Loss
January 1 through August 21, 2018

	Jan 1 - Aug 21, 18
Ordinary Income/Expense	
Income	
Training	700.00
Total Income	700.00
Gross Profit	700.00
Expense	
Computer and Internet Expenses	125.00
Credit Card Fees	3.00
Office Supplies	49.22
Over/Under	0.05
Postage	5.45
Production Supplies	
Ink	64.20
Misc.	105.08
Total Production Supplies	169.28
Repairs and Maintenance ▶	107.00 ◀
Total Expense	459.00
Net Ordinary Income	241.00
Net Income	**241.00**

Figure 7-7: Profit & Loss

Notice that the amount of the bill from the vendor, *$107.00*, ($100.00 plus $7.00 provincial tax) displays in the Repairs and Maintenance GL account.

Note: There is no need to look at this report on a non-accrual (cash) basis, because this system is rarely used in Canada.

Figure 7-8 displays the Balance Sheet set to the accrual basis.

| Dates | Custom | ▼ | As of 08/21/2018 📅 | Show Columns |

Report Basis: ● Accrual ○ Cash   Show Filters

5:12 PM
08/19/18
Accrual Basis

Best Custom T-Shirts C1_L7_A
Balance Sheet
As of August 21, 2018

	Aug 21, 18
ASSETS	
Current Assets	
Chequing/Savings	
Chequing	15,507.99
Merchant Credit Card	200.00
Online Credit Card	197.00
Petty Cash	100.00
Total Chequing/Savings	16,004.99
Total Current Assets	16,004.99
Fixed Assets	
Furniture and Equipment	2,500.00
Total Fixed Assets	2,500.00
Other Assets	
Start-up Costs	400.00
Total Other Assets	400.00
TOTAL ASSETS	18,904.99
LIABILITIES & EQUITY	
Liabilities	
Current Liabilities	
Accounts Payable	
Accounts Payable	112.00
Total Accounts Payable	112.00
Credit Cards	
First Bank Credit Card	67.20
Total Credit Cards	67.20

Figure 7-8: Balance Sheet

Notice that the total amount of *$112.00* (the amount owed plus all taxes) displays in the Accounts Payable GL account.

Examining the Accounts Payable Aging Reports

Next, we will examine the two Accounts Payable Aging reports. Figure 7-9 displays the A/P Aging Summary report.

▣		A/P Aging Summary					_ ☐ ✕
Customize Report	Comment on Report	Memorize	Print	E-mail ▼	Excel ▼	Hide Header	Coll

| Dates | Custom | ▼ | 08/21/2018 📅 | Interval (days) 30 | Through (days past due) 90 |

Show Filters

4:57 PM
08/19/18

Best Custom T-Shirts C1_L7_A
A/P Aging Summary
As of August 21, 2018

	Current	1 - 30	31 - 60	61 - 90	> 90	TOTAL
Equip. Repair ▶	112.00 ◀	0.00	0.00	0.00	0.00	112.00
TOTAL	112.00	0.00	0.00	0.00	0.00	112.00

Figure 7-9: A/P Aging Summary report

This report shows the total amount owed to each vendor. Currently, the report lists the bill in the *Current* column because, as of *08/21/2018*, the bill is not past the due date of *09/05/2018*.

Figure 7-10 displays the A/P Aging Detail report.

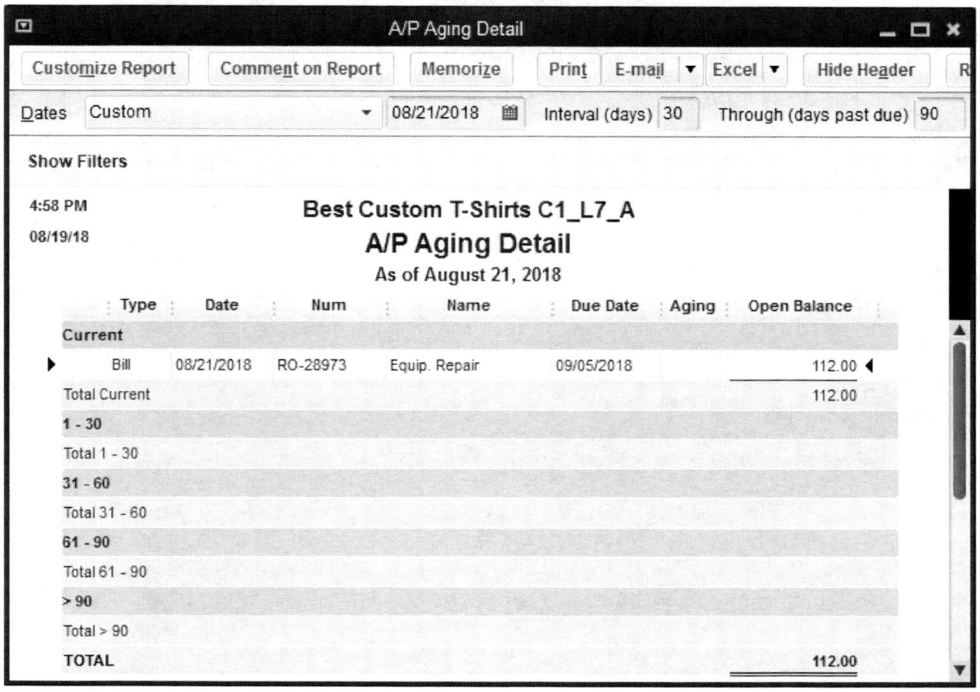

Figure 7-10: A/P Aging Detail report

This report presents the same information in a vertical format by category instead of by vendor. Every bill is sorted by the number of days past the due date.

However, if the report date changes to the date one day after the bill is due, *09/06/2018* (Figure 7-11), the bill moves into the column *1 - 30*. This means that the bill is between one and thirty days overdue.

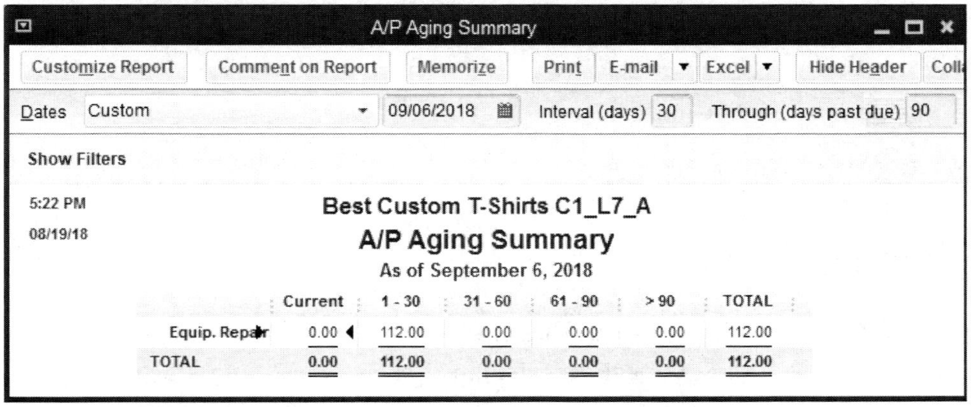

Figure 7-11: A/P Aging Summary report, dated 09/06/2018

Finally, using the QuickZoom tool, the detail report shown in Figure 7-12 displays the number of days the bill is overdue, *1*, in the *Aging* column.

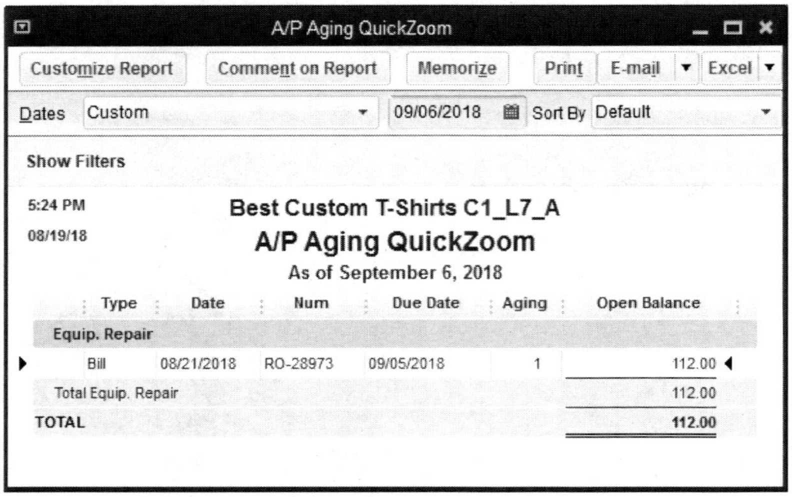

Figure 7-12: A/P Aging QuickZoom report, dated 09/06/2018

Exercise 7.2: Reading Accounts Payable Aging Reports

In this exercise, you will run an Accounts Payable Aging report for Best Custom T-Shirts.

1.   Ensure that the company file you worked on in the previous exercise is still open.

2.   Click **Reports > Vendors & Payables > A/P Aging Summary**. The A/P Aging Summary report appears.

3.   Set the date to **8/21/2018**, and then click the **Refresh** button. The bill from Equip. Repair for $112.00 appears in the *Current* column.

4.   Set the date to **10/15/2018**, and then click the **Refresh** button. The bill moves to the *31-60* column.

5.   Position the mouse pointer over the amount, *$112.00*, until the QuickZoom tool appears, then double-click. The A/P Aging QuickZoom report appears. Notice that the number of days the bill is overdue (*55*) appears in the *Aging* column.

6.   Close the report windows without memorizing any reports.

Leave the company file open for the next exercise.

Entering Payables

After a business begins to prepare for sales by purchasing production supplies or merchandise, credit entries usually start. The portion of the Purchases Cycle (Figure 7-13) now shows more options before reaching the Banking Cycle. The lesson about paying bills later in this course will provide more information about the Purchases Cycle.

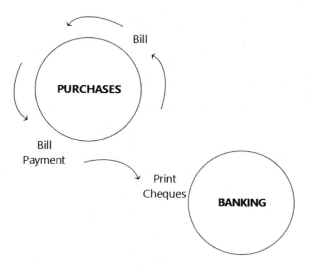

Figure 7-13: Purchases Cycle

Now, we will examine another bill for Best Custom T-Shirts to learn more about the Enter Bills form. Figure 7-14 shows the purchase of labels for the printed T-shirts. This is a special type of expense called ***Cost of Goods Sold (COGS)***. These expenses become part of the product. Other expenses, such as the T-shirts themselves, reach COGS a different way, which will be covered in a later lesson.

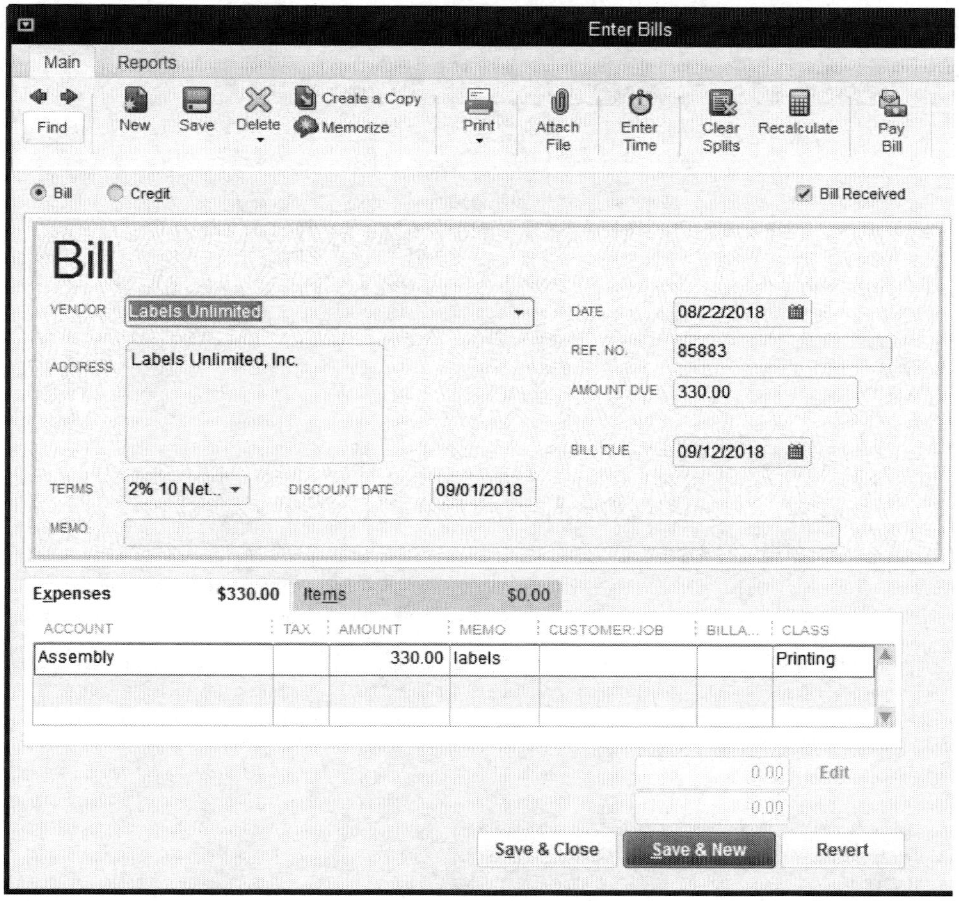

Figure 7-14: Enter Bills form, bill for labels without tax code

Notice the icons on the ribbon. The icons on the left, from *Find* to *Create a Copy* and *Memorize*, appear on all forms with a ribbon. Bill forms are rarely printed, but can be if needed. We will cover the *Recalculate* icon in this lesson and the *Pay Bill* icon in a later lesson.

You will enter information from the vendor's invoice in the required fields. The VENDOR, DATE, and AMOUNT fields must all be entered from the invoice. You can enter the bill and save it without entering the REF. NO., which is the number on the invoice, but you then risk entering a duplicate that QuickBooks won't warn you about. So, it is best to enter the REF. NO. any time you enter a bill.

The other fields you must enter are the GL account in the ACCOUNT field and the class in the CLASS field. You will select the correct choice based on your knowledge of the appropriate account and class for the label purchases. When you first start working in a new company file, you will need to familiarize yourself with where you should place transactions based on previous records.

Because a discount is part of the payment terms, the DISCOUNT DATE field populates when the vendor payment terms auto-fill.

The Enter Bills form in Figure 7-14 was saved and re-opened to show one mistake. The tax code was not entered. While it is necessary to complete this field, the bill will save without it. We will now go through the process of correcting the bill.

Notice in Figure 7-15 that after entering the tax code, *G*, the AMOUNT DUE at the upper right is *330.00*. Also notice that a GST tax of *16.50* appears.

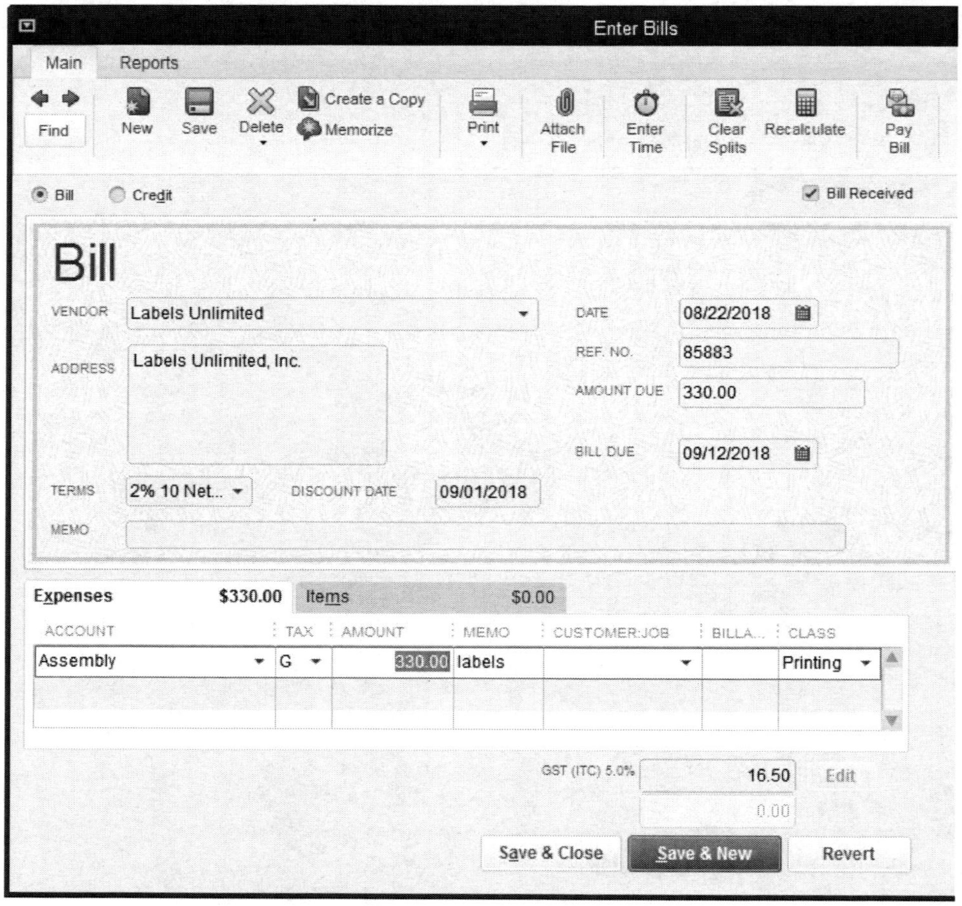

Figure 7-15: Bill for labels with tax code entered

If you click the Save & Close button now, the message in Figure 7-16 appears. QuickBooks wants you to be sure you are ready to save the transaction.

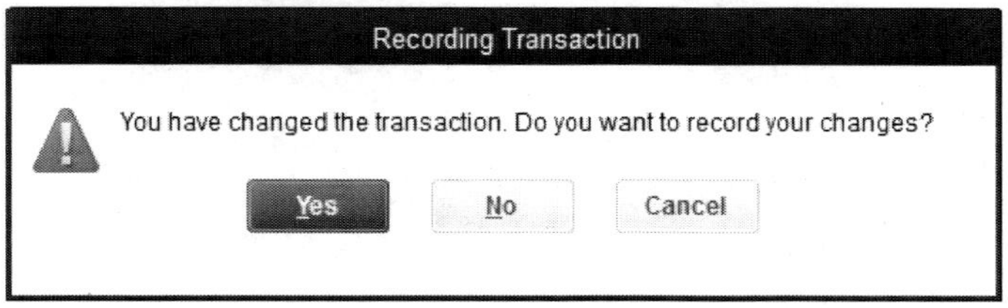

Figure 7-16: Message pop up when saving changed transaction

However, one step remains incomplete because if you click *Yes*, the message in Figure 7-17 appears.

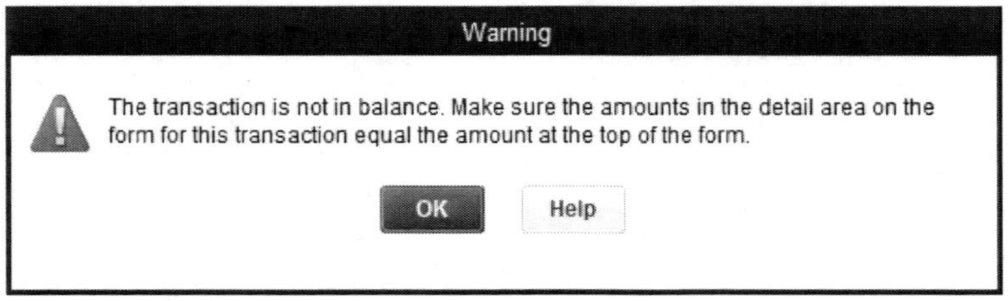

Figure 7-17: Message pop up for transaction not in balance

Figure 7-17 tells you the transaction is not in balance. This is due to adding the tax code. The vendor needs to be paid both for the labels and the tax. Click OK and return to the form. Then, click the Recalculate icon and QuickBooks will balance the transaction. The AMOUNT DUE at the top now equals the label purchase plus the tax, *$346.50*, as shown in Figure 7-18.

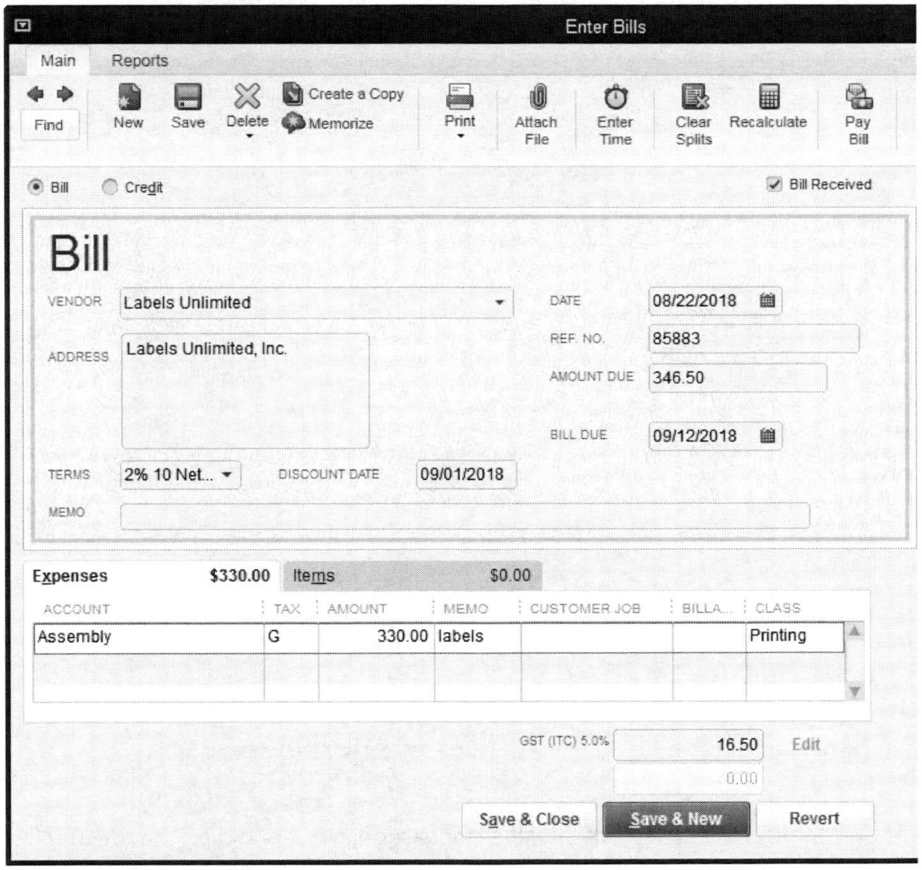

Figure 7-18: Result of clicking the Recalculate icon

Then, click the Save & Close button to bring up the changed transaction warning one more time, but this time you can click Yes to save the transaction.

You are now ready to check the financial reports and Accounts Payable Aging reports to see the results of your work.

Duplicating Transactions

The Create Duplicate button is a useful feature because it reduces data entry; however, you must take care to use it correctly. When administrative overhead bills, like the phone bill, contain a lot of information, like account numbers that print in the memo on the cheque, duplicating and just updating the *Date*, *Ref. No.*, and *Amount* saves a lot of time. You can also handle a series of similar bills more quickly by using the duplicate feature. However, any transactions involving inventory usually need to be entered in a blank form.

For this example, you need to enter several phone bills. For some reason. the one from the prior month, for $52.00, pre-tax, arrived late and now you also need to enter the next one. After completing the current month's form, for the pre-tax amount of $56.00, make sure you tab out of the last field you enter before saving it. Then, click the Create a Copy icon on the ribbon. Figure 7-19 shows the form before clicking the icon.

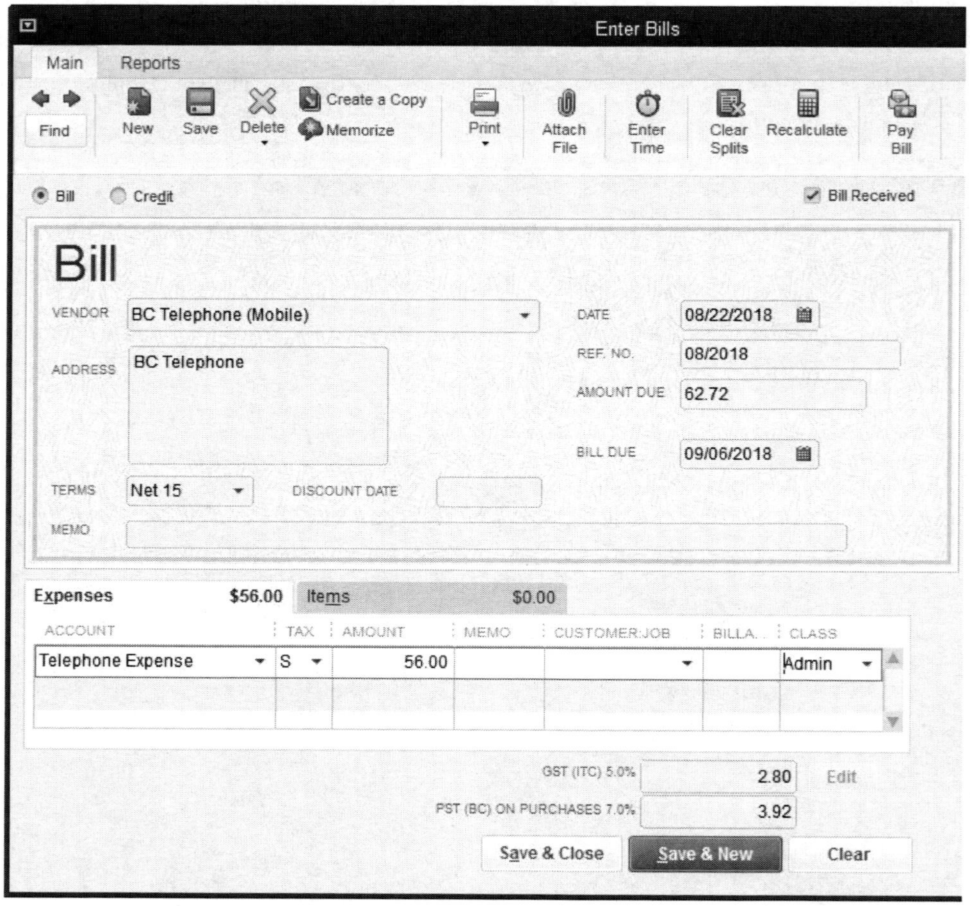

Figure 7-19: Bill before clicking Create a Copy icon

Note that the lower right button reads *Clear*. This means the transaction is still in the edit mode and has not yet been saved.

When you click the Create a Copy icon, the warning message in Figure 7-20 will appear.

Figure 7-20: After clicking Create a Copy icon

After clicking either Yes or No in the warning message in Figure 7-20, the message shown in Figure 7-21 appears.

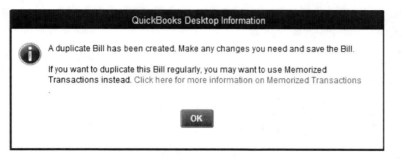

Figure 7-21: After clicking Yes on previous message

Click OK to proceed.

If you clicked No in the message in Figure 7-20, you can continue editing the bill; no duplicate exists. If you clicked Yes, then a duplicate bill is created, as shown in Figure 7-22.

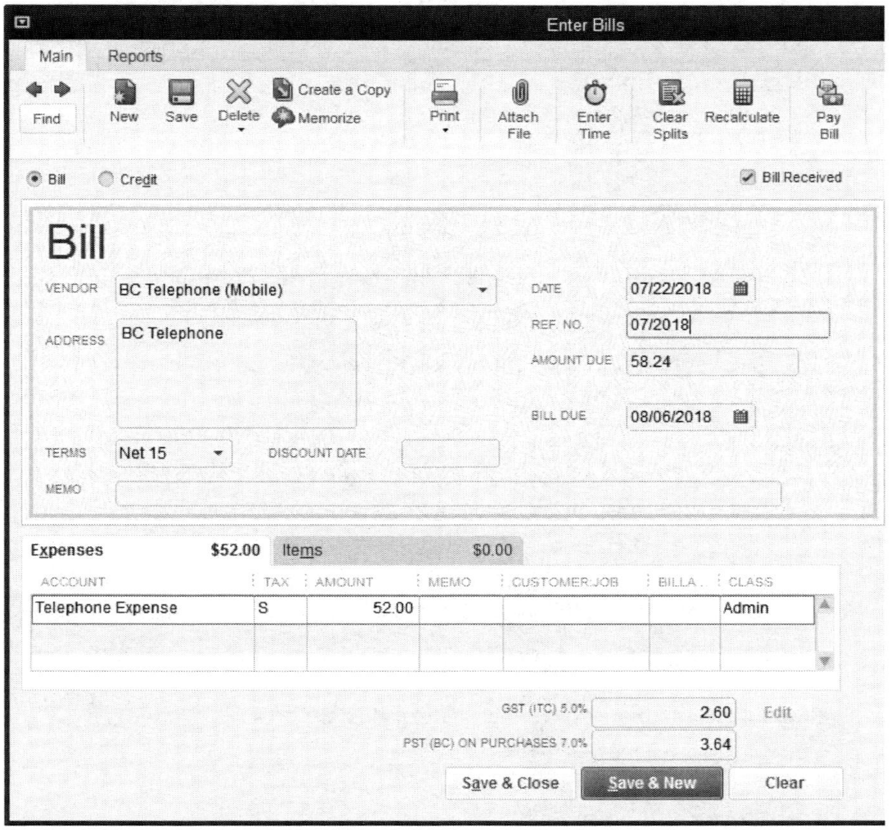

Figure 7-22: Duplicated bill

Update the *Date*, *Ref. No.*, and *Amount*, and click the Save & Close button.

You can also perform this process by opening a saved bill. In that case, when opened, the bill shows the Revert button instead of the Clear button. When duplicated, the Revert button becomes the Clear button. Always check that the due dates are correct and double-check the audit report to make sure you do not change an existing bill. You always need to see the Clear button to safely enter information on a duplicated transaction.

Exercise 7.3: Preparing for Production - Purchasing

In this exercise, you will make another COGS purchase for ink for Best Custom T-Shirts' printing press. You previously purchased ink by credit card for the training program. Because they only used the ink for training, not products they planned to sell, that expense did not go into COGS. This purchase will be posted to COGS. Then you will enter an additional entry for the following month that will post to the same account.

1. Ensure that the company file you worked on in the previous exercise is still open.

Enter a bill for the purchase of ink.

2. Click **Vendors > Enter Bills**. The Enter Bills form appears.

3. In the *VENDOR* drop-down menu, select **Ink Suppliers**. The account, address, and tax fields all auto-fill.

4. In the *DATE* field, type: **08/24/2018**.

5. In the *REF. NO.* field, type: **590351**.

6. In the *ACCOUNT* drop-down menu, change the GL account from the expense GL account, *Production Supplies:Ink,* to the COGS GL account *Ink*.

   Note: Forms auto-fill with the last GL account selected for the name used. This is a QuickBooks Preference selection.

7. In the *TAX* drop-down menu, select **G**.

8. In the *AMOUNT* field, type: **365.00**, then press **TAB**. Notice that the total in the *AMOUNT DUE* field changes to *383.25* to reflect the amount you entered plus tax.

9. In the *CLASS* drop-down menu, select **Printing**.

Duplicate the bill.

10. Click the **Create a Copy** button in the ribbon. Click **Yes** in the pop up message to record the bill. Then, click **OK** to dismiss the duplicate created pop up message.

11. Update the reference number to: **590352**.

12. Update the date to: **9/5/2018**. Keep the amount the same.

13. Click the **Save & Close** button.

Create a portable file to turn in as part of this lesson's assignments.

14. Save the company file as a portable file in the *1767-Student-Files\Lesson 7\MyProjects* folder.

    Note: This is the file you will turn in.

15. If you plan to perform the Practice the Skill exercise, close the company file but leave QuickBooks open; otherwise, close the company file and exit QuickBooks.

Lesson Summary

Now that you have completed this lesson, you should be able to:

☑ Understand how customer and vendor credit transactions differ in QuickBooks.

☑ Enter credit purchases.

☑ Understand how credit purchases affect reports.

Key Terms

Term	Definition
Billing	The activity of sending invoices to customers for payment.
Bill of Lading	A shipping document for products that proves the products were shipped or have arrived at their destination.
Cost of Goods Sold (COGS)	A sub-section of the Profit & Loss for expenses associated directly with producing revenue.
Matching Principle	Entering costs in the same period as the revenue generated by the costs.
Overhead	Expenses not directly associated with producing revenue that must be paid whether any revenue is earned.
Recognition Principle	Entering transactions as of the date they occur, not when they are paid.
Statement	A document that lists outstanding invoices not yet paid. The amounts may also be summarized by the length of time overdue.
Payment Terms	The description of payment requirements and/or options to apply discount percentages to payment amounts owed, if they are paid within a specified time period.

Activity 1: Matching Forms to Balance Sheet Accounts

In the second column in the table below, identify the Balance Sheet account affected by the transaction.

Transaction Form	Balance Sheet Account
Make Deposits	
Write Cheques	
Credit Card Purchase/Charge	
Enter Bills	
Create Invoices	

Balance Sheet Account:

1.   Chequing

2.   Credit Card

3.   Accounts Receivable

4.   Accounts Payable

Activity 2: Bills and Accounts Payable Aging Report

If you enter a bill dated *08/12/2018* and the vendor payment terms are *2% 10 Net 15*, what is the due date and, if the bill is not yet paid, in which column in the Accounts Payable Aging report will it appear when the report date is set to *08/31/2018*?

Due Date:_ _____

Column: _____

Accounts Payable Aging columns:

1.   Current

2.   30

3.   60

4.   90

5.   > 90

Practice the Skill

This Practice the Skill exercise is designed to reinforce the skills you have learned. In this exercise, you will enter the current utility bill and then duplicate it for the prior month's bill, which was not received previously.

1.   If necessary, launch **QuickBooks** and open **Best Custom T-Shirts C1_L7_B (Portable).QBM** from the *1767-Student-Files\Lesson 7\PTS* folder.

2.   Open the Enter Bills form and enter a bill for the vendor *BC Power & Light*.

3.   Set the date to *08/25/2018*, the GL account to *Utilities*, the tax code to *S*, the pre-tax amount to *$126.89*, and the class to *Plant* (because the power is for the printing press). (The Amount on the top half of the form should change to *$142.11*.)

4.   Specify payment terms of *Net 07* because the bill states the payment is due in seven days.

5.   You need the account number to print on the cheque. Enter *861346583* in the memo field on the top half of the form.

6.   Duplicate the bill you just entered. When prompted, specify to make the change in payment terms in the first bill permanent. Set the date to *07/25/2018* and the pre-tax amount to *$114.62*.

7. Save the duplicate bill and when prompted, specify to make the change in payment terms permanent.

8. Save the company file as a portable company file and add the letters PTS to the end of the file name (*Best Custom T-Shirts C1_L7_<your name> PTS (Portable).QBM*). Turn this file in to your instructor.

9. Close the company file.

Course Project Exercise

Two bills came in for you to enter for Blue Heron Spa. North Island Spa Supplies delivered the March 23, 2017 order of linens and spa supplies for the pre-tax amount of $626.00, using the tax code *S*. You notice that the payment terms entered on the bill in QuickBooks do not match the vendor invoice. When you ask, your supervisor tells you that you should change the payment terms permanently to *1% 10 Net 30*. You also notice that the bills from the vendor have no reference number, and nothing is entered on prior bills. The supervisor agrees that using the same date as the bill for the reference number is okay. The second bill came in from Comox Florists, also dated March 23, 2017. The reference number is *030892*, the pre-tax amount is *$61.00*, and the tax code is *S*. As you don't see a GL account for flowers, try checking the previous bills to see if you can find the correct GL account to use. You also need to enter payment terms of *Net 15* and make them permanent.

Filename:	Blue Heron Spa Inc 2018 C1_L7_A (Portable).QBM
Admin password:	BluSpa18
New company name:	Blue Heron Spa, Inc._C1_L7 <your name>

Perform the following tasks:

1. Restore the portable file and change the company name as indicated in the table.

2. Enter a bill for North Island Spa Supplies, using the information provided.

3. Determine which GL account to use for the Comox Florist bill. (If necessary, ask your instructor for assistance.)

4. Create a bill for Comox Florists, using the information provided.

5. Create a portable file to turn in to your instructor.

6. Close the company file.

Quiz Questions

For each question, select the best answer.

1. Which of the following statements is true?

   a. The correct QuickBooks form when billing the customer is the Statement.

   b. The correct QuickBooks form when vendors bill the company is the Write Cheques form.

   c. The correct QuickBooks form for a customer invoice is the Sales Receipts form.

   d. The correct QuickBooks form for a vendor invoice is the Enter Bills form.

2. Which statement correctly pairs form debits and credits to GL accounts?

    a. The Enter Bills form debits an expense and credits Accounts Payable.

    b. The Write Cheques form debits an expense and credits Accounts Payable.

    c. The Credit Card Purchase/Charge form debits Chequing and credits an expense.

    d. The Enter Bills form debits an expense and credits Chequing.

3. Which of the following statements is true?

    a. Amounts the customers owe the business are held in the Undeposited Funds GL account until paid.

    b. Amounts the business owes to others are held in the Accounts Payable (A/P) GL account until paid.

    c. Amounts the business owes to others are held in the Accounts Receivable (A/R) GL account until paid.

    d. Amounts the customers owe the business are held until paid in the Cost of Goods Sold (COGS) GL account until paid.

Lesson 8: Creating Invoices for Sales

Lesson Objectives

In this lesson, you will learn how credit affects sales, examine accounts receivable transactions and enter an invoice, and learn how to charge the correct sales tax. You are already aware that *all* accounting in Canada is done on an accrual basis, following the guidelines of the International Financial Reporting Standards (IFRS). Upon successful completion of this lesson, you should be able to:

☐ Understand how credit sales affect reports.

☐ Enter credit sales.

☐ Charge correct sales tax.

Accrued Sales and Sales Tax Collection

This lesson focuses on the selling side of accrued transactions for Best Custom T-Shirts. In Lesson 7, you were introduced to invoices and terms for credit purchases. In this lesson, you'll see the same concepts applied to sales.

Selling products to consumers also involves collecting sales taxes. You will learn how to set up and pay sales taxes in later lessons. For now, we will provide what you need to know to complete the appropriate forms.

When a business invoices for a sales transaction during a sales tax reporting period, the tax for that period must be paid, even if the business has not yet collected the tax from its customers. This is because it's a sales tax and the business has made a sale.

Reporting Credit Sales Transactions

Objective L-8.1 Understand how credit sales affect reports

The Create Invoices form affects reports the same way as the Enter Bills form. The Create Invoices form uses the balance sheet GL account Accounts Receivable to hold the sale amount in suspense until paid.

The Accounts Receivable (A/R) Aging reports show data the same way as the Accounts Payable (A/P) Aging reports. Figure 8-1 shows the A/R Aging Summary report before any invoices have been entered.

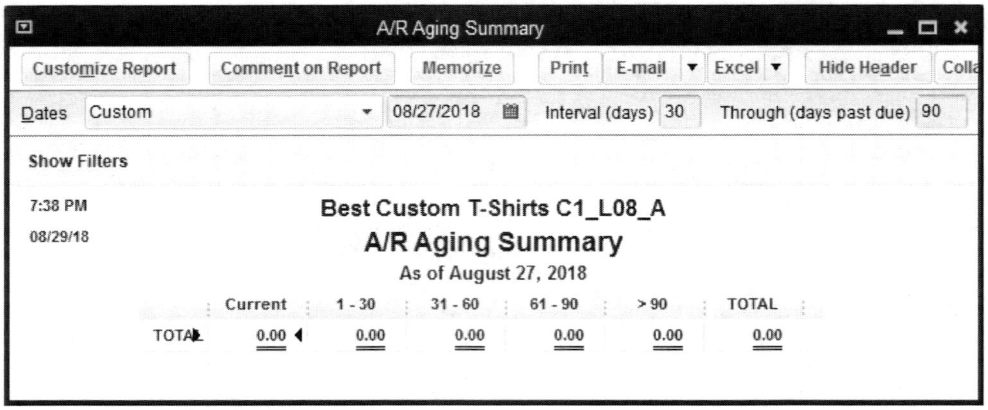

Figure 8-1: A/R Aging Summary report before transactions

The date on the invoice combined with the payment terms calculates the due date. The summary report provides an overview of the customer's account. The invoice appears in the Current column if it is not late. If the invoice is not paid on time, the amount appears in one of the columns approximating the number of days overdue. The detail report provides the exact number of days overdue for each invoice.

Entering a Credit Sales Transaction

All sales transactions in Best Custom T-Shirts received payment on the date of the sale. For this reason, the Enter Sales Receipts form served the dual role of recording the sale and the payment information. Now, however, the business is developing relationships with customers and arranges sales based on payment terms. You will enter these sales in the Create Invoices form.

Figure 8-2 displays the Create Invoices form with an invoice from Best Custom T-Shirts to the city for its share of the training program.

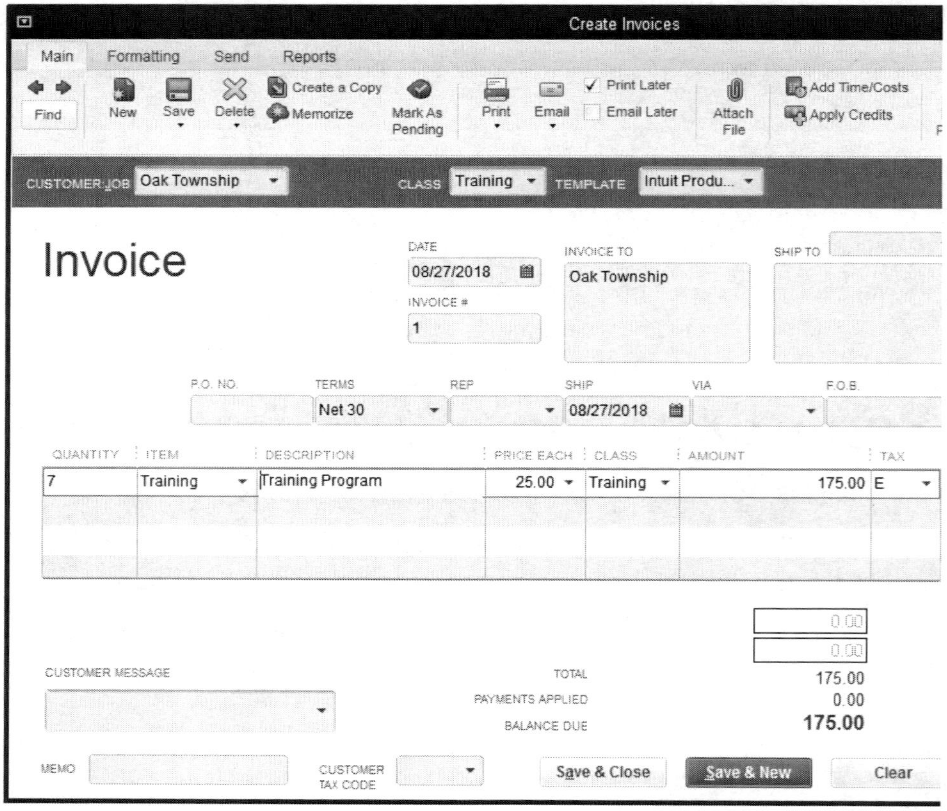

Figure 8-2: Create Invoices form for training

The city agreed to pay $25 per student. Seven students enrolled. The invoice specifies the Training item. Entering *7* in the QUANTITY field and *25.00* in the PRICE EACH field calculates and auto-fills the AMOUNT field (*175.00*). The city agreed to terms of *Net 30*. The date of *08/27/2018* starts the clock on the due date.

The Journal report in Figure 8-3 shows the results of the Create Invoices form in the accounting records.

8:13 PM
08/29/18

Best Custom T-Shirts C1_L08_A
Journal
August 27, 2018

Trans #	Type	Date	Num	Adj	Name	Memo	Account	Debit	Credit
34	Invoice	08/27/2018	1		Oak Township		Accounts Receivable	175.00	
					Oak Township	Training Program	Training		175.00
								175.00	175.00
TOTAL								**175.00**	**175.00**

Figure 8-3: Journal report for invoice

The debit goes to the Accounts Receivable GL account. This increases what others owe the business. The credit goes to the Training GL income account.

Examining a Credit Sales Transaction in the Financial Reports

Figure 8-4 displays the Balance Sheet. Notice the invoice amount of $175.00 in the Accounts Receivable GL account.

Balance Sheet			
Customize Report	Comment on Report	Memorize	Print E-mail ▼ Excel

Dates Custom ▼ As of 08/27/2018 📅 Show Columns Tot

Report Basis: ● Accrual ○ Cash   Show Filters

8:09 PM
08/29/18

Best Custom T-Shirts C1_L08_A
Balance Sheet

Accrual Basis   **As of August 27, 2018**

	Aug 27, 18
ASSETS	
Current Assets	
Chequing/Savings	
Chequing	15,507.99
Merchant Credit Card	200.00
Online Credit Card	197.00
Petty Cash	100.00
Total Chequing/Savings	16,004.99
Accounts Receivable	
Accounts Receivable	175.00
Total Accounts Receivable	175.00
Total Current Assets	16,179.99

Figure 8-4: Balance Sheet

Figure 8-5 displays the Profit & Loss. Notice that the $700 Best Custom T-Shirts collected and entered as a sales receipt for training fees is combined with the $175 invoice to calculate a total of $875 in training income, or revenue.

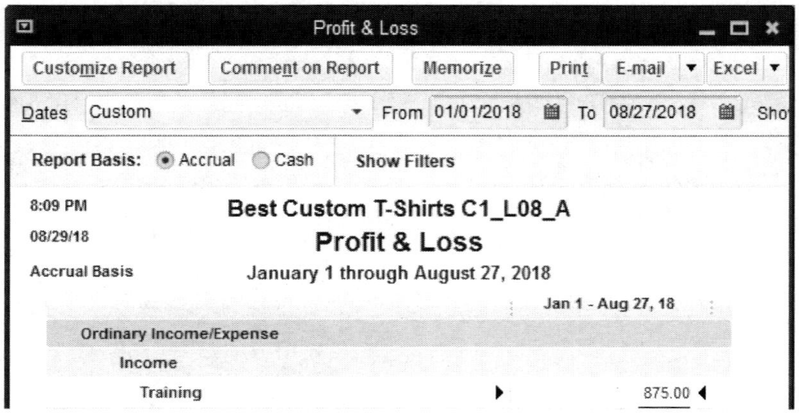

Figure 8-5: Profit & Loss

Examining the Accounts Receivable Aging Reports

In Figure 8-6, the A/R Aging Summary report dated 08/27/2018 shows the invoice as current.

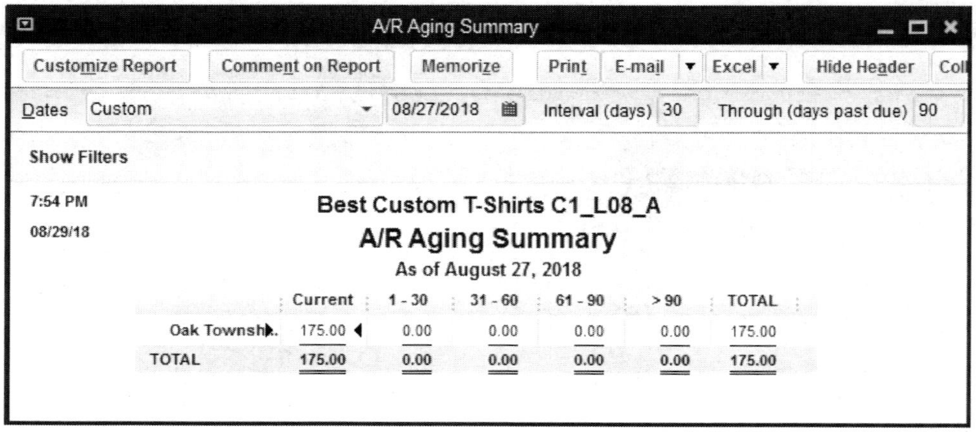

Figure 8-6: A/R Aging Summary report

In Figure 8-7, the A/R Aging Detail report dated 09/30/2018 shows the invoice as being four days late because the invoice was not paid on time according to the invoice payment terms (*Net 30*).

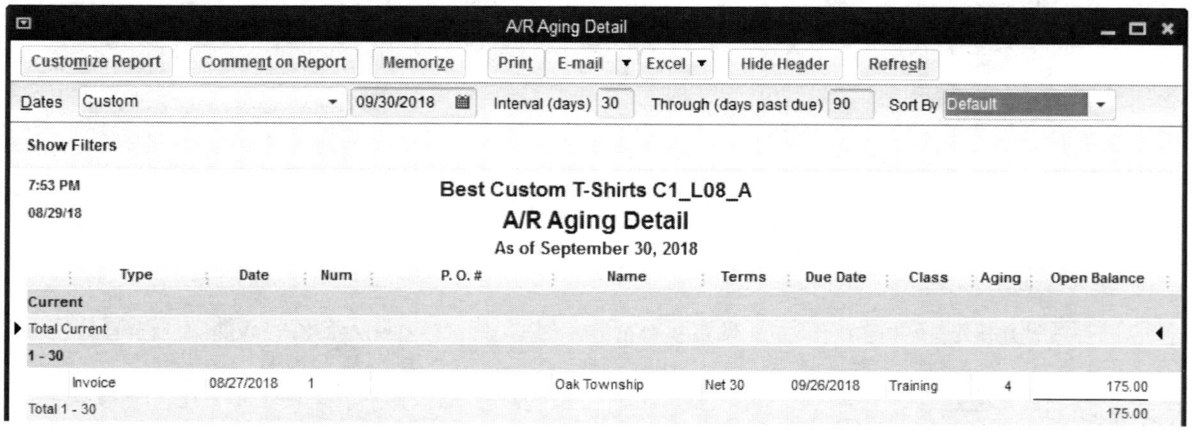

Figure 8-7: A/R Aging Detail report

Exercise 8.1: Reading Financial Statements

In this exercise, you'll open financial reports and memorize one report.

1. Launch **QuickBooks** if necessary, and restore **Best Custom T-Shirts C1_L8_A (Portable).QBM** from the *1767-Student-Files\Lesson 8\StarterFiles* folder. Save the restored company file as **Best Custom T-Shirts C1_L8_<your name>.QBW** in the *1767-Student-Files\Lesson 8\MyProjects* folder.

2. Change the Company Name to **Best Custom T-Shirts C1_L8_<your name>**.

3. Click **Reports > Customers & Receivables > A/R Aging Summary**. The A/R Aging Summary report appears.

4. Set the date to **8/27/2018**, and then click the **Refresh** button. The invoice for Oak Township for $175.00 appears in the *Current* column.

5. Position the QuickZoom tool over the *$175.00* in the Current column and double-click. The A/R Aging QuickZoom report appears

6. Position the QuickZoom tool over *Invoice*, then double-click. The Create Invoices form opens to show the invoice. Notice that the terms are Net 30 and that the invoice is assigned to the Training class.

7. Close the Create Invoices form and the A/R Aging QuickZoom report.

8. In the A/R Aging Summary report, set the date to **09/30/2018**, and then click the **Refresh** button. The invoice moves to the *1-30* column.

9. Set the date to **10/31/2018**, and then click the **Refresh** button. The invoice moves to the *31-60* column.

10. Close the A/R Aging Summary report without memorizing it.

11. Click **Reports > Company & Financial > Profit & Loss by Class**. The Profit & Loss by Class report appears.

12. In the *From* date field, type: **01/01/2018**, and in the *To* date field, type: **09/30/2018**, then click the **Refresh** button. Notice that Total Income is $875.00, which reflects the $700 Best Custom T-Shirts collected and entered as a sales receipt for training fees and the $175 invoice to Oak Township.

13. Click the **Customize Report** button. The Modify Report: Profit & Loss by Class dialog box appears.

14. Click the **Header/Footer** tab.

15. In the *Report Title* field, after the displayed text, type: – **End of 3rd Qtr.**, and then click **OK**.

16. Click the **Memorize** button. The Memorize Report dialog box appears.

17. Select the **Save in Memorized Report Group** check box and ensure that **Accountant** (the default report group) displays in the drop-down menu.

18. Click **OK**.

19. Close the Profit & Loss by Class report.

Leave the company file open for the next exercise.

Entering Receivables

Objective L-8.2 Enter credit sales

Best Custom T-Shirts will start selling design services to other businesses on credit. They need to start using Invoice forms instead of Sales Receipts because it's a credit sale. They are continuing to prepare for printing operations, but do not yet sell products. Once product sales begin, the sales department will enter most of the invoices. You still need to know how to complete Invoice forms for sales, so you can update or correct them as needed. The QuickBooks Sales Cycle (Figure 8-8) now shows more options before reaching the Banking Cycle.

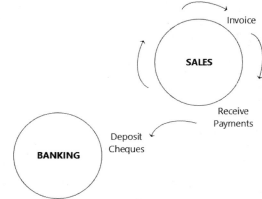

Figure 8-8: Sales Cycle

The Create Invoices form (Figure 8-9) has several more icons in the ribbon than the Enter Bills form.

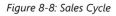

Figure 8-9: Create Invoices form

The *Mark As Pending* icon is unique to the Create Invoices form. If you click it, the icon changes to the *Mark As Final* icon, shown in Figure 8-10.

Figure 8-10: Mark As Final icon

The Mark As Pending icon allows a **pro forma** or proposed invoice to be created. This can be sent to a customer without entering the invoice into the accounting records. The invoice only posts and creates a journal entry when you click the Mark As Final icon. When you click the Mark As Final icon, the icon image changes back to *Mark As Pending*.

Note: Adding the words *Pro Forma* to the Create Invoices form title helps make clear that the invoice is only a proposed invoice. You will learn how to do this in a later lesson.

When you click the Mark As Pending icon, the PENDING NON-POSTING stamp (Figure 8-11) will appear on the Invoice form, indicating that the form has not yet been posted to the accounting records.

PENDING
NON-POSTING

Figure 8-11: PENDING NON-POSTING stamp

The Create Invoices form has the same required elements as other forms. You have used the CUSTOMER:JOB, DATE, ITEM (that maps to a GL account), AMOUNT, and CLASS fields in the Sales Receipts form. If a quantity is involved, the QUANTITY, multiplied by the PRICE, calculates and auto-fills the AMOUNT. Otherwise, you can manually fill in the AMOUNT field.

While the INVOICE # field may look like the REF. NO. field on the Enter Bills form, the INVOICE # field is different. This field is more than a text field. It both auto-numbers and accepts text. QuickBooks starts all auto-numbering fields with the number *1*. But businesses do not always want to disclose to their customers a low number of invoices because this indicates they are a new business. Instead, they may choose to start their numbering system with a six- or seven-digit number, such as *100000*. Other businesses may have a special numbering system they maintain in a system other than QuickBooks.

Note: This is **QB Global** information that you need to remember.

All QuickBooks auto-numbering fields work the same way. After QuickBooks begins an auto-number field with *1* or the number you enter, here's what happens. The next time you use the form, the field increments by one. But any number you enter in the field will also increment by one, even if you add letters. Let's say you need to split an invoice into two parts and want to add a letter to the number. The first part is *1111A* and the second part is *1111B*. The next invoice after that will auto-number as *1112B*; the letters never increment. Using a numbering system developed outside of QuickBooks can add a step to the invoicing process but ensures that the numbering makes sense.

The Create Invoices form has several fields that the Enter Bills form does not have. Some involve information to ship the product. You can enter information in the SHIP TO address block. If you complete the SHIP TO field in the Customer Name record, then it auto-fills. You only need this address if the customer's warehouse is in a different location than their headquarters. The other shipping fields include VIA and F.O.B. (free on board). VIA is usually the shipping method. F.O.B. is another type of agreement between the purchaser and seller that determines who pays the freight and from which location.

Two additional fields are the P.O. NO. field, where you enter the customer's sales order number, and the REP drop-down menu that lets you select the sales representative for the order. The customer's sales order number becomes the purchase order number for the business.

Adding a Sales Representative

The last field we'll cover is the REP field. The partners want to track who brought in sales. They won't collect commissions themselves, but when they hire sales representatives, they will need to pay commissions to them. All sales representatives need to be entered in QuickBooks as vendors. The partners do not all have vendor records. Taylor Green is set up as a vendor and we will add her as a sales rep.

Figure 8-12 shows the Edit Sales Rep form. You can click **Lists > Customer & Vendor Profile Lists > Sales Rep List** to display the Sales Rep List. Then, click **Sales Rep > Edit Sales Rep** to access this form.

Figure 8-12: Edit Sales Rep form

Notice that Taylor Green has been added as a vendor. She can now be selected in the *Sale Rep Name* drop-down menu. QuickBooks automatically provided the initials GT (last name, first name) but initials are easier to understand using the first name, last name protocol. Typing *TG* corrected this to the desired initials.

Exercise 8.2: Entering an Invoice

In this exercise, you will add a new customer and create an invoice for design services for Best Custom T-Shirts. You will also see the effect of the invoice on the memorized P&L report.

1. Ensure that the company file you worked on in the previous exercise is still open.

2. Click **Customers > Create Invoices**. The Create Invoices form appears.

3. In the *CUSTOMER:JOB* drop-down menu, select **<Add New>**. The New Customer form appears.

4. In the *CUSTOMER NAME* field, type: **A1 Painting**.

5. Click the **Payment Settings** tab.

6. In the *PAYMENT TERMS* drop-down menu, select **1% 10 Net 30**.

7. Click the **Sales Tax Settings** tab.

8. In the *TAX CODE* drop-down menu, select **S Standard Taxes (GST/PST)**.

    Note: Usually, you would also enter the customer's business number, which is their sales tax registration number.

9. Click **OK**. The New Customer form closes, and the information populates the relevant fields in the Create Invoices form.

10. In the *CLASS* drop-down menu, select **Design**.

11. Set the *DATE* field to **08/28/2018**.

12. In the *REP* drop-down menu, select **TG Green-V, Taylor**.

13. In the *ITEM* drop-down menu, select **Design**. You may see a message about Sales Tax Codes; if so, select the **Do not display this message in the future** check box and click **OK**.

14. In the *AMOUNT* field, type: **500.00**, and then press **TAB**. The *BALANCE DUE* field should display *560.00*.

15. Click the **Save & Close** button. If the Information Changed pop up message appears, click **No**.

Check the memorized P&L report.

16. Click **Reports > Memorized Reports > Accountant > Profit & Loss by Class – End of 3rd Qtr**. The memorized P&L report opens. Notice that the report now includes an additional column – one for the Design class, which shows the $500 invoice to A1 Painting. Total Income is now $1,375 (an increase of $500), even though the money has not yet been received.

17. Close the report.

Leave the company file open for the next exercise.

Charging Correct Sales Tax

Objective L-8.3 Charge correct sales tax

Sales tax in Canada has both national and provincial aspects. Each province and territory has its own system and rules, some of which are similar. Specifying your province in QuickBooks during setup loads the correct information to use in transactions. You still need to keep QuickBooks up-to-date to apply current sales tax rates and to charge customers the correct amount of sales tax.

You or the business's CPA can decide what types of revenue and expenses will have tax collected and paid to the government. The www.canadabusiness.ca/government/taxes website provides current information for businesses in any location in Canada.

Table 8-1 shows the three types of Canadian sales tax and what the initials mean. The business's location determines the combination of taxes you need to collect. The PST tax name may vary, depending on the province.

Table 8-1: Types of sales tax

Tax initials	Meaning
GST	Goods and Services Tax
HST	Harmonized Sales Tax
PST	Provincial Sales Tax

The possible taxes that a business may need to collect and pay are:

- PST only
- GST only
- GST/PST (submitted separately)
- HST, which combines PST and GST

Because Best Custom T-Shirts is a new business and expects to earn more than $30,000 each year, the partners registered for a GST/PST account with the Canada Revenue Agency (CRA). Only Québec has its own agency, Revenue Québec. The agency gave the partners an account number and designated reporting period (month, quarter, year). The partners will use the number when they file a sales tax return to report and remit the taxes collected. They also registered and obtained a number and reporting period for their province, British Columbia. The provinces and territories have different thresholds for registering. Figure 8-13 shows where you enter the number in the Company Information dialog box.

COMPANY IDENTIFICATION

CRA Business Number [   ] RT [0001]
The 9-digit business number plus 4 digit account number
the Canada Revenue Agency assigned to your business.

QST Registration No. [   ]
The 10 digit number Revenu Québec assigned to your business
when you registered to collect Québec Sales Tax.

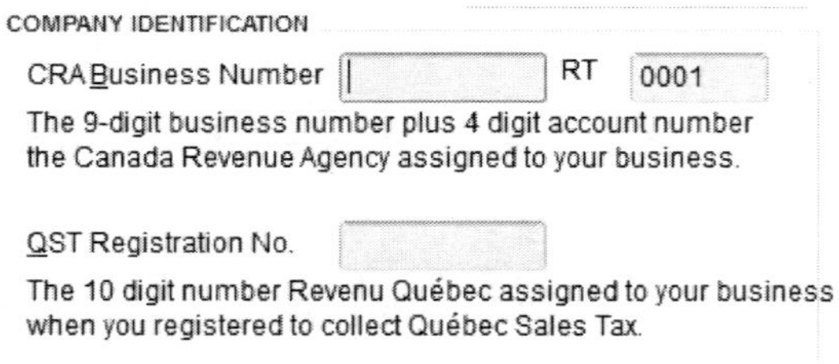

Figure 8-13: Company Information dialog box—Company Identification section for sales tax numbers

The tax system also factors in taxes the business pays. The GST or HST combination allows a business to deduct certain taxes it has paid before remitting the net from the taxes it collects. The deduction is called an *input tax credit*. The eligible expenses include most overhead costs and business start-up costs, as well as goods for resale for which GST has been paid.

QuickBooks prepares for tax filings by posting the eligible taxes paid as debits to the Sales Tax Payable GL account. Remember, debits decrease liability accounts. Figure 8-14 displays the GST/HST Payable Register, which shows the taxes from the bills entered to date in the Balance Sheet GL liability account. Each tax amount decreases the GL account balance. Invoices to customers will start adding credits to the account.

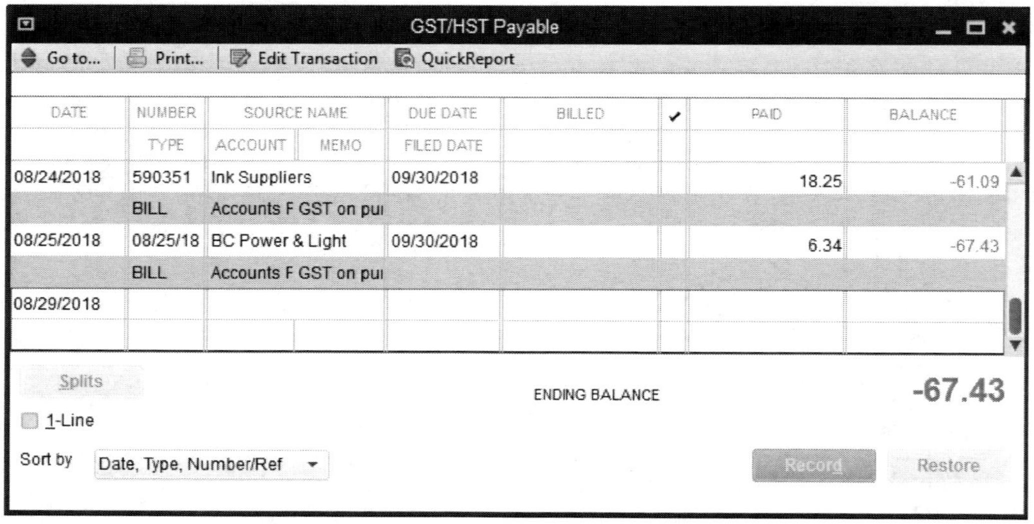

Figure 8-14: GST/HST Payable Register

Although most goods are taxable, you need to know the Provincial rules that apply to the business's location. The PST in British Columbia exempts certain clothing for children under the age of 15. Even adult clothing bought for children is not taxable. While Best Custom T-Shirts plans to make only adult clothing, it needs to keep this in mind. Any new business needs to know the regulations that affect it.

QuickBooks assigns codes to the different types of taxes, as shown in the Sales Tax Code List (Figure 8-15).

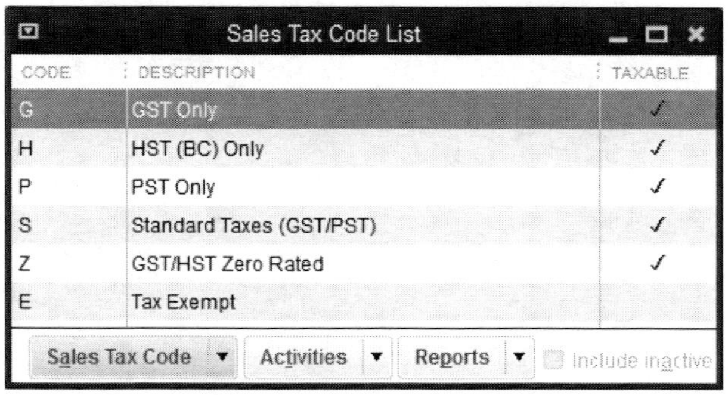

Figure 8-15: Sales Tax Code List

One other term to note is *GST/HST Zero Rated*, which applies if exporting goods or for a variety of food or medical costs. QuickBooks also offers the ability to charge the correct tax if you sell outside your province or country. While that is beyond the scope of this course, sample files in the software provide examples.

Exercise 8.3: Viewing Sales Tax Information

In this exercise, you will view sales tax information.

1. Ensure that the company file you worked on in the previous exercise is still open.

2. Click **Lists > Chart of Accounts**. The Chart of Accounts appears.

3. Scroll down in the *NAME* column, and then double-click **GST/HST Payable**. The GST/HST Payable Register appears, which shows the taxes billed and paid to date.

4. Close the GST/HST Payable Register and the Chart of Accounts.

5. Click **Sales Tax > Sales Tax Code List**. The Sales Tax Code List appears, which displays a list of Canadian tax codes and their descriptions.

6. Close the Sales Tax Code List.

Create a portable file to turn in as part of this lesson's assignments.

> **Note:** This is the file you will turn in.

7. If you plan to perform the Practice the Skill exercise, close the company file but leave QuickBooks open; otherwise, close the company file and exit QuickBooks.

Lesson Summary

Now that you have completed this lesson, you should be able to:

☑ Understand how credit sales affect reports.   ☑ Charge correct sales tax.

☑ Enter credit sales.

Key Terms

Term	Definition
Pro forma	A draft invoice that can be sent to a customer without entering the invoice into the accounting records. It is marked with the *PENDING NON-POSTING* stamp.
Sales Tax	The percentage of a sale collected by the business and remitted to the government.

Activity 1: Finalizing Pro Forma Invoices

Determine whether the following statement is true or false.

If you open an invoice and you see the *PENDING NON-POSTING* stamp on the Invoice form, the A/R Aging report will include the invoice.

Activity 2: Numbering Invoices

If the last invoice number you entered was *638925A*, which number will QuickBooks auto-assign next?

1. 638925B
2. 638926B
3. 638926A

Practice the Skill

This Practice the Skill exercise is designed to reinforce the skills you have learned. In this exercise, you'll enter a second invoice for design services for Best Custom T-Shirts and add another partner, Jordan Smith, as a sales representative.

1. If necessary, launch **QuickBooks** and open **Best Custom T-Shirts C1_L8_B (Portable).QBM** from the *1767-Student-Files\Lesson 8\PTS folder*.

2. Add Jordan Smith to the Sales Rep List and enter his initials using the first name, last name protocol.

    Hint: Click **Lists > Customer & Vendor Profile Lists > Sales Rep List** to display the Sales Rep List. Then, click **Sales Rep > New** to add Jordan Smith as a Sales Rep.

    Note: If the pop up message stating that Jordan Smith is not entered as a Vendor and asking if you want to add him appears, click **OK**. The Quick Add window opens and you can add him as a Vendor.

3. Open invoice number 2 for A1 Painting.

    Hint: Click **Reports > Customers & Receivables > Open Invoices** to display the Open Invoices window.

4. Create a copy of the invoice to duplicate it and accept the new invoice number, *3*.

5. Update the new invoice with the following information: The date is *08/29/2018*. The pre-tax amount is *$450*. The sales representative is *Jordan Smith*. Save the invoice.

Note: When you are prompted to make the sales representative change permanent for all past and future transactions, click **No**. This keeps Jordan Smith as the Rep for this transaction but doesn't make the change permanent for the customer.

6. Save the company file as a portable company file and add the letters PTS to the end of the file name (*Best Custom T-Shirts C1_L8_<your name> PTS (Portable).QBM*). Turn this file in to your instructor.

7. Close the company file.

Course Project Exercise

The owners of Blue Heron Spa run a special for spa services. Customers can purchase five treatments now if they pay the price of four treatments within thirty days. Employees who sell the package to customers receive a commission. Two new customers, Charlotte Johnson and Becky Flynn, both buy the package from the same employee, Emily Jackson. Emily Jackson is a new sales rep. Date both invoices *March 15, 2017*. Enter *Net 30* as the payment terms in each invoice. Use the *Package 5 for 4* item. The price of the package is *$400*.

Filename:	Blue Heron Spa Inc 2018 C1_L8_A (Portable).QBM
Admin password:	BluSpa18
New company name:	Blue Heron Spa, Inc._C1_L8 <your name>

Perform the following tasks:

1. Restore the portable file and change the company name as indicated in the table.

2. Add the new customers Charlotte Johnson and Becky Flynn.

3. Add the new sales rep Emily Jackson.

4. Create two invoices for the scenario described above.

5. Create a portable file to turn in to your instructor.

6. Close the company file.

Quiz Questions

For each question, select the best answer.

1. Which report provides the exact number of days an invoice is overdue for payment?

   a. Profit & Loss

   b. A/R Aging Detail

   c. Balance Sheet

   d. A/R Aging Summary

2.   Which statement about the effect of entering a Create Invoices form in the accounting records is correct?

   a.   Accounts Receivable decreases.

   b.   When marked as final, the invoice is removed from accrual reports.

   c.   When marked as pending, the invoice still appears in accrual reports.

   d.   The invoice debits Accounts Receivable and credits Revenue.

3.   Which statement about the Canadian sales tax system is true?

   a.   Every province and territory follows the same system.

   b.   Registering for the national sales tax also registers a business for the provincial tax.

   c.   Businesses making over $30,000 per year must register for GST/PST.

   d.   Reporting periods are the same for all businesses.

Lesson 9: Modifying the Chart of Accounts

Lesson Objectives

In this lesson, you will add and edit GL accounts in the Chart of Accounts list, then review your changes. Upon successful completion of this lesson, you should be able to:

☐ Apply the accounting equation to the Chart of Accounts.

☐ Review changes to the Chart of Accounts.

☐ Enter and modify GL accounts.

Organizing and Updating GL Accounts

The Chart of Accounts is the primary list in QuickBooks. This list organizes all transaction entries in the accounting system for reports. Learning to navigate the Chart of Accounts is like learning your way around a house. If you're in one room, you know which room is through which door. Sometimes houses need more room and undergo remodeling. The same holds true for the Chart of Accounts. Just like a house, any additions or changes to GL accounts must build on the existing structure. Also like an actual house, you need to perform spring cleaning. Over time, additions or changes to the Chart of Accounts can result in inconsistencies that can cause confusion.

In this lesson, you will update the Best Custom T-Shirts company file. You will also review the accounting equation and its relationship to the GL accounts and the different types of accounts.

Several previous lessons covered aspects of the list of GL accounts. You already know much of what you need to make changes to the Chart of Accounts. In this lesson, you will learn additional skills you can apply to this and other lists.

Choosing GL Account Types, Names, and Numbers

Objective L-9.1 Apply the accounting equation to the Chart of Accounts

From one business to the next, you will find many similar GL accounts in the Chart of Accounts. These GL accounts exist to provide management accounting, which should be the primary purpose of accounting. Many of these accounts exist to provide totals for tax purposes. Each business usually needs to track optional information for tax calculations. Even if the information is not be needed for tax reporting, the business managers need the information to manage the business. Determining where businesses spend their money and the sources of income is very important in evaluating the health of the business.

In a previous lesson, you learned that organizing information the way people naturally remember it can prevent confusion. Usually people know the order of numbers or letters without even thinking about it. For this reason, QuickBooks organizes the Chart of Accounts by placing GL accounts of the same account type in alphabetical order. You can also move accounts around in the Chart of Accounts or display the list in more than one way. Using the QuickBooks numbering system is an even better method for organizing the list order. It keeps the list order the way you want it. However, even within a numbered chart, you still need to keep the account names in alphabetical order to make finding them easier.

Placing similar GL accounts together is critical to organizing the Chart of Accounts. The best way to accomplish this is to establish a hierarchy in the Chart of Accounts. This means that one account becomes the **header account** (also known as the parent account), and related accounts become **sub-accounts**. The header GL account name unites the sub-accounts. The sub-accounts may be drawn from accounts within the same account type. Capitalizing header account names makes them easy to identify. For example, a GL account named *COMMUNICATION* could be the header for various telephone expenses. Another one named *INTERNET* could include the costs for maintaining a web presence.

Grouping accounts in a hierarchy has other benefits. Grouped accounts can provide sub-totals in reports for the entire group of sub-accounts under a header. This provides a higher-level look at your accounts because it is less detailed than an account-by-account report. The hierarchy can also work with the collapse feature in QuickBooks reports so that only the top header accounts of each account type appear on in the reports. This feature is only available in the desktop version of QuickBooks. However, if you do not have the hierarchy feature and have only alphabetical capability, you can use short prefixes for similar accounts, like *UTIL-Powe*r and *UTIL-Water* to indicate that the accounts belong together as utilities.

QuickBooks creates certain GL accounts automatically. These accounts work with the software program and cannot be deleted. However, they can be renamed or hidden so they don't appear in the list. Examples include Sales Tax Payable and Payroll Payable.

Reviewing the Accounting Equation

Before adding or changing any GL accounts, decide where they belong based on the information in Table 9-1. You saw this table about the accounting equation and the QuickBooks Chart of Accounts in an earlier lesson. The table shows the relationships between the accounting equation sections and account types in QuickBooks. These account types appear in the same order as they do in the Chart of Accounts.

Table 9-1: Financial Statements and Equation/Report Sections and Sub-sections Aligned with GL/Account Types

Financial Report	Equation Section	Equation Sub-Section	Report Sub-Section	Chart of Accounts Sections and GL Account Type
Balance Sheet	Assets		Current Assets	Bank
Balance Sheet	Assets		Current Assets	Accounts Receivable
Balance Sheet	Assets		Current Assets	Other Current Asset
Balance Sheet	Assets		Fixed Assets	Fixed Asset
Balance Sheet	Assets		Other Assets	Other Asset
Balance Sheet	Liabilities		Liabilities	Accounts Payable
Balance Sheet	Liabilities		Liabilities	Credit Card
Balance Sheet	Liabilities		Liabilities	Other Current Liability
Balance Sheet	Liabilities		Liabilities	Long Term Liability
Balance Sheet	Equity		Equity	Equity
Income Statement	Equity	Income	Ordinary Income and Expense	Income
Income Statement	Equity	Expense	Ordinary Income and Expense	COGS
Income Statement	Equity	Expense	Ordinary Income and Expense	Expense
Income Statement	Equity	Income	Other Income/Expense	Other Income
Income Statement	Equity	Expense	Other Income/Expense	Other Expense

As a reminder, the accounting equation is Assets = Liabilities plus Equity. Each section of the accounting equation represents either debits or credits. The relationship between the section and debit or credit also determines whether the debit or credit increases or decreases a GL account in that section. Whatever increases the account is considered the normal balance for the account. Asset section GL accounts increase with debits and their normal balance has more debits than credits. Both the Liability and Equity sections increase with credits and their normal balance has more credits than debits. This keeps the accounting equation balanced.

Posting to certain GL accounts creates the opposite effect—the section decreases. These GL accounts are known as **contra accounts**. They have the opposite debit or credit balance from what is normal for their section. When you see these on financial reports, the account balance appears with a negative sign or in parentheses. This occurs regardless of whether the account has a debit or credit balance. The accounts with a normal balance display as positive numbers. Table 9-2 shows the main contra accounts you'll find in many accounting systems. Notice that while Table 9-1 only shows report sub-sections, Table 9-2 adds sub-totals. The reason for providing the sub-totals is that not every report sub-total has a matching header.

Table 9-2: Equation Sections and Contra GL Accounts

Equation	Section Increased by (normal)	Section Decreased by (contra)	Account Type	Report Sub-section	Report Sub-total	Contra GL Account
Assets	Debit	Credit	Fixed Asset	Fixed Assets	Fixed Assets	Accumulated Depreciation
Equity (Direct Expense)	Credit	Debit	COGS	Ordinary Income and Expense	Gross Profit	Expenses directly producing income
Equity (Overhead)	Credit	Debit	Expense and Other Expense	Ordinary Income and Expense	Total Expense	Overhead (Expenses indirectly producing income)

There are many more types of accounts than what QuickBooks offers. For example, a long-term note receivable (term greater than 1 year) should be in an account category called Long-Term Assets. The value of the first year of expected payments on the note would be a current asset and the balance would be long term. However, QuickBooks does not provide that category and the accounting system works on the accounts that QuickBooks provides. This means that the determination of account names might not be what you expect or are trained to use, though the functionality is provided.

You can produce a sub-total for anything you need with a new header account in the correct section. If you have only one GL account for a type, you might not need a header account.

Any time you enter a new GL account in the Chart of Accounts, you first need to specify the type of account you want to create. QuickBooks does not ask you for the section of the accounting equation. The account types often, but not always, contain the name of the equation section. For example, an account or sub-section such as *Expenses,* which will eventually be netted out to Equity, is known as an Expense until it becomes Equity. Knowing which account type belongs in which section is the first step in creating a new GL account.

QuickBooks has two main sections on the Balance Sheet report, Assets and Liabilities & Equity. They match each side of the accounting equation. Liabilities & Equity contains sub-sections for each of those. Each account type is also a sub-section of its accounting equation section.

The key point to remember when choosing an account type for either assets or liabilities is this: If a new GL account is not a specific type such as Bank, Fixed Asset, or Credit Cards, then it's either Current or Other. **Current** means the assets are **liquid** or can be converted to cash within a year. For example, Accounts Receivable is in the Current Assets report section because the business expects to receive the payments within a year. Accounts Payable is in the Current Liabilities section for the same reason. Anything not fitting into an account type as Current is Other. **Other** means non-current or miscellaneous. The one exception is Long Term Liability. This account type is usually used only for loans lasting more than one year.

Naming GL Accounts

Once you begin creating or updating a GL account, you need to keep several points in mind:

- Do not repeat the type of account in the account name.

- Do not repeat a header account name in a sub-account name.

- Keep the name short.

- Make sure the name is obvious.

Finally, colons are reserved for all names in QuickBooks. You can use a colon in text fields such as descriptions or memos. The colon is used to show the header account and the sub-account on one line; for example, UTILITIES: Water. Combining one or more sets of characters and punctuation in this manner is a data function called *concatenation.*

Note: This is **QB Global** information for any list with hierarchical elements.

Numbering GL Accounts

The major sections for any Chart of Accounts follow a standard numbering system. If you turn on the numbering in QuickBooks Preferences, accounts already in the Chart may be numbered for you. However, they might not be the numbers you want. Figure 9-1 shows the Company Preferences tab of the Accounting Preferences, where you can specify whether to use account numbers.

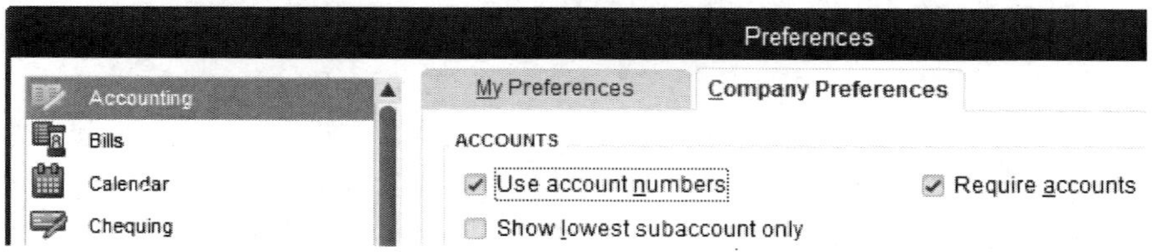

Figure 9-1: Preference dialog box—setting for using account numbers

Select the *Use account numbers* check box to enable the numbering feature. If you do not want any header accounts to appear, select the *Show lowest subaccount only* check box to prevent them from appearing on reports. The *Require accounts* option, which is selected by default, ensures that you enter a GL account for every transaction. If the check box is not selected, QuickBooks will place transactions without a GL account in Uncategorized Income or Uncategorized Expenses.

When you create a new GL account, QuickBooks does not number it for you or remind you if you forget to add the number. It does allow up to seven characters in the GL number entry field. The characters do not all have to be numbers. Using a four-digit number does not leave enough space for sub-accounts. A five-digit number is enough, as shown in Table 9-3.

Table 9-3: Chart sections and standard numbering

Chart Section	GL Number section
Assets	10000
Liabilities	20000
Equity	30000
Income	40000
COGS	50000
Expense	60000
Other Income	70000
Other Expense	80000

Some accounting systems also have a section starting with *9* for tax entries, which can be placed into the Other Income or Other Expense sections in QuickBooks, as needed.

You can make GL accounts numbers easier or more difficult. For example, the number 10100 is easier to remember than 10101. You should use single digits at the end of the number only for sub-accounts several tiers under the header account. The major sections and headers should have two-to-three zeros at the end.

As mentioned earlier, within any numbered section and sub-section, you should keep the names of the accounts in alphabetical order. QuickBooks automatically does this. However, because you can move accounts, they may become unordered.

QuickBooks displays the GL account numbers in reports. While not all business owners like this feature, it makes finding reports easier when the number is associated with the account name. But you can switch the numbers off, as needed. To do this, open the Company Preferences tab of the Accounting Preferences and deselect the *Use account numbers* check box. The accounts will revert to alphabetical order without numbers.

Using the numbering system has another benefit. It allows you to have multiple accounts with the same name because the number is different. Otherwise, every account name must be unique.

Posting to Header GL Accounts

If you use GL numbers, consider how QuickBooks handles transactions posted to header accounts. While QuickBooks allows you to post to header accounts, it does not show the total in any reports, except as described below. QuickBooks treats anything posted to a header account like a miscellaneous entry. While it belongs in the same area of accounts as the header describes, it doesn't fit in any of the other accounts.

For example, under the UTILITIES header, you may have separate accounts for your utility bills: Water, Power, and Garbage. Someone processes a recycling bill and, because it's not one of the sub-accounts, posts it to the header, UTILITIES. QuickBooks duplicates the header account under the header at the bottom of the other sub-accounts; for example, UTILITIES – Other. Since this generated account uses the same number as the header, it is out of order with the sub-accounts.

Instead, you might want to create a sub-account named *Misc.* You can give it a number that places it below the other sub-accounts in the list. In this case, you can ignore the alphabetical order, because people usually look for the *Misc.* account at the bottom of any list.

The first column of Figure 9-2 shows how posting to a header account produces an additional GL account. The second column shows how it looks when you post to a numbered miscellaneous account instead of the header account.

QUICKBOOKS (no Misc. Account)	Use of Numbered Misc. Account
68000 · UTILITIES	68000 · UTILITIES
68110 · Garbage	68110 · Garbage
68120 · Power	68120 · Power
68130 · Water	68130 · Water
68000 · UTILITIES – Other	68199 · Misc.

Figure 9-2: Comparing the QuickBooks method for miscellaneous entries to using a numbered system with a designated GL account for miscellaneous entries

Entering and Changing GL Accounts

Objective L-9.2 Enter and modify GL accounts

Unlike some accounting systems, QuickBooks offers great flexibility in organizing the Chart of Accounts. Other systems do not allow any changes after an account is created and numbered, except to the name of a GL account or type. QuickBooks allows you to change the account numbers, the hierarchy, and, in many cases, the account type. This flexibility can be especially useful if a GL account that normally carries a credit balance changes to regularly carry a debit balance and, as a result, you want to move the account from the Liability section to the Asset section. QuickBooks allows only accounts of the same type to be grouped together.

First, let's add a new expense GL account named *Printing*. Every business incurs printing costs of some kind, such as business cards and stationery. Printing for advertising purposes would be posted to an advertising GL account. Figure 9-3 shows the Add New Account: Choose Account Type window. You can access this window by clicking **Lists > Chart of Accounts** to display the Chart of Accounts. Then, perform one of the following three options:

- Click **Edit > New Account** in the Menu Bar.
- Press **CTRL+N**.
- From the Chart of Accounts window, click the **Account** drop-down menu and select **New**.

Note: The options are **QB Global**. The same options work for many lists after you open them.

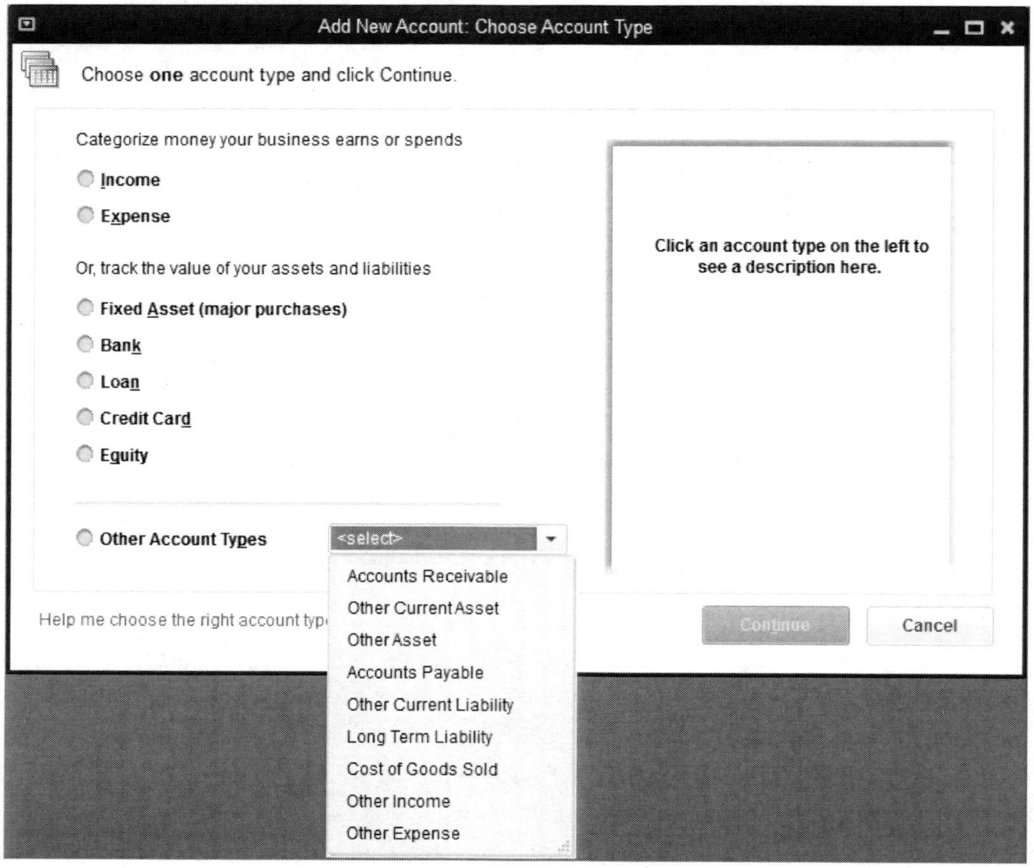

Figure 9-3: Add New Account: Choose Account Type window

You first need to pick an account type. QuickBooks provides the most common ones with radio buttons. The rest you can find in the drop-down menu to the right of the *Other Account Types* radio button. Clicking one of the selections from the drop-down menu automatically selects the radio button. For now, click the Expense radio button. Then, click the Continue button. The Add New Account window opens, shown in Figure 9-4.

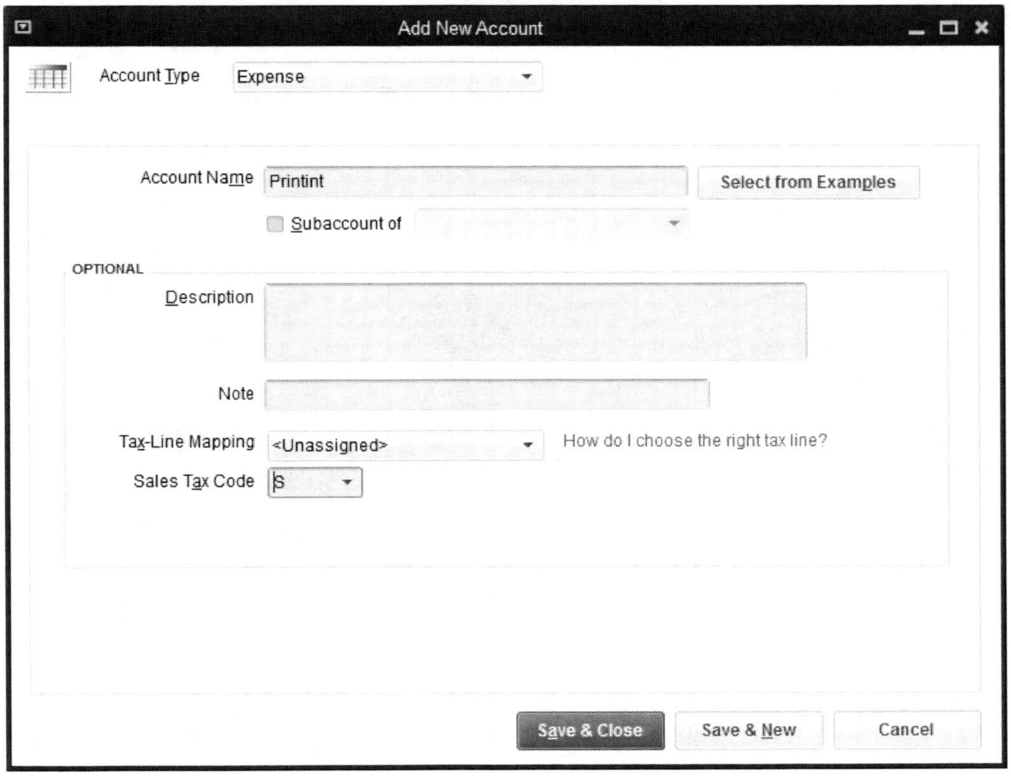

Figure 9-4: Add New Account window

Notice that the word *Printing* is spelled incorrectly. For now, we'll ignore this mistake and show how to correct the mistake after you save the account. You can add an additional description as needed in the Description text box. The correct tax code *S* is selected.

Note: Tax-Line Mapping is not part of this course.

After you click the Save & Close button, the GL account displays in the Chart of Accounts window, as shown in Figure 9-5.

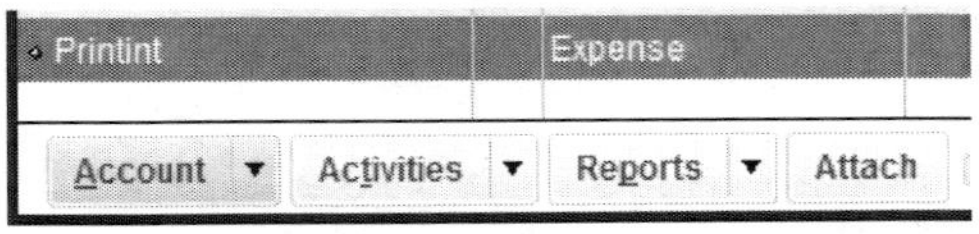

Figure 9-5: Incorrectly spelled new GL account

If you double-click the GL account, the QuickReport for the account will appear. To edit the account, open the Edit Account window (Figure 9-6). The commands are similar to what you used to create a new account. Open the Chart of Accounts, then perform one of the following three options:

- Click **Edit > Edit Account** in the Menu Bar.
- Press **CTRL+E**.
- From the Chart of Accounts window, click the **Account** drop-down menu and select **Edit Account**.

Note: The options are **QB Global**. The same options work for many lists after you open them.

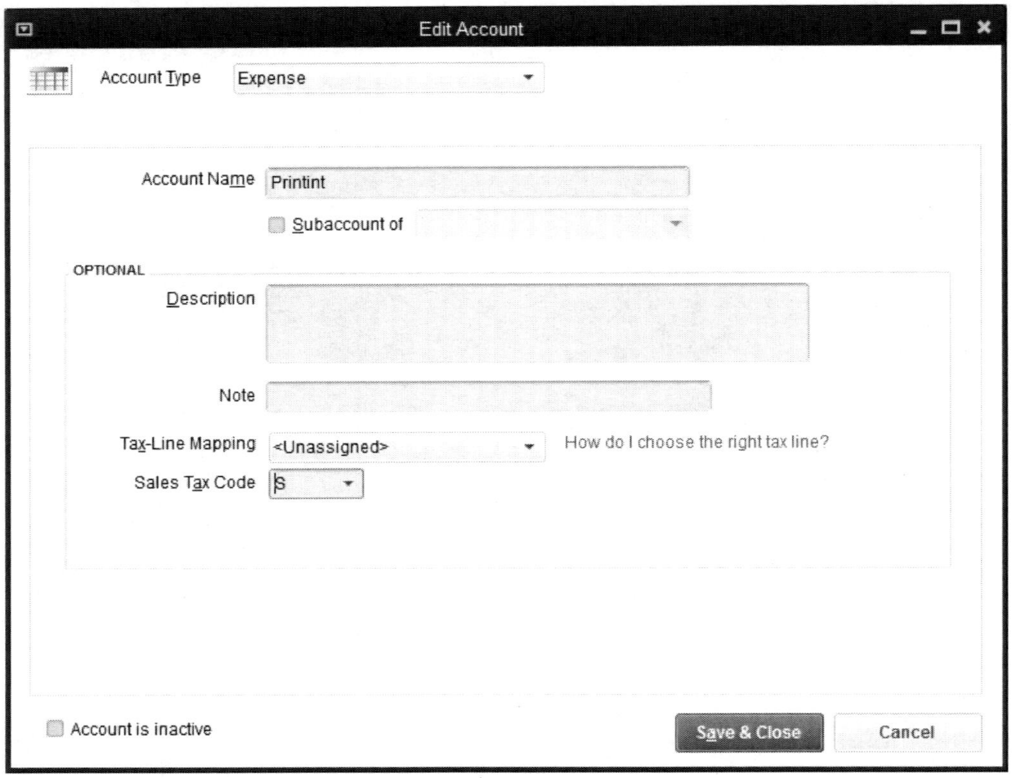

Figure 9-6: Edit Account window

The Edit Account window has several features. Besides correcting the spelling, you can change the account type and add a description, just like in the Add New Account window. Notice the *Account is inactive* check box at the lower left. If it is selected, it hides the account so that it does not appear in the Chart of Accounts. You cannot access the account anywhere in QuickBooks until the check box is deselected.

Next, we will create a hierarchy between accounts. The Best Custom T-Shirts partners request that you create two new GL accounts: Legal and Accounting. These both belong under Professional Fees. When grouping similar accounts, you can draw from accounts above or below the header account in alphabetical order. Only the order under the header matters. Figure 9-7 shows the Add New Account window in which *Legal* is being made a sub-account of *Professional Fees*.

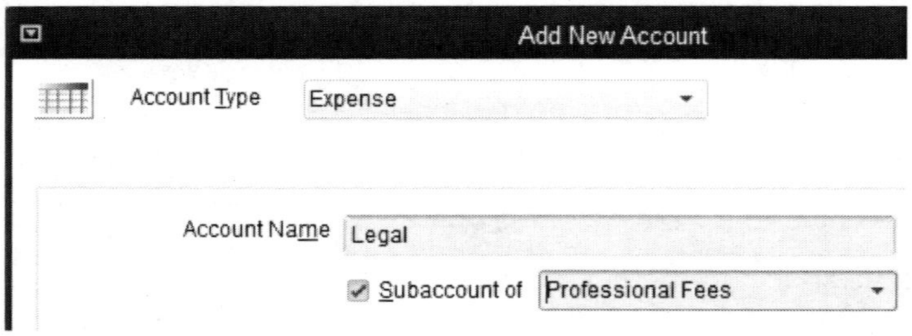

Figure 9-7: Add New Account window—creating a sub-account

Selecting the *Subaccount of* check box allows the drop-down menu to open.

Note: Even with account numbers, typing the first few letters of a list entry will show the options starting with those letters. This is **QB Global** information.

After editing and capitalizing Professional Fees to show that it is a header account, the new GL accounts appear in the Chart of Accounts, as shown in Figure 9-8.

◇ PROFESSIONAL FEES	Expense
◇Accounting	Expense
◇Legal	Expense

Figure 9-8: Result of header account creation

After turning on the numbering preference in the Company Preferences tab of the Accounting Preferences (Figure 9-1), the same accounts appear in the Chart of Accounts as shown in Figure 9-9.

◇ 66700 · PROFESSIONAL FEES	Expense
◇Accounting	Expense
◇Legal	Expense

Figure 9-9: Result of header account creation with account numbers

QuickBooks assigned the number *66700* to the Professional Fees account during file creation. Because the two new accounts have no numbers, they appear in alphabetical order. Figure 9-10 shows the header account when the numbering preference is turned on.

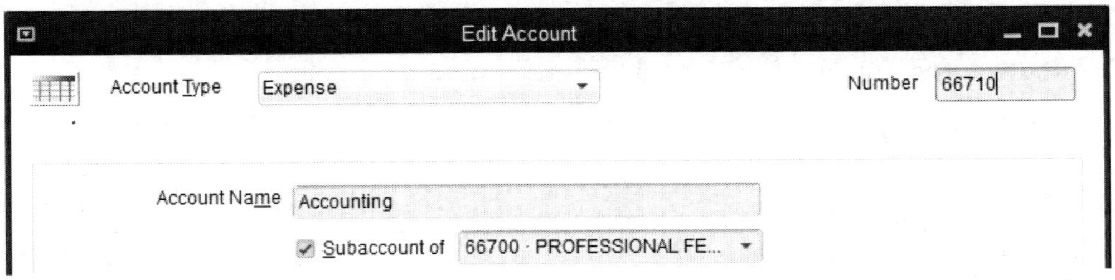

Figure 9-10: Addition of number to existing GL account

You need to evaluate the number QuickBooks provided. Is it okay or does it need to be changed? The 60000 series belongs to expenses, so this is fine. The account name starts with *PRO*, and the letter *P* is in the second half of the alphabet. Within the 60000 series, 66000 is past the middle of the series. This is a good place for the GL header account in the numbering system because the number and the letter have similar qualities.

You could use a lower number like 61000. But then all the GL accounts before the letter *P* would have to fit between 60000 and 61000. The key is to leave enough room for additional GL accounts without crowding too many accounts into a small range of numbers.

Next, we will add numbers to the new GL accounts.

Note: If you add many sub-accounts, you might need to use single digits.

In Figure 9-10, notice how the header account PROFESSIONAL FEES fills the entire *Subaccount of* drop-down menu. This is where skillful abbreviation can help. After editing the GL account and adding a number to the Legal sub-account, the GL accounts appear in the Chart of Accounts as shown in Figure 9-11. The sub-accounts are correctly numbered and remain in alphabetical order.

◇ 66700 · PROF. FEES	Expense
◇66710 · Accounting	Expense
◇66720 · Legal	Expense

Figure 9-11: Post addition of GL numbers and abbreviating header account

Exercise 9.1: Adding and Changing GL Accounts

In this exercise, you will enter several new GL accounts for Best Custom T-Shirts, modify an account, and create a hierarchy for the new accounts.

Note: In the company file you will use for all exercises in this lesson, the account numbers are turned off.

1. Launch **QuickBooks** if necessary, and restore **Best Custom T-Shirts C1_L9_A (Portable).QBM** from the *1767-Student-Files\Lesson 9\StarterFiles* folder. Save the restored company file as **Best Custom T-Shirts C1_L9_<your name>.QBW** in the *1767-Student-Files\Lesson 9\MyProjects* folder.

2. Change the Company Name to **Best Custom T-Shirts C1_L9_<your name>**.

3. Click **Lists > Chart of Accounts**. The Chart of Accounts window opens.

4. Press **CTRL+N**. The Add New Account: Choose Account Type window opens.

5. Click the **Expense** radio button.

6. Click the **Continue** button. The Add New Account window opens.

7. In the *Account Name* field, type: **Computers**.

8. Click the **Save & New** button. A blank Add New Account window opens.

9. In the *Account Name* field, type: **Software**.

10. Select the **Subaccount of** check box.

11. In the *Subaccount of* drop-down menu, select **Computers**.

12. Click the **Save & New** button. A blank Add New Account window opens.

13. In the *Account Name* field, type: **Hardware**.

14. Select the **Subaccount of** check box.

15. In the *Subaccount of* drop-down menu, select **Computers**.

16. Click the **Save & Close** button.

17. In the Chart of Accounts window, click **NAME** at the top of the account list. The new accounts sort alphabetically.

18. Select the GL account **Computer and Internet Expenses**.

19. Press **CTRL+E**. The Edit Account window opens.

20. In the *Account Name* field, replace the existing text with: **Internet**.

21. Click the **Save & Close** button.

22. Close the Chart of Accounts window.

Leave the company file open for the next exercise.

Reviewing the Chart of Accounts

Objective L-9.3 Review changes to the Chart of Accounts

After you make changes to the Chart of Accounts, you will want to review them. From the Chart of Accounts window, you can access the Account Listing (Figure 9-12) from the Reports drop-down menu at the bottom of the window. To see the full account name on the screen, you may need to click-and-drag the three vertical dots to re-size the Account column.

Figure 9-12: Account Listing

The Account Listing concatenates the header accounts with the sub-accounts, placing a colon between them. In Figure 9-12, notice that the concatenated accounts appear on one line. While this listing displays the hierarchy, you can't see it as easily as you would be able to in a report. In a complex Chart of Accounts, you can easily miss an incorrect entry if you check only the Account Listing.

Instead, you should view the accounts the way they would appear in financial reports. This can seem challenging at first because QuickBooks only shows the GL accounts in default reports if they have transactions during the reporting period. However, you can compensate for this. First, open the Profit & Loss report. Do not change the dates. Click the Customize Report button. In the Display tab, click the Advanced button. The Advanced Options dialog box appears, as shown in Figure 9-13.

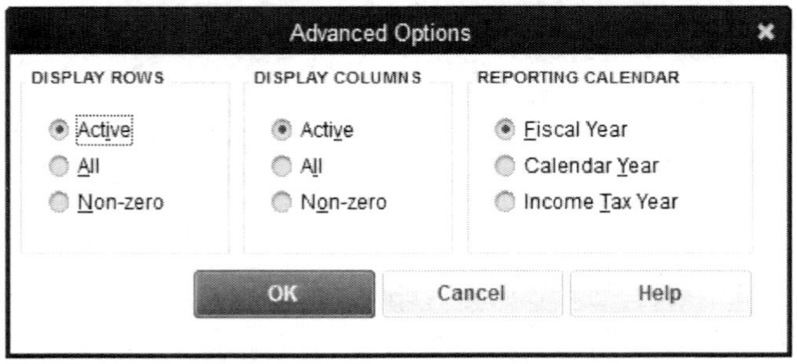

Figure 9-13: Advanced Options dialog box with default settings

The default for financial reports is to have the Active radio button selected. As described earlier, this shows only GL accounts with transactions that occurred during the date range specified in the report. Clicking the All radio button in the DISPLAY ROWS section will produce the result shown in Figure 9-14.

Figure 9-14: Profit & Loss with Display Rows set to All

Now, you can clearly see the hierarchy and the numbers. You can examine your work and make sure you generated the correct results. The report also shows the 66700 · PROF.FEE – Other GL account. If transactions are posted to the header account, they will appear in this account. It is better, though, to avoid posting to header accounts and instead create appropriate sub-accounts.

Exercise 9.2: Reviewing GL Accounts

In this exercise, you'll open the Profit & Loss report, change the advanced settings so that all accounts will appear, and memorize the report.

1. Ensure that the company file you worked on in the previous exercise is still open.

2. Click **Reports > Company & Financial > Profit & Loss Standard**. The Profit & Loss report opens.

3. Click the **Customize Report** button. The Modify Report: Profit & Loss dialog box opens.

4. In the *Display* tab, click the **Advanced** button. The Advanced Options dialog box opens.

5. In the *DISPLAY ROWS* section, click the **All** radio button, and then click **OK**.

6. In the Modify Report: Profit & Loss dialog box, click the **Header/Footer** tab.

7. In the *Report Title* field, type: **ALL ROWS** at the end of the existing text.

8. Click **OK**.

9. Scroll through the report and notice the header accounts and their respective sub-accounts that appear in the hierarchy.

10. Click the **Memorize** button (or press **CTRL+M**). The Memorize Report dialog box opens.

11. Select the **Save in Memorized Report Group** check box, and ensure that **Accountant** (the default value) is selected in the drop-down menu.

12. Click **OK** to save the report to the Accountant Memorized Report group.

13. Close the Profit & Loss report.

Leave the company file open for the next exercise.

Finding, Sorting, and Moving GL Accounts

You can easily find, sort, and move GL accounts in the Chart of Accounts window. You can use the *Look for account name or number* field, shown in Figure 9-15, to locate information in the Chart of Accounts.

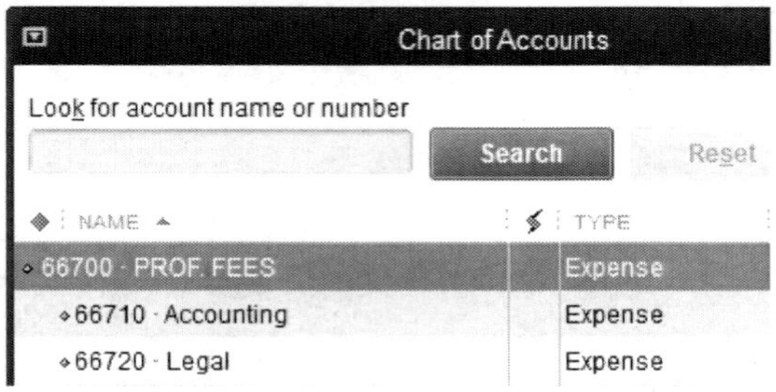

Figure 9-15: Look for account name or number *field*

When the diamond appears to the left of the NAME column, the list is not in the default order; that is, the list has been sorted by clicking one of the column headings. However, if you had moved an account manually by clicking-and-dragging it within its account type, clicking the diamond reverts the list back to the default view.

QuickBooks may not allow you to move an account unless it is in the default view; instead, it will display a warning message. The message tells you that you can't move anything until you click the diamond next to the name and restore the list to its original order.

If you have not turned on numbering, new GL accounts that you add will appear at the beginning of that account type. You can click the NAME column header to view the entire list in alphabetical order.

If numbering is turned on, the numbers sort first followed by the account type. If you turn off numbering and the click the NAME column header, the accounts will no longer appear in order by account type, but in alphabetical order. By clicking the TYPE column, you can restore the sort order to display account type first, and then alphabetically within account type.

Finally, you can perform several of these actions by clicking a GL account. If you click and hold the tiny diamond to the left of a GL account, a four-headed arrow will appear. If you continue holding, you can drag the account within its account type to move it up or down. A dashed horizontal line appears to mark the account's new location. You can also create a hierarchy by clicking and holding the tiny diamond and moving the account to the right. A vertical line appears, indicating that the account you are moving will become a sub-account. You can also move a sub-account to the left to make it a header account.

Exercise 9.3: Arranging GL Accounts

In this exercise, you'll open the Chart of Accounts, start to move one account, respond to a warning, finish moving it, and then move another account.

1.   Ensure that the company file you worked on in the previous exercise is still open.

2.   Open the Chart of Accounts.

3.   Click the **TYPE** column header. The list sorts in order of account type.

4.   Scroll through the list to find the new expense account *Computers* that you added in Exercise 9.1.

5.   Click and hold the small **diamond** to the left of *Computers*. The header account and both sub-accounts become highlighted.

---

6. While continuing to hold, move the accounts below the *Internet* account. A Warning message appears stating that you cannot move the account unless the list is in its original order.

7. Click **OK** to dismiss the Warning message.

8. Click the large **diamond** to the left of *NAME*.

9. Click and hold the small **diamond** to the left of *Computers*. The header account and both sub-accounts become highlighted.

10. While continuing to hold, move the accounts below the *Internet* account.

11. Click and hold the small **diamond** to the left of the expense account *Internet*, and move the account below *Interest Expense*.

12. Close the Chart of Accounts.

Create a portable file to turn in as part of this lesson's assignments.

13. Save the company file as a portable file in the *1767-Student-Files\Lesson 9\MyProjects* folder.

    Note: This is the file you will turn in.

14. If you plan to perform the Practice the Skill exercise, close the company file but leave QuickBooks open; otherwise, close the company file and exit QuickBooks.

Lesson Summary

Now that you have completed this lesson, you should be able to:

☑ Apply the accounting equation to the Chart of   ☑ Review changes to the Chart of Accounts.
    Accounts.

☑ Enter and modify GL accounts.

Key Terms

Term	Definition
Concatenation	Text manipulation with formulas or software code that unites multiple sections or strings of text into one. Also refers to the placement of a character, such as a colon, between strings of text.
Contra account	GL account with a normal balance that is the opposite of the section in which it is located.
Current	In accounting terminology, assets or liabilities that can be converted to cash within a year.
Header account	GL account with accounts ordered beneath it. A header account may also be the sub-account of another header account.
Liquid	In accounting terminology, convertible to cash within a year.
Other	In accounting terminology, assets or liabilities that are non-current or miscellaneous.
Sub-account	GL account beneath a header account. A sub-account may also be the header or header account of other accounts.

Activity 1: Choosing Account Numbers

Of the numbers given, what is the best choice for the header account: Computers?

1. 67800

2. 69465

3. 62100

4. 65100

Activity 2: Choosing Account Types

Match the following descriptions of GL accounts with the correct account type.

Account Types:

1. Income

2. Other Current Asset

3. Credit Card

4. Expense

5. Bank

Account descriptions:

a. Record money owed to the business that is expected to be received within a year.

b. Record credit card purchases until the statement arrives.

c. Records transactions for a new chequing account.

d. Revenue from training courses.

e. Purchases of office supplies.

Practice the Skill

This Practice the Skill exercise is designed to reinforce the skills you have learned. In this exercise, you'll add GL accounts, create a hierarchy, and check your work.

1. If necessary, launch **QuickBooks** and open **Best Custom T-Shirts C1_L9_B (Portable).QBM** from the *1767-Student-Files\Lesson 9\PTS folder*.

2. Add the following three income accounts using the first one as the header: Print Production, Standard, and Custom.

3. Change the name of the Bank Service Charges expense account to *Bank Fees*.

4. Save the company file as a portable company file and add the letters PTS to the end of the file name (*Best Custom T-Shirts C1_L9_<your name> PTS (Portable).QBM*). Turn this file in to your instructor.

5. Close the company file.

Course Project Exercise

The owners of the Blue Heron Spa want to track their advertising costs more closely. They ask you to rename the Advertising and Promotion GL account to Advertising. You also need to add the following four sub-accounts to Advertising: Direct Mail, Events, Media, and Print.

Filename:	Blue Heron Spa Inc 2018 C1_L9_A (Portable).QBM
Admin password:	BluSpa18
New company name:	Blue Heron Spa, Inc. C1_L9 <your name>

Perform the following tasks:

1. Restore the portable file and change the company name as indicated in the table.

2. Rename the Advertising and Promotion GL account to *Advertising*.

3. Add the Direct Mail, Events, Media, and Print GL expense accounts as sub-accounts of ADVERTISING.

4. Create a portable file to turn in to your instructor.

5. Close the company file.

Quiz Questions

For each question, select the best answer.

1. Which statement correctly describes a contra account?

    a. The balance always has more debits than credits.

    b. The balance is the same as what would be considered normal for its section.

    c. The balance always has more credits than debits.

    d. The balance is the opposite of what would be considered normal for its section.

2. Which of the following actions is not allowed when you create or edit a GL account?

    a. Using a colon in the name.

    b. Changing the account name.

    c. Making the account a sub-account.

    d. Changing the account number.

3. Which reports best show the hierarchy of the Chart of Accounts when you want to review changes?

    a. Account Listing

    b. A/R Aging Detail

    c. Financial reports (Balance Sheet and Profit & Loss)

    d. Journal

Lesson 10: Banking and Bill Payments

Lesson Objectives

In this lesson, you will pay bills, receive cheques for invoices, and make payment adjustments. Upon successful completion of this lesson, you should be able to:

☐ Pay bills according to terms.

☐ Adjust customer invoices.

☐ Receive and deposit multiple cheques.

Paying and Receiving Payment for Bill and Invoice Transactions

After you make purchases and sales using credit transactions, you need to note the delay until payment. Everyone wants to maintain good relationships after agreeing to payment terms. The vendors and customers of a business both develop trust when payments arrive on time, but sometimes business plans don't work. Expected sales do not happen. You may have more stock in the warehouse than money in the bank. In most circumstances, businesses can work together when a problem arises. Achieving on-time payments and avoiding late payments and fees is best for everyone. It builds goodwill in business relationships.

Most businesses schedule payments on a regular cycle. They may be scheduled weekly or every other week. If any of the vendors have short payment terms, they can determine the schedule. For example, if one vendor wants payment within ten days, then a once-a-week bill-paying cycle might be necessary.

Before making any payments, you usually need approval. Best Custom T-Shirts wants to review the A/P Aging report before paying any bills. Business owners may want to delay or speed up payment. You cannot determine this from the report alone. You will go through a process to export the report and the owners will tell you which bills to pay.

Most of the time, receiving payments goes smoothly. Cheques arrive on time with the invoice numbers you need to post payments in the accounting records with the correct amounts. But if the customer's accounting department makes a mistake, then you need to know how to handle the problem when the cheque arrives.

When everything goes well, the business's accounting system records match the customers' and vendors' accounting system records. The business's A/P Aging report for a vendor will have the same total as the vendor's customer A/R Aging report for the business. If they don't match, the receipt of payment is often the first time anyone will become aware of it. You must report any problems you find when receiving payments to the responsible person or department.

Paying Bills

Objective L-10.1 Pay bills according to terms

In this section, we will focus on the Pay Bills window, which is part of Bill Payment in the Purchases Cycle (Figure 10-1). In this window, you select existing bills and apply payments. When you save the transactions, you will create one or more journal entries as the Bill Payment type. The payment posts the debits (decreases) to the Accounts Payable GL account in the Liabilities section and the credits (decreases) to the Chequing GL account in the Assets section.

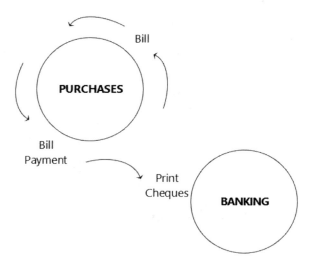

Figure 10-1: Purchases Cycle

It is important to understand that the business owner or other designated person, such as the Chief Financial Officer (CFO), decides which bills you will pay and when you will pay them. The person who approves bill payment may have his or her own access to the accounting system, or may expect you to print or export the A/P Aging Detail and/or A/P Aging Summary reports to Excel.

The CFO first verifies the chequing account balance. The business may also have a line of credit. If the amount needed to pay the bills exceeds the chequing account balance, then you may be authorized to transfer money from the line of credit account into the chequing account to cover the shortage.

After you receive approval to pay the bills, you can click **Vendors > Pay Bills** to open the Pay Bills window (Figure 10-2), which shows all the existing bills and their due dates.

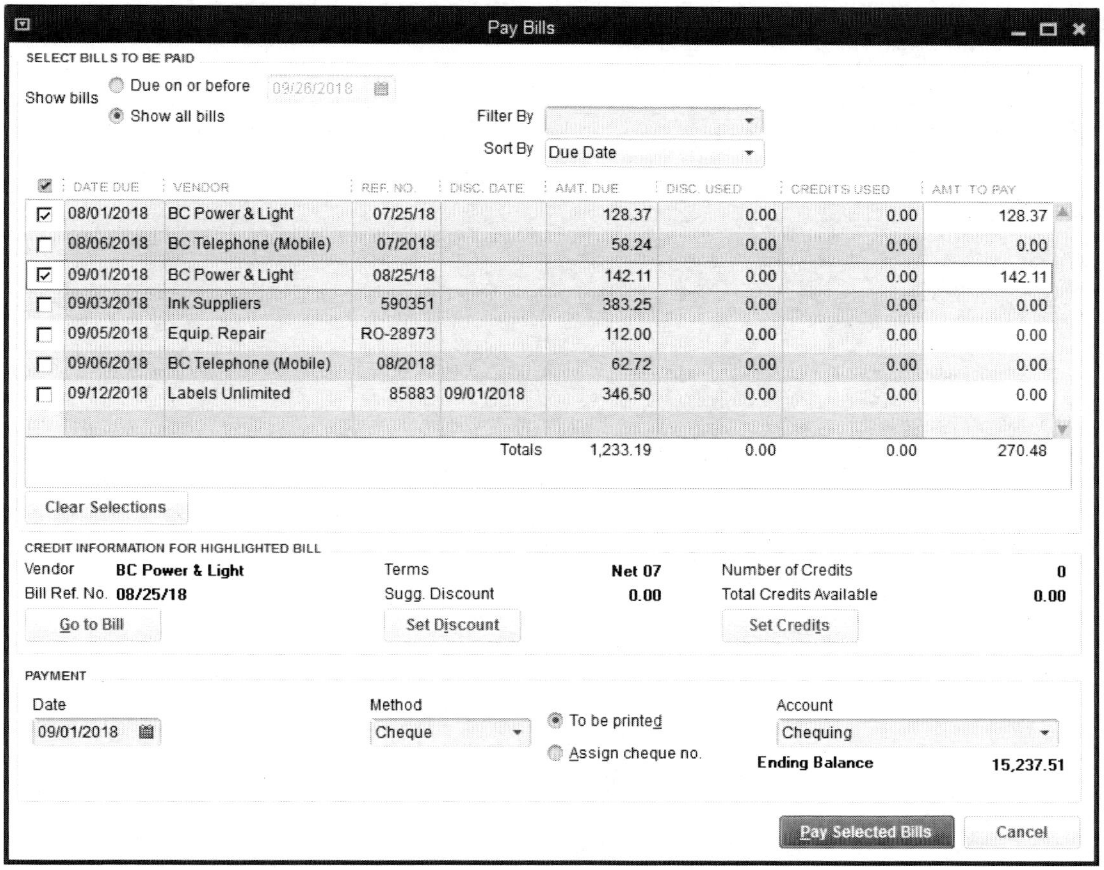

Figure 10-2: Pay Bills window

Depending on the length of the list, you can scan the list to find the bills you want to pay, or you can filter the list by vendor or due date. Figure 10-2 shows two bills selected for BC Power & Light. Recall that in our scenario from a previous lesson, the utility bills for August had been overlooked, so there are two bills listed for each utility vendor (BC Power & Light and BC Telephone (Mobile)). Also, notice that the number at the lower right for Ending Balance indicates what the balance in the Chequing GL account will be after paying the bills that are selected in the Pay Bills window.

If you need to look more closely at any bill, you can open it from the Pay Bills window. Click anywhere in the bill line, and then click the Go to Bill button in the lower left, above the date. This action will open the Enter Bills form for the bill, which you can then edit.

You may be writing cheques for some payments and sending others electronically. This determines the form of the payment: cheque or EFT. You can select all the bills you plan to pay by the same payment type at one time. QuickBooks creates one Bill Payments form for each vendor, with multiple bills on each as needed. For cheques, make sure you click the *To be printed* radio button in the Pay Bills window before you click the Pay Selected Bills button. (The use of the *Assign cheque no.* radio button for the EFT payment option will be described shortly).

In the Pay Bills window, click the check box to the left of a bill to select it. After you have selected all the bills you want to pay for a particular payment type, you need to turn your attention to two more fields. First, make sure the date is correct in the Date field based on the date the CFO told you to use for issuing the cheques. This date becomes the date of the journal entry and the date printed on the cheque. Second, make sure you select the correct chequing account in the Account field if you have more than one. Then click the Pay Selected Bills button.

QuickBooks may take a moment to process the payments. Each vendor bill payment becomes a journal entry and populates the Bill Payments form (Figure 10-3).

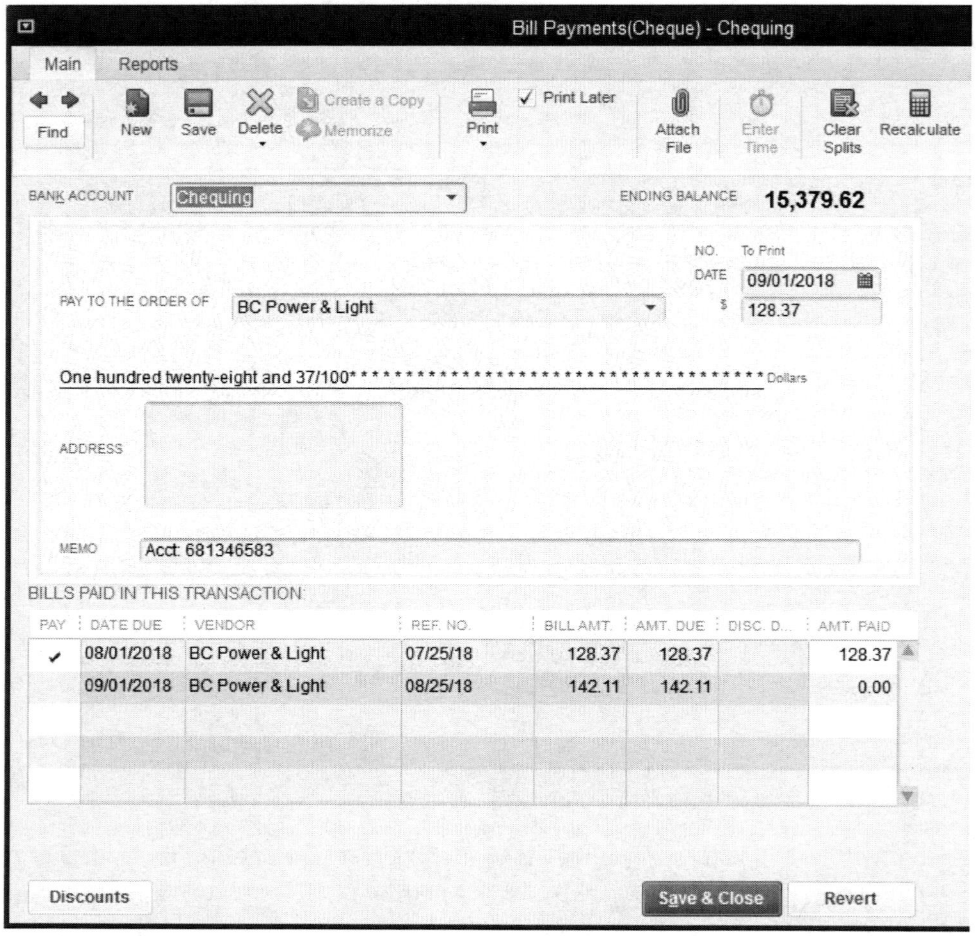

Figure 10-3: Bill Payments form

The Bill Payments form is like the Write Cheques form. The differences are that, instead of Expenses and Items tabs, the Bill Payments form lists only the paid and outstanding bills, and the form is connected to the Enter Bills form.

You can also edit the Bill Payments form. For example, if a vendor has two bills in the same amount and you discover you selected the wrong one, you could correct that in the Bill Payments form. Deselecting one bill allows you to select another if the total amount paid remains the same. You can change the amount if, for some reason, the cheque clears the bank in a different amount. Although rare with printed checks, this can happen. Then, you can enter another bill or credit to resolve the difference.

Figure 10-3 shows the result of deselecting the second BC Power & Light bill in the Pay Bills window, and then clicking the Pay Selected Bills button. You can see that only the first bill due on 08/01/2018 is selected (a check mark appears in the PAY column). What can be confusing about the Bill Payments form is that all bills from the vendor appear in the form. The text BILLS PAID IN THIS TRANSACTION refers only to the selected bill(s).

Notice in the upper right of Figure 10-3, the field NO. reads *To Print*. Until you assign a cheque number and print the check, this text will appear in the Bill Payments form.

Let's say you receive word that the owners want to set up an EFT payment for this vendor to avoid missing another payment. You'll keep the first bill payment as a cheque to be printed and make the second payment an EFT-OUT. For the EFT-OUT payment, click the *Assign cheque no.* radio button in the Pay Bills window. When you click the Pay Selected Bills button, the Assign Cheque Numbers dialog box will appear (Figure 10-4).

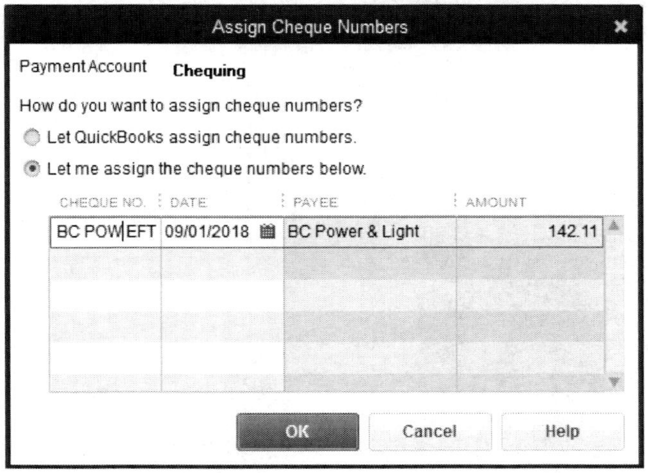

Figure 10-4: Assign Cheque Numbers dialog box

You can enter text in the CHEQUE NO. field in the dialog box. If you want, you can include the vendor's initials in the CHEQUE NO. field to help identify the vendor, as shown in Figure 10-4.

Note: While there is an EFT payment type, choosing it eliminates the option of entering anything in the CHEQUE NO. field when you pay the bill. Leaving the payment method set to Cheque (in the Pay Bills window) allows you to add text.

As you can see in Figure 10-4, you still have the option to let QuickBooks assign cheque numbers. For EFTs, entering your own text is the better option. In our example, a few initials indicate that BC Power is receiving the EFT payment.

Note: Usually, EFT payments are generated by the vendor. You need to watch carefully for these on the bank statement.

After you click OK in the Assign Cheque Numbers dialog box, the processing completes. Then the Payment Summary dialog box appears (Figure 10-5).

This dialog box asks if you want to pay more bills. If you click the Done button, you'll exit the Pay Bills process. If you click the Pay More Bills button, you'll return to the Pay Bills window, in which you can select the next set of bills you want to pay.

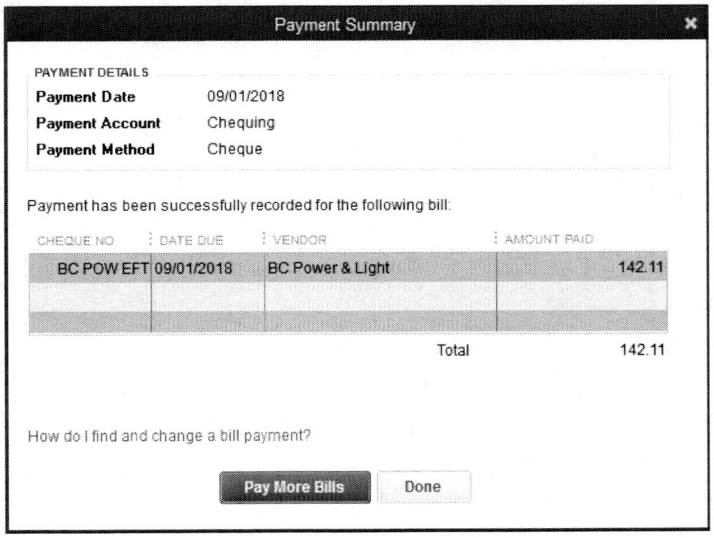

Figure 10-5: Payment Summary dialog box—pay more bills

In our example scenario, let's assume you select the Ink Suppliers bill in the Pay Bills window next, click the *To be printed* radio button, and then click the Pay Selected Bills button. The Payment Summary dialog box appears as shown in Figure 10-6. Notice that it is similar to the Payment Summary dialog box that appears in Figure 10-5, but contains the additional button, Print Cheques.

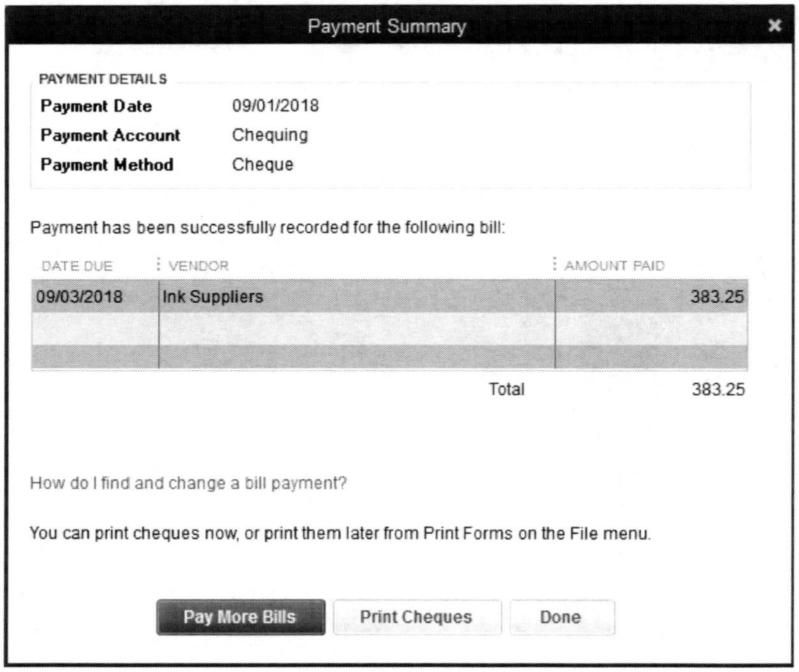

Figure 10-6: Payment Summary dialog box—print cheques

Before you print the cheques, you can view the status of the bill payments in the Chequing GL register (Figure 10-7).

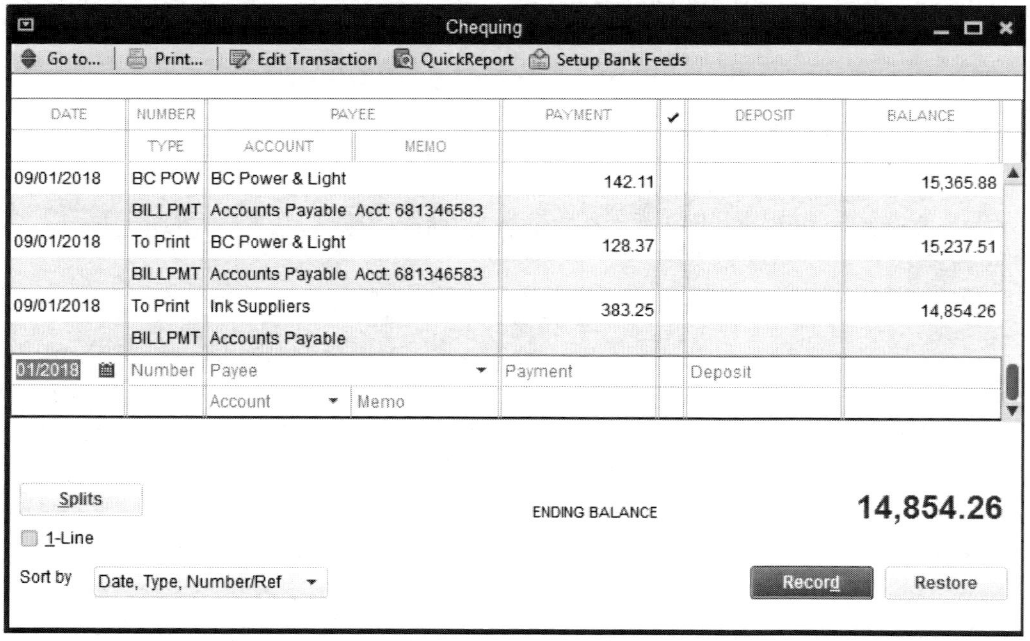

Figure 10-7: Chequing GL register

Figure 10-7 shows the EFT to BC Power & Light with the NUMBER text entered (shortened to fit) as *BC POW*. The two cheques waiting to be printed do not yet have cheque numbers and instead say *To Print*. After they are printed, the cheque numbers will appear.

Printing Cheques

If you don't click the Print Cheques button in the Payment Summary dialog box, you can open the Select Cheques to Print dialog box (Figure 10-8) by clicking **File > Print Forms > Cheques**.

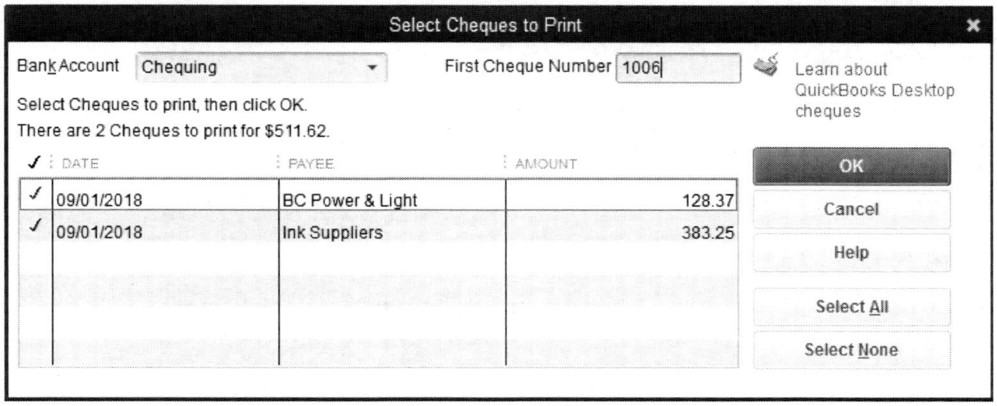

Figure 10-8: Select Cheques to Print dialog box

The Select Cheques to Print dialog box displays the total number of cheques needed, the starting cheque number, and the total dollar amount of the cheques to print.

Notice that in Figure 10-8, the cursor is in the First Cheque Number field. Continuing with our scenario, suppose that the two selected cheques are the first two cheques to be printed from QuickBooks. QuickBooks would display the number *1* in the First Cheque Number field, but you can easily edit that value to reflect the correct number for the first cheque you want to print—and in our scenario, the correct number is *1006*. QuickBooks will remember that 1007 should be the next cheque number. After you load the cheque paper in the printer (and ensure that the correct account is selected in the Bank Account drop-down menu), click OK.

The Print Cheques dialog box appears (Figure 10-9).

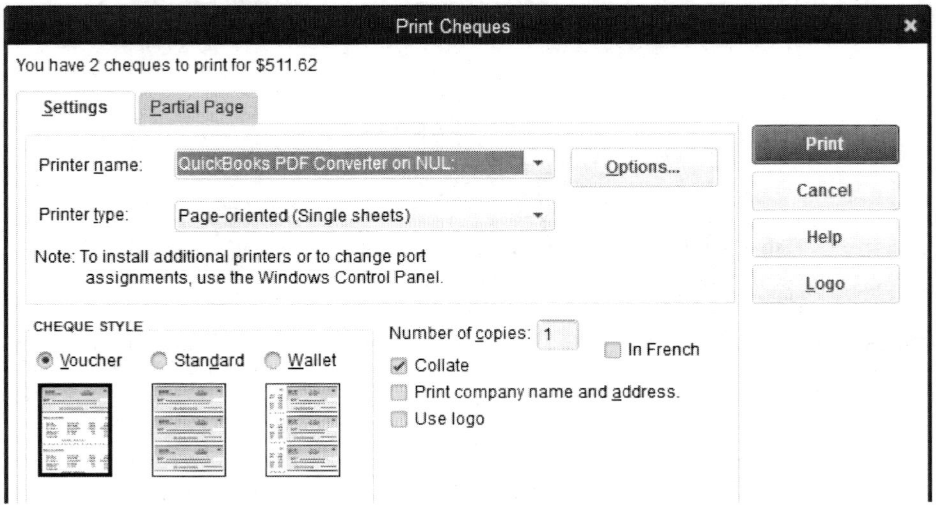

Figure 10-9: Print Cheques dialog box

Select the appropriate printer and any other options specific to printing in your office, and then click the Print button. Examine the printed cheques to be sure they printed correctly.

After you print the cheques, the Print Cheques - Confirmation dialog box (Figure 10-10) will appear and ask if the cheques printed correctly.

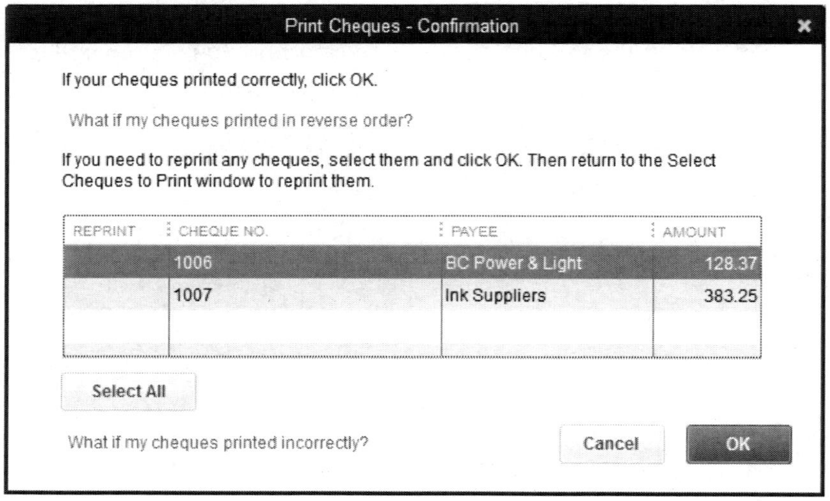

Figure 10-10: Print Cheques - Confirmation dialog box

If they did not, you can select any cheques that you want to re-print by clicking in the REPRINT column to the left of the cheque number, as shown in Figure 10-11.

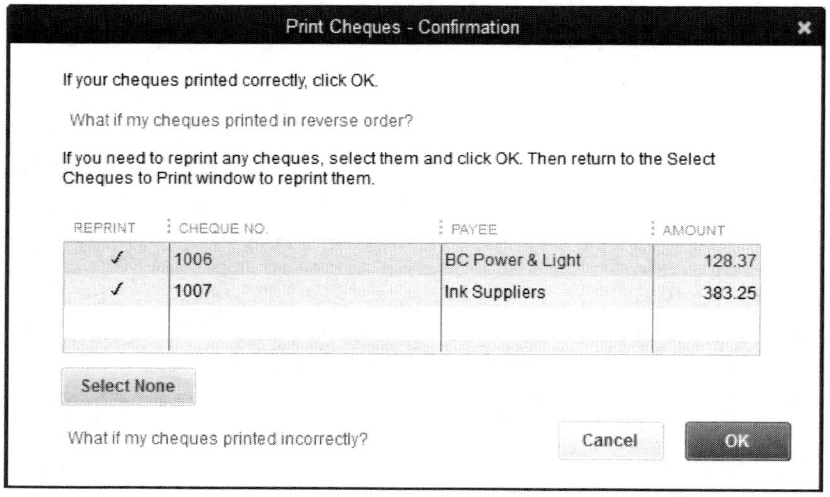

Figure 10-11: Print Cheques - Confirmation dialog box—select cheques to re-print

Click OK to close the dialog box. The selected checks are marked for re-printing and will appear in the Select Cheques to Print dialog box the next time you open it.

To return to the Select Cheques to Print dialog box (Figure 10-12), click **File > Print Forms > Cheques**.

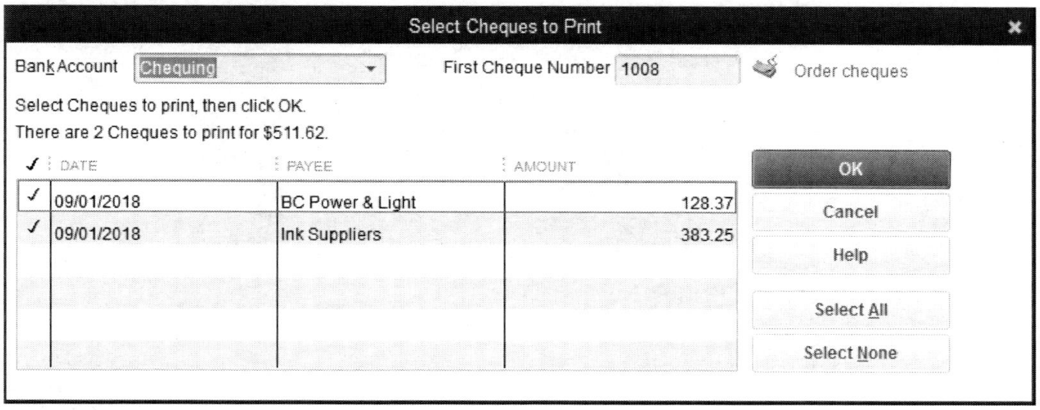

Figure 10-12: Select Cheques to Print dialog box – adjusted First Cheque Number

Notice that QuickBooks assumes the cheques are unusable and auto-fills the next cheque number in the First Cheque Number field, *1008*. You can manually change the number if necessary by typing the correct number in the field. After you successfully print the cheques, the Chequing register will display the cheque numbers in the NUMBER column, as shown in Figure 10-13.

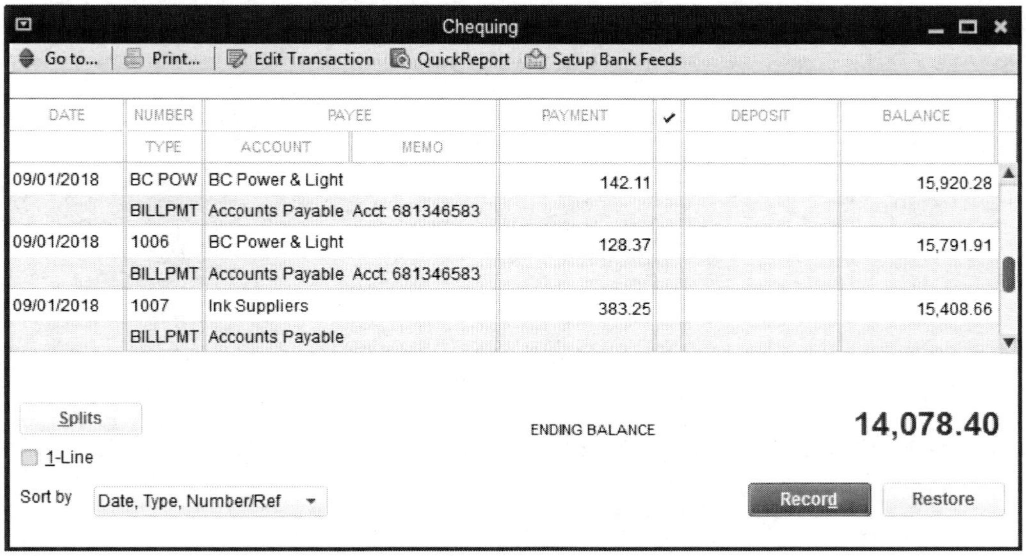

Figure 10-13: Chequing register showing cheque numbers

If for some reason the cheques printed correctly but the cheque numbers are incorrect, you can edit the cheque numbers directly in the register. A message will appear when you press TAB to move out of the field asking if you want to make the change.

If you make a mistake, miss a chance to re-do the cheque printing, and need to re-print a cheque, you can do so directly from the Bill Payments form. You can find the cheque or bill payment through the Chequing register or Vendor Centre. Open the Bill Payments form and deselect the Print Later check box, as shown in Figure 10-14.

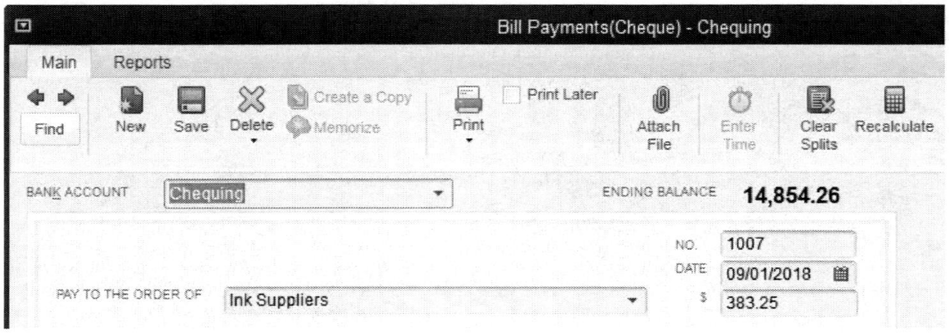

Figure 10-14: Bill Payments form—Print Later check box deselected

When you select the Print Later check box, the NO. field changes to *To Print*, as shown in Figure 10-15. When you are ready to print the checks, you can then return to the Bill Payments form to complete the process.

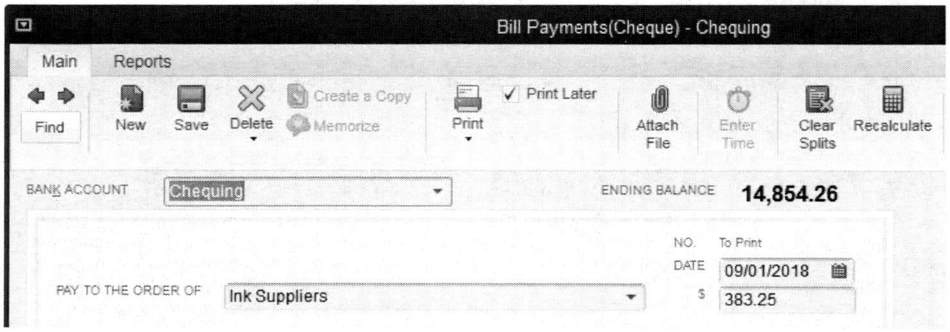

Figure 10-15: Bill Payments form—Print Later check box selected

After successfully printing the cheques, you can prepare the cheques for signature following your business's procedure.

You might also need to report issued cheques to the bank electronically. You can compose a Journal report with all the bill payments made on a specific day, as shown in Figure 10-16.

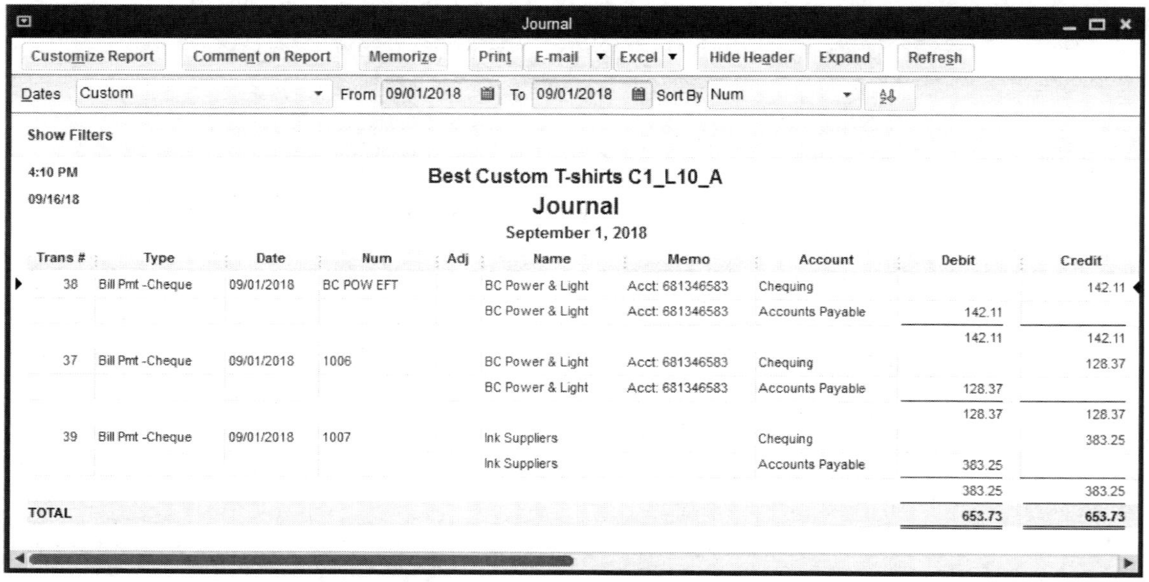

Trans #	Type	Date	Num	Adj	Name	Memo	Account	Debit	Credit
38	Bill Pmt -Cheque	09/01/2018	BC POW EFT		BC Power & Light	Acct: 681346583	Chequing		142.11
					BC Power & Light	Acct: 681346583	Accounts Payable	142.11	
								142.11	142.11
37	Bill Pmt -Cheque	09/01/2018	1006		BC Power & Light	Acct: 681346583	Chequing		128.37
					BC Power & Light	Acct: 681346583	Accounts Payable	128.37	
								128.37	128.37
39	Bill Pmt -Cheque	09/01/2018	1007		Ink Suppliers		Chequing		383.25
					Ink Suppliers		Accounts Payable	383.25	
								383.25	383.25
TOTAL								653.73	653.73

Figure 10-16: Journal report—bill payments

In Figure 10-16, you can also see that each bill payment debits the Accounts Payable GL and credits the Chequing GL. The payments in the figure happened to be the only bill payments on 09/01/2018, but you could click Customize Report and specify to filter the report to show only the Bill Pmt - Cheque transaction type. The default sort setting for the Journal report is by transaction numbers. In Figure 10-16, however, the report has been customized to sort by values in the *Num* column. You can sort by any field in the report by clicking the column header of your choice.

You can then export the report to Excel. Files going to or from banks usually need to be in ***comma separated values (CSV)*** format. You can select this option in the Send Report to Excel dialog box.

Applying Vendor Discounts

Continuing with our scenario, let's assume you still need to pay one more bill to Labels Unlimited, as shown in the Pay Bills window (Figure 10-17).

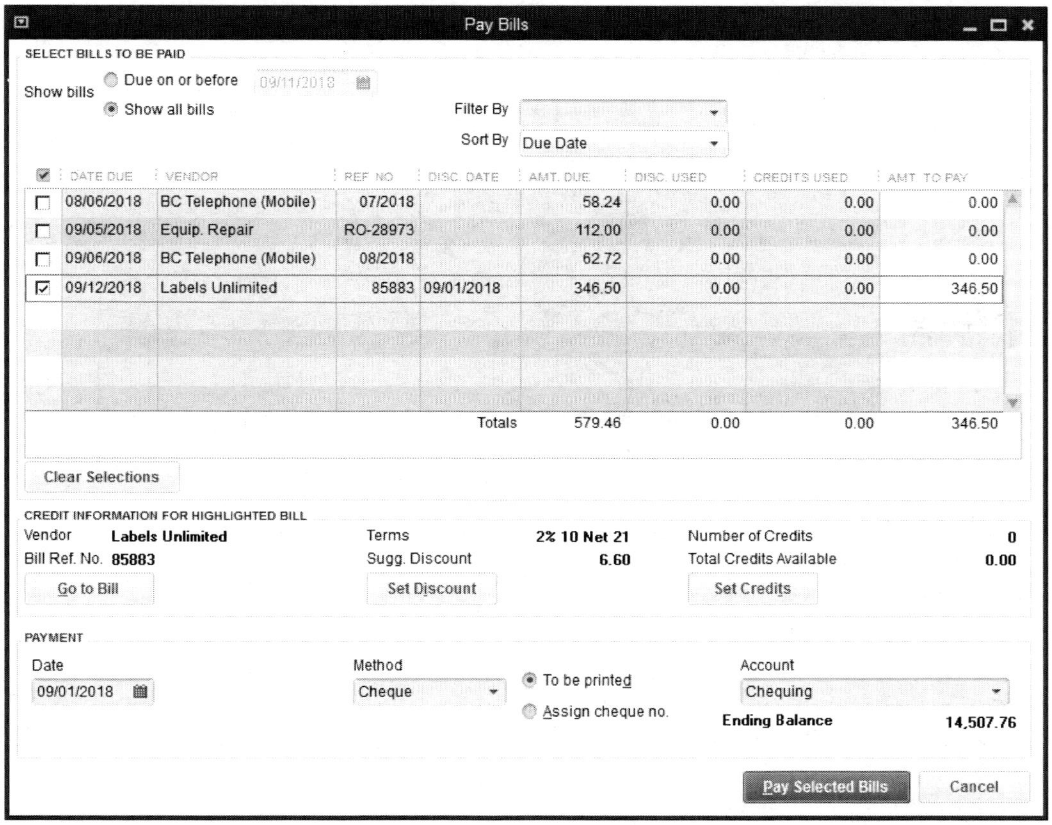

Figure 10-17: Pay Bills window—bill with eligible discount

The vendor payment terms for Labels Unlimited offer a $6.60 discount if paid by 09/01/2018. Select the check box to select the bill, and then click the Set Discount button to open the Discount and Credits dialog box, shown in Figure 10-18.

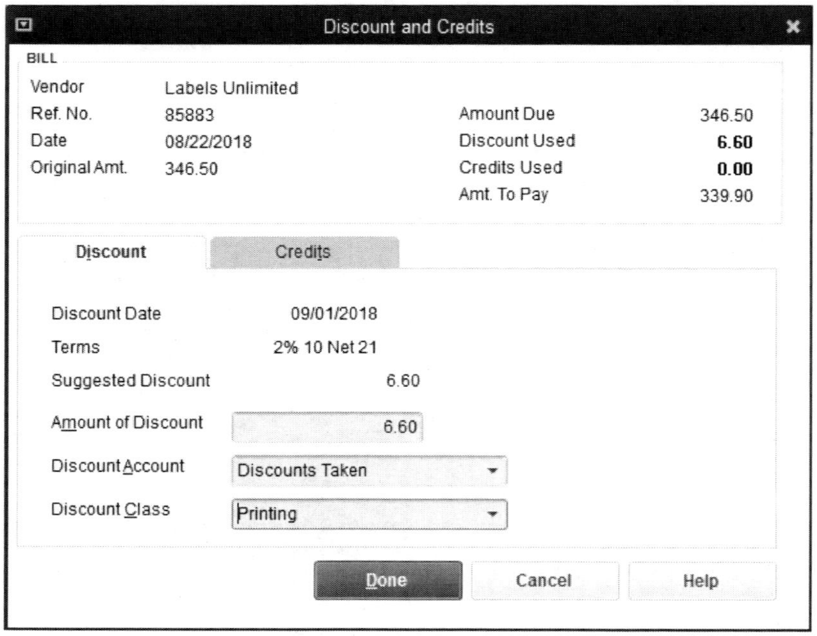

Figure 10-18: Discount and Credits dialog box

Notice the Discount Account field in Figure 10-18. The Discount Account is an income type account (because vendor discounts are considered income). Figure 10-19 shows the bill in the Pay Bills window with the discount applied and the remaining balance.

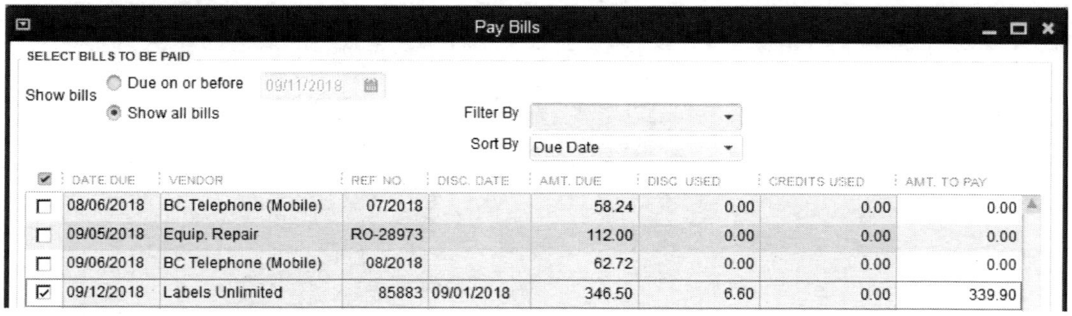

Figure 10-19: Remaining bill amount

Note: If you want to apply a discount or credit but are not paying the bill immediately, you can keep the discount or credit attached to the bill. To do this, change the amount to zero and click the Pay Selected Bills button.

Exercise 10.1: Paying Bills and Applying Discounts

In this exercise, you will pay four bills and print three cheques.

1.   Launch **QuickBooks** if necessary, and restore **Best Custom T-Shirts C1_L10_A (Portable).QBM** from the *1767-Student-Files\Lesson 10\StarterFiles* folder. Save the restored company file as **Best Custom T-Shirts C1_L10_<your name>.QBW** in the *1767-Student-Files\Lesson 10\MyProjects* folder.

2.   Change the Company Name to **Best Custom T-Shirts C1_L10_<your name>**.

3.   Click **Vendors > Pay Bills**. The Pay Bills window opens.

Select the bills to pay by cheque.

4. Select the check boxes to the left of both **BC Telephone (Mobile)** bills and the **Equip. Repair** bill.

5. In the *PAYMENT* section at bottom of window, change the Date to **09/05/2018**.

6. Select the **To be Printed** radio button, if necessary.

7. Click the **Pay Selected Bills** button. The Payment Summary dialog box opens, indicating that payments have been successfully recorded for three bills.

Begin the process to make an electronic funds transfer (EFT) payment.

8. In the Payment Summary dialog box, click the **Pay More Bills** button to pay an EFT. The Pay Bills window re-opens.

9. Select the check box to the left of **Web Hosting**.

10. Ensure that the date is set to **09/05/2018**.

Apply a discount.

11. Click the **Set Discount** button. The Discount and Credits window opens.

12. In the *Amount of Discount* field, type: **1.68**.

13. Ensure that the *Discount Account* field displays **Discounts Taken**.

14. In the *Discount Class* drop-down menu, select **Admin**.

15. Click the **Done** button. Notice in the Pay Bills window that the AMT. TO PAY column for Web Hosting now displays the discounted amount, *$166.32*.

Specify a descriptive cheque number.

16. Click the **Assign cheque no.** radio button.

17. Click the **Pay Selected Bills** button. The Assign Cheque Numbers dialog box opens.

18. In the *CHEQUE NO.* field, type: **WEB EFT**.

19. Click **OK**. The Payment Summary dialog box opens, indicating that the payment has been successfully recorded.

20. Click the **Done** button.

Print the cheques.

21. Click **File > Print Forms > Cheques**. The Select Cheques to Print dialog box opens.

22. Ensure that the *First Cheque Number* field displays **1010**.

23. Verify that both cheques are selected (check marks should appear to the left of each check).

24. Click **OK**. The Print Cheques dialog box opens.

25. Print the cheques according to your instructor's preference.

Verify the bill payments in the Journal report and memorize the report.

26. Click **Reports > Accountant & Taxes > Journal**. The Journal report opens.

27. Click the **Customize Report** button. The Modify Report: Journal dialog box opens.

28. In the *Display* tab, set the *From* and *To* dates to **09/05/2018**.

29. Click the **Filters** tab, and then select **Transaction Type** in the *FILTER* list box.

30. In the *Transaction Type* drop-down menu, select **Bill Payment**.

31. Click the **Header/Footer** tab and, in the *Report Title* field, type: – **Payments** at the end of the text.

32. Click **OK** to return to the Journal report.

33. Expand the window if necessary and view the report details. Notice that each bill payment debits the Accounts Payable GL and credits the Chequing GL.

34. Press **CTRL+M**. The Memorize Report dialog box opens.

35. Select the **Save in Memorized Report Group** check box, and ensure that **Accountant** (the default value) displays in the drop-down menu.

36. Click **OK** to save the report in the Accountant Memorized Report group.

37. Close the Journal report.

Leave the company file open for the next exercise.

Depositing Multiple Cheques

Objective L-10.2 Receive and deposit multiple cheques

In this section, we will learn more about the Receive Payments step in the Sales Cycle (Figure 10-20).

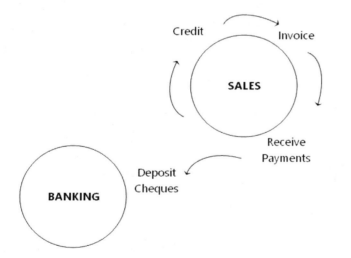

Figure 10-20: Sales Cycle—Receive Payments

When you finish receiving payments, the journal entry creates debits (increases) in the suspense GL account Undeposited Funds and credits (decreases) the Accounts Receivable GL account. These are both in the Assets section.

Once you receive all payments, then you use the Make Deposits form to select the cheques in each deposit. The deposit creates the journal entry as the payment type. This debits (increases) Chequing and credits (decreases) Undeposited Funds. Both are GL accounts in the Asset section.

Receiving Payments

Several possible scenarios exist when a cheque arrives. Each situation has a solution. You need to take the correct action based on the processes. You also need to understand what QuickBooks does in each situation. Here are the three scenarios:

1. The amount paid matches the invoice amount in QuickBooks.

2. The amount paid is less than the invoice amount.

3. The amount paid is greater than the invoice amount.

If the cheque amount matches the invoice amount, you simply receive it. The most direct way to enter the received cheque is by using the Find tool. In the Find window, in the Simple tab, select *Invoice* in the Transaction Type drop-down menu, and then enter the invoice number from the cheque.

Note: You can also click **Banking > Make Deposits** to open the Make Deposits form, and then select the customer. If you have more than one A/R account, finding the invoice is more difficult as you may need to change the A/R account using the drop-down menu. Using the Find tool and the invoice number selects the correct A/R account.

After you locate and open the invoice, click the Receive Payments icon in the button bar to display the Receive Payments form. Figure 10-21 shows a received payment from the Blue Heron Spa company file. In this figure, the cheque amount matches the invoice amount.

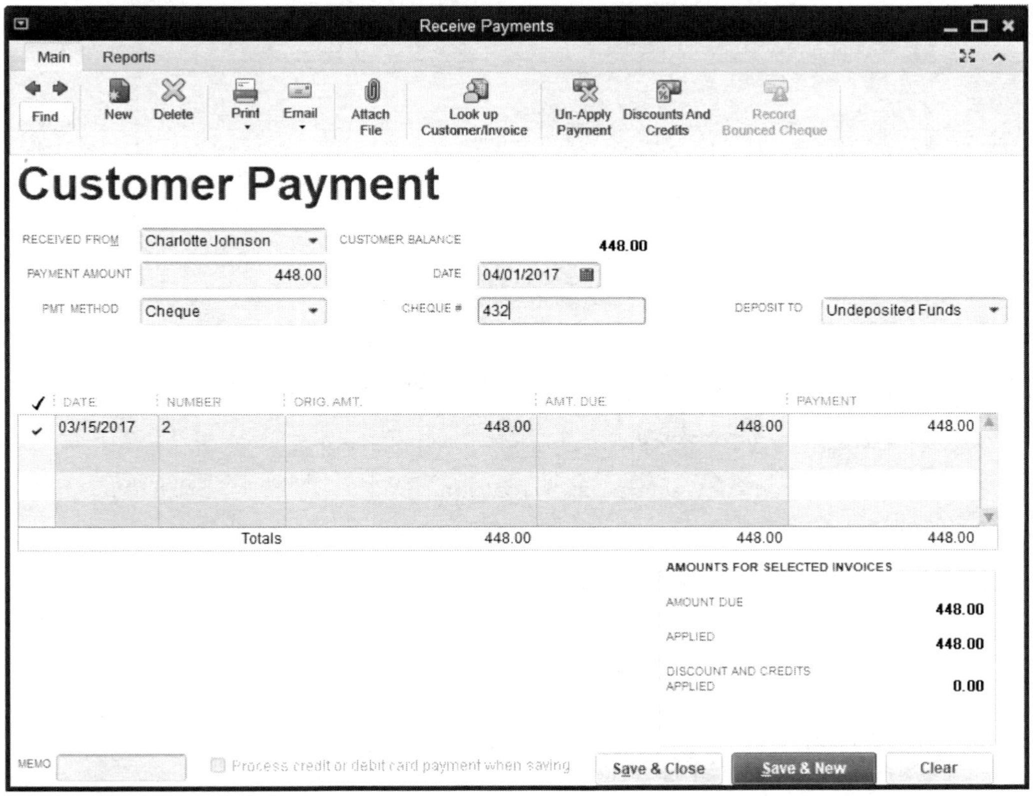

Figure 10-21: Receive Payments form

The required fields in the Receive Payments form are the customer, amount, and date. Always enter the deposit date and not the cheque date. This is the official date the business received the funds. Specifying the payment method is optional but can help you locate a transaction later.

If the amount is an exact match for only one invoice, QuickBooks places a check mark to the left of the invoice in the Receive Payments form. It can locate the invoice no matter where it is in the list of invoices. If the amount matches more than one invoice, the check mark goes in front of the oldest invoice. If the invoice is not the correct one, you need to deselect the check box next to the incorrect invoice, and then select the correct invoice.

If the amount paid is less than the invoice amount

Now let's work through a cheque amount that is less than the invoice amount. Figure 10-22 shows the Receive Payments form for customer *A1 Painting*. They sent a cheque for $554.40 for invoice 2. This is less than the amount of the invoice but allowable because the customer payment terms are 1% 10 Net 30.

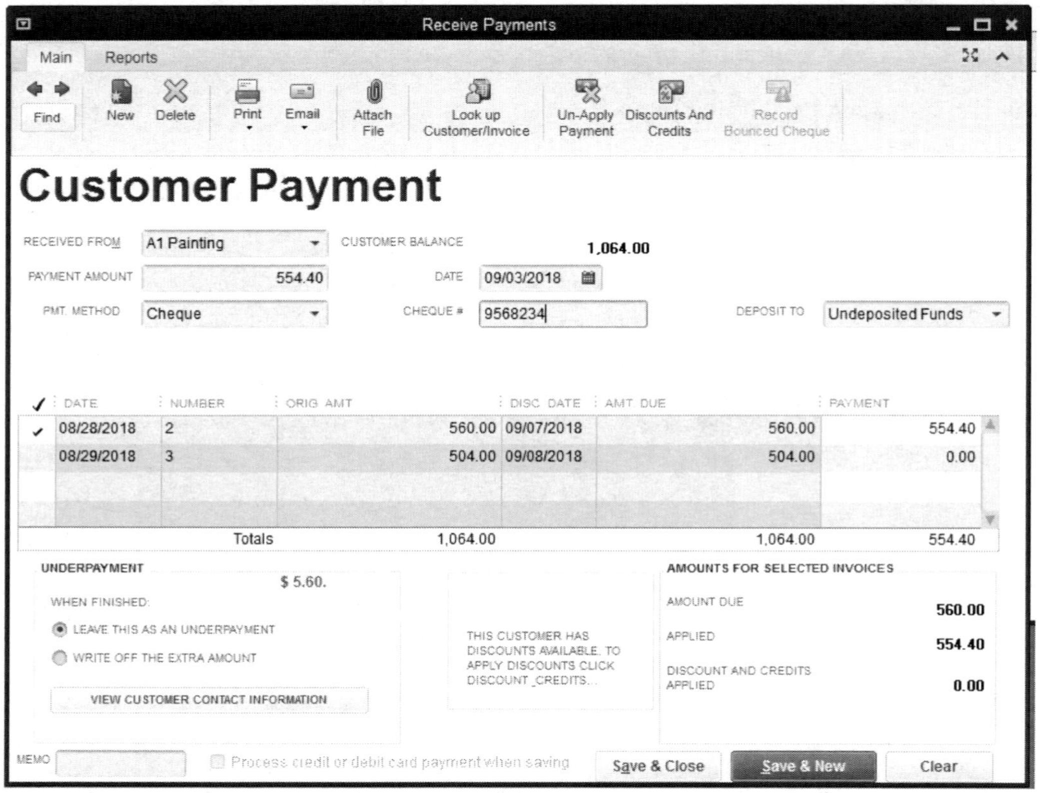

Figure 10-22: Receive Payments form with underpayment

In the *UNDERPAYMENT* section in the lower left, notice that the LEAVE THIS AS AN UNDERPAYMENT radio button is selected.

Note: Do not select the WRITE OFF THE EXTRA AMOUNT radio button in the *UNDERPAYMENT* section. (Writing off a balance uses a different process.)

You have several options for what to do next.

QuickBooks will apply the cheque amounts to the invoices even if they don't match. Matching may not always be correct, so you have to verify what you see in the form.

If no invoice matches the cheque amount, QuickBooks automatically applies the cheque amount to the oldest invoice that appears at the top of the list. A mismatch between the cheque and an invoice usually happens for one of two different reasons:

1. The customer pays multiple invoices with one cheque.
2. The customer takes the discount offered in the terms.

If the customer skips an invoice or takes a discount, you may have to deselect any selected invoices except the one you want. Then, apply the discount using the following process.

1. Click the appropriate line in the detail section of the form to ensure you apply the discount to the correct invoice.
2. Click the Discounts and Credits button in the ribbon, which opens the Discount and Credits dialog box (Figure 10-23).

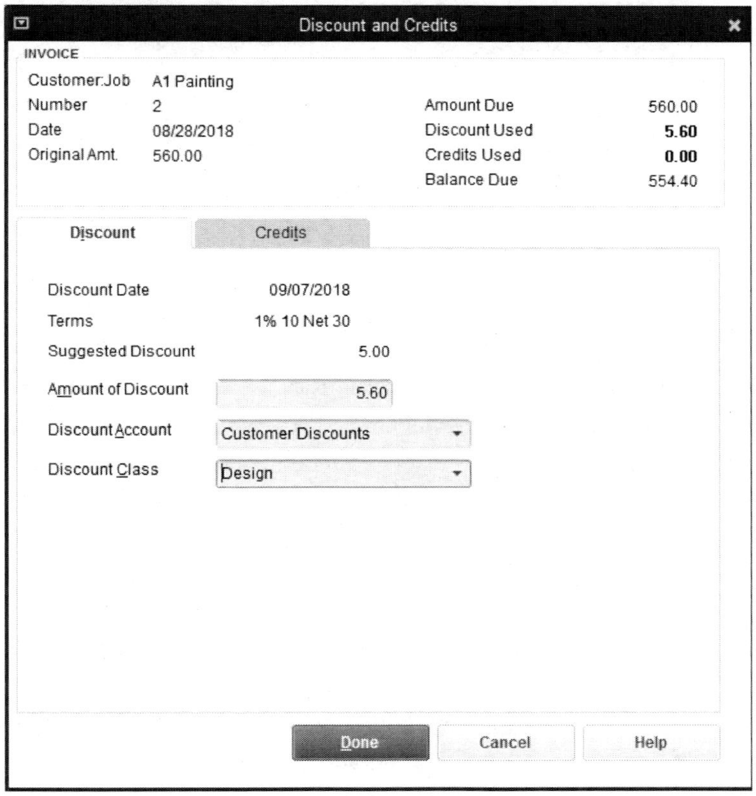

Figure 10-23: Discount and Credits dialog box—apply discount

3. In the Discount and Credits dialog box, click the Discount tab.
4. Enter the amount of the discount, select the correct GL account and class, and then click Done.

Note: If the cheque date is past the date allowed by the payment terms, notify your supervisor and do not apply the discount.

Figure 10-24 shows the Receive Payments form after applying the discount. The customer Discount GL is a COGS type.

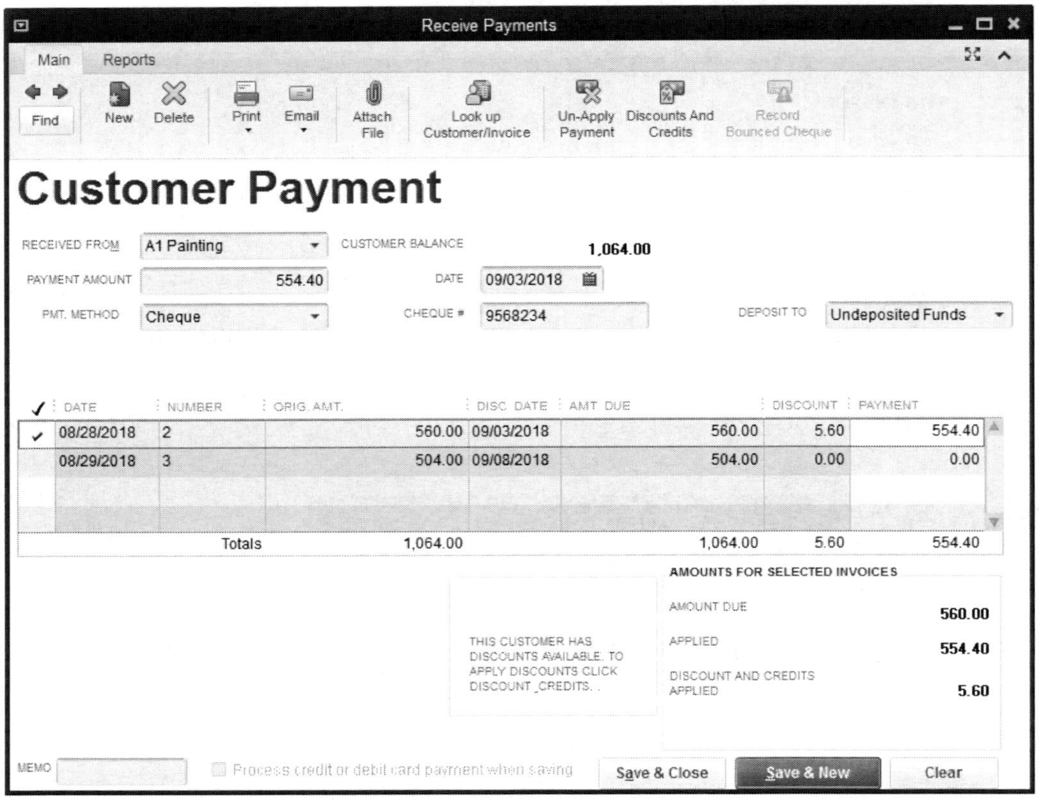

Figure 10-24: Receive Payments form—discount applied

The customer may also pay less than the invoice amount without a discount. The original invoice may have been updated and the customer's accounting department didn't receive it. Or the customer may deduct a fee for sending payment by wire, which can happen with international customers. If the cheque amount is correct, you will create and apply credits, which is covered later in this lesson.

If the amount paid is greater than the invoice amount

If the cheque amount is more than the amount of the invoice, QuickBooks applies the amount to the oldest invoice first and then to the next one until the amount is fully applied. You may need to change the selection if the amount is for only one invoice. You can change the selection even after saving the Receive Payments form, but QuickBooks will still allow you to receive the entire amount, even if it is not completely applied. If you have an overage, you will see a message informing you about this. After you save the Receive Payments form, a message appears asking if you want to refund the amount or keep it as a credit.

Sending refunds is a decision your supervisor and/or the CFO or business owners needs to make. You can choose to keep the overpayment as a credit until they make a decision. However, you need to let the person or department who handles customer relations know about this. They can resolve the problem with the customer. Figure 10-25 shows an overpayment from Oak Township.

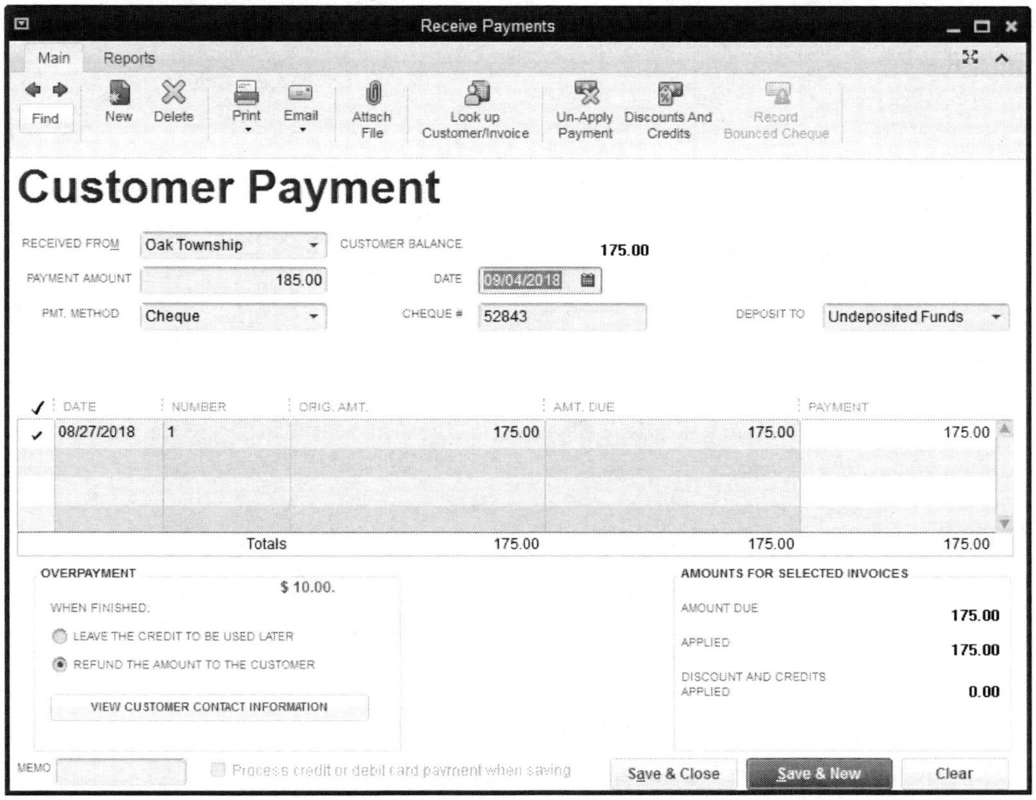

Figure 10-25: Receive Payments form—overpayment from Oak Township

After entering the customer, deposit date, and payment amount, select the REFUND THE AMOUNT TO THE CUSTOMER radio button in the *OVERPAYMENT* box. If you are not sure if the amount will be refunded, select the LEAVE THE CREDIT TO BE USED LATER radio button. Click the Save & Close button and come back to this form later to issue the refund.

If you do refund the amount later, open the same Receive Payments form and select the REFUND THE AMOUNT TO THE CUSTOMER radio button. Click the Save & Close button. A warning message will appear asking if you want to record your changes. Click Yes. The Issue a Refund form opens, as shown in Figure 10-26.

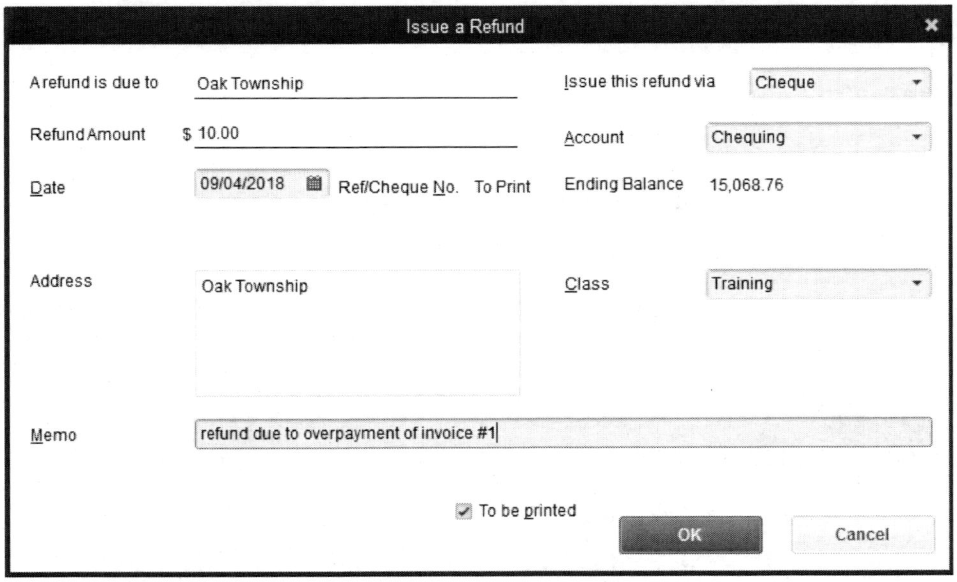

Figure 10-26: Issue a Refund form

After completing the refund information, including whether to print the cheque by selecting or deselecting the *To be printed* check box, click the OK button. Then follow the process for printing cheques, making sure the cheque number is correct.

Depositing Received Payments

After you finish receiving payments, you need to prepare the deposit. Click **Banking > Make Deposits** to open the Make Deposits form and the Payments to Deposit form. In the Payments to Deposit form, select only the cheques included in the deposit, then click OK to add the selected cheques to the Make Deposits form. You must ensure that the number you enter for the deposit will match the number on the bank statement. You may be posting the deposit before or after it actually goes to the bank. If after, take care that the total deposit in QuickBooks matches the deposit amount. Be sure to choose the same date the deposit went to the bank or will go to the bank. Check the Undeposited Funds account in the Chart of Accounts and make sure it has a zero balance.

Exercise 10.2: Applying Payments and Discounts to Invoices

In this exercise, you'll receive a cheque for $449.46 with a discount of $4.54 on an adjusted amount of $454.00. You will leave an underpayment for an adjustment in the next exercise.

Find and open an invoice.

1. Ensure that the company file you worked on in the previous exercise is still open.

2. Press **CTRL+F**. The Find window opens.

3. In the *Simple* tab, in the *Invoice #* field, type: **3**.

4. Press **ENTER** (or click the **Find** button). The invoice will appear at the bottom of the window.

5. Make sure the invoice is highlighted and click the **Go To** button. The Create Invoices form opens displaying the invoice from A1 Painting.

Process a received payment.

6. Click the **Receive Payments** icon in the button bar. The Receive Payments form opens.

7. Set the date to: **09/06/2018**.

8. In the *PMT. METHOD* drop-down menu, select **Cheque** if necessary.

9. In the *CHEQUE #* field, type: **9568238**.

10. In the *PAYMENT AMOUNT* field, type: **449.46**, and then press **TAB**. The UNDERPAYMENT section appears in the Receive Payments form.

Apply the discount.

11. Click the **Discounts and Credits** icon in the button bar. The Discount and Credits dialog box opens.

12. In the *Amount of Discount* field, type: **4.54**.

13. In the *Discount Account* drop-down menu, select **Customer Discounts**, if necessary.

14. In the *Discount Class* drop-down menu, select **Printing**.

15. Click the **Done** button to apply the discount and return to the Receive Payments form. Notice the underpayment of *$25.00*.

16. In the *UNDERPAYMENT* section, click the **LEAVE THIS AS AN UNDERPAYMENT** radio button, if necessary.

17. Click the **Save & Close** button, and then close the Create Invoices form and the Find window.

Make the deposit.

18. Click **Banking > Make Deposits**. The Make Deposits and Payments to Deposit forms open.

19. In the Payments to Deposit form, select the payment for **449.46** (a check mark should appear to the left of the date).

20. Click **OK**. The Make Deposits form populates with the deposit information. Notice that the date is set to *09/06/2018*.

21. Click the **Save & Close** button.

Leave the company file open for the next exercise.

Adjusting Customer Invoices

Objective L-10.3 Adjust customer invoices

Because customer payments do not always match the invoice amount, you might need to create and apply a credit transaction to the invoice. Most businesses have policies about how this happens and who makes the decision.

Creating and Applying Customer Credits

Let's assume that the customer A1 Painting, has a balance due on invoice #3 of $25.00. You need to know to whom to report this. You'll see in the customer record for A1 Painting that the sales rep is Jordan Smith. Because he is also a business owner, he can authorize an invoice adjustment. A1 Painting feels they should pay one fewer hour for design services, at $25 per hour including tax, to which Jordan agrees.

To make the adjustment to the invoice, open it and click the Refund/Credit icon in the button bar. The Create Credit Memos/Refunds form opens (Figure 10-27). You can also open this form by clicking **Customers > Create Credit Memos/Refunds**.

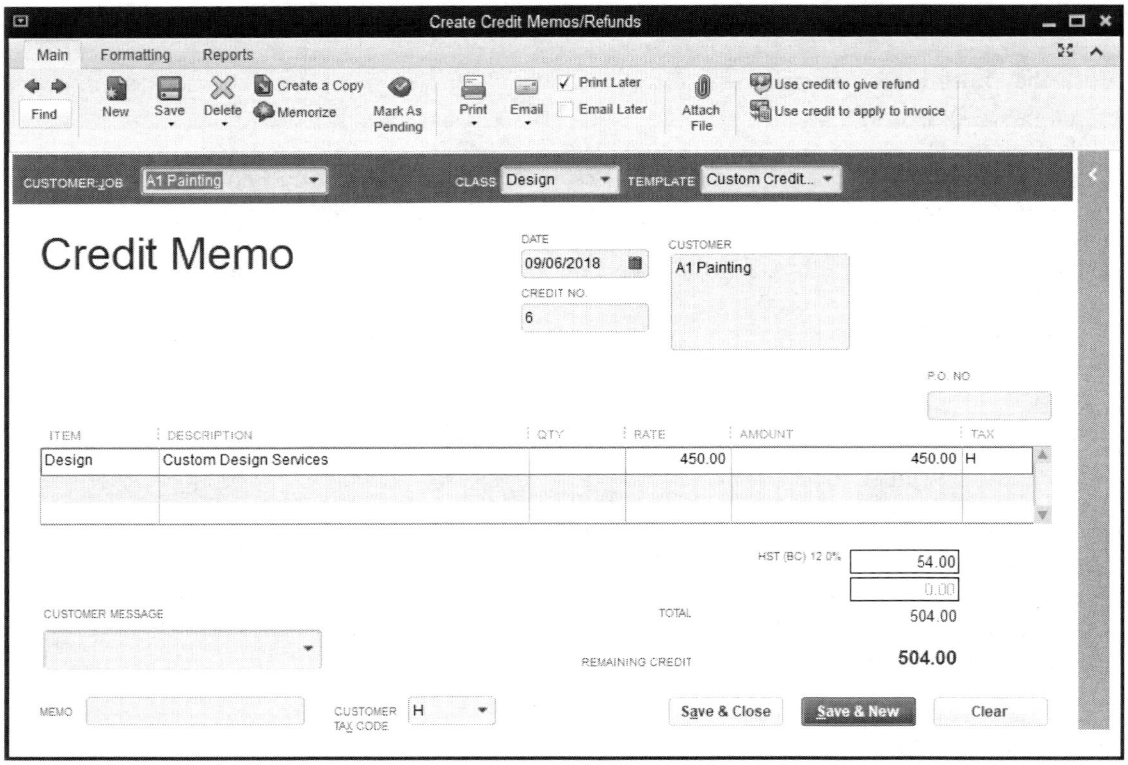

Figure 10-27: Create Credit Memos/Refunds form

All items in the invoice will appear in this form. You enter the credit of $22.32 before tax. The class is *Design* and the date is *09/06/2018*. Figure 10-28 shows the completed Create Credit Memos/Refunds form.

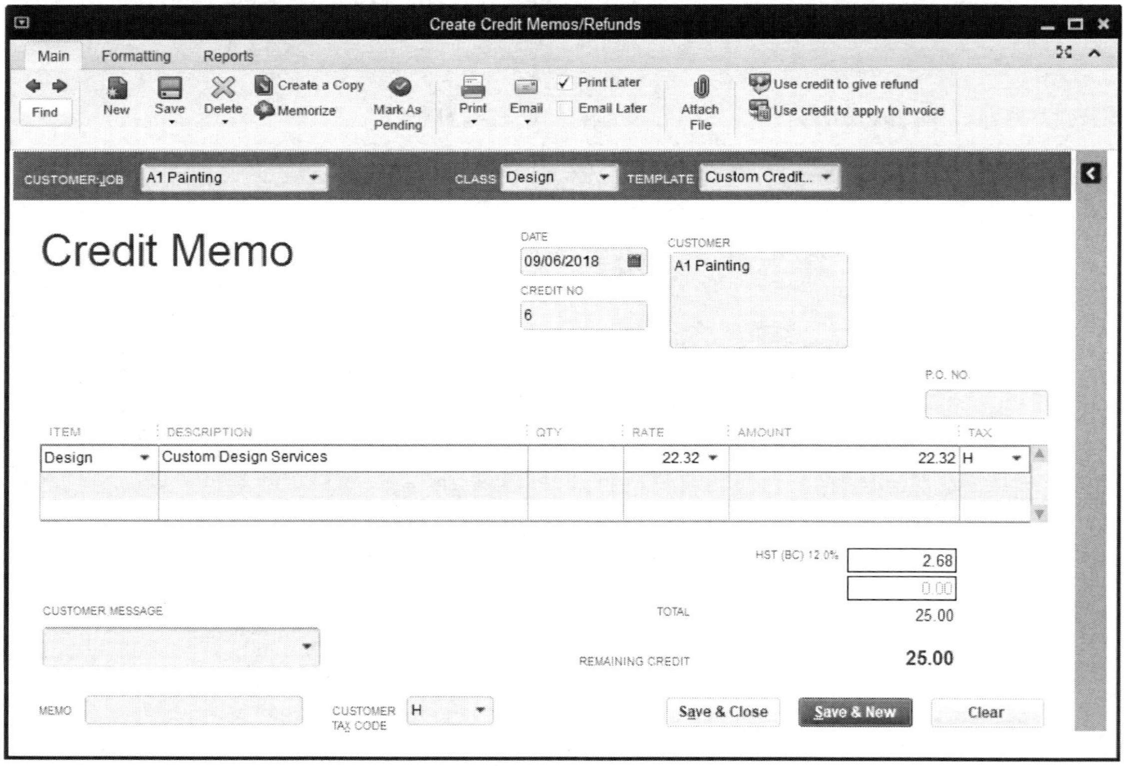

Figure 10-28: Create Credit Memos/Refunds form—completed

After completing the Create Credit Memos/Refunds form, click the *Use credit to apply to invoice* icon in the button bar. A warning message may appear asking about changing the tax code. Click the No button and the Apply Credit to Invoices dialog box opens (Figure 10-29).

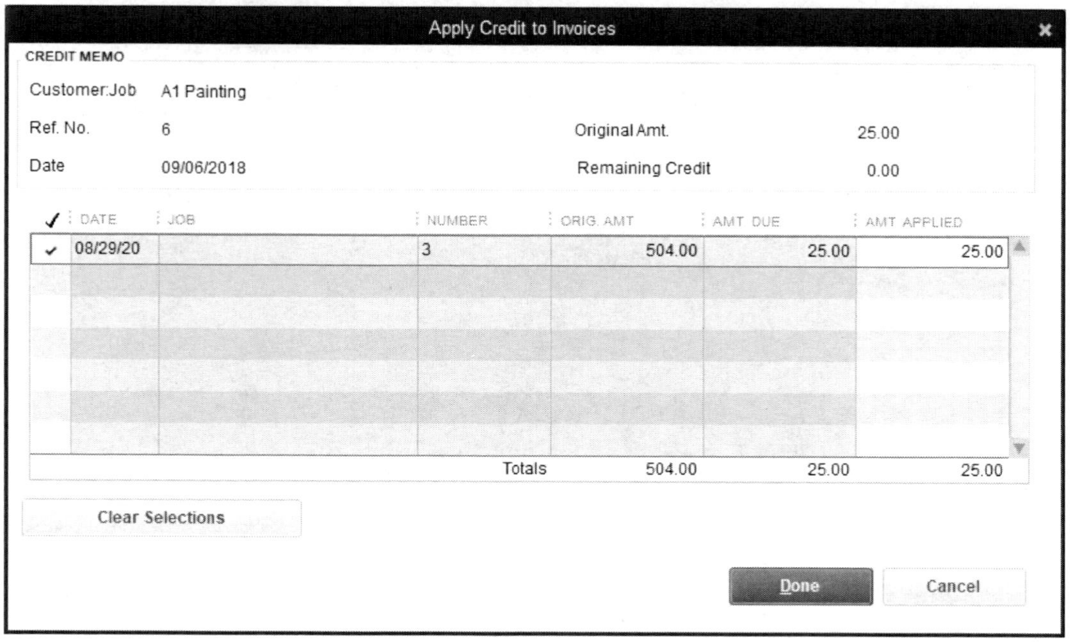

Figure 10-29: Apply Credit to Invoices dialog box

Click the Done button to apply the credit to the invoice. Click the Save & Close button in the Create Credit Memos/Refunds form to complete the process, which applies the credit to the invoice, leaving a balance of *$0.00*.

If you do not apply the credit from the Create Credit Memos/Refunds form, QuickBooks asks you what you want to do with the credit (Figure 10-30).

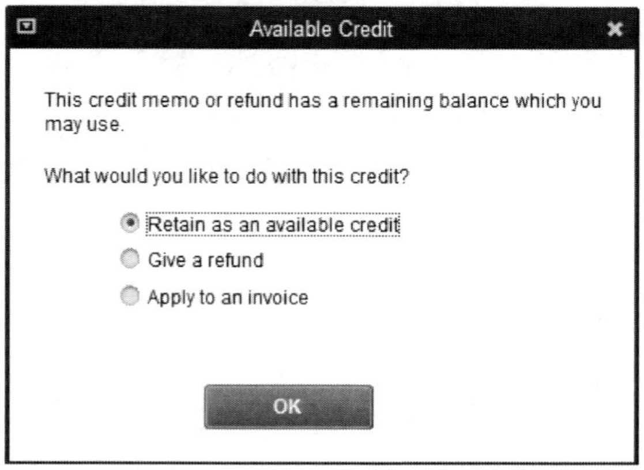

Figure 10-30: Available Credit message

You will often delay applying a credit memo to an invoice and will retain the default choice, *Retain as an available credit*. The *Give a refund* radio button opens a cheque writing form. The *Apply to an invoice* radio button performs the same function as clicking the *Use credit to apply to invoice* icon in the Create Credit Memos/Refunds form.

After you apply the credit memo, you can still make changes. The process is similar to changing the bills on a bill payment. Figure 10-31 shows the Apply Credits dialog box. Notice that a separate credit (Credit No. 4) had been applied previously.

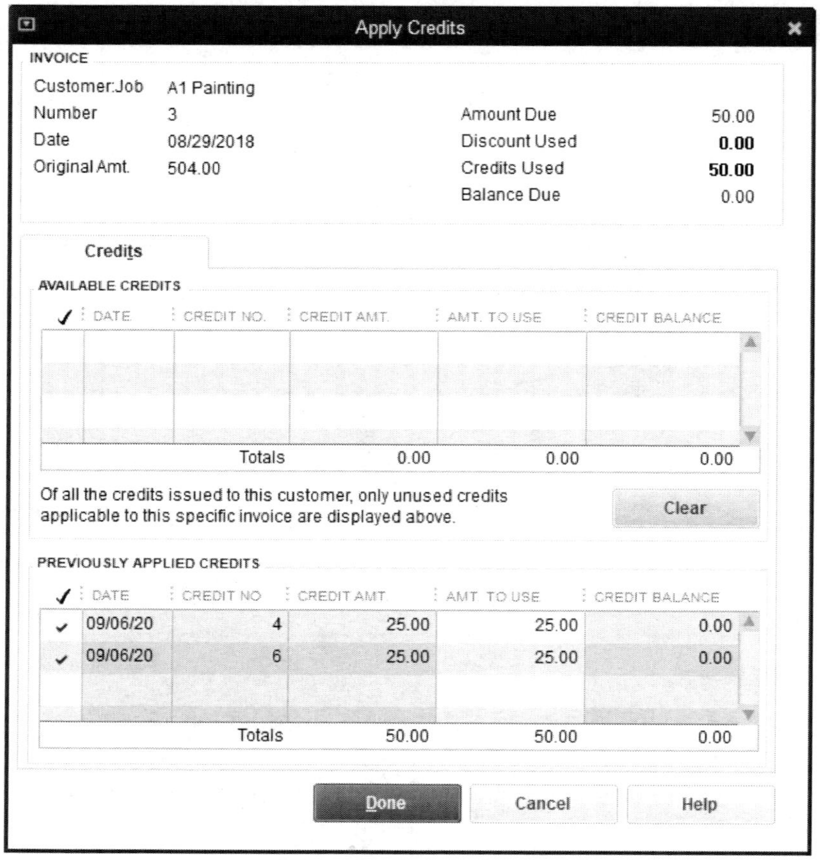

Figure 10-31: Apply Credits dialog box—examine application of credit memo

You can access the Apply Credits dialog box by clicking the Apply Credits icon in the button bar of the Create Invoices form. If there are no discounts, you will only see the Credits tab. The available credits appear in the top half of the dialog box. The previously applied credits appear in the bottom half. Clicking the checkmark removes the credit from the invoice and the credit moves from the lower half to the upper half of the form.

Handling an NSF Cheque

If, for some reason, a customer does not have enough money in the bank account to cover a cheque, the cheque will bounce—it will be sent back for *Non-sufficient Funds (NSF)*.

When you receive notice from the bank that a cheque is NSF, it means that the invoice is now unpaid. However, because you already recorded and deposited the payment in QuickBooks, the transaction needs to remain in the accounting system. QuickBooks has a simple method for handling the NSF cheque.

Let's assume that Tim Jones' cheque has bounced. Open the Create Invoices form and press CTRL+H to display the transaction history. Open the payment to display the Receive Payments form (Figure 10-32).

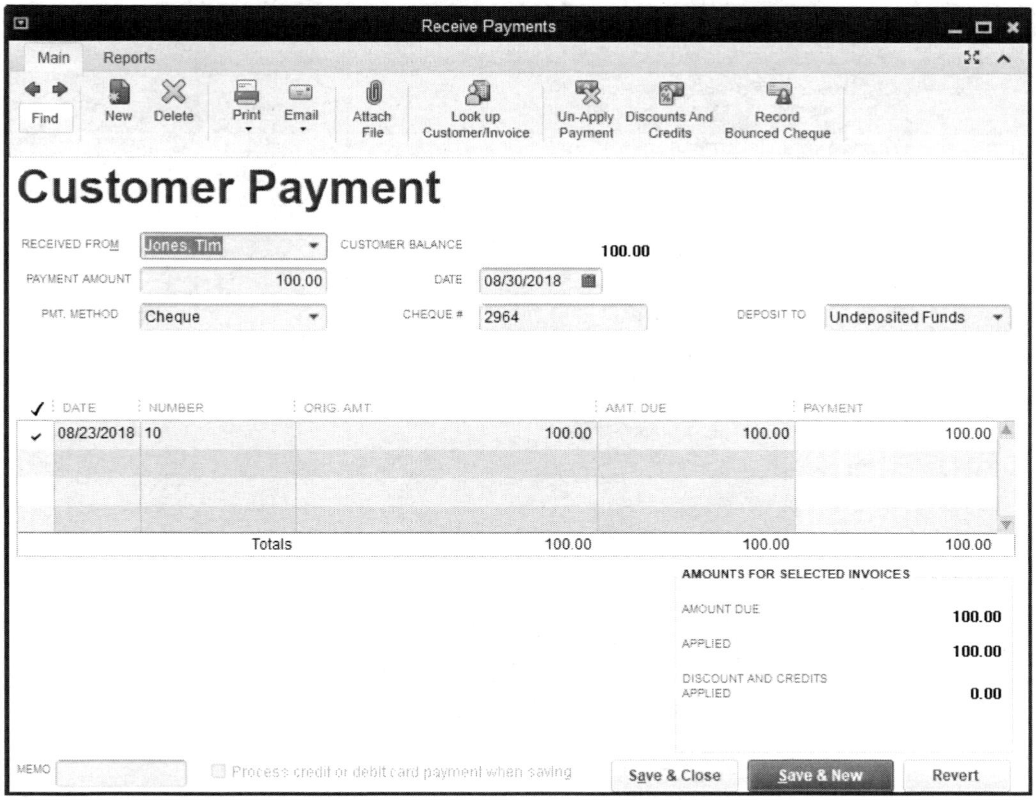

Figure 10-32: Receive Payments form—customer paid with a bad cheque

Click the Record Bounced Cheque icon in the button bar. The Manage Bounced Cheque form opens. Complete the form by specifying the bank fee, date, expense account, class, and customer fee. Figure 10-33 shows a completed Manage Bounced Cheque form.

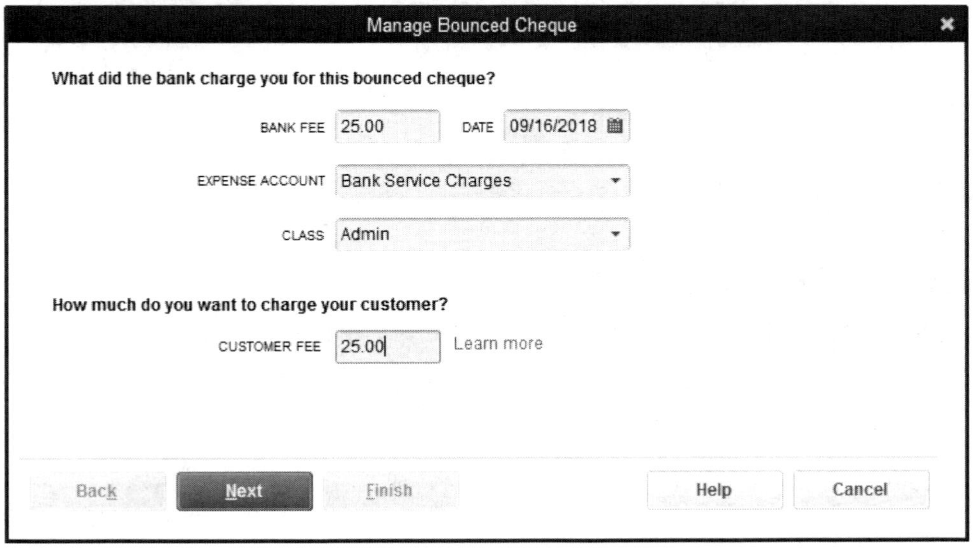

Figure 10-33: Manage Bounced Cheque form—completed

After you complete the form, click the Next button. The Bounced Cheque Summary dialog box opens (Figure 10-34).

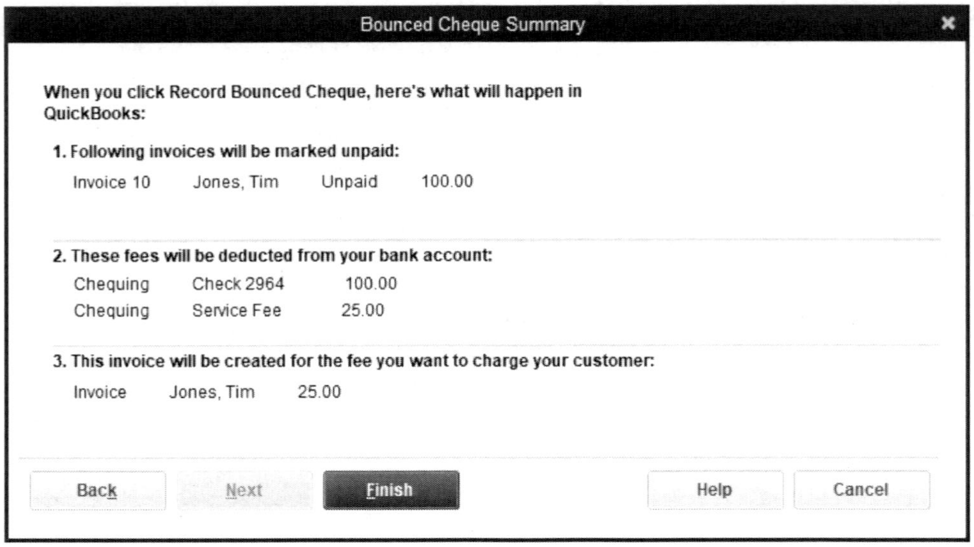

Figure 10-34: Bounced Cheque Summary dialog box

Click the Finish button to post the NSF transaction. The stamp shown in Figure 10-35 will appear in the Receive Payments form.

BOUNCED CHEQUE

Figure 10-35: Bounced Cheque stamp

As Figure 10-34 indicates, the invoice is marked unpaid, the invoice amount and bank fee are deducted from the business's bank account, and a new invoice is created for the bank charges incurred due to the returned cheque. However, QuickBooks does this with journal entries that are programmed to become invoices. In the Journal, you will see journal entries. On the A/R Aging report, you will see invoices. While the same item from the original invoice shows in the invoice for the NSF cheque, sales for the item do not double. QuickBooks posts the bank fee to an income GL account it creates, called Returned Cheque Charges. Alternatively, you can create an item for NSF cheques and bank fees and place it in a new invoice for the total amount of the NSF cheque and any fees.

Exercise 10.3: Creating and Applying Credit Memos and Handling NSF Cheques

In this exercise, you'll enter and apply a second credit memo for A1 Painting, and learn how to handle a bounced (NSF) check.

Enter and apply a credit memo.

1. Ensure that the company file you worked on in the previous exercise is still open.

2. Click **Customers > Customer Centre**. The Customer Centre opens.

3. Select **A1 Painting** from the list on the left, and then double-click the **Invoice 3** transaction. The Create Invoices form for Invoice 3 opens.

4. Click the **Refund/Credit** icon in the button bar. The Create Credit Memos/Refunds form opens.

5. Set the *Date* to **09/06/2018**, if necessary.

6. In the *AMOUNT* field, type: **22.32**.

7. Click the **Use credit to apply to invoice** icon in the button bar. If an Information Changed warning message pops up, click the **No** button. The Apply Credit to Invoices dialog box opens.

8. Ensure that invoice **3** is selected (there should be a check mark to the left of the date). QuickBooks may have auto-selected it because the balance due is the same as the credit memo.

9. Click the **Done** button to apply the credit to the invoice.

10. In the Create Credit Memos/Refunds form, click the **Save & Close** button. Notice that the invoice is now stamped as PAID.

11. Close the Create Invoices form and the Customer Centre.

Post an NSF transaction in the accounting records.

12. Press **CTRL+F**. The Find window opens.

13. Ensure that the *Transaction Type* drop-down menu displays **Invoice**.

14. In the *Invoice #* field, type: **10**.

15. Click **Find**. Invoice *#10* for *Jones, Tim* appears.

16. Click the **Go To** button. The Create Invoices form for Tim Jones opens.

17. Press **CTRL+H** to display the *Transaction History – Invoice* dialog box.

18. Ensure that the payment is selected, and then click the **Go To** button. The Receive Payments form for Tim Jones opens.

19. Click the **Record Bounced Cheque** icon in the button bar. The Manage Bounced Cheque form opens.

20. In the *BANK FEE* field, type: **25.00**.

21. Change the *DATE* to **09/04/2018**.

22. In the *CLASS* drop-down menu, select **Admin**.

23. In the *CUSTOMER FEE* field, type: **25.00**.

24. Click the **Next** button. The Bounced Cheque Summary dialog box opens.

25. Click the **Finish** button to post the NSF transaction in the accounting records.

    Note: You can use this method only for an invoice payment. In a later lesson, you'll learn about an alternative method if a cheque that is received with a sales receipt or deposit bounces.

26. Click **Window > Close All** to close all open windows in the QuickBooks desktop.

Create a portable file to turn in as part of this lesson's assignments.

27. Save the company file as a portable file in the *1767-Student-Files\Lesson 10\MyProjects* folder.

    Note: This is the file you will turn in.

28. If you plan to perform the Practice the Skill exercise, close the company file but leave QuickBooks open; otherwise, close the company file and exit QuickBooks.

Lesson Summary

Now that you have completed this lesson, you should be able to:

☑ Pay bills according to terms.   ☑ Adjust customer invoices.

☑ Receive and deposit multiple cheques.

Key Terms

Term	Definition
Comma Separated Values (CSV)	A file that holds plain text as a series of values separated by commas. Most applications can read CSV files, and you can open and read one with a text editor. Most often, CSV files are used to import or export banking information.
Non-sufficient Funds (NSF)	A term that describes a situation in which a customer's bank account doesn't have enough funds to cover a cheque.

Activity 1: Selecting Bills to Pay

What do you need to know before selecting bills to pay in the Pay Bills window?

1.   Date of bill

2.   Form of payment

3.   Bank balance

4.   Method of payment

Activity 2: Choosing the Correct Process for Receiving Payments

What is the correct process to follow if a customer payment is less than the invoice amount?

1.   Call the customer and ask them why the payment amount is incorrect.

2.   Process the payment and do nothing else.

3.   If the cheque shows a discount, and the cheque date is not within the number of days allowed by the payment terms, apply the discount.

4.   If the cheque shows a discount, and the cheque date is within the number of days allowed by the payment terms, apply the discount.

Practice the Skill

This Practice the Skill exercise is designed to reinforce the skills you have learned. In this exercise, you will pay bills, apply a discount, receive payments, and adjust an invoice.

1. If necessary, launch **QuickBooks** and open **Best Custom T-Shirts C1_L10_B (Portable).QBM** from the *1767-Student-Files\Lesson 10\PTS folder*.

2. Pay the bill from Insurance Brokerage, Ltd. They will be paid using an EFT-OUT. The date is 09/17/2018.

3. Apply the suggested discount of $2.50 to the bill from Labels Unlimited, using the class Admin. Then pay the bill with a cheque dated 09/17/2018.

4. Receive cheque number 9568245 from A1 Painting for $554.40, and deposit it on 09/17/2018.

5. Receive cheque number 16928 from Pride's Grocery Store for $255.00 and apply the amount to their outstanding invoice on 09/17/2018.

6. Create a credit memo for Pride's Grocery Store for $22.32 pre-tax for design services and apply it to the balance on their invoice on 09/17/2018.

7. Receive cheque number 57329 from Star Car Wash for $329.28 and apply the amount to their outstanding invoice on 09/17/2018.

8. Enter a discount of 6.72 for Star Car Wash using the Design class and the GL Customer Discounts account.

9. Deposit the cheques received on 09/17/2018.

10. Save the company file as a portable company file and add the letters PTS to the end of the file name *(Best Custom T-Shirts C1_L10_<your name> PTS (Portable).QBM)*. Turn this file in to your instructor.

11. Close the company file.

Course Project Exercise

The Blue Heron Spa needs several vendor bills paid and customer payments processed. All the bills except Comox Florists, which accepts only EFTs, use the cheque payment form. The payment date for all payments is 03/31/2017. Print the cheques for the 03/31/2017 payment date only. The starting cheque number is 984. Both customers pay their invoices on 04/01/2017. Charlotte Johnson pays in full using cheque number 432. However, Becky Flynn had a problem with one of her treatments and paid only $336.00 with cheque number 692. Create a credit memo for Becky for $100.00 pre-tax and apply it to the invoice. Then, deposit both cheques on 04/01/2017.

Filename:	Blue Heron Spa Inc 2018 C1_L10_A (Portable).QBM
Admin password:	BluSpa18
New company name:	Blue Heron Spa, Inc. C1_L10_<your name>

Perform the following tasks:

1. Restore the portable file and change the company name as indicated in the table.

2. Open the Pay Bills window and pay all bills except the one for Comox Florists, using the information provided in the scenario.

3. Repeat Step 2 for Comox Florists, but use the EFT designation.

4. Print the cheques using the information provided in the scenario.

5. Accept customer payments from both customers using the information provided in the scenario.

6. Create a credit memo for Becky Flynn for the underpayment.

7. Deposit the cheques from both customers using the information provided in the scenario.

8. Create a portable file to turn in to your instructor.

9. Close the company file.

Quiz Questions

For each question, select the best answer.

1. What can you not do after a bill payment is saved and the cheque clears the bank?

    a. Change the date.

    b. Change the total amount on the bill payment.

    c. Change the bills paid.

    d. Change the memo.

2. How does QuickBooks process a cheque amount greater than any one invoice on a cheque?

    a. QuickBooks first applies the amount to the invoice with the smallest amount, and then to invoices with the next smallest amount.

    b. QuickBooks first applies the amount to the invoice with the largest amount, and then to invoices with the next largest amount.

    c. QuickBooks first applies the amount to the oldest invoice, and then to the next oldest invoices.

    d. QuickBooks first applies the amount to the newest invoice, and then to the next newest invoices.

3. Under what conditions can you issue a customer credit?

    a. The decision to reduce the original invoice amount is approved by the business.

    b. The customer decides they should not pay as much as charged.

    c. The customer took a discount on the invoice.

    d. The cost of what the customer purchased decreased.

4. What happens when you complete the Manage Bounced Cheque form?

    a. The invoice will be marked unpaid, and the process ends.

    b. An invoice will be created for the bank fee that you pass along to the customer, and the process ends.

    c. The invoice total is increased by the amount of the bank fee, and the process ends.

    d. The invoice will be marked unpaid, the fees for the invoice and the bank charge will be deducted from the business's bank account, and an invoice will be created for the bank fee that you pass along to the customer.

Lesson 11: Reconciling Banking

Lesson Objectives

In this lesson, you will reconcile bank, credit card, and merchant accounts. Upon successful completion of this lesson, you should be able to:

- [ ] Reconcile the chequing statement.
- [ ] Reconcile the credit card statement.
- [ ] Reconcile the merchant account.

Proving the Accounting Records

Reconciling the business accounting records with banking records is an essential task, to be done monthly. This confirms that the movement of funds in and out of the business are reflected in the bank records. Then the business can be confident about the accuracy of both their accounting and the bank's.

A useful outcome from bank reconciliations includes identifying transactions that are **outstanding**. For example, these may be cheques that do not clear, or missing deposits. Sometimes transactions are only **in transit**, which means that they may have occurred close to the end of the month. Therefore, they do not appear on the bank statement in the same period as in the accounting records. If a cheque remains uncleared for more than one cycle, following up is important. This is particularly important at the end of the fiscal year. Accurate financial statements are required for decision-making purposes and reporting to ownership. The Canada Revenue Agency (CRA) may want to see bank reconciliations as well, to confirm transactions.

Chequing account statements follow the calendar month. Sometimes they may end a day or two early if the last days of the month are on the weekend. Credit card statements usually do not follow a calendar month. This means one statement crosses over the end of the year. Posting all the transactions dated through the end of the year is important to capture all occurring expenses. The statement may have two reconciliations; one to the end of fiscal year and one to the end of the statement.

Merchant credit card accounts require different handling. Remember, a merchant account allows the business to accept credit cards for sales by using an account processor. The merchant account processor accepts credit cards and holds that money until the next batch deposit, which is usually within 48 hours. Merchant statements do not always follow calendar months. These statements provide only the summary amounts for the batches, or groups of individual transactions, they processed. This means you may need to reconcile, on a batch basis, the GL account for credit card sales and resultant deposits to the GL bank account.

Reconciling batches at the end of a period requires the detail of all the transactions in a batch. You can obtain this by downloading comma separated values (CSV) files from the merchant account's web site. Then, you can match the transactions against the individual credit card transactions in the accounting records on an entry-by-entry basis.

QuickBooks has an easy-to-use reconciliation process. First, let's review several terms before proceeding. The **cleared balance** is the same amount that the bank or credit card company considers the **ending balance**. A cleared balance is understood to mean the ending balance in QuickBooks. The ending balance for one period becomes the starting balance for the next period. The starting balance on the bank statement plus cleared deposits and minus cleared payments equals the ending balance. For a credit card statement, the total amount owed is the starting balance plus the charges and minus the payments. The QuickBooks reconciliation always starts with entering the ending balance and the ending date from the statement.

The last term unique to QuickBooks is the **register balance**. The register balance is the balance in the Chequing GL register as of the last date of the period the statement covers. The difference between the ending or cleared balance on the statement and the register balance on the same date is all the transactions in transit that still need to clear. The term register balance appears on the reconciliation reports.

Before describing the processes, here's a reminder that the reconciliation process is where all the monetary transactions meet. Figure 11-1 shows the Banking portion of the QuickBooks Cycles.

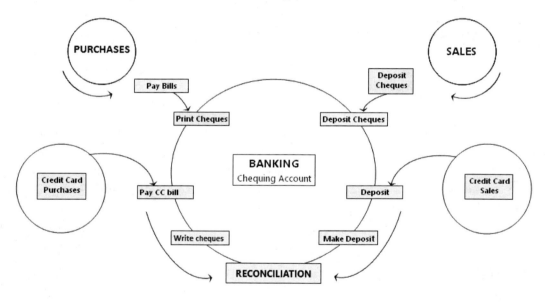

QuickBooks Cycles

Figure 11-1: Banking Cycle

Reconciling the Chequing GL Account

Objective L-11.1 Reconcile the chequing statement

Once you receive the bank statement, the reconciliation process can begin. Some businesses may want you to download the bank statement or will provide an electronic copy. Some may wait for it to arrive in the mail. The business Chequing account could be connected electronically to the QuickBooks automatic updating service. (That process is not covered in this course.) However, any automatic downloads of transactions need to be monitored closely because sometimes they can download more than once.

Usually, the bank statement includes scans of the cleared cheques. If not, scans of deposits may be available online if needed. All you really need to start the reconciliation process is the bank statement.

Click **Banking > Reconcile**. The Begin Reconciliation form appears (Figure 11-2).

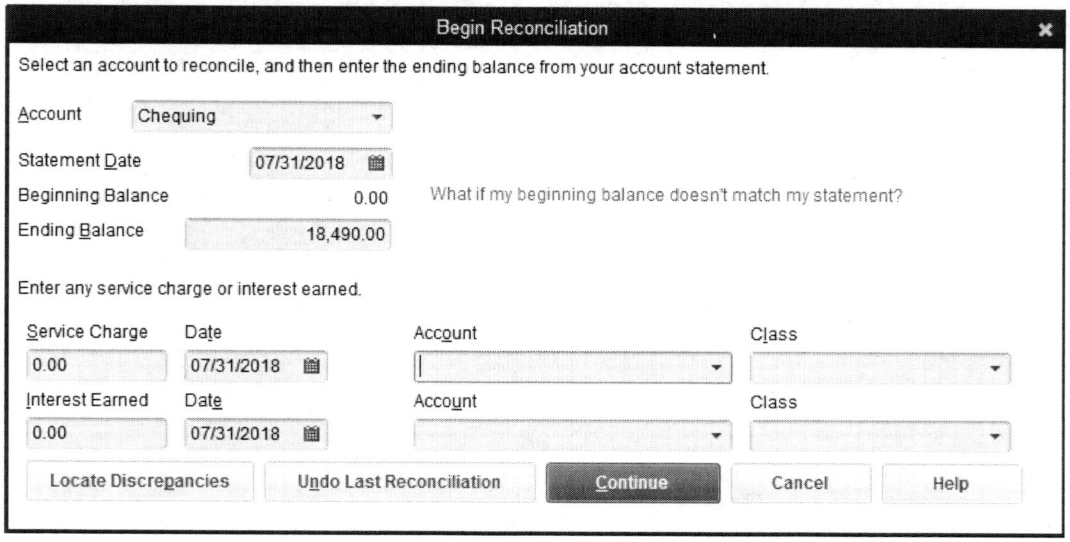

Figure 11-2: Begin Reconciliation form

Before going further, make sure that the beginning balance QuickBooks shows in the Begin Reconciliation form matches the bank statement. Because the account for Best Custom T-Shirts opened in July, the beginning balance shown in Figure 11-2 is correct at zero.

Next, enter the ending date and ending balance from the bank statement. In the scenario shown in the images, the first bank statement ends on 07/31/2018 and the ending balance is 18,490.00. After entering this information, click the Continue button to advance to the Reconcile window.

Note: The Begin Reconciliation form includes an Undo Last Reconciliation button. If you click this button you will receive a warning message. Proceeding past the warning should only be done with great care. Sometimes it is necessary to undo a reconciliation, but always check with your supervisor. In a situation where a reconciliation must be undone and performed again, the Excel reports you export at the end of the reconciliation process can be invaluable. These reports will allow you to see what was on the original reconciliation and can help you re-do your work.

The Reconcile Window

Figure 11-3 shows the Reconcile – Chequing window. Each account has its own window.

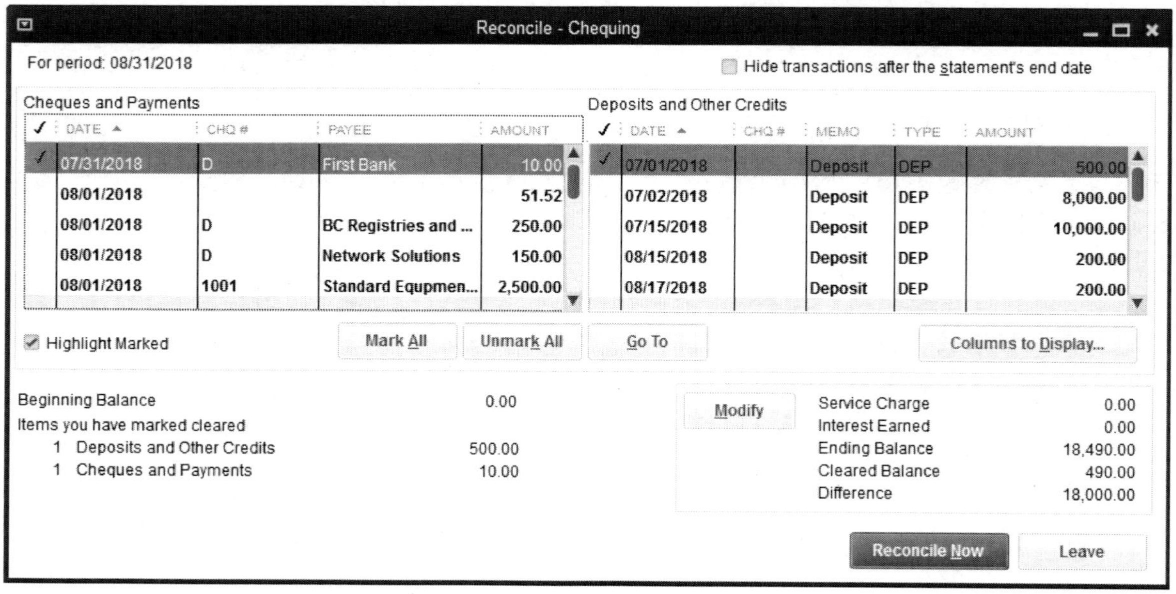

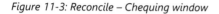

Figure 11-3: Reconcile – Chequing window

The window contains two list boxes—the Cheques and Payments list box displays on the left side, and the Deposits and Other Credits list box displays on the right side. The transactions display in order by date. When the Reconcile window first opens, the first transaction on each side is highlighted in green. The green highlight simply indicates the currently-selected transaction.

Each side of the Reconcile window contains helpful features. You can click a column header to sort the column from smallest to largest or from largest to smallest. Click the header once to sort; click it again to sort in the reverse order.

You can also open any transaction in either list box by double-clicking it; this will allow you to examine or edit it. Also, if you find any missing transactions, you can add them while the window is open. These will automatically appear in the Reconcile window after you save it.

Notice the *Hide transactions after the statement's end date* check box above the Deposits and Other Credits list box. You can select this check box to hide transactions with dates after the statement end date. This gives you fewer transactions to sift through in each list box and can make the reconciliation process easier.

Marking Transactions as Cleared

Clicking anywhere on a transaction displays a checkmark in the left-most column. The checkmark indicates that you are marking the transaction as "cleared." In Figure 11-3, two transactions are marked as cleared: the bank fee debit on the left and the first deposit on the right.

As you find each transaction in the window that matches the statement, click it to mark it as cleared. In the lower left, under the *Items you have marked cleared* heading, the transaction count and dollar amounts for the Deposits and Other Credits and Cheques and Payments items update to show the current totals for cleared items. In Figure 11-3, the amount of the single 500.00 deposit and the single 10.00 bank fee are reflected in this section.

In the lower right, notice the Ending Balance, Cleared Balance, and Difference totals. The Ending Balance shows the amount you enter in the Begin Reconciliation window. As you mark transactions as cleared, the Cleared Balance updates to show the current total. As the Cleared Balance increases, the Difference is updated. The Difference total shows the difference between the Ending Balance and the Cleared Balance.

In Figure 11-3, the Ending Balance is $18,490.00. The Cleared Balance is $490 (which represents the cleared First Bank payment for $10.00 and the cleared $500 deposit). The Difference is $18,000.00. The remaining amount or Difference that needs to be cleared is $18,000 in deposits. Then the Difference becomes zero and the reconciliation is complete. If only deposits clear, the deposits equal the Cleared Balance. When cheques also clear, then the Difference is a net number of all the cleared deposits and cheques.

Completing the reconciliation systematically is easiest. You can begin with either the Cheques and Payments (cheques, EFTs, debit card transactions) on the left, or the Deposits and Other Credits (deposits, EFTs) on the right. Clicking a cleared transaction again will remove the checkmark and the transaction is no longer considered cleared.

Peeking at the Register

You should also understand that when you mark a transaction as cleared in the Reconcile window (the transaction displays a checkmark in the left column), that same transaction will display an asterisk in the Chequing register. Figure 11-4 shows how the cleared deposit (marked in the Reconcile window in Figure 11-3) appears in the Chequing register.

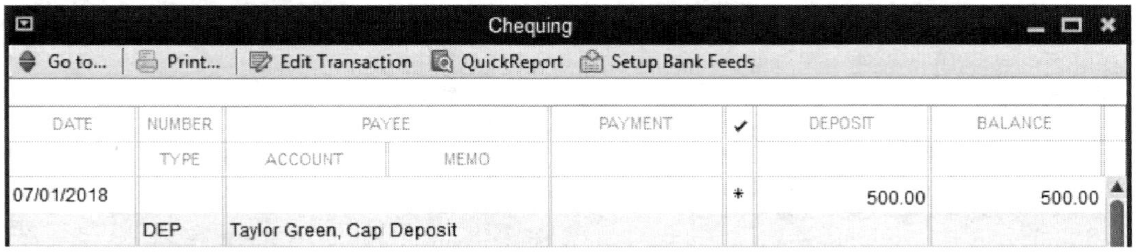

Figure 11-4: Chequing register showing transaction marked as cleared but not yet reconciled

After you reconcile, the asterisk in the register will turn into a checkmark.

Note: To view the chequing register from the Reconcile window, right-click an item in either list box, then click Use Register.

Tips for Making Reconciliation Easier

You may find after you do this a few times that other features can be useful. For example, if the bank statement has separate sections for deposits and EFTs, adding the letters *EFT* to the deposit memo sorts them separately from the deposits.

The care you take with dating transactions correctly also helps. When they are in order by date and type, finding them becomes much easier. For example, if you consistently enter a *D* in the cheque number field for the debit card purchases, they'll sort together, but separately from the cheques.

The most important thing to understand is that you should only enter numbers in the Chequing GL account that appear on the bank statement. Sometimes, you will have numbers that do not match, but having a clear one-to-one match between the accounting records and the bank statement saves time and prevents confusion.

The statement usually subtotals the transactions for four or more sections. The credits or deposits are in one section and you may see a second section for EFT-IN transactions. The debits are usually divided into cheques and debit card or electronic withdrawals. As shown in Figure 11-3, at the lower left, QuickBooks only gives you two totals, one for the debits or deposits in the accounting system and the other for the credits or withdrawals. You can still use this to good advantage.

If you start marking the cheques or bank debits as cleared until the total withdrawals in the window match the bank statement subtotal, it verifies that you did this part correctly. If you add to the cheque subtotal the subtotal of all the remaining debits from the bank statement, then you'll know the total for cheques and debit card or EFT-OUT transactions. When you reach this number on the screen in the lower left in *Items you have marked cleared*, then you can be confident the amount for all debits is correct.

The exception is the bank fees and interest. Each may be listed separately on the statement, so you need to remember to include each in its appropriate section. While QuickBooks does offer places to enter fees and interest at the start of the reconciliation process, using the Write Cheques or Make Deposits forms offers the chance of making a correction later, if needed. Then you repeat the process for the bank deposits, or credits on the statement.

Once the Difference in the lower right reaches zero, you are done. If you do not reach zero, you cannot finish. Re-check the ending balance. Then re-check every checkmark. If needed, unmark all the transactions and start over until you do reach zero. Then you can click on the Reconcile Now button.

Running Reconciliation Reports

When you click the Reconcile Now button, the Select Reconciliation Report dialog box appears (Figure 11-5). You have the choice of running the summary report or the detailed report. Running both reports is best, which is the default selection.

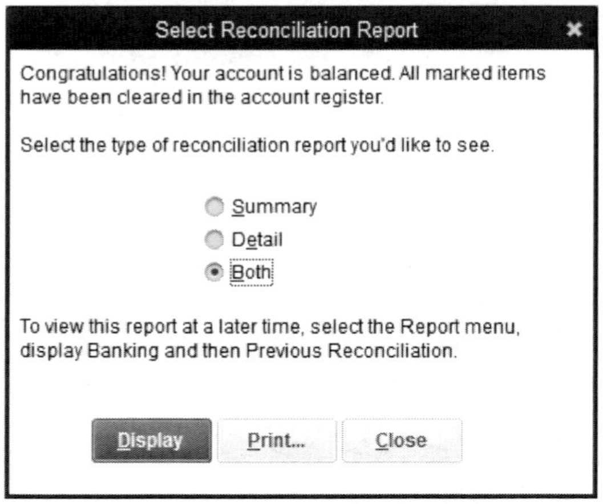

Figure 11-5: Select Reconciliation Report dialog box

The protocol in some businesses is to print the summary report for attaching to the hard-copy bank statement. You can later see either report as a pdf from the Reports menu. The detail report may still be important, even if it is not normally retained for the files.

After you click the Display button, the message in Figure 11-6 appears. The message reminds you that you will see both the cleared and uncleared transactions as of the ending statement date, plus any new transactions after the statement date.

Figure 11-6: Reconciliation Report message

You can safely dismiss this message by clicking OK. The selected report(s) appear. Figure 11-7 shows the summary report. Notice the line *Register Balance* that appears immediately below *Cleared Balance*.

	Reconciliation Summary	
Customize Report	Comment on Report	Memorize	Print	E-mail ▼	Excel ▼

Show Filters

7:43 PM
09/21/18

Best Custom T-shirts C1_L11_A
Reconciliation Summary
Chequing, Period Ending 07/31/2018

	Jul 31, 18
Beginning Balance	0.00
Cleared Transactions	
Cheques and Payments - 1 item	-10.00
Deposits and Credits - 3 items	18,500.00
Total Cleared Transactions	18,490.00
Cleared Balance	**18,490.00**
Register Balance as of 07/31/2018	18,490.00
New Transactions	
Cheques and Payments - 21 items	-6,235.25
Deposits and Credits - 7 items	2,755.54
Total New Transactions	-3,479.71
Ending Balance	**15,010.29** ◄

Figure 11-7: Reconciliation Summary report

For the detail report, follow these two simple steps and export the report. If you ever need to re-do a reconciliation, it will be easier if the reconciliation is captured in an Excel file.

1. Use the Customize Report button and make three changes in the columns:

    a. Add the Memo field.

    b. Add the Debit and Credit fields.

    c. Remove the Amount field.

2. Export the report to Excel and save it. Often, you can keep an entire year of reports in one file.

Figure 11-8 shows the Reconciliation Detail report before the changes, and Figure 11-9 shows the Reconciliation Detail report after the changes.

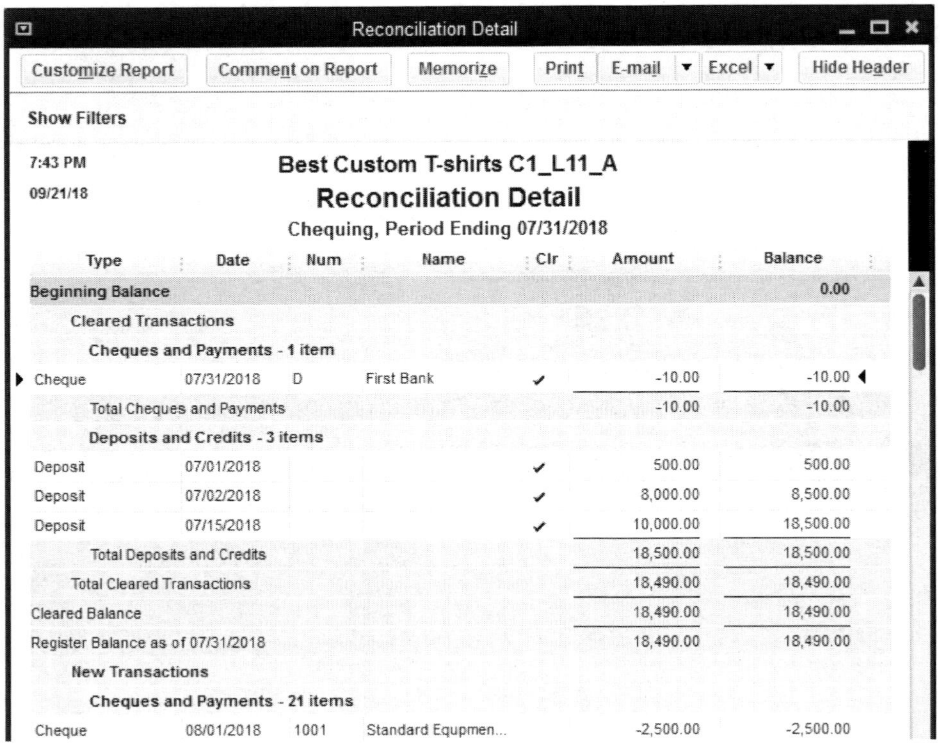

Figure 11-8: Reconciliation Detail report before changes

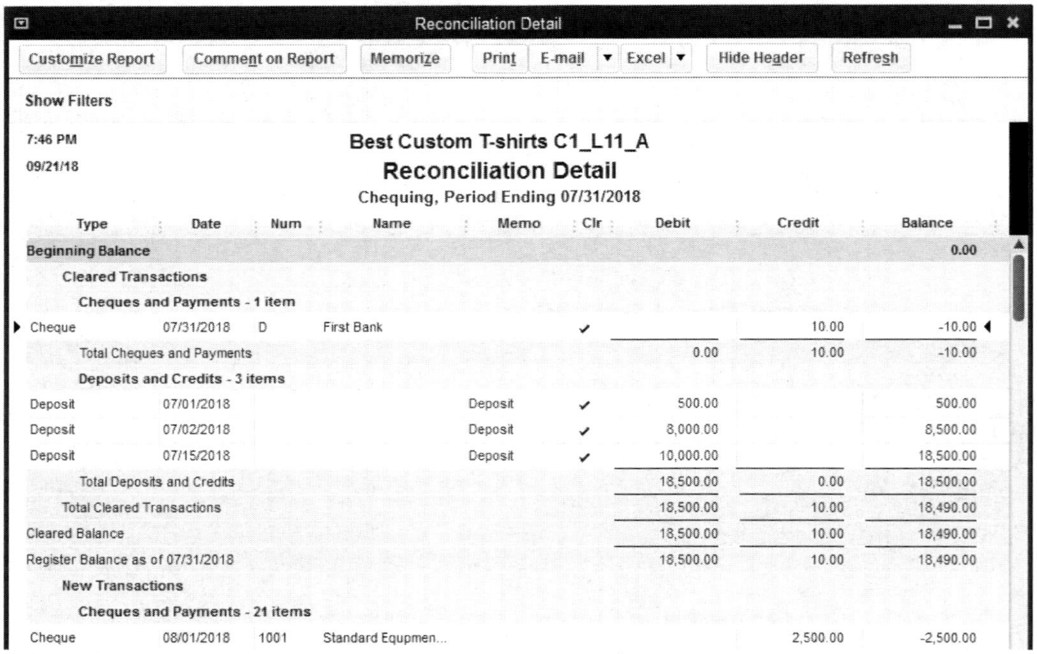

Figure 11-9: Reconciliation Detail report after changes

When you finish with the detail report, the warning message shown in Figure 11-10 appears, asking if you want to memorize the report. You cannot memorize bank reconciliation reports. This is the one message in which you do *NOT* want to select the *Do not display this message in the future* check box. If you suppress the display of this message, you may accidentally lose reports that you customize. Simply click the No button.

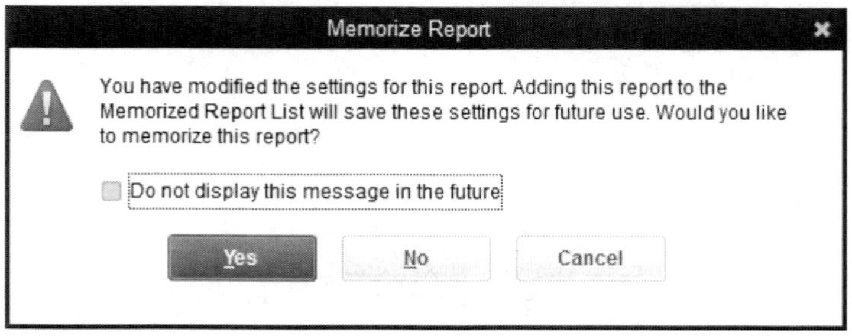

Figure 11-10: Memorize Report warning message.

Before finishing, look at the uncleared items list in the detail report. Which cheques have not cleared? Did any deposits not clear? You need to decide if they are only in transit or require further attention. Uncleared deposits should only be in transit. Cheques may take a cycle or more to clear. Notify the person who needs to know if any cheque fails to clear after two reconciliations. Also, verify that the register balance in the report as of the end of the statement date matches the balance in the Chequing GL account register as of the end of statement date. If you find discrepancies, usually they are due to a dating issue.

Exercise 11.1: Reconciling the Chequing GL Account

Note: Steps 17-23 and 27-29 of this exercise require Microsoft Excel. If Excel is not installed, skip these steps.

In this exercise, you will reconcile the Chequing GL for Best Custom T-Shirts for August 2018.

1. Launch **QuickBooks** if necessary, and restore **Best Custom T-Shirts C1_L11_A (Portable).QBM** from the *1767-Student-Files\Lesson 11\StarterFiles* folder. Save the restored company file as **Best Custom T-Shirts C1_L11_<your name>.QBW** in the *1767-Student-Files\Lesson 11\MyProjects* folder

2. Change the Company Name to **Best Custom T-Shirts C1_L11_<your name>**.

Begin the reconciliation.

3. Click **Banking > Reconcile**. The Begin Reconciliation form appears.

4. Select the **Chequing** GL account in the *Account* drop-down menu, if necessary. The beginning balance is 18,490.00.

5. In the *Statement Date* field, set the date to **08/31/2018**, if necessary.

6. In the *Ending Balance* field, type: **15685.99**, if necessary.

7. Click the **Continue** button. The *Reconcile – Chequing* window opens.

8. Click the **CHQ#** column header on the left side. The cheque numbers and memos entered in the cheque number fields sort by number.

9. On the left side, in the *Cheques and Payments* list box, select each of the cheques written in August, except for cheque #1005, written for $100 to Greg Lee, because this did not clear. Checkmarks appear to the left. The total of the cleared cheques on the statement should be 2,730.50.

10. Select all the debits, EFTs and transfers dated in August. The *Cheques and Payments* total under *Items you have marked cleared* should now be 3,304.01.

Note: Transfers from the bank GL accounts do not have a memo that appears in the reconciliation window. Transfers to the bank GL accounts show in the memo field.

11. On the right side, in the *Deposits and Other Credits* section, select all deposits and transfers for August. The total of *Deposits and Other Credits* under *Items you have marked cleared* should be 500.00. Notice that the Cleared Balance matches the Ending Balance, and the Difference is zero.

		Reconcile - Chequing						_ □ ×	

For period: 08/31/2018 ☐ Hide transactions after the statement's end date

Cheques and Payments

✓	DATE	CHQ # ▲	PAYEE	AMOUNT
	09/17/2018	INSUR EFT	Insurance B...	728.00
	09/05/2018	WEB EFT	Web Hosting	168.00
	09/16/2018	1	A1 Painting	554.40
	09/16/2018	2	A1 Painting	25.00
✓	08/01/2018	1001	Standard Eq...	2,500.00

Deposits and Other Credits

✓	DATE ▲	CHQ #	MEMO	TYPE	AMOUNT
	09/01/2018		Deposit	DEP	554.40
	09/04/2018		Deposit	DEP	185.00
	09/06/2018		Deposit	DEP	449.46
	09/17/2018		Deposit	DEP	582.40
	09/17/2018		Deposit	DEP	584.28

☑ Highlight Marked   Mark All   Unmark All   Go To   Columns to Display...

Beginning Balance	18,490.00	Modify	Service Charge	0.00
Items you have marked cleared			Interest Earned	0.00
3 Deposits and Other Credits	500.00		Ending Balance	15,685.99
9 Cheques and Payments	3,304.01		Cleared Balance	15,685.99
			Difference	0.00

Reconcile Now   Leave

Finish reconciling, and then customize and export a report.

12. Click the **Reconcile Now** button. The Select Reconciliation Report dialog box opens. Click the **Detail** radio button.

13. Click the **Display** button. If the Reconciliation Report message appears, click **OK** to dismiss the message. The Reconciliation Detail report opens.

14. Click the **Customize Report** button in the button bar.

15. In the *Display* tab, under *COLUMNS,* select **Debit** and **Credit**. Deselect **Amount**.

16. Click **OK**. The revised report opens.

17. In the Reconciliation Detail report, click the **Excel** drop-down button and select **Create New Worksheet**.

18. Ensure that the **Create new worksheet** and **in new workbook** radio buttons are selected.

19. Click the **Advanced** button. The Advanced Excel Option dialog box opens.

20. If the **Include QuickBooks Export Guide worksheet with helpful advice** check box is selected, deselect it, then click **OK**.

21. Click the **Export** button to open the Reconciliation Detail report in Excel.

22. Look at Uncleared Transactions. Only the uncleared cheque for $100.00 to Greg Lee should be listed.

23. Look at the Register Balance as of 08/31/2018. The amount of 15,585.99 should match the Chequing register balance as of the same date.

Check the register.

24. In the QuickBooks window, click **Banking > Use Register**, ensure that **Chequing** displays in the Use Register dialog box, then click **OK**.

25. In the Chequing register, scroll up to view the 08/24/2018 date (the last date in August for which there is an entry). Notice that the Balance is 15,585.99.

26. Carefully close the register without changing any transactions.

Rename the worksheet, then save the Excel file.

27. In Excel, double-click the **Sheet1** sheet tab, type: **Ex 1**, then press **ENTER** to rename the worksheet.

28. In Excel, click **File > Save As**, navigate to the *1767-Student-Files\Lesson 11\MyProjects* folder, select the text in the *File name* field and type: **<your name> Lesson 11 Reconciliation**, then click the **Save** button.

29. Minimize the Excel application window, and then close the Reconciliation Detail report without memorizing it.

Leave the company file open for the next exercise.

Reconciling the Credit Card GL Account

Objective L-11.2 Reconcile the credit card statement

QuickBooks will let you reconcile most GL accounts on the Balance Sheet. Return to the Begin Reconciliation form. Then, select the account you need to reconcile. For the credit card statement, ensure the starting balance matches, and then enter the ending date and the ending balance. After you are in the Reconcile window, begin checking off the transactions. You can use the same method described for the Chequing account reconciliation. Start with one section of the statement until the total in the reconciliation window matches a section on the statement, then proceed to the next section.

If any interest is charged on the statement, simply enter another Credit Card Purchase/Charge Form. Enter the credit card company as the vendor. Use the Credit Card Refund/Credit Form and the correct GL account for interest expenses. Often, the refunds are in their own section.

Figure 11-11 shows the *Reconcile Credit Card – First Bank Credit Card* window. The statement period ends on 08/06/2018. Because the credit card statement was paid in full before the due date, the balance is zero. Selecting the charge on the left, the refund on the right, and the payment brings the balance to zero. Follow the same procedures as for the Chequing account statement after finishing.

Figure 11-11: Credit card statement reconciliation

Exercise 11.2: Reconciling the Credit Card GL Account

Note: Steps 16-21 of this exercise require Microsoft Excel. If Excel is not installed, skip these steps.

In this exercise, you will reconcile the credit card statement for Best Custom T-Shirts through 09/06/2018.

1. Ensure that the company file you worked on in the previous exercise is still open.

2. Click **Banking > Reconcile**.

3. In the *Account* drop-down menu, select **First Bank Credit Card.** The beginning balance is 0.00.

4. In the *Statement Date* field, set the date to **09/06/2018**, if necessary.

5. In the *Ending Balance* field, type: **67.20**.

6. Click the **Continue** button. The Reconcile Credit Card – First Bank Credit Card window appears.

    Note: The Reconcile Credit Card window has a REF # instead of the CHQ #. You may leave the column blank. It is best to leave the transactions in the default order.

7. On the left side, in the *Charges and Cash Advances* list box, select the only charge showing. A checkmark appears to the left. The total cleared charges on the statement is 84.00 and this number appears under *Items you have marked cleared.*

8. On the right side, in the *Payments and Credits* list box, select the only refund for 16.80. The total of Payments and Credits under *Items you have marked cleared* is 16.80. The Cleared Balance matches the Ending Balance of 67.20 and the Difference is zero.

9. Click the **Reconcile Now** button. The Make Payment dialog box appears with the default option selected.

10. Leave the **Write a cheque for payment now** radio button selected and click **OK**. Two windows appear—the Write Cheques form and the Select Reconciliation Report dialog box.

Select and customize the detail report.

11. In the Select Reconciliation Report dialog box, click the **Detail** radio button.

12. Click the **Display** button. If the Reconciliation Report message appears, click **OK**. The Reconciliation Detail report opens.

13. Click the **Customize Report** button in the button bar.

14. In the *Display* tab, under *COLUMNS*, select **Debit** and **Credit**. Deselect **Amount**.

15. Click **OK**. The revised report appears.

Export the report.

16. In the Reconciliation Detail report, click the **Excel** drop-down button and select **Create New Worksheet**.

17. In the Send Report to Excel dialog box, change the default selection by clicking the **in existing workbook** radio button.

18. Click the **Browse** button, navigate to the *1767-Student-Files\Lesson 11\MyProjects* folder, click the **<your name> Lesson 11 Reconciliation** workbook to select it, then click the **Open** button. This step specifies that QuickBooks will create a new worksheet in the workbook you created in Exercise 11.1.

19. Click the **Export** button to view the new worksheet with the Reconciliation Detail report for the credit card in Excel.

   Note: You will see all Excel files temporarily close. Any unsaved changes are kept.

Rename the worksheet, then save the Excel file.

20. In Excel, double-click the **Sheet1** sheet tab, type: **Ex 2**, then press **ENTER** to rename the worksheet. The workbook now contains two worksheets.

21. In Excel, click **File > Save**, then minimize the Excel application window.

22. In QuickBooks, close the Reconciliation Detail report without memorizing it. You will see the Write Cheques form.

Pay the outstanding balance for the credit card.

23. In the *NO.* field on the Write Cheques form, type: **9/7/18** over the cheque number.

24. In the *DATE* field, type: **09/07/2018**.

25. In the *CLASS* field, select **Admin**.

26. Click the **Save and Close** button.

Leave the company file open for the next exercise.

Reconciling the Merchant GL Account

Objective L-11.3 Reconcile the merchant account

You reconcile the merchant statement to confirm that all processed transactions are accurate in the accounting records. Additionally, you confirm that all the sales and refunds arrived at the bank. Even with the electronic processing of transactions, human error can cause mistakes. The key to reconciliation is to use the detail from the processor about the batch deposits.

Note: If you are using QuickBooks integrated credit card processing, you may have fewer or different steps.

The merchant statement does not have beginning or ending balances because the merchant processor is not a depository for the business; accumulated funds are deposited by the batch to the business's bank account and the total is cleared to zero. The statement lists the batch totals deposited into the Chequing account and the fees taken out of the Chequing account. Ensure that the deposit amount on the statement is the same as the deposit amount in the Chequing GL account.

All credit card processors charge a fee for processing payments. It is usually removed as an EFT-OUT from the chequing account by the merchant account and you must record it. Online credit card processors may take the fee out of the funds they collect for you and deposit the total amount minus the fee. For that type of EFT, you should record the entire amount of the sale, and then record the fee expense separately. Other online processors let you decide when you want to move your funds from their account to yours. Then you record the individual amounts again with the total sale minus the fees that equal the transfer amount.

Usually, the batch detail includes a list of every charge and refund in a CSV file. Overall, what you would look for is the total transactions by date, by type of card, and by batch number. Sometimes one type of credit card is batched apart from the others. Other cards are batched together.

You also reconcile each batch deposited into the Chequing account. Enter zero for the ending balance and use the date of the deposit. Locate and select the transactions for that batch. The transactions will be in order by date in the Reconcile window. You can then use the Transfer Funds Between Accounts form (click **Banking > Transfer Funds**) to move the funds from the Merchant GL account to the Chequing GL account. The reconciliation difference will become zero after you check off the transfer. Figure 11-12 shows the Transfer Funds Between Accounts form.

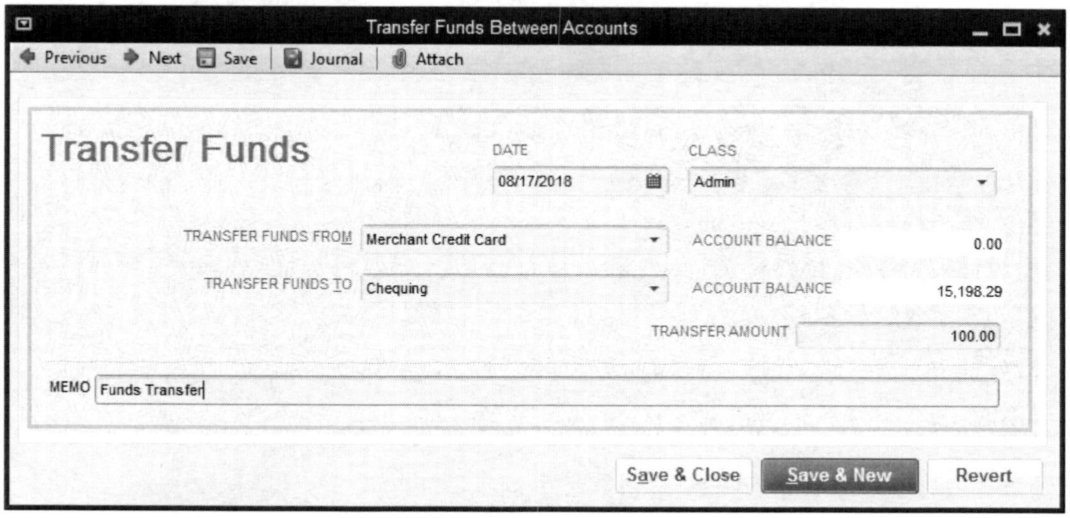

Figure 11-12: Transfer Funds Between Accounts form

Usually, the batches take a day or more from the date of the sale until they reach the bank. This means that at the end of each month, amounts often remain in the Merchant GL account. All this means is that these deposits are in transit.

Figure 11-13 shows the Reconcile – Merchant Credit Card window.

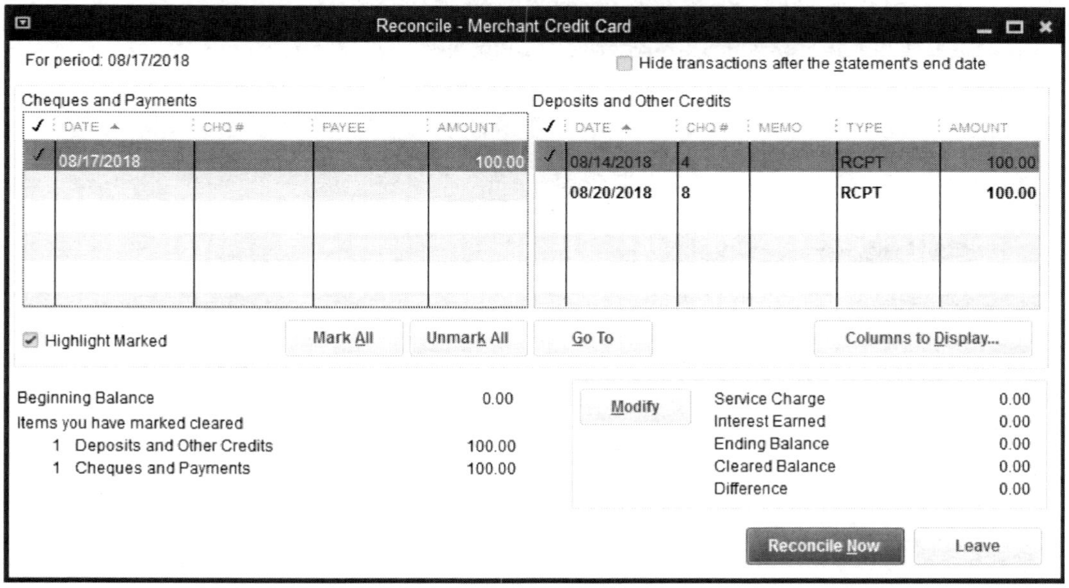

Figure 11-13: Merchant batch reconciliation

The Ending Balance and Cleared Balance are both zero. This reconciliation is for the 100.00 charge on 08/14/2018. The batch arrived in the Chequing account on 08/17/2018. Fees will be deducted later. You enter the transfer for the batch amount in the Transfer Funds Between Accounts form, as shown in Figure 11-12. Both the batch deposit transaction and transfer are selected in Figure 11-13 to complete the reconciliation.

Exercise 11.3: Reconciling the Merchant GL Account

Note: Steps 21-26 of this exercise require Microsoft Excel. If Excel is not installed, skip these steps.

In this exercise, you will reconcile one batch of credit card transactions for Best Custom T-Shirts for 08/20/2018.

1. Ensure that the company file you worked on in the previous exercise is still open.

2. Click **Banking > Reconcile**.

3. In the *Account* drop-down menu, select **Merchant Credit Card**. The beginning balance is 0.00.

4. In the *Statement Date* field, set the date to **08/23/2018**.

5. In the *Ending Balance* field, type: **0.00**.

6. Click the **Continue** button. The Reconcile – Merchant Credit Card window appears.

    Note: The Merchant GL account is the same type as the Chequing GL account. Both are bank types, so the column headings are the same.

7. On the right side, in the *Deposits and Other Credits* list box, select the only transaction (for 100.00). The total of Deposits and Other Credits under *Items you have marked cleared* is 100.00. The Cleared Balance does not match the Ending Balance of 0.00; the Difference is 100.00.

8. Click **Banking > Transfer Funds**. The Transfer Funds Between Accounts form opens.

9. In the *DATE* field, enter: **08/23/2018**.

10. In the *CLASS* field, select **Admin**.

11. In the *TRANSFER FUNDS TO* field, select **Chequing**.

12. In the *TRANSFER AMOUNT* field, type: **100.00**.

13. Click the **Save & Close** button.

14. On the left side of the Reconcile window, in the *Cheques and Payments* list box, select the transfer of 100.00. A checkmark appears to the left. Under *Items you have marked cleared*, the Cheques and Payments field reads 100.00 and the Difference is now zero.

15. Click the **Reconcile Now** button. The Select Reconciliation Report dialog box appears.

Select and customize the detail report.

16. In the Select Reconciliation Report dialog box, select the **Detail** radio button.

17. Click the **Display** button. If the Reconciliation Report message appears, click **OK**. The Reconciliation Detail report opens.

18. Click the **Customize Report** button in the button bar.

19. In the *Display* tab, under *COLUMNS,* select **Debit** and **Credit**. Deselect **Amount**.

20. Click **OK**. The revised report appears.

Export the report.

21. In the Reconciliation Detail report, click the **Excel** drop-down button and select **Create New Worksheet**.

22. In the Send Report to Excel dialog box, select the **in existing workbook** radio button.

23. Click the **Browse** button, navigate to the *1767-Student-Files\Lesson 11\MyProjects* folder, click the **<your name> Lesson 11 Reconciliation** workbook to select it, then click the **Open** button.

24. Click the **Export** button to view the new worksheet with the Reconciliation Detail report for the Merchant GL account in Excel.

    Note: You will see all Excel files temporarily close. Any unsaved changes are kept.

25. In Excel, double-click the **Sheet1** sheet tab, type: **Ex 3**, then press **ENTER** to rename the worksheet. The workbook now contains three worksheets.

26. In Excel, click **File > Save**, then close the Excel application window. Submit the **<your name> Lesson 11 Reconciliation** Excel workbook file to your instructor.

27. Close the Reconciliation Detail report without memorizing it.

28. Save the company file as a portable file in the *1767-Student-Files\Lesson 11\MyProjects* folder.

    Note: This is the file you will turn in to your instructor, along with the Excel workbook.

29. If you plan to perform the Practice the Skill exercise, close the company file but leave QuickBooks open; otherwise, close the company file and exit QuickBooks.

Lesson Summary

Now that you have completed this lesson, you should be able to:

☑ Reconcile the chequing statement.   ☑ Reconcile the merchant account.

☑ Reconcile the credit card statement.

Key Terms

Term	Definition
Cleared Balance	The prior period's ending balance plus and minus all cleared transactions. In QuickBooks, analogous to Ending Balance.
Ending Balance	The prior period's ending balance plus and minus all transactions. In QuickBooks, analogous to Cleared Balance.
In Transit	Transactions in the accounting records that do not yet appear on the bank statement.
Outstanding	Transactions that have not yet cleared the bank.
Register Balance	The balance that shows in the chequing register. This should equal the statement ending balance plus and minus all uncleared transactions.

Activity 1: Recognizing the Role of Uncleared Transactions

Which of the following statements about the reconciliation process is true?

a. The starting balance on a chequing statement equals the register balance from the prior period if outstanding transactions exist.

b. The register balance does not equal the cleared balance when outstanding transactions exist during the period.

c. The register balance equals the cleared balance when outstanding transactions are in transit.

d. The ending balance on a chequing statement equals the starting balance plus the cheques and minus the deposits.

Activity 2: Using the Reconciliation Window

Answer this question *Yes* or *No* and explain your answer. If you are reconciling a GL account and the difference in the Reconcile window is not zero, can you complete the reconciliation?

Practice the Skill

This Practice the Skill exercise is designed to reinforce the skills you have learned. In this exercise, you'll complete a reconciliation by entering any missing transactions, as needed.

1. If necessary, launch **QuickBooks** and open **Best Custom T-Shirts C1_L11_B (Portable).QBM** from the *1767-Student-Files\Lesson 11\PTS* folder.

2. Open the Begin Reconciliation window for the Chequing GL account. The ending date is 09/30/2018 and the ending balance is 15,252.34. (Do not enter the bank fees in this window.)

3. Use the Find tool to locate the completed Write Cheques form to First Bank for the July 2018 bank service charge and duplicate it for 09/30/2018. Correct the memo to read 09/30/2018.

4. The bank statement has 1,194.48 in cheques, 1,684.71 in EFT-OUT, and the 10.00 fee for a total of 2,889.19. Cheque 1012 did not clear. Deposits total 2,355.54 and transfers total 100.00 for a total of 2,455.54. Complete the reconciliation.

5. Customize the Detail Reconciliation report by adding the Memo, Debit, and Credit columns, and removing the Amount column.

6. Export the report to a new Excel workbook named **<your name> Lesson 11 PTS** and turn this file in with your portable file.

7. Save the company file as a portable company file and add the letters PTS to the end of the file name (*Best Custom T-Shirts C1_L11_<your name> PTS (Portable).QBM*). Turn this file in to your instructor.

8. Close the company file.

Course Project Exercise

The Blue Heron Spa has received the February CIBC Chequing bank statement ending 02/28/2017, and it needs to be reconciled. The ending balance is 42,721.84. The outstanding cheques are: 267 to 270 and 984 to 985. The only EFT-OUT is in transit. The cheques total 21,927.64. There is no bank fee.

The deposit on 02/28/2017 is also in transit and deposits dated after the ending date are outstanding. Total deposits equal 53,392.50.

Reconcile and export the summary and detail reports without customizations into the same Excel file, without the QuickBooks Export Guide worksheet. Save the workbook as **<your name> Lesson 11 Course Project** and rename the tabs Summary and Detail.

Filename:	Blue Heron Spa Inc 2018 C1_L11_A (Portable).QBM
Admin password:	BluSpa18
New company name:	Blue Heron Spa, Inc. C1_L11 <your name>

Perform the following tasks:

1. Restore the portable company file and change the company name as indicated in the table.

2. Open the Begin Reconciliation form and enter the statement end date and balance.

3. Clear the transactions as described in the scenario and finish reconciling.

4. Export the summary and detail reports without customizations to new worksheets in one new Excel file, and rename the tabs.

5. Create a portable file to turn in to your instructor.

6. Close the company file and exit QuickBooks.

Quiz Questions

For each question, select the best answer.

1. What is the purpose of reconciling GL accounts that process funds in and out of the business?

    a. Reconciling ensures that the register balance is correct.

    b. Reconciling ensures that the outstanding balance equals the register balance.

    c. Reconciling verifies outstanding transactions.

    d. Reconciling transactions with the bank statement verifies that both you and the bank processed them correctly.

2. Which statement about the ending balance on a credit card statement is true?

    a. The starting balance plus the charges and interest, and minus the payments, is the ending balance owed.

    b. When the ending balance equals the register balance, transactions are still in transit.

    c. The starting balance minus the charges plus the payments and interest is the ending balance.

    d. When the ending balance is zero, nothing is currently owed.

3. Which statement about the Merchant Credit Card GL account is true?

    a.   The outstanding balance is held by the merchant processor.

    b.   No transactions are ever in transit.

    c.   You should always reconcile the batch to zero.

    d.   Fees are always deducted from batches.

QuickBooks

Premier 2018

Level 1

Appendices

Appendix A

Capstone Project

Appendix B

Courseware Mapping

Appendix C

Glossary of Terms

Appendix D

Index

Appendix A: Capstone Project

The Capstone Project exercise encompasses many of the skills you have learned in the course and gives you an opportunity to showcase what you have learned. For this project, you will be asked to complete a set of entries and compose reports in a QuickBooks company file.

Complete the following tasks.

1. Launch QuickBooks and restore the portable file **West End Computers Inc. - base 2018 (Portable).QBM**. Save as **West End Computers Inc - <your name>**. Password: **WestComp18** (case sensitive).

2. Change the Home page so that the Sales Receipts icon does not show.

3. Add two customers (Gerald Davis, Maybrook School) with Net 30 terms. Add one vendor: Hardware Central with the terms Due on receipt.

4. Change the Desktop View/My Preferences to *Save the current desktop*.

5. Add the expense GL account Software. Edit the Chequing Account GL to read: 1-Chequing Account.

6. Add the main email for Bradford Accounting services: clients@bradfordaccounting.com.

7. Paul Lesko just brought in his computer for repair for the first time. Enter his name in the correct list.

8. Prepare a detailed report showing all the entries for the Weekly Cash Sales for All Customers for 01/17/2017 and memorize it in the Customers Group with the name: Detail Weekly Cash Sales.

9. Shannon Cranston asks that her new computer be shipped. Enter an invoice dated 02/03/17 using the S110 Delivery Charge item, quantity 1 (use the default tax) for $50.00. She drops off cheque #4729 on 02/04/2017, but this won't be deposited until 02/06/2017.

10. Gerald Davis brings in his cell phone on 02/04/2017 and they can repair it while he waits. They charge him $75 using the S101 Service item instead of $50, because it is a rush. He pays with cheque #3492 before he leaves. His cheque goes to the bank on 02/06/2017.

11. Maybrook School receives a quote for computer repairs of 2 hours. The shop completes the work on 02/07/2017. Enter the transaction based on their payment terms.

12. Make a report showing the sales and banking transactions from 02/04/2017 to 02/06/2017, including the status of Undeposited Funds. Make the title: Sales and Banking and memorize it in the Customers group.

13. Adventure Travel Inc. needs a credit issued for 1 hour of S105 Installation & Assembly applied to their invoice #5 on 02/08/2017.

14. Jeremy Greene's cheque #239 is returned NSF on 02/09/2017. The bank charges $20 and the business $50.

15. The business contracts with a new computer repair person, Alonzo Garcia. He'll bill the business for his services on terms, Net 15.

16. Prepare a detailed report that only shows the open (unpaid) bills from Microsoft as of 01/31/2017. Title the report: Microsoft and memorize it in the Vendors group.

17. Enter a bill for Bell Canada for Telephone Expense of $133 (use the default tax code) for the Feb 2017 bill on 02/10/2017. Then pay the bill on 02/13/2017 assigning cheque #152.

18. Enter a new vendor, Delivery Express, assign the Sales Tax Settings code "H", then write cheque #153 for $25.00 pre-tax on 02/14/2017.

19. On 02/15/2017 enter a credit card purchase from Guelph Line Office Supplies for Office Supplies Expense of $75.00 pre-tax (use the default tax code) on the RBC Visa Payable card.

20. Enter a debit card purchase from Hardware Central on 02/16/2017 for $56.00 pre-tax using the "H" tax code for small tools and equipment.

21. Enter a Sales Receipt for 2 hours of S105 Installation & Assembly for New Vision Optical on 02/17/2017 using the sales tax code "H". Payment is by cheque #21683, deposited on 02/18/2107.

22. Reconcile the 1-Chequing Account on January 31, 2017. The beginning balance is zero. The ending balance is $45,146.78. Cheque #151 and the 01/30/2017 deposit have not cleared.

23. Run the Summary Balance Sheet for 02/28/2017 and add to Favourites.

24. Run the Standard Balance Sheet for the same date, make it a Favourite, then collapse it and memorize it under the name Balance Sheet-Collapsed in the Accountant Group.

25. Run a report for 01/01/2017 to 02/28/2017 that shows the equity sub-sections. Change the name to Equity Sub-Sections and memorize it in the Accountant Group.

26. Locate the two reports from the last two steps and run them at the same time. Then add "-2" to the names and memorize them again as new reports in the Accountant Group.

27. Run a Journal report for the month of February 2017. Change the default sort to "date." Title it February Journal (by date) CAPSTONE" and memorize it in the Accountant Group.

28. Run accrual reports for the month of February that provide all GL accounts in the Accounting Equation. Change the title to "Accounting Equation #1" and "Accounting Equation #2." Memorize them in the Accountant Group.

29. Run the reports in the previous step, change the basis to Cash, add the word "CASH" to the title and memorize them as new reports in the Accountant Group.

30. Create a portable file named **West End Computers Inc - <your name>.QBM** to turn in to your instructor.

Appendix B: Courseware Mapping

Learning Objectives		Lesson
L-0.1	Recognize the edition of QuickBooks used in this course	
L-0.2	Describe the purpose of the Accounting Cycle	Introduction
L-0.3	Identify Transaction Cycles used in QuickBooks	
L-1.1	Find, open, save, rename, and close QuickBooks files	
L-1.2	Interpret message pop ups correctly	
L-1.3	Locate Purchases and Sales Cycle Forms	
L-1.4	Compare form usage to General Journal Entries	Lesson 1
L-1.5	Navigate forms	
L-1.6	Verify data entry settings	
L-2.1	Know how revenue, investments, and loans differ	
L-2.2	Use QuickBooks classes	Lesson 2
L-2.3	Correctly complete the QuickBooks Make Deposits form	
L-3.1	Match GL accounts to financial reports	
L-3.2	Produce detail and summary reports	
L-3.3	Define non-accrual (cash) accounting	
L-3.4	Find transactions	Lesson 3
L-3.5	Correct transactions	
L-3.6	Review your work	
L-4.1	Identify if an accrual entry is necessary in purchases	
L-4.2	Enter cash purchases using cheques	
L-4.3	Enter credit card purchases	Lesson 4
L-4.4	Process Petty Cash reimbursements	
L-5.1	Identify when an accrual is required as opposed to a cash-based sale	
L-5.2	Enter sales receipts	
L-5.3	Make deposits	Lesson 5
L-5.4	Issue cash refunds	

Learning Objectives		Lesson
L-6.1	Navigate Centres	
L-6.2	Create vendor name records	
L-6.3	Create customer name records	Lesson 6
L-6.4	Edit name records	
L-6.5	Access and update related lists	
L-6.6	Memorize and export reports	
L-7.1	Understand how customer and vendor credit transactions differ in QuickBooks	
L-7.2	Understand how credit purchases affect reports	Lesson 7
L-7.3	Enter credit purchases	
L-8.1	Understand how credit sales affect reports	
L-8.2	Enter credit sales	Lesson 8
L-8.3	Charge correct sales tax	
L-9.1	Apply the accounting equation to the Chart of Accounts	
L-9.2	Enter and modify GL accounts	Lesson 9
L-9.3	Review changes to the Chart of Accounts	
L-10.1	Pay bills according to terms	
L-10.2	Receive and deposit multiple cheques	Lesson 10
L-10.3	Adjust customer invoices	
L-11.1	Reconcile the chequing statement	
L-11.2	Reconcile the credit card statement	Lesson 11
L-11.3	Reconcile the merchant account	

Appendix C: Glossary of Terms

Account – A place in the accounting records for tracking funds.

Accounting Basis – The method by which the accounting system reports revenue and expenses.

Accounting Cycle – Period of time to complete one entire fiscal period of accounting.

Accrual Basis – The accounting basis used to report revenue and expenses when services or goods change hands.

Amortization – Transferring annual amounts from the Balance Sheet to the Profit and Loss statement through amortization expense.

Asset accounts – General Ledger accounts that represent tangible objects such as inventory, machines, and buildings, as well as bank accounts that contain the funds the business has received. They also represent amounts owed to the business, prepaid amounts, and so on.

Assets – What the business owns.

Balance – The value in an account at any given time. Balance can also refer to the total amount of money owed to a third party, such as a vendor or credit card company.

Balance Sheet – A summary report showing totals for Assets, Liabilities, and Equity.

Bank Statement – A monthly summary from the bank showing the prior month's ending balance, all withdrawals and deposits the bank processed or cleared, and the current month's ending balance.

Batch – A group of credit card transactions transmitted for processing.

Bill – QuickBooks form used to record purchase transactions.

Bill of Lading – A shipping document for products that proves the products were shipped or have arrived at their destination.

Billing – The activity of sending invoices to customers for payment.

Bookkeeping – The process of entering business transactions into the records of an accounting system.

Break-Even – The point at which the debits equal the credits in the Income Statement.

Capital – Money or assets available for starting or investing in a business.

Capital Cost Allowance – A government incentive to purchase capital equipment by providing tax relief, often at a rate greater than the asset depreciates on the books.

Capital Expenditure – The purchase of an asset.

Capital investment – The funds or other assets that the owners of the business invest in the business.

Capitalized – An item that it is purchased as an asset rather than as an expenditure. It appears in the Balance Sheet rather than in the Profit & Loss statement.

Cash Basis – The accounting basis used to report revenue and expenses when payments for services or goods leave or arrive at the bank.

Chart of Accounts – The list of all the different types of General Ledger accounts in your QuickBooks file.

Chartered Professional Accountant (CPA) – Licensed accounting professional.

Class – A QuickBooks category, such as a cost or income centre, to which you can assign a transaction. A class could represent a physical location, an entire line of business within the company, or one store among multiple stores the business operates.

Cleared Balance – The prior period's ending balance plus and minus all cleared transactions. In QuickBooks, analogous to Ending Balance.

Comma Separated Values (CSV) – A file that holds plain text as a series of values separated by commas. Most applications can read CSV files, and you can open and read one with a text editor. Most often, CSV files are used to import or export banking information.

Company file – QuickBooks term that describes a QuickBooks file for any entity, either personal or business. The company file is a database that stores financial data, templates, transaction records, customizations, and preferences.

Concatenation – Text manipulation with formulas or software code that unites multiple sections or strings of text into one. Also refers to the placement of a character, such as a colon, between strings of text.

Contra account – GL account with a normal balance that is the opposite of the section in which it is located.

Cost of Goods Sold (COGS) – A sub-section of the Profit & Loss for expenses associated directly with producing revenue.

Credit – Usual Balances found in Sales and Liability accounts; used to decrease Asset accounts.

Current – In accounting terminology, assets or liabilities that can be converted to cash within a year.

Customer – Company or individual that buys goods or services from a business.

DBA – Short for *doing business as*; a registered legal alias for the business.

Debit – Usual Balances found in Asset accounts; used to decrease Liability accounts.

Depreciable Property – Property expected to last more than one year, which therefore needs to be expensed over its lifetime.

Depreciation – The loss in value of an asset due to devaluation from use. This is also a measure of utility over time.

Discount – A reduction in the sale amount for merchant accounts, often for credit card fees.

Double-entry Bookkeeping – A system of bookkeeping that requires each business transaction be entered in two different accounts in the accounting records and that both entries are equal and have an "opposing" effect. Double-entry bookkeeping ensures that the accounting records stay in balance.

Electronic Funds Transfer (EFT) – Money that is sent electronically from one bank account to another without the need for a person to write and mail a paper cheque.

Ending Balance – The prior period's ending balance plus and minus all transactions. In QuickBooks, analogous to Cleared Balance.

Equity accounts – General Ledger accounts that represent the amount of money the owners invest in the business, plus the historical record of profitability over the life of the business.

Field – Place to enter data on a form.

Financial Statements – The Balance Sheet and Income (Profit and Loss) Statement, which show the financial condition of a company in summary form.

Fiscal Year – Refers to financial matters or items associated with taxation. In accounting, a fiscal year is the period of time in which the Accounting Cycle is completed and is the basis for filing taxes. A fiscal year may or may not follow a calendar year.

Form – Data entry window for transactions in QuickBooks.

General Journal Entries – Records of a financial transaction recorded in a company's General Journal. When you use a QuickBooks form to record a transaction, QuickBooks automatically makes the proper entries and properly debits and credits the appropriate accounts. You can also enter transactions into the General Journal manually, but you should have a thorough understanding of accounting principles and best practices. Manual entries are best left to qualified professionals.

General Ledger (GL) Accounts – The accounts into which accounting transactions are entered. GL accounts appear in the Chart of Accounts.

GST – Goods and Services Tax – the Canadian national tax.

Header account – GL account with accounts ordered beneath it. A header account may also be the sub-account of another header account.

In Transit – Transactions in the accounting records that do not yet appear on the bank statement.

Income Statement – A summary report showing totals for the sub-sections of Equity: Income and Expense.

Interest – Fees charged by the lender for the use of the lender's funds.

Internal Name – An entity name that shows only on documents that stay inside the company. The internal name is a subset of the legal name and must be unique.

International Financial Reporting Standards (IFRS) – A common set of accounting principles, standards, and procedures. These principles ensure that everyone knows the accounting transactions accurately represent business activities and maintain integrity in reporting. Adherence to these principles ensures that financial reporting is transparent and consistent across organizations.

Inventory – Products stocked for sale.

Invoice – QuickBooks form used to enter sales transactions.

Items – QuickBooks term for the pairing of the name of an income or expense with a GL account.

Job – A specific project that you perform for a customer that you want to track.

Journal – A location in the company file where every detail of every transaction you enter is stored.

Journal report – The detail report that includes all transactions in the accounting records.

Legal Name – The official entity name as it appears in documents such as cheques or statements.

Liabilities – What a business owes.

Liability accounts – General Ledger accounts that represent obligations that must be paid to another person, business, or entity, such as payroll, credit card debt, or utility bills.

Line of Credit – A line of credit is set by the bank with a ceiling based on the business's financial position. The outstanding balance fluctuates with the business's cash flow requirements but cannot exceed the ceiling. Interest is generally calculated monthly and charged against the line by the bank.

Liquid – In accounting terminology, convertible to cash within a year.

Loan – Money borrowed from a lending institution that the borrower will repay with interest.

Loan Proceeds – The funds provided by the lender to the business.

Loss – A financial decline in which a business has more expenses than income during a given time period.

Make Deposits form – A QuickBooks data entry form that allows you to enter bank deposits.

Matching Principle – Entering costs in the same period as the revenue generated by the costs.

Merchant Fees – Fees that the payment processor, such as a credit card provider, charges a business for the ability to accept payment using their credit card.

Multi-user Mode – Setting that allows multiple users to work in a file at the same time.

Net – The difference between two numbers, such as a debit and a credit.

Net Income – The total of all GL accounts in the Income Statement.

Non-sufficient Funds (NSF) – A term that describes a situation in which a customer's bank account doesn't have enough funds to cover a cheque.

Other – In accounting terminology, assets or liabilities that are non-current or miscellaneous.

Outstanding – Transactions that have not yet cleared the bank.

Overhead – Expenses not directly associated with producing revenue that must be paid whether or not any revenue is earned.

Payment Terms – The description of payment requirements and/or options to apply discount percentages to payment amounts owed, if they are paid within a specified time period.

Petty Cash – An account that represents an amount of cash that the business keeps on hand for cash-based purchases.

Pro forma – A draft invoice that can be sent to a customer without entering the invoice into the accounting records. It is marked with the *PENDING NON-POSTING* stamp.

Profit – A financial gain in which a business has more income than expenses during a given time period.

PST – Provincial Sales Tax.

QuickBooks Global – Information that applies everywhere in QuickBooks.

Recognition Principle – Entering transactions as of the date they occur, not when they are paid.

Register – A QuickBooks window for viewing transaction details of GL accounts that appear on the Balance Sheet.

Register Balance – The balance that shows in the chequing register. This should equal the statement ending balance plus and minus all uncleared transactions.

Remittance Advice – Information about what a cheque payment is for. It is usually located on a removable section of the cheque or on an attachment, or it may appear only in the memo section of a cheque.

Revenue – Funds a business receives as payment from customers for products or services.

Sales Tax – The percentage of a sale collected by the business and remitted to the government.

Shareholder Loan – Money loaned to a business which the shareholder has personally borrowed from a bank.

Single-user Mode – Setting that allows only one user to work in a file at a time.

Start-up Costs – Costs owners pay before business activities begin.

Statement – A document that lists outstanding invoices not yet paid. The amounts may also be summarized by the length of time overdue.

Sub-account – GL account beneath a header account. A sub-account may also be the header or header account of other accounts.

Suspense Account – A GL account that serves as a temporary holding place for transactions until they can be posted.

Unrelated Income – Funds a business receives that do not come from the business activities of selling products and services.

Vendor – Company or individual that sells goods or services for you to purchase.

Appendix D: Index